Women and Girls in the Hindi Public Sphere

Women and Girls in the Hindi Public Sphere

Periodical Literature in Colonial North India

SHOBNA NIJHAWAN

OXFORD
UNIVERSITY PRESS

OXFORD
UNIVERSITY PRESS

Oxford University Press is a department of the University of Oxford. It furthers the University's objective of excellence in research, scholarship, and education by publishing worldwide. Oxford is a registered trademark of Oxford University Press in the UK and in certain other countries

Published in India by
Oxford University Press
YMCA Library Building, 1 Jai Singh Road, New Delhi 110001, India

First published in 2012

ISBN 13: 978-0-19-807407-6
ISBN 10: 0-19-807407-7

Typeset in Adobe Garamond Pro 11/13.2
by Le Studio Graphique, Gurgaon 122 001
Printed in India by Artxel, New Delhi 110 020

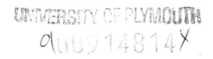

To

my parents
Veena and Subhash Chander Nijhawan

Contents

Figures and Boxes

Figures

Boxes

Preface

When I first introduced my project to a librarian at a Hindi archive and told her that I was interested in the literary activities of women in the Hindi public sphere of the early twentieth century, she was surprised by my desire to consult women's periodicals. She politely suggested that it might make more sense to consider another publishing genre carrying 'real' literature. Clearly, she considered periodicals inferior as source material and argued for novels, short stories, and poetry published in monographs and collections. Hers was not a singular voice. Yet, after conducting my research on women's periodicals, I am convinced more than ever that these forms of print contain enormous potential to learn about the literary, cultural, and socio-political developments of the time as reflected upon by women writers in Hindi. Especially from a literary point of view, the periodical represented the primary site upon which new literary genres in Hindi prose and poetry took shape and were experimented with.

The primary sources for this book stem from archival research conducted at the Hindī Sāhitya Sammelan Pustakālay in Allahabad. The Hindī Sāhitya Sammelan (Society for Hindi Literature) was founded in 1910 in Benares and was shifted to Allahabad the following year, where it developed into one of the most influential literary institutions in the years to follow. Established to provide a forum for discussion for writers, editors, publishers, and a public interested in Hindi, the society launched many Hindi publications and regularly held annual conferences. Since its inception, the Hindī Sāhitya Sammelan was a proponent of standardized Khaṛī Bolī Hindi in the Nāgari script as the national language of the Indian nation, and was thus deeply involved in language politics of the time. Today, the institution carries a much-frequented reference library. Most of the women's periodicals that I consulted there were edited or co-edited by women of the elite and middle classes from the United Provinces of Agra and Oudh.

Retrieving information about the circumstances under which Hindi women's periodicals were published, and on the numbers and spread of their issues, was a challenging and sometimes daunting venture. Many of the publications either no longer existed or had disintegrated in archives and libraries. Unlike British-Indian official documents (parliamentary papers, court records, and official proceedings) that for the most part have been well maintained in Indian and British archives, many vernacular documents—'gendered' literature in particular—do not generally find the wherewithal to guarantee their due preservation. Many women's periodicals in the archive were so fragile and yellowed that turning their pages required much care, but of course they had also not been produced with durability in mind. In the process of binding them into volumes they had often been stripped of their cover pages as well as their advertisements on the first pages. The bound volumes showed missing pages, and sometimes missing issues, which interrupted debates and serialized features.

Still, while mining the archives, I felt excited about reading the very periodical issues which readers of the early twentieth century had leafed through. I eagerly awaited the next issue from the hands of the librarian in order to continue reading a serialized novel or essay. Even though my diachronic reading of these women's periodicals is not comparable to that of their target audience, their spirit, in a sense, was transmitted to me—a reader in the twenty-first century—through these now brittle pages. There was also a sense of privilege in being able to read these documents, thanks to funding, my knowledge of Hindi and my access to the archive. I often paused to let my thoughts dwell on the possible encounters of the readers with these texts. With what expectations had women read these periodicals? Which contributions had they selected first? What features had the children liked most? Had their fathers joined them in solving the riddles? What made a family subscribe to a periodical in the first place? And how may a reader today write about women's periodicals of the past?

I have also treated the periodicals as a rich archive from which to gather information about domesticity, political emancipation, and language politics. At the same time I acknowledge the periodical as a genre in its own right and as an instigator of change, not merely a witness thereof. This leads to two objectives of this book: (i) to trace the development of women's, girls', and children's periodical's in the early twentieth century, and (ii) to discuss selected writings mostly by women for women, girls, and children as they emerged in the Hindi public sphere.

To attune the reader to the contributions in women's periodicals (of which a number appear in full translation in Part Two), I cite from a contribution to *Grihalakshmi*, a women's periodical published from Allahabad. The passage describes the arrival of the periodical in the house of Sushila, a young woman, whose friend Shanta is visiting her.

Sushila: Listen, sister, someone is knocking at the door. Maybe the postman has come. I'll be right back. (She leaves).

Sushila: Who is it? The postman?

Postman: Yes, today I've brought something that looks like a book.

Sushila: Pass it here. (Sushila takes the book. She is very happy and returns). Sister, *Grihalakshmi* has come! (She hands it over to Shanta). We'll both read it and benefit doubly.

Shanta: Yes sister, it is wonderful that *Grihalakshmi* (Mārgśīrṣ, s. 1973 [November/December 1916]) has come just today, while I'm still here. (She looks at the table of contents). Sister Sushila Devi, I mostly love to first read those articles that narrate of important, brave, and devoted wives. So, I'll read out the story titled 'Kichak and Draupadi as dutiful wives'. But before narrating a story, one must know the name of the author. The author is *śrimatī* Damayanti Deviji. Listen. (She reads out the entire story).[1]

The arrival of the periodical is described here as a joyous moment. Shanta is particularly happy to be able to take a look at *Grihalakshmi* at her friend's house. Each issue was likely to have passed through the hands of many readers in a household and shared with the neighbourhood. The process of reading is described as one in which the periodical is read aloud and not digested in solitude and quiet. Its readers have specific preferences regarding the contributions: Shanta first selects an article about heroic and devoted women. After reading the story, the friends even discuss the contents:

Sushila: Sister Shanta, the lady has written this essay skilfully; but there's a mistake. She has presented Draupadi as the wife of Arjuna only. This assumption is wrong. Draupadi was married to the five Pandavas.

Shanta: Yes sister, I've also read this in 'The illustrated Mahabharata'.[2]

Inspired by this negligence of the author, the friends embark on a long discussion about Draupadi and the epic, referring to other publications on the topic. They are depicted as informed readers who draw connections between multiple sources of information. This passage suggests a possible encounter with a periodical, or, at the very least, it expresses what Sundar Rani, the female author, seems to have envisioned.

Sundar Rani also touches upon how editorial and authorial control was moderated by readers as consumers who themselves selected pieces they would read from a variety of articles and messages found in the periodical. Periodicals may thus be read as disseminators of ideologies pertaining to women's roles in public and private. They may be understood as part of yet another discursive formation of womanhood, this time with women as driving forces. Yet, it were not only editors who interspersed their opinions in the periodical; readers, too, made use of their possibilities to intervene in debates by way of readers' letters and submissions that entered into dialogue with debates of the day. Margaret Beetham (1996) has drawn attention in her socio-historical work on British-Victorian women's periodicals to a shared base of power amongst periodicals' editors, writers, and readers.

While an editor may have determined what was suitable for publication and may have made use of the power to censor or change what was written by contributors, periodicals themselves were commodities that depended on buyers, if not for profit then at least for sustainability. Essential to the success of women's periodicals was that editors catered to women's and men's expectations as readers and (ideological and financial) supporters of women's periodicals, respectively.

Notes

1. Dekho bahin, koī kivāṛ bajā rahā hai, śāyad ḍākiyā (posṭ men) āyā ho. Abhī dekh kar ātī hūṅ. (Jāti hai).

Suśīlā: Kaun, ḍākiyā hai kyā?

Ḍākiyā: Hāṅ, lo āj to yah ek kitāb sī hī āyī hai.

Su: Lāo. (Suśīlā kitāb liye baṛī khuś huī ātī hai). Lo bahin, *Gṛhalakṣmī* ā gaī. (Hāth meṅ detī hai). Ek panth do kāj hī sahī. Donoṅ paṛh bhī leṅgī.

Śāntā: Hāṅ bahin, yah to bahut acchā huā ki *Gṛhalakṣmī* (*Mārgśīrṣ*, s. 1973) āj āyī, jab ki maiṅ bhī yahīṅ hūṅ. (*Gṛhalakṣmī* kī viṣay-sūcī dekhtī hai). Bahin suśīlā devī! Merā man to jyādatar un lekhoṅ meṅ lagtā hai, jo ki kisī pahlī, vīr-pativratā' kā ho, isse maiṅ to 'kīcak aur dropadī kā pātivrat dharm' vālā lekh paṛh kar sunātī hūṅ. Lekh sunāne se pahile lekhikā kā nām batānā cāhie. Lekhikā iskī haiṅ 'śrimatī damayantī devī jī'. Lo suno; (sārī kathā sunā jātī hai) Sunder Rani, 1917, '*Do sakhiyoṇ kā śikṣā-prad vārtālāp*' [A conversation between two friends on education], *Grihalakshmi* [March/April 1917 (Caiṭra 1974)]: 14–5).

2. Su: Hāṅ, bahin śāntā! Lekh to śrīmatī jī ne bahut acchā likhā hai; parantu truṭi ek yah rah gaī ki śrīmatī jī ne yah darśāyā hai ki dropadī arjun hī kī strī thīṅ; parantu yah vicār iskā ğalat hai. Dropadī kā vivāh to pāṅcoṅ pāṇḍavoṅ se huā thā.

Śā.: Hāṅ bahin, maiṅne bhī 'sacitra mahābhārat' meṅ aisā hī paṛhā hai (*Grihalakshmi* [March/April 1917 (Caiṭra 1974)]: 15).

Acknowledgements

Roland Barthes describes a 'punctum' as 'a sting, speck, cut [...] that accident which pricks me (but also bruises me, is poignant to me)' (Barthes 1981: 27). Such a punctum pricked me on towards completion of this book. Similarly, what Barthes (1981: 59) says about photographs that animate the spectator and are animated by him/her holds true for the women's periodicals I investigated. Women's periodicals of the early twentieth century sent me on many adventures, goading me endlessly. Along this journey, I was accompanied by people who have been very kind and are dear to me.

I thank Vasudha Dalmia, Francesca Orsini, Barbara Metcalf, Trinh T. Minh-ha, Lawrence Cohen, Raka Ray, and Colleen Lye for their encouragement, critique, and for sharing their knowledge with me while I was writing my dissertation, which forms the basis for this book. My enthusiasm was especially kindled by Vasudha Dalmia, Doktormutter and friend, who has gently guided me for more than a decade, reminding me that projects cannot be completed overnight. I also thank my mother Veena Nijhawan for reviewing all of my translations from Hindi. Balraj Persaud has been the most thorough and critical reader of this manuscript, offering suggestions and advice that go well beyond of what I could have expected from a research assistant. My sincere thanks also to Vasudha Dalmia, Rukun Advani, Michael Nijhawan, Joan Judge, and Khyati Nagar who read and commented on the manuscript or parts thereof, and to the anonymous reviewer of Oxford University Press. This present work is indebted to the pioneering works of Vasudha Dalmia and Francesca Orsini who have both laid the foundation for this and future work to emerge in the field of modern Hindi language and literature.

The Hindī Sāhitya Sammelan in Allahabad, from where I gathered most of my primary sources, was a wonderful place to begin archival research. I am grateful to the chief librarian, Sadhana Chaturvedi, and to the research staff, particularly Asha Dvivedi. Alka and Hari Om Agarwal with Gaurav welcomed me in Allahabad. Shabitri Yadav, little Sushil (now himself father of a son), and the Jain family accompanied me as I made my first notes in Delhi. Their warmth and generosity is deeply appreciated.

Research in the Hindī Sāhitya Sammelan, the Allahabad Public Library, and the Oriental and India Office Collection at the British Library in London was made possible by two grants from the Department of South and Southeast Asian Studies (Summer 2002, Fall 2003) and by the Graduate Division Research Grant (Summer 2003), all from the University of California at Berkeley. The manuscript was completed with the support of the York University Travel and Research Grant (Fall 2005), the Social Science and Humanities Research Council Research Grant (Summer 2006), the Faculty of Arts Research Grant (Winter 2006), and a joint grant from the Faculty of Liberal Arts and Professional Studies and the Office of the Vice-President for Research and Innovation (Fall 2010), all administered through York University in Canada. This support is gratefully acknowledged.

Sharing my work with the *Rewriting South Asian History Dissertation Writing Workshop* under David Szanton has been as valuable as the *Women Studies Dissertation-Writing Seminar* led by Meg Conkey. Sujata Mody, Trina Chaudhuri, Rina Mehta, Elizabeth Greene, and Nicole Thesz in California were all best friends while Mita Bannerjee, Irka Mohr, and Subin Nijhawan in Germany, and Laura Feldt and Jamie Tsai in Toronto made life away from the desk meaningful. Bangle, Shankar, Callie (†2011), and Costello (†2008) were valuable companions in their quietude, meows, and woofs. Kim Nishida, Annette Doeberlin, and Shao Kang Tat successfully made me switch off my brain when necessary and Theresa Kersten, Gloria Saito, Anthony Godfrey, Claire Lyons, and Wanda Malcolm helped me find courage, strength, and inner peace. I thank the 'punctum' of the deck of 223 Taurus Avenue in Oakland, the Rapunzel Tower on Ward Street in Berkeley, as well as Earl Bales Park in Toronto for inspiration and grounding.

My sincere gratitude goes to Michael Nijhawan. In all situations and at all times, he had an open ear for my thoughts on women's periodicals and gave me much appreciated feedback—all mistakes that remain are of course mine. He also let me occupy the kitchen table for nearly a decade without ever complaining or spilling anything over my papers.

The acknowledgements (as anything else in my life) would be incomplete without including Mayur Marcel: Thank you for your reassurances that you love me as high as the sky, as hot as lava, and as round as a ball. Thank you for your hugs, kisses, and smiles. I love you.

Note on Transliteration and Translation

The system of diacritical marks followed in this book is based on that outlined in *Hindi and Urdu since 1800: A Common Reader* by Christopher Shackle and Rupert Snell (1990: 26). Personal names, place names, periodical titles, and the major Indian vernacular languages are not presented with diacritics; the same holds for Indian words current in English. The inherent vowel 'a' in words of Sanskrit origin ending on an unmodified consonant has been omitted unless it occurs as part of standardized English spelling. For the sake of readability of the English language text, the Hindi-sounds 'च' and 'छ' have both been transliterated as 'ch'.

All translations from Hindi to English, unless specified otherwise, are by me.

In citations, English words in italics indicate English usage within the Hindi original.

Part One

Women's and Girls' Periodicals

1 The Periodical as a Genre

An Introduction

The Participatory Framework of Hindi Women's and Girls' Periodicals

Hindi women's and girls' periodicals emerged at the historical conjuncture marked by a shift in mainstream north Indian discourse from social reform to nationalism. During this period of social transition and political emancipation, Hindi women's periodicals became a medium for elite and middle-class women to think in new idioms, communicate with strangers, and find a collective identity across local forms of connectedness. Furthermore, with women as editors, contributors, and target audience, these periodicals became early printed forms of female self-expression. Formatted to the size of a handy booklet, they contained several features: an editorial with extensive news coverage on topics pertaining to women, as well as political commentary; discursive prose consisting of essays and articles about social reform and nationalism—mostly centring on the woman question—as well as such diverse topics as science, virtue, and advice on domestic issues including health, lifestyle, cooking, child rearing, and household management. They also contained narrative prose consisting of short stories, biographies, and (serialized) novels; a section on poetry; book reviews; and readers' letters. Periodicals furthermore carried illustrations, photographs, advertisements, inserts, and occasional special issues.

The very composition of such periodicals represents the diversity of interests and anticipated political stances taken by a spatially dispersed readership. The periodicals were also effective in forging bonds among a newly imagined yet heterogeneous community of women. However, the readership—by default upper class and Hindu—was addressed as an entity, indicated by the terms *strī jāti* (womenkind), *strī samāj* (women's society), *strī gaṇ* (women's group), and even *Hindī bhāṣiṇī nārīsamāj* (the Hindi-speaking women's community), or through the more intimate kinship terms mother and sister. Accordingly, men were conceptualized as an integral group with the equivalent terms *puruṣ jāti*, *puruṣ samāj*, or *puruṣ gaṇ*, and occasionally also as brothers (bhāī), but not as fathers. Men were seen as partners and were by all means asked to give advice, but to do so in a companionate rather than a paternalistic or condescending manner.

In spite of their classification as 'women's' and 'girls'' periodicals, the editors of these periodicals did not exclude men as readers and contributors. On the contrary, they encouraged them to make their views public by sending in contributions and letters. The women's periodicals, then, attracted a much larger audience (as readers and writers) than the term women's and girls' periodical suggests. The question arises how we are to understand the explicit or indirect addressing of male readers in the periodicals. One could simply explain repeated references to a male readership as a play by editors who did not want to appear too women-focused. Women's publishing was not an established institution. Excluding men as readers and writers could have very well jeopardized these young ventures by women. Besides, it would have been practically impossible to exclude men, who mostly provided the financial means for subscription, and who would adjudicate the appropriateness of a periodical for women. In fact, it can be argued that the contributors deliberately chose to involve men in their projects. The women's, girls', and children's periodicals intended to create a critical, open, and discursive public for *all* future subject-citizens and not just a distinct women's or counter public. Writers were aware that their demands for female liberation would not be successful without men's support. And yet a new and sometimes subversive discourse gained strength in the women's periodicals, contesting what male reformers had long deemed appropriate for women.

Based on this contestation of norms and codes of conduct as laid out by men, the contributors to women's and girls' periodicals were not *determined* by mainstream, male-dominated public discourse; they creatively and strategically negotiated, subverted, and redeployed the terms of public discourse in the language of public reasoning. Contributions by women appeared next to those written by men. So it would be misleading to posit male and female writings against each other: any classification of contributions along the lines of gender would gloss over alliances between women and men who were both arguing in the new language of public discourse. Bannerji (1991: 60) has argued that it is crucial to be aware of the ways women shared a base with male reformers of the time, as much as they resisted patriarchy when articulating themselves within colonial, local, and patriarchal discourses. Women's periodicals operated on the grounds of such shared spaces and inevitably created new spaces for women in society. In this process, women and men reset the boundaries set by patriarchy, colonialism, and nationalism. More than other literary genres, the polyphonic character of the women's periodical, its spread and diverse modes of transmission, and its capacity to engage immediate issues of public interest were conducive to public interventions.

The present book highlights the socially interactive and participatory framework created by women's and girls' periodicals in an environment marked by social reform, anti-colonial sentiment, as well as emerging nationalist and feminist thought. Editors, along with eminent and less-known authors of the Hindi literary and political establishments, as well as a large number of subscribers, female and male, were all part of the making of women's and girls' periodicals. The lay writers did not engage in creative writing or journalism as a profession, but occasionally contributed to debates carried out in these periodicals or raised topics of their own interest. The open form of the periodical as a genre made it possible for an increasing number of lay people to reprocess knowledge production and contestation.

This direct involvement was particularly advantageous for women in north India as social constraints on their physical movement in public domains were still operative in the early twentieth century. Women from the upper and middle classes rarely worked for an income and were economically and socially dependent on the male head of the household. Unless a woman had received formal education at home or in school and her elders approved of her spending time in reading, it was not possible to subscribe, let alone contribute, to a periodical, despite the lower subscription rates that periodicals such as *Jyoti* (Light) offered students and women. We are thus dealing with writers and readers who enjoyed the privilege of some education, leisure time, as well as the financial and ideological support of a joint family. And yet, the periodical also reached female members in middle-class households without formal education, to whom stories, essays, and news were read out aloud. Women's periodicals carried special sections of interest to children and unmarried girls, and also addressed men specifically. A periodical was thus likely to pass through many hands for different reasons—instruction, entertainment, and surveillance.

Middle-class Women in Nationalist Narratives

A growing body of literature emerging during recent decades has come to focus on those women who have often been ignored in nationalist narratives or who have not been taken seriously as political actors.[1] Such scholarship sheds light on a forgotten woman's agency and responds to patriarchal (re)castings of women by showing how women actively carved out spaces for themselves and for other women. The present study from the Hindi heartland, the United Provinces, seeks to complement this new historical visibility of individual women and women collectives from Bengal, Bombay, Maharashtra, and the United Provinces. The antecedents of women's large-scale involvement in the nationalist movement, I demonstrate, are to be found in these reasonably numerous, but decidedly involved contributors to Hindi women's periodicals of the early twentieth century. Even radical feminist thought that fell on unfertile ground in the mainstream Hindi public (Talwar 1989: 229–30) was expressed in some Hindi women's periodicals.

Official colonial records testify to the presence of women's voices in political and journalistic activities, though such representations are sometimes derogatory and fragmentary (Spivak 1985a; Visweswaran 1996: 90). Women therein are denied the status of 'proper subjects' in British colonial as well as nationalist discourses (Visweswaran 1996: 124). This present study of privileged and yet—in their perception—subjugated elite and middle-class women and their interventions in a male-centred discourse complicates assumptions of the containment of women's agency that Visweswaran (1996) unravels in British colonial sources. The sources that I have consulted in this work allow the conclusion that women, while working from within patriarchal moulds, defined and created themselves as responsible citizen-subjects of a nation-to-be. Their discourse was not an alternative or separate one, but part of the literary and political public. Women's periodicals were as much subject to colonial examination and censorship as other publications. The *Selections from Indian-Owned Newspapers Published in the United Provinces* (hereafter *Selections*) were weekly publications of the colonial government that listed not only the postal circulation numbers of registered women's periodicals in the quarterly lists of reported newspapers and periodicals, but also provided abstracts of articles published in these periodicals. The women's periodical *Stri Darpan*, for example, was mentioned in the political rubric of the *Selections* over many years on topics as diverse as indentured labour, World War I, Hindi/Urdu language, the Montagu–Chelmsford reforms, and demands for home rule. *Chand*, another women's periodical, fell under censorship of the Press Ordinance in the 1920s and was banned from educational institutions after it had serialized a nationalist rendering of colonial history (Orsini 2002: 271). Such censorship confirms my earlier hypothesis that women's periodicals were considered quite a serious source of political information. At the same time, women's periodicals, and sometimes even girls' and children's periodicals, offered a loophole for publications that might have otherwise been proscribed by the colonial government. Proscriptions were made at the discretion of the British colonial official in charge; many proscribed poems and nationalist songs listed in the bibliography of proscribed literature (Shaw & Lloyd 1985) are comparable to the texts in these periodicals, where they apparently fell through colonial screening. They shared not only contents and titles, but also format and ornamentation, though the proscribed texts were mostly printed on much cheaper paper.

Two dominant ideas are related to middle-class women and the emergence of Hindi women's periodicals in the early twentieth century. First, women who came from family backgrounds which granted them the freedom to engage with the printed word were conceptualized as a coherent readership in their own right. Second, the women's periodical as a genre was recognized, if not as a profitable enterprise, at least as a new commodity in the growing publishing industry, which also prompted the emergence of different kinds of women's periodicals and periodicals for unmarried women and girls. The rise of the vernacular press in colonial north India was intrinsically linked to the growth of a Hindi reading public.[2] As Dalmia (1997: 147) has shown, neither colonial authorities nor indigenous rulers were regarded as offering political and social orientation in the Hindi public sphere. This task was accomplished by the newly emerging middle classes, amongst whom, as I will demonstrate, were also women.

The colonial context determined the nature of participation and articulation in a public sphere via a notion of difference; it assigned inferiority to the middle classes, even more so to the women emerging in the Hindi public. The colonial policy of difference did not recognize colonized people as emancipated enough to represent public opinion. Until the nineteenth century, European residents of British India exclusively enjoyed the status of citizen-subjects. They formed 'the public', and it was through the Anglo-Indian press that public opinion was expected to be disseminated (Chatterjee 1993: 22). Indigenous public discourse was essentially understood as one of tradition, custom, and religion. There existed Indian-owned political periodicals;[3] however, they were more or less excluded from the dominant public sphere constituted by British officials and Anglo-Indian residents. This had important ramifications for the process in which textual knowledge was produced and circulated in vernacular publics. Not only did the British try to control this production and circulation,[4] for all those Indian individuals and communities, including women, who were attempting to find a voice, it became important to gain control over textual production and consumption. The question of literacy, authority over the written word and its circulation, and the challenges of the printed word for traditional forms of knowledge and social relations were issues tied into the project of shaping and containing a public sphere in the colonial context.

To some extent, British colonial legislators encouraged the emergence of 'citizens' as spokesmen and representatives of 'public opinion'. This can be seen in the role granted to Indian social reformers. However, it is very obvious that this position was only tolerated under colonial hegemony. Until the mid-nineteenth century, the Indian public sphere had not yet formed the constitutional public of Habermas' (1962) model.[5] This was doubly true for the female citizen, for even though women and womanhood were centrally featured in colonial discourses, women had rarely participated in them, especially not in the Hindi belt. The existence of a link between women and the public sphere, however, was well recognized: activities of British women were attributed to a secure and gendered British public sphere that enabled women to participate therein. Such a public sphere, at times, also served as a model in the Indian context. Women writers repeatedly referred to the British public sphere as an exemplary model, picturing the large number of 'awakened' British people reading newspapers and books:

> The poorest of the poor women, domestic servants, flower vendors—wherever you look, in their leisure time they have a newspaper or some book in their hands. The consequence of this is that all of them are not only acquainted with the state of their country and the world as well as with matters of progress, wisdom, and science; they are also filled with love for their country and knowledgeable about the good and evil that are found in their nation. Male and female readers can themselves draw a comparison with India's dormant women's community.[6]

The reference to literate, responsible, and patriotic British citizens was meant to stimulate the Indian public and promulgate vernacular periodicals for Indian women. But even if the British public sphere was a reference point for the urban Indian elite and middle classes, the British model was not to be merely imitated. While it is true that the British were highly regarded for technological inventions and innovations such as the printing press, modern scientific developments, forms of economic organization, as well as modern methods of statecraft, when it came to private and spiritual matters, British superiority was overtly contested (Chatterjee 1989: 237–8). While the 'spiritual'–'material' distinction laid out by Chatterjee (1989) may not be adequate to describe the project of female editors—after all they were discussing supposed private matters in the public world rather than relegating them into the spiritual realm—it is important to understand the repercussions of colonial modernity on educated Indian women as it manifested itself in women's periodicals.[7]

Far from being a homogenous group of professionals, the term 'middle class' describes urban and upwardly mobile groups which by and large followed the trends expressed in vernacular and English writings on culture and politics. The majority of the Indian middle classes, as well as a large number of public figures of the nineteenth and twentieth centuries, came from the Indian gentry and the newly emerging professional classes. Most had been raised in multilingual environments and had a background in languages such as Sanskrit, Persian, and at least two Indian vernaculars. As aspirants to the lucrative employment in the British Indian administrative system, male members of these middle classes were also introduced to western education in the English medium. The financial stimulus and security along with the social uplift of employees in the Indian civil service also impacted their private lives. Victorian ideals of partnership, domesticity, and education became new catchphrases for these middle classes. In turn, the intelligentsia publicized their newly acquainted knowledge to their own communities. Their objectives ranged between consolidating anti-colonial opinions and securing political power for their own privileged class (Naregal 2002: 220–5). This is also reflected in the literature published for women.

Besides those employed in the administrative system, barristers, lawyers, law officers, doctors, medical assistants, college and school teachers, engineers, writers, publishers, and the owners of printing presses all belonged to the newly emerging middle classes.[8] As this variety of professions suggests, it is difficult to speak of a homogenous middle class. It is however possible to identify some common interests and behavioural patterns of this professional class. Misra (1961: 307) notes that other than the landholders, traders, and industrialists, the 'professional classes were the first to break through caste or regional barriers and to develop a sense of unity and solidarity'. It may be added that they were also amongst the first who introduced the female members of a family to formal education and printed literature. Moreover, they constituted the bulk of subscribers to women's and girls' periodicals. Their surnames, as given at the beginning of articles and readers' letters, indicate that the majority of contributors (and readers) were Brahmins, Kayasths, and Khatris.[9]

Even though only scant information on the reading experience itself can be traced, it has been possible to retrieve information on the circulation of periodicals through editorials, readers' letters, and contributions that specifically address their readers. Information on occasional contributors does not go beyond the name, place of origin, and the personal information that the writers chose to include in their submissions. From this it was nevertheless possible to deduce that the majority of subscribers and many occasional contributors came from municipal cities and towns through which the East Indian Railways passed (see Figure 1). The large catchment area of Hindi women's periodicals included Allahabad (also known as Prayag) and its immediate surroundings (such as the divisions of Banda and Fatehpur), as well

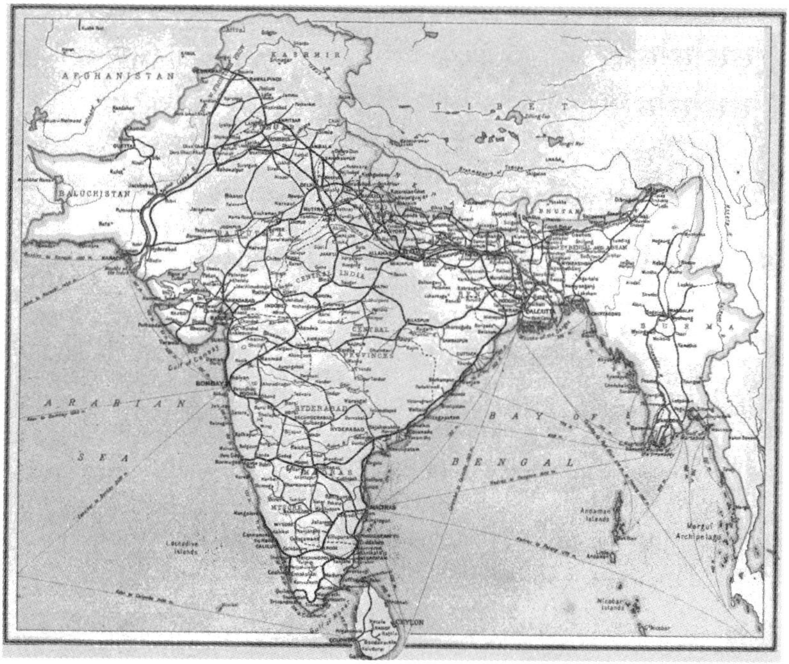

FIGURE 1 India 1909—an artist's rendition of the railways in India. Railway lines in the United Provinces, with a total length that increased from 2.571 miles in 1891 to 3.423 miles in 1901, and to 3.636 miles in 1904, not only provided the necessary infrastructure for the transportation of commercial goods, crops, and people, but also facilitated the spread of news and ideas.

as neighbouring towns and districts within a span of 100 miles such as Benares (also known as Kashi) and Mirzapur. There were copious submissions from the northern and north-western parts of the United Provinces, including Lucknow, Kanpur/Cawnpore, Unnao, Jhansi, and Rohilkhand, as well as further north-west—the districts Agra (which included the divisions Mathura/Muttra and Farrukhabad) and Meerut (which included Aligarh and Dehra Dun). Along the route of the Grand Trunk Road and East Indian Railways that ran up to Punjab, we find contributors from Kapurthala, Amritsar, Ambala, and Patiala. Other occasional submissions came from Jodhpur and Bikaner in Rajputana, Hyderabad in the south, Kashmir in the north, and Bombay in the west. There were Hindi translations of Bengali works in Hindi women's periodicals but no explicit submissions *from* Bengal, though it is widely known that Bengali periodicals pioneered women's literature in this genre (Borthwick 1984; Murshid 1983).

Gender, Tradition, and the Politics of Nationalism

Against the background of social reformist and nationalist movements in early twentieth-century British India, what was the relationship of the political struggles for women's rights with national liberation at large? In this context, I concur with Basu (1976), Forbes (1981, 1998), and Kumar (1993), who read women's self-organization and their relationship to nationalism as acts of conciliation and congruence. Women's associations, these authors argue, were constantly pressured to reassess any nonconformist claims. As I show in this book, to the writers of women's periodicals—male and female alike—women's emancipation was inextricably linked to nationalist claims. But was it possible to launch a movement for women's liberation alongside or as part of the nationalist movement, or did the mainstream nationalist movement contain the emergence of feminist activism? There is no simple answer to this question and it seems that women's organizations were also divided on the issue. Organizations such as the All India Women's Conference (estd 1927) sought to mobilize women in the name of a universal sisterhood, but they also carried a clause in their constitution declaring that they would keep out of party politics (Forbes 1981: 59). Other organizations functioned as auxiliary branches of political associations and usually complied when demands specific to women were kept off the political agenda because they did not conform to patriarchal norms. Women activists who wished to foreground feminist demands had to strategically position themselves in the dominant political discourse in which they claimed a public voice. Editors and writers of women's periodicals had well recognized the constraining facets of nationalist ideology and yet they made use of the periodicals to articulate specific women's demands.[10]

Regardless of whether or not one wishes to perceive the nationalist movement in its constrictive dimension, Ray (1994) writes for the Bengali case: '[O]ne must not overlook the fact that whatever the form, the actual act of women's sharing in activities outside the household meant a departure from the traditional ethos, and lent a radically new dimension to their horizon'. This new dimension was also being presented in Hindi women's periodicals. Every public debate in which women's periodicals engaged came with a new positioning with regard to politics, tradition, and gender. Sometimes, the alliance tended more towards being submerged in nationalist politics, in other instances the implementation of women's rights stood at the forefront of the agenda. From our perspective today, it becomes evident that women's periodicals were creating a network of female activists that would add immense force to nationalist politics from the mid-1910s up to India's Independence.

In this book, I describe many contributions to women's periodicals as feminist. It is not from the lack of another suitable word, such as emancipated (*svadhīn*) or awakened (*jāgṛit*), that I use this term anachronistically. I am aware that Hindi equivalents of the term feminism, such as *strī pakṣ*, are not encountered before the 1930s and that feminists in past and present themselves reject(ed) the adjective to describe their activism. However, I find the term useful to describe writings in women's periodicals of the early twentieth century because of their controversial nature.[11] Hindi women's periodicals were instrumental in developing among women a feeling of self-worth, a process that can be labelled 'feminist' to the extent that it was couched in an overall perception of women as political subjects. Women's periodicals not only redefined gender roles within the domestic sphere, they also tackled women's new roles as members of a nation-to-be. By persevering on the use of the term 'feminism', I would like to contribute to the feminist scholarship that has conceptualized the struggles of non-western women as multilayered and multidimensional (Sangari & Vaid 1989; Mohanty et al. 1991; Tharu & Lalita 1991). As Mohanty (1991a, 1991b) argues, western feminist theory has often fallen into the trap of homogenizing and 'freezing' third world women into generalized statements about women's oppression, dependency, subjugation, and lack of agency. Responsible scholarship, she argues (Mohanty 1991a), conceptualizes third world women as a political rather than an essentialist analytical category. Other scholars from the fields of feminist and postcolonial studies concur with her proposition that scholars refrain from homogenizing women (Spivak 1994, 1993; Sinha 1994, 2000). My work speaks to these debates by showing that Hindi writers, who launched debates on gender in their very own vernacular, certainly interacted with western feminist debates, but were not determined by them.[12]

Crucial to the British Indian colonial context in which Hindi women's periodicals are situated is the project of nation formation. Women's periodicals can certainly be categorized as social feminist documents, putting the nation first and women's interests second. In the same manner, Indian women's movements of the colonial period may be described as social-reformist and nationalist movements; such descriptions, however, discount their feminist legacy. In this work, I especially wish to consider the extent to which women writers and activists—in their role as citizen-subjects—thought beyond immediate nationalist concerns and redefined nationalist frameworks.

Female pioneers of the women's movement in India like Tarabai Shinde (1850–1910), Pandita Ramabai Saraswati (1858–1922), Sarojini Naidu (1879–1949), and many women of the Nehru family—Uma, Svarup/Sarup, and Rameshwari—were all well informed about feminist movements in Europe and the United States. They had either travelled abroad or were introduced to western thought through literature and theatre that circulated in colonial public spheres. They had established friendships with British and American women, and read English-language publications that circulated in the empire such as British women's magazines and publications promulgated by the missionary presses. They were well informed about anti-imperial movements from all around the world as such success stories travelled between countries (Jayawardena 1994: 7). In the early twentieth century, Japan's victory in the Manchurian War (1905) and its model character for modernization, industrialization, and militarization, revolutions in Turkey (1908) and Russia (1917), as well as a diversity of achievements by individual women and women's collectives found their way into the Hindi press. Male and female contributors to women's periodicals were attuned to the changing roles of women all around the world and often referred to western and non-western women's movements or women's support of political movements as positive examples of change.[13]

Notwithstanding, such texts also suggest that the writers were cautious when it came to describing political events in western feminist and emancipatory terms. However, the refusal to adopt western feminist concepts from movements for equality and enfranchisement did not make the periodicals less feminist than their western counterparts. The writers, male and female, exhibited a deep understanding of women's subjugation and articulated their opinions in women's periodicals. They investigated the causes for women's oppression and sought answers on how to remediate social ills. Women's periodicals are thus excellent sources to display this feminist consciousness in the Hindi vernacular.

Print Capitalism and the Participation of Women in the Hindi Public Sphere

Periodicals were not the only medium through which women gained a public voice, though, as I argue in this book, they were the most effective medium in the United Provinces. Apart from print literature, extra-discursive forces also need to be examined in order to determine women's actual involvement in shaping the Hindi public sphere, particularly before the 1920s, when women's political organizations and educational institutions in the Hindi belt were scarce (Orsini 2002: 306). Women's organizations acted as 'safe havens' for women from the respectable classes who participated in public discourse from a gendered vantage point (Thapar–Björkert 2006: 66). But the paucity of such venues in the United Provinces confounded such interaction. Simultaneous to the emergence of women's organizations in Allahabad, women's periodicals such as *Stri Darpan* and *Grihalakshmi* became the central medium for women to communicate across familial local forms of connectedness.[14] The literary sphere created for women, men, and children in the early twentieth century was one of the ways to bypass physical restrictions imposed on women from conservative backgrounds. Women who themselves 'spoke' in this sphere would also constitute the many 'unseen faces and unheard voices' from ordinary middle-class homes that Thapar-Björkert (2006) accredits to the nationalist struggle. The texts investigated in this book, for the most part, stem from this seemingly unassuming category of women as editors, readers, writers, and literary activists of the 1910s and 1920s.

The formation of public opinion was not only kindled by the vernacular press and newly-emerging literary, political, social, and religious institutions. Pre-colonial forms of public participation continued to function alongside print technology. Public oratory and performance genres drew semi-literate and predominantly rural audiences into the public sphere (Freitag 1991: 10). But such public gatherings, for the most part, excluded female participants from the middle classes. Any investigation of the formation of public opinion that wishes to accommodate the voices of middle-class women has therefore to consult forms of written (published as well as unpublished) communication. Furthermore, it is important to consider print vernaculars as the languages of Indian publics. Stark (2007) in her seminal study of commercial book publishing in the second half of the nineteenth century, has done so for five such languages (Hindi, Urdu, Sanskrit, Arabic, and Persian), and refined Anderson's (1983) concept of print capitalism and its importance of establishing imagined communities that would constitute the nation. With the case study of the Naval Kishore Press (estd 1858) in Lucknow, Stark (2007) argues that print was linked not only to the dissemination of knowledge and education, but also to the revitalization of India's cultural and literary heritage. Print technology in the nineteenth century had, for example, been vital to religious reformist and revivalist discourses as print enabled the spread of religious pamphlets and other publications to large audiences, including women (Metcalf 1990: 19). Stretching from orthodox to modernist writings, print technology enriched oral modes for the transmission of religious knowledge. Print was used to disseminate new ideas and values well beyond elite circles, as Minault (1998: 105) has described for the Muslim community in British India:

> Print was integral to the process of religious change as it made scriptures in translation available to all who could read, and it was important in the process of social change as well, as the ability to read increasingly became a marker of social and cultural status. Print also permitted individuals to gain information for themselves, and to communicate with others across the barriers of purdah and the boundaries of family, neighbourhood, and region that so often stood in the way of women's education.

The use of print technology, as the citation indicates, was intended to foster women's education in social, cultural, and religious matters. Furthermore, as Hindi women's periodicals demonstrate, print also provided political education.

Apart from contributing to women's periodicals, women also wrote personal narratives (Ghosh 1986; Mukherjee 1988; Karlekar 1991; Sarkar 1999) and pamphlets on educational and domestic matters (Walsh 1997; Banerjee 1996), as well as health issues (Gupta 2001). The language used was a vernacular close to the lingua franca of the female readership. English was only gradually becoming the second language of the Hindi public, and only a small number of women were well versed therein.[15] They were, however, often the ones propelling the development of the periodical.

As the number of printed literature and literate audiences with access to the media increased, periodicals gained importance. Dwivedi (1995 [1911]: 112), the leading Hindi literary critic and editor, noted in 1911 at a literary assembly:

> The number of newspapers and books has increased significantly as have the research topics; the language is also more refined and pure as compared to before. There are several weekly papers and monthly books that are being edited with great skill. New papers are being launched. The number of thematic books is on the rise. Very old papers mainly contained poetry, drama, and entertainment, as well as very simple articles and news. Topical books were also in a wretched state. This has changed. There has been much progress. Compared to before, editors are now taking their duty seriously. More attention is being paid to the beauty [of language], to education and the well-being of the community as well as to popular opinion.[16]

Entrepreneurs, too, had found a new market among women readers. Increasingly, women's periodicals contained advertisements promoting health and hygiene products, as well as recommending 'suitable' literature for women and children.[17] It is against this background of a gendered Hindi readership and gendered genre that I have developed the two broad arguments in this book. First, women's and girls' periodicals functioned as a field of literary production in which multiple discourses intermingled. I do not conceptualize this discursive field in terms of a 'minority discourse', despite a range of factors that would allow a reading of women's literature in terms of such a minority voice. Against the background of the nationalist movement, we need to understand the significance of Hindi women's and girls' periodicals in their capacity to create a socio-politically informed readership which goaded debates on 'private' issues of domesticity and engendered questions of political awakening.

By encouraging readers' participation in the making of the periodical, and in permitting different voices and opinions, the authoritative potential of the editorial process was not exploited to mould women into ideal domestic figures, as may have been the case in late nineteenth-century women's and girls' periodicals that were edited by men for women. The editorial boards of Hindi women's periodicals of the early twentieth century no longer regulated textual production in quite the way it had been done earlier, and this holds true even for women's periodicals that were edited by men. Unlike the Hindi and Gujarati periodicals discussed by Dalmia (2004) and Shukla (1991) respectively, to the Hindi contributors of the early twentieth century, the periodical was a site to expose patriarchal, social, and political ideologies that negatively impacted the lives of women. The ensuing debates created diverse representational, but always negotiable, models of womanhood and citizenship. The domestic sphere, for example, remained the central field of action for women, but engaging in the public was also no longer taboo. Hindi women's and girls' periodicals aimed at creating responsible female citizens with creative modes of reporting and the utilization of various genres that appealed to upper- and middle-class society sometimes through their familiarity and sometimes through their novelty. Speaking to and on behalf of women, writers identified diverse causes for women's subjugation and exploitation. Their calls for education and mobilization of women and girls shifted from social reformist discourse to an assertion of rights that were no longer contingent upon male benevolence. Writers and editors appealed to their male and female readership to consider an amelioration of the status of women a *pre*condition for Indian Independence. These developments took root at a time that witnessed significant changes in Indian nationalist politics—changes that paved the way for Indian Independence and the partition of the subcontinent.

My second argument is directed at the development of women's and girls' periodicals as a publishing *genre*. I opt for an understanding of the periodical as a genre in its own right despite the difficulty of accommodating the periodical within a taxonomy of literary forms. My discussion of the form of periodicals as it developed in the early twentieth century may allow for sub-classifications of periodicals into domestic, feminist, and religious periodicals, as well as girls' and ladies' magazines. For the most part, however, they remain a combination thereof. The dozen or so periodicals that I have consulted for this work provide enough evidence for strong conclusions to be drawn regarding women's literary and political mobilization. But more importantly, this work intends to further open the field to scholarship on periodicals on an all-India basis out of which there might emerge an even larger, supra-regional study of *Indian* women's periodicals. At all times, it is my aim to read and analyse women-edited women's and girls' periodicals in their importance as a new genre for women and girls.

Once women readers were addressed as a separate audience of a gendered genre, the preliminary steps were laid to develop the sense of national- and female-imagined community that was to become characteristic for the period under consideration. Like other national leaders, women editors were recognizing that the participation of *all* prospective citizens in rural and urban areas across the provinces was required in the anti-colonial struggle. This included members of different religious communities as well as of all classes and castes. Women's periodicals consciously associated themselves with processes of nationalization. It needs to be stressed, however, that these periodicals did not focus only on urban elites when it came to their audiences. In fact, they reached out to readers in small towns and villages, succeeding in addressing audiences which were often neglected by other political organs. By putting the so-called woman question as it manifested itself in quotidian life onto their agenda, women's periodicals went beyond the understanding of politics that centred on constitutional, economic, and administrative reforms in order to achieve dominion status. Addressing even more diverse social issues related to caste, class, and the rural–urban divide, the periodicals contested the 'successive' approach of the Indian National Congress, arguing that social reform—which was bracketed out of the political agenda of the Indian National Congress—was a precondition for political independence, not a logical consequence thereof.

Gandhian Politics and the Nationalization of Women's and Girls' Periodicals

Whereas the Indian National Congress was from its inception in 1885 more concerned with constitutional reform than with representing the Indian people, in the first two decades of the twentieth century the founding members of India's first nationally recognized political party were joined by a new generation of zealous politicians. The latter gradually took the lead in nationalist politics and were critical of co-operating with colonial rule in the way of their moderate predecessors, considering such moderation detrimental to the demand for self-government. With the advent of Mohandas Karamchand Gandhi on the Indian political stage after World War I, Indian nationalism entered a new phase. The Indian National Congress, once a countrywide group of educated elite with representation in the provincial legislatures and in the Imperial Legislative Council (McLane 1988), turned venturesome and sought to mobilize larger sections of society, including women (Ray 1994, 1995).

The momentum created through the involvement of Mohandas Karamchand Gandhi in Indian nationalist politics after World War I gave women's national responsibilities larger recognition. Gandhi's political methods of *ahimsa* (non-violence), *satyagraha* ('truth-force'), *swaraj* and *swadeshi* (self-government), spoke to the masses and led to heightened patriotic fervour in the 1920s. His call for a boycott of British produce and support of the manufacture of Indian produce spoke equally to women as consumers. His non-cooperation movements depended on women's active involvement. Under Gandhi's tutelage, women's participation in the nationalist struggle against British colonial rule became key to the success of the movement.

What was the relationship between Gandhian politics and women's and girls' periodicals? It has often been assumed that the women's movement in India originated in the 1920s as an integral part of the non-cooperation campaigns under the leadership of Mahatma Gandhi (Agnew 1979; Basu 1976; Mazumdar 1976). Indeed, Gandhi's views on women as not merely objects of reform and humanist reasoning 'but as self-conscious subjects who could, if they chose, become arbiters of their own destiny' (Kishwar 1985a: 1691) gained ascendancy amongst those involved in the nationalist movement. Gandhi's role in drawing women from all classes into the nationalist struggle has been acclaimed by Agnew (1979) and Kishwar (1985), among others. In that context it has been described either as the perpetuation of 'patriarchal control of women' or as a 'liberating potential for women' (Forbes 1981: 52–4). Gandhi recognized women's potential for the nationalist struggle and conceptualized women as active participants in the non-cooperation movements. He politicized women's responsibilities in the family and declared women's public involvement a respectable activity. From my discussion of women's and girls' periodicals and women's columns of mainstream periodicals as they were creating a critically informed public, it becomes obvious that Gandhi himself drew on a network of middle-class and elite women who had already emerged in the literary and political spheres. This was not merely true for the Hindi belt: Anagol's Maharashtrian case study of women's periodicals has also made the point that Indian feminism has pre-Gandhian roots that may be found in women's literary production (2005: 17). More than that, the periodicals would go on to interact with Gandhian politics: *Stri Darpan*, for example, reprinted a number of Gandhi's writings and also thematized Gandhian politics in its fictional sections, such as in the story 'Suśilā', where the spinning wheel emerges as economic and spiritual saviour for a widowed woman.[18] Often, the periodicals' deliberations were far more radical than Gandhi's views on women's roles, such as in response to a reader's letter, in which the editors of the young women's periodical *Kumari Darpan* suggest public engagement of young women in the nationalist movement as an alternative to marriage and not a temporary diversion from it.[19]

By the late 1910s, after nearly one decade of publication, women's periodicals identified social problems, such as the condition of women and the lack of education, as pressing national concerns. Even a women's periodical with the primary agenda of religious education, such as *Arya Mahila*, remade itself in the light of these political and literary developments.[20] Within the process of expressly nationalizing the women's, girls', and children's periodicals, a new development can be witnessed. The periodicals that had first addressed women, girls, and children as separate audiences collapsed these gendered divisions and began conceptualizing women and girls and men alike as future citizens of an independent nation. In this process, the women's periodical also collapsed the responsibilities of women and men in both public and private spheres, a move fed by the feminist consciousness of women's periodicals. Literary voices in the women's and girls' periodicals thus laid the foundation for women's participation in the nationalist movement and the formation of women's movements in the Hindi-speaking belt as well as India-wide organizations. Like organizations and institutions outside the fold of the Indian National Congress that set into motion the uprisings of peasants and the working classes, editors of Hindi women's and girls' periodicals considered it their duty to prepare women to join men in the struggle against colonial domination while also safeguarding specific women's interests.

This book is divided into two parts: Part One discusses the format, structure, and thematic categories of women's periodicals and analyses the trajectory of five women's periodicals (Chapter Two) as well as two girls' periodicals (Chapter Three) that I selected from a pool of periodicals because they seemed the most representative for the purposes of this work. In examining the development of the periodical *genre*, I situate the periodical in its specific historical, cultural, political, and social context relying on recent scholarship which has emphasized the importance of periodicals for the emergence of Indian nationalism and the creation of a Hindi public sphere in colonial north India (Dalmia 1997; Orsini 2002). This approach can provide a better understanding of the range of possibilities contained in the periodical genre with regard to the formation of the Indian nationalist movement, the Indian women's movement, and the Hindi literary sphere.

Chapters Four and Five revolve around thematic discussions of domesticity and the Hindi movement. 'Genre and Domesticity' investigates debates on domesticity and gender roles as they centre on notions of responsibility and accountability. The contributions examined in this chapter add a new dimension to the mainstream nationalist debates on womanhood, significantly broadening women's roles and making women's 'private' lives intersect with men's lives in the public world. 'Woman' thereby is no longer an essentialist 'frozen' category, as women begin to participate in the debates on womanhood and nationalism. Even though women's household, marital, and child-rearing responsibilities are never completely overthrown, the contributions convey a shift in argumentation: what validates a woman's and a girl's domestic duties is not her biological gender, but an acquirable skill. Consequently, not only a woman, but also a man can *learn* domesticity. This realization apart, the domestic sphere in itself gained public importance and crystallized as a constitutive part of nationalist politics. With the necessary familial (especially male) support, it was possible for women to engage in both spheres not only through their writing, but also through physical involvement in nationalist politics. In this context, doubled responsibilities of women at home and in public emerged.

'Hindi and the Question of Comprehensibility' has two objectives: first, to discuss how women's periodicals contributed to debates over Hindi as a national language and literature and second, to analyse the language used in women's periodicals. To follow the analysis of the Hindi language, some knowledge of Hindi will be of advantage to the reader, even though I also describe my findings by analysing the Hindi quotes for the reader of English. The chapter is organized chronologically and thematically around the Hindi movement. Many writings in women's periodicals rejected the mainstream Hindi nationalist agenda of standardized and Sanskritized Hindi. Instead, they chose to publish in a language that came close to the lingua franca of the targeted audiences and which nevertheless claimed the status of a national language. Moreover, writers who were not always native speakers of a Hindi dialect, retained the flexibility of Hindi and created a language different to the one envisioned by the Hindi literati. Hindi women's periodicals were thus vital not only in shaping and creating political discourse on women and society; they also envisioned the creation of modern Hindi as a national language *and* the language of the people. The chapter draws on numerous quotes in the Hindi original to discuss the language of women.

In Chapters Four and Five, I discuss individual text portions selected from the periodicals, and not the periodical as a whole—as I did in Chapters Two and Three. The genre of the periodical, however, continued to be crucial to the ways women (and men) thought of their roles and responsibilities in public and private spheres. Messages not appropriate for one genre (such as economic independence for women in a domestic advice text) were easily articulated in another one (such as the short story in which a woman in distress finds herself a job). For the early twentieth century, Orsini (2002: 284) has identified genres such as the confession, the epistolary and the social novel as hybrid genres. On the other hand, Dalmia (2003) looks at the Hindi literary sphere of the late nineteenth century and argues that genres remained separate and were used by writers who knew of readers' and critics' expectations towards the respective genres. In women's periodicals of the early twentieth century, as I show, a new flexibility manifested amidst reasonably clear definitions of genre. This flexibility allowed for new contestations—feminist and nationalist ones.

Part Two is conceptualized in the form of a reader with a general introduction to the format and structure of women's and girls' periodicals. It is divided into sub-genres, each of which carries descriptions thereof, as well as sample readings. In providing a number of full-text translations of representative and otherwise significant texts from women's periodicals, it is my hope that the reader can appreciate this glimpse into the richness, creativity, and diversity of the literary archive out of which the texts at hand have emerged. I have adopted this framework from Beetham & Boardman's (2001) anthology of Victorian magazines for my 'offerings' to the field of women's writing. Women's magazines were shipped to different parts of the empire (Beetham & Boardman 2001: 3); indeed the similarities in formal features, scope, and design bear striking similarities, but Hindi women's periodicals were not a derivative of Victorian women's magazines as to show.

Apart from the works that combine socio-historical and literary analysis in the field of South Asian studies pioneered by Dalmia (1997) and Orsini (2002), I am indebted to the methodologies shared with me in private conversations with Joan Judge and her large-scale international research project on new approaches to Chinese women's periodicals in the early twentieth century. This book's structure has also benefitted immensely from Beetham's monograph (1996) and the work she co-edited with a collective of scholars tapping Victorian periodicals (Ballaster et al. 1991; Beetham & Boardman 2001). Moving back and forth between works on China of the early twentieth century and Victorian Britain has produced a productive tension for my work: Judge's project, with which I had the honour of being marginally involved, taught me the concepts of horizontal and vertical readings of women's periodicals, which ultimately gave the book its structure. I, thus, read women's periodicals as a conglomerate of texts that may be approached 'horizontally' when tapping special topics of women's periodicals (parts of Chapters Three to Five). At the same time, it has been indispensable to undertake numerous 'vertical' readings of the individual periodicals at hand to chart their individual developments over time (specifically Chapter Two). While I also read horizontally in Chapters Three to Five when discussing how periodicals interacted in the Hindi public sphere and shaped each other's form and content, the purpose of these chapters is to show how the sub-genres in the women's periodical intermixed while also maintaining their specific form. While horizontal and vertical readings, thus, intermittently intersect, a conceptual distinction has provided the necessary clarity to analyse women's periodicals as a genre as well as historically specific texts.

Notes

1. Basu 1976; Agnew 1979; Forbes 1981, 1988; Schomer 1983; Sarkar 1989; Ray 1994, 1995; Sinha 1997, 2000; Anagol 2005; Mohan 2005; Thapar-Björkert 2006.

2. For the year 1845, the *Imperial Gazetteers* listed one vernacular paper in the United Provinces that was not written in English or Persian. This number increased to sixty-nine in 1881, and in 1891, 101 vernacular papers were published—mostly in Hindi, Urdu, and Bengali. In the early twentieth century there existed around 119 papers out of which there were three daily newspapers, three newspapers that were published several times a week, eleven English papers, and 103 vernacular papers—out of which sixty-nine were in the Arabic script and thirty-four in the Hindi Nāgari script (*Imperial Gazetteer of India*, 1908: 137). Between 1880 and 1904, the number of registered newspapers circulated via mail in the United Provinces had increased from 15,93,199 to 3,80,99,910 (*Imperial Gazetteer of India* 1908: 95).

3. Allahabad was a centre of publication of influential English and Hindi periodicals of the late nineteenth century, such as *Leader*, *Hindi Pradip*, *Independent*, and *Hindustan Review*, as also of the first decade of the twentieth century, such as *Abhyuday*, *Maryada*, and *Saraswati* (Orsini 2002: 35f, 63f, Appendix).

4. The earliest press regulation and censorship laws date to 1799 when Governor General Lord Wellesley promulgated that all periodicals were to undergo censorship before they could receive permission for publication. There followed censorship law modifications in 1813 and in 1823 new regulations for registration and license requirements lasted until 1835, when several repressive regulatory measures were loosened. Such pre-1857 regulations, however, pertained mainly to European publishing ventures. After the political uprising of 1857, the British made efforts to control the vernacular public sphere through thoroughly implemented legislative mechanisms that inhibited the ownership of printing presses along with a required licensing of newspapers, books, and other printed materials. The Press and Registration of Books Act (1867), the infamous Dramatic Performance Bill (1876) that was issued in response to the rise of political and social criticism in drama plays, the Vernacular Press Act (1878), the Newspaper (Incitement to Offences) Act (1908), and the Indian Press Act (1910) are examples of the regulatory control exercised by the colonial government, which had the power under such acts to confiscate printing machinery and issue search warrants without judicial notification (Dalmia 1997: 232). Without question, such legislation created immense constraints on the development of an openly accessible public sphere as editors were directly held liable for the publication of supposedly seditious or rebellious content. Furthermore, it resulted in a segmentation of the public sphere into different communal formations, as the sphere of religion and community affairs was the only space allocated to indigenous organization and legislature. The legislative measures, however, also represent a tacit recognition of an already existing public sphere, although through the eyes of the colonial

administration, it was corrupted and uncontrolled. As the censorship acts also reveal, Indian elites, including women, made use of print media in a way that called for British control.

5. The concept of the public sphere has emerged as a category of modern political philosophy and social theory, which, in Jürgen Habermas' (1962) rendering, has an essentially normative core: the ideal of an open and democratic public discourse in which politicians and those in power are accountable and can be held responsible for their actions. If we trace the concept genealogically in European thinking, 'public sphere' is not simply a sociological category to describe the empirical existence of a public sphere of communicative practices. Rather, it is assumed that the public sphere constitutes an ideal form of discourse with certain requirements, such as open access to any participant in public discourse beyond class, gender, and racial distinction, along with the assurance of a reciprocal relationship between anticipated forms of social and political conduct, as well as practical possibilities for their realization. Central to Habermas' model of the public sphere is that, ideally, neither class nor property provides access to the public sphere but rationality. 'Public sphere' is thus also a term that emerges as a modern response to feudalism, authoritarianism, and repressive regimes. It is closely linked to the emergence of the democratic nation-state and its new model of citizenship.

6. Garīb se garīb striyāṅ, gharoṅ kī dāsiyāṅ, phūl becne vālī, kisī ko bhī dekho - avakāś ke samay akhbār yā koī pustak hāth meṅ hogī. Isī kā pariṇām hai ki sab kī sab na keval apne deś kī avasthā, unnati aur jñān-vijñān se paricit haiṅ; balki deś-bhakti se pūrṇ aur apnī jāti kī burāī bhalāī samajhne vālī haiṅ. Unkī tulnā bhārat kī soī huī strī jāti se pāṭhak pāṭhikāyeṅ svayam kar sakte haiṅ. (Subhadradevi, 1928, '*Yorop kī striyāṅ*' [European women], *Stri Darpan* [June]: 849)

7. Chatterjee (1989: 237–8) claims that the nationalist ideology in Bengal was constructed as if in two spheres, each with different underlying assumptions about the domain of culture. In the 'material' sphere, processes of modernization were considered advantageous. The 'spiritual' sphere, however, was defined by parameters set by indigenous culture. According to the nationalist logic, it was deemed necessary to 'cultivate the material techniques of modern western civilization while retaining and strengthening the distinctive spiritual essence of the national culture' (Chatterjee 1989: 237–8). This acceptance and rejection complicates the notion of 'derivative' versus 'autonomous' discourses of nationalism, as Chatterjee (1986) discusses in his monograph.

8. Smaller and larger landholders belonged to the landed middle class. Employees in higher and lower commerce (bankers, brokers, gold merchants, larger traders, manufacturers of sugar, as well as large shopkeepers) constituted the industrial and commercial middle classes (Misra 1961).

9. The contributors signed their submissions with their first name, surname, and with *Śrīyut*, *Śrīmatī*, *Yuvak*, *Vidyārtī*, or *Paṇḍit* as mode of address or title.

Some Brahmin last names were Bajpeyi, Bhargava, Bhatt, Chaturvedi, Dar, Dikshit, Dvivedi, Garg, Ghosh, Joshi, Malaviya, Narayan, Nehru, Pandey, Pathak, Prasad, Sharma, Shukla, and Tivari. Kayasth/Khatri last names were Mehrotra, Mitra, Sahay, Saksena, Shrivastav, Tandon, and Varma. Other common surnames of contributors were Kumar, Jain, Jaini, Gupta, Khanna, and Sinha. Some women contributors are listed with their first names only, followed by the respectful suffix Devi, Kumari, or Rani. Occasionally, they use their first name along with that of their husband or father ('faithful wife of...' or 'dutiful daughter of...'). A few contributions were anonymous and signed as 'a humble patriot' (*ek vinīt deśbhakt*), 'a believer in equal rights' (*ek samtā vādī*), 'a supporter of woman's education' (*strī-śikṣā prem*), or 'a well-wisher of self-government' (*svadeś hitaiṣiṇī*).

10. See for example the poem 'You want home rule?', Part Two, pp. 314–5.

11. The term 'feminist' had been a controversial one even in western 'feminist' discourses. Simone de Beauvoir critiqued any feminist struggle, if it was undertaken in isolation of the class struggle. Until the 1970s, she refused to call herself a feminist (Moi 1985: 91). Similarly, Helene Cixous refused the label feminist if feminism was predicated upon a 'bourgeois egalitarian demand for women to obtain power in the present patriarchal system' (Moi 1985: 103). Though there is widespread agreement on the definition of feminism and feminist criticism as exposure of patriarchal practices, these two examples of French 'feminists' illustrate the fluidity and constant redefinitions of the term and the denial to reduce a struggle solely to women's issues. Conceptually, however, I find it useful to speak of feminist writers and texts to broaden what has academically been defined as feminism by South Asian, Asian, and African–American women, as do Talwar (1989) for Hindi and Anagol (2006) for Marathi women's periodicals of the early twentieth century. hooks (1981, 1984), Moraga and Anzaldua (1981), as well as Alice Walker (1983) have, since the 1980s, significantly broadened the very category of feminism and pointed to the patronizing attitude of western feminists (for a discussion, see Johnson-Odim 1991).

12. As my forthcoming work on political reportage in women's periodicals demonstrates, Hindi print media of the early twentieth century drew on gendered transnational discourses that went beyond the well-known interactions between colony and the British mainland. The contributions in women's periodicals suggest that news about women's social liberation and political emancipation stemmed not only from Europe and the United States, but also from the immediate colonial neighbourhood and plantation colonies as well as from East Asia and Inner Asia, thus suggesting that coalition building and sisterhood were conceptualized in a more global framework (Nijhawan 2009).

13. Such as in '*Striyāṅ aur Deśbhakt*' [Women and Patriotism], where Raj Kumar Pandey praises North American women for their unequalled struggle during the American War of Independence (Raj Kumar Pandey 1917).

14. The Prayāg Mahilā Samiti was established 1909 by Rameshwari Nehru and the Bharat Stri Mahamandal, the first *all-India* women's organization, held its first meeting in Allahabad in 1910 under the leadership of Saraladevi Chaudhurani. The very first women's organizations had been established under the tutelage of social reformers. There existed several women's branches of sectarian social reform associations such as the Arya Samaj and the Brahmo Samaj as well as branches of national associations such as the National Social Conference, of which the Bharat Mahila Parishad (established 1905) was an auxiliary organization (Forbes 1998). For a detailed listing and description of women's organizations, see Kumar (1993) and Forbes (1998). Both scholars discuss the three major all-Indian women's organizations, the Women's Indian Association (WIA, estd 1917), the National Council of Women in India (NCWI, estd 1925), and the All-India Women's Conference (AIWC, estd 1927) in detail.

15. A reasonable number of early periodicals (not specifically intended for women) were bi-lingual: *Samacar Sudha Varshan* (1854) was a daily running from Calcutta in Hindi and Bengali, as was *Sudhakar*. *Banaras Akhbar* was published in Hindi and Urdu; *Martand* (1846) consisted of five columns (Hindi, Urdu, Bengali, Persian, and English). The all-Indian women's periodical *Stree Dharma* (1918) was published in four languages (English, Hindi, Malayalam, and Tamil).

16. Patroṅ aur pustakoṅ kī saṅkhyā ab bahut baṛh gaī hai; vivecanīya viṣayoṅ kā vistār bhī adhik hai; bhāṣā bhī pahle kī apekṣā adhik parimārjjit aur viśuddh ho gaī hai. Kaī ek sāptāhik patr aur māsik pustakeṅ yogyatāpūrvak sampādit hotī haiṅ. Naye-naye patr nikalte jāte haiṅ. Sāmayik pustakoṅ kī bhī saṅkhyā dinodin vṛddhī par hai. Bahut purāne patroṅ meṅ viśeṣ karke kavitā, nāṭak, haṅsī-dillagī kī bāteṅ aur bahut hī sādhāraṇ lekh aur samācār rahte the. Sāmayik pustakoṅ kī bhī nikṛṣṭ avasthā thī. Vah bāt ab nahīṅ rahī. Ab bahut kuch unnati huī hai. Sampādak-samudāy apne karttavya ko ab pahle kī apekṣā adhik samajhne lagā hai. Surūci kā bhī adhik khayāl rakkhā jātā hai, lokśikṣaṇ kā bhī, aur jan-samudāy ke hit tathā mat-bāhulya kā bhī. (Dwivedi 1995: 112)

17. See Part Two, pp. 315–21.

18. Chaturbhuj Ji Divaniya, 1927, '*Suśīlā*' [Sushila], *Stri Darpan* (January): 7–16. For a discussion of this story see Chapter Four, pp. 154–5; for the full story see Sneha Desai's translation (Nijhawan 2010: 411–8).

19. R. Nehru and R.K. Vancu, 1922, '*Laṛkiyoṅ se bātcit*' [Conversation with girls], *Kumari Darpan* (May): 40. For a discussion of this editorial see Chapter Four, pp. 161–2; for a full translation see Part Two, pp. 249–50.

20. See Chapter Two, subsection *Arya Mahila*, pp. 65–70.

2 Women's Periodicals

Women's periodicals emerged in the Hindi public sphere many decades after the first Hindi political and literary periodicals had been launched.[1] Titles such as 'Women's Mirror', 'Lakshmi of the Home', and 'Arya Woman' indicate that these were self-proclaimed women's periodicals primarily addressing a female readership.[2] Whereas literature directed at women was not new to the twentieth century, what was new was the increasing number of female authors and editors. These new literary voices operated separately, but not disconnected from male-dominated political, literary, and journalistic networks of the early twentieth century.

Four Hindi women's periodicals in particular, along with two self-proclaimed young women and girls' periodicals mark a shift from the reformist literatures of the nineteenth century that had prioritized normative notions of Indian femininity to a more critical writing that engendered new spheres of activity for women.[3] These periodicals—*Stri Darpan* (1909–28), *Grihalakshmi* (1909–1929), *Arya Mahila* (1917–*c*1948), *Chand* (1922–1940s), and the women's column 'Mahila Manoranjan' of the Hindi literary periodical *Madhuri* (1922–50)—will be discussed in detail in this chapter, and *Kumari Darpan* (1916–1920s) and *Kanya Manoranjan* (1913–19??) will be discussed in Chapter Three. Unlike earlier women's literature, these periodicals no longer exclusively contained practical and moral advice for the domestic middle-class woman. They now carried political news from South Asia and the rest of the world, as well as commentary and opinion pieces on social reform, the nationalist struggle, and worldwide women's movements. The socio-political events of the day were also dealt with in the expansive fictional sections.

The periodicals not only provided a forum for those women writers and readers who were already involved in public activities, they also appealed to a larger women's community to recognize oppressive social and patriarchal structures, and to liberate and emancipate themselves by means of reading and writing. Hence, a women's periodical no longer exclusively provided information geared to the perfection of household skills, even if it claimed to be doing so in its self-descriptions, as is the case with *Grihalakshmi*, *Arya Mahila*, and *Chand*. Instead, it broadened the knowledge offered to women from domestic advice to national politics and international news. Most importantly, up to the 1930s, it sought to develop a sense of self-respect in women, as well as recognition of their roles in a family, society, and nation. Given such a thematic expansion, the columns in women's periodicals also became more diverse.

Women's periodicals of the early twentieth century were subject to experimentation and constant revision. They carried both, new and old, literary genres at a time when Hindi literature was gaining importance on the political stage. Because of their creative and experimental nature, the particular features discussed in the following text as well as the examples given in Part Two of the book are characteristic but not exhaustive of these periodicals. While testing the genre of the women's periodical, writers rethought and renewed existing literary trends and traditions of prose narrative. Features such as the editorial, letters to the editor, book reviews, (international, national, regional, and local) news, essays on society, culture and politics, travelogues, biographies, short stories, and serialized novels—also characteristic of the periodical genre as it had emerged in late seventeenth-century Europe (White 1970), in early twentieth-century China (Chin 2006), and in British India (Dalmia 1997)—were found in Hindi women's periodicals alongside domestic advice, Hindu devotional songs and prayers, as well as renderings from the Indian epics and moral-didactic tales from Sanskrit classics. Dalmia notes that even though in the late nineteenth century 'new grids of private and public, male and female, were coming into being, there existed already, or came into existence simultaneously, challenges to these newly constituted spheres, some in genres *reproduced*, some in genres *introduced*' (2004: 402–3).[4] Correspondingly, in Hindi women's and girls' periodicals there was an adoption of and experimentation with indigenous genres of the *vartā*, *kathā*, romance, and commentary. In addition, new columns such as 'Grandmother's Stories', 'Homemade Remedies', 'Musical Scores', and 'Recipes' were introduced granting oral knowledge entry into the world of print. It is thus not only that texts were taken from the periodical and put into more functional and sturdier formats such as the monograph and collection; it was also that popular oral narrative was collected in the heterogeneous and polymorphous genre of the periodical.[5]

All these features were shaped by the new literary needs and tastes that developed in urban centres, at times claiming ancestry in a Sanskrit literary tradition (Dalmia 1997: 274), and at others drawing on sources that stemmed from popular and folkloric genres and recorded oral histories (Blackburn & Dalmia 2004: 16). Das attributes these experimentations to the multilingual environment of the time as well as to the versatility of its writers who were familiar with a diversity of vernacular texts and genres (1991: 2). In his ambitious project of writing a supra-regional history of *Indian* literature he holds that writers transcended linguistic and literary barriers, which made it possible for literature to be inspired by indigenous literary traditions, as well as by newly introduced western literary models (Das 1991: 56). Contributors to women's periodicals took these different literary traditions into account when choosing genres familiar and useful to them while also giving them new meanings. Ramanujan provides another useful argument applicable to women's periodicals' form as text and context when pointing to the self-reflexivity of texts (and genres) in their respective vernaculars (1992: 171). Texts turn into the contexts of new texts and in the case of women's periodical, texts formed each other's contexts, at times even with intersections not only within one periodical issue, but also between periodicals.

How can such observations contribute towards a theory of the periodical as a genre? While literary texts are often 'rescued' from periodicals and brought into an established and recognizable genre (Beetham 1990: 25), the periodical has historically acted as more than a springboard for entry into the literary canon. It would be too simple to define the periodical as a loose collection of ephemeral articles, from which some proceed into a higher stage of publication and others lose their significance once they are succeeded by the next periodical issue. With Beetham (1990) I argue that the periodical is not 'a kind of nursery in which certain kinds of development in other forms can take place' (1990: 25). Instead, what might seem a random mix of texts is undergirded by a resilient formula that remains popular even today (Beetham 1990: 24). The periodical has peculiar characteristics, including its intervallic nature, its heterogeneous character, and its participatory dimension, the two latter of which specifically allow for immediate involvement of subscribers. In her attempt to identify the periodical as a publishing genre, Beetham (1990: 29), whose work focuses on women's periodicals of Victorian Britain, writes:

> The periodical is an open form in a number of ways: it resists closure because it comes out over time and is, in that respect, serial rather than end-stopped. *Its boundaries are fluid and it mixes genres and authorial voices; all this in a time-extended form seems to encourage readers to produce their own readings.* Yet, in complete opposition to these formal qualities are another set of qualities, which are equally characteristic. Each number of the periodical is a self-contained text and will contain sub-texts which are endstopped or marked by closure. And each periodical positions its readers in terms which construct for that reader a recognizable self. [...] Any periodical will display both sets of characteristics, although each will mix them differently. (Emphasis mine)

The characteristics outlined by Beetham are also valid for Hindi women's periodicals, whose editors conceptualized their project as a dialogic endeavour rather than as a normative project. Their emphasis lay on publishing the writings of eminent *and* non-professional writers, and this openness towards literary styles and topics is what most characterized women's periodicals. Rameshwari Nehru, the editor of *Stri Darpan*, for example, was particularly proud that women, adolescents and girls, all submitted contributions to the periodical. She not only praised their involvement in the making of *Stri Darpan* but also their love for Hindi as it was spreading amongst women.[6] Mahadevi Varma, as editor of *Chand*, was meticulous about the periodicals' style, literary standard, and outer appearance. She wrote introductions to articles, added her own illustrations and gave the periodical 'the stamp of aesthetic taste and meticulous craftsmanship' (Schomer 1983: 225) that would bring the periodical to bloom in the mid-1930s. By claiming literary openness, both editors aimed at creating a critically engaged public. How women were called upon to awaken by supplying the periodical with their own readings and writings forms the mainstay of this book and a period of over two decades will be analysed.

Historically, literary critics have paid much attention to the distinction between a text's outer form (particular literary styles and genre) and its inner form (attitude, intonation, and so on). Drawing on classical texts of genre theory that date back to Aristotle, Wellek and Warren argue that the theory of genres 'classifies literature and literary history not by time or place (period or national language) but by specifically literary types of organization or structure' (1956: 226). They acknowledge that the concept of genre is linked to social institutions, arguing that '[o]ne can work through, express oneself through, existing institutions [literary kinds based on the Aristotelian distinction of the drama, the epic and the lyric], create new ones, or get on, so far as possible, without sharing in polities or rituals; one can also join, but then reshape, institutions' (Ibid.).

Concepts such as those propounded by Wellek and Warren stand in a literary-critical tradition that seeks to separate the social and political field from that of literature, claiming the universal applicability of literary genres on the basis of western categorizations. As new scholarship has demonstrated, it is more productive to undertake genre analysis and socio-historical analysis simultaneously rather than separately (Dalmia & Blackburn 2004; Dalmia & Damsteegt 1999). Women's periodicals frequently incorporated and created new styles of literary expression. They mastered the conglomerate of what Bakhtin (1986: 62) defined as primary and secondary speech genres: primary speech genres constitute most of everyday talk and secondary (complex) speech genres are primarily written, artistic, and scientific forms of communication. 'During the process of their formation,' Bakhtin writes, secondary speech genres 'absorb and digest various primary (simple) genres that have taken form in unmediated speech communion' (Ibid.).

Literary critics have furthermore made the point that genres reflect the literary taste of a particular readership. A reader is likely to select a work according to his or her familiarity with an existing genre or curiosity about a new genre. Similarly, an author is likely to select a genre depending on the message s/he intends to spread. Dalmia (1999) has explored readers' expectations towards literary genres by drawing attention to the novel *Parīkṣā Guru* (1882) written by the Hindi writer, Shrinivasdas. She has shown that the author's expectations of reader responses informed the stylistic structure of the novel. Identifying different literary traditions (oral, western, and Indian) that have informed Shrinivasdas' prose narrative, Dalmia (1991: 172–3) argues that the latter deliberately created a new style of writing with explicit directions for the potential reader:

[I]n considering the formal aspirations of *Parīkṣā guru* it needs to be remembered that the new reader was also the old reader, therefore certain older expectations were carried over into the new. This was reflected in the fact that the new novel referred to two narrative traditions in its title, the religious-didactic tradition of the vārtā as also the worldly-secular of the novel, contained in the modifying adjective *saṅsārī*. But it also invoked as its models works as various as the Mahabharata, the Gulistan, *Strībodh* ('Instruction for Women', one of the many manuals for women in circulation at the time), the novel of Oliver Goldsmith and the essays of Lord Bacon and the *Spectator*, the eighteenth-century moral weekly in English. A further important model was the collection of *nīti-kathā* or didactic tales which was not explicitly referred to but frequently cited, the Hitopadesha.

Such cross-references to old and new genres are also a reality in women's periodicals. They seemed particularly suited to sustain processes of public opinion-making. More so, as Orsini (2002: 123) has argued, 'journals created their own authority as spaces for public debate conducted in the name of public opinion; they were vehicles for both normative and critical understandings of the public sphere. They were also the only space for new literary experiments'. Subscribing to a *woman's* periodical, however, was also bound to female and male readers' expectations of the genre. Traditionally known to impart 'suitable education' for the domestic woman, the new periodicals discussed here are testimony to a redefinition of 'useful knowledge'. This redefinition was fostered through conflating old and new genres within one and the same article, as well as within the covers of a women's periodical.

As I wish to explore the connections between the emergence of periodical literature for women, girls and children and socio-political conjunctures,[7] I ask how the variety of literary genres bore upon women's, girls', and children's periodicals. How did the women's periodical *as a publishing genre* become important at this crucial historical conjuncture in the formation of a national Hindi language and literary canon? Are they perhaps 'minor literature' because they are considered irrelevant to the Hindi literary canon and the world of politics; or because they address supposedly insignificant audiences? Are these texts doubly discredited for being written by women *and* published in the periodical, which formal qualities and literary standards may be distinct from single-authored monographs? Or could we understand 'minor literature' in the way Deleuze and Guattari (1990) have, namely, as the political contribution of underprivileged groups to mainstream public discourse? Such an approach, which recognizes the political significance and collective value of 'minor literature' as well as the revolutionary force of 'minor literatures' for all literature, also makes it possible to recognize the nature of resistance contained in women's periodicals. Bearing in mind that as a form of 'resistance literature' women's writings have long been excluded from the academic disciplines of literary studies and critical theory, it might even be necessary to use the term 'minority literature', as suggested by Harlow (1987) in an attempt to carve out a discursive space for marginalized literatures that have been excluded from processes of canonization.

Without engaging in an extended discussion on which terminology most accurately describes Hindi women's periodicals, my aim in engaging with various connotations of the terms 'minor' and 'literature' has been to address a range of issues around which the argument of this book is woven. More than any other form of literary media, these periodicals covered a range of political and social issues in both prose and poetry. Not only did their contributions from a diversity of writers allow for diverse literary styles and modes of argument at a time during which political discourse was often split along communal lines, a number of viewpoints concerning a single topic could be articulated within one editorial framework. In a way, the periodical by virtue of its heterogeneity and periodicity became a major force in the shaping and contestation of political and literary regimes of knowledge.

Most Hindi women's periodicals that circulated in the United Provinces between 1909 and the 1920s were launched in Benares and Allahabad, the two major publication centres in the heart of the Hindi belt and the Hindi movement. With the growth of print technology, a range of vernacular publications began to disseminate news and literature through channels different from official colonial ones, even though these publications continued to remain under surveillance and possible censorship. A number of smaller presses published religious and mythological literature, sex manuals, poetry, sensational novels, and romance narratives. Mostly poorly printed and on low-quality paper, these publications were affordable and constituted the most popular literature of the time. While the Hindi literati was debating possible common grounds of popular and elite conceptions of what constituted literature in the 1920s (Kumar 2000: 133), and gradually began dismissing a certain type of immensely popular literature as 'low literature' (Gupta 2001: 51), it is more than likely that this literature circulated in the houses of readers of women's periodicals.[8]

In the late nineteenth century, Allahabad had become the centre for educational, journalistic, and nationalist activities (Bayly 1975). By the early twentieth century, the city had become the centre of Hindi publishing. It was not only the capital of the United Provinces, with the provincial government and the High Court located in the city, it also hosted the headquarters of the Indian National Congress and literary institutions such as the first Hindi public library, Bhārati Bhavan Pustakālay (estd 1889). Allahabad also attracted the educated middle classes, most prominently Bengalis, Kashmiri Brahmins, local Brahmins, and Kayasths, who aspired to employment as British administrative and educational bureaucrats. Two of the five earliest educational institutions of higher education for women, the Crosswaithe High School (estd 1895) and the Prayāg Mahilā Vidyāpith (estd 1922) were located in Allahabad as part of Allahabad University.[9] The symbiotic relationship between education and literary activities particularly benefited newcomers to the Hindi literary scene. Female college students, such as Mahadevi Varma, found in women's periodicals an opportunity to publish their writings.[10] Schomer (1983: 135) describes the political and literary atmosphere of the city and its residents as follows:

> This composite new class of lawyers, doctors, teachers, administrators, and clerks created the genteel modern culture of Allahabad, a culture characterized by the high valuation it placed on formal education, a belief in the power of the printed word, a relative openness to new ideas, and a passion for voluntary associations of all sorts. In the second half of the nineteenth century, Allahabad became a city of reform movements, educational institutions, printing presses, libraries, and journalism. It was in this atmosphere that a self-conscious Hindi literary life began to develop.

Women's periodicals also emerged as part of Hindi literary life. In the following, I attempt to use five case studies in order to highlight some of the developments of women's periodicals in the Hindi public of the 1910s and 1920s. Four questions regarding the conceptualization and significance of *Stri Darpan*, *Grihalakshmi*, *Arya Mahila*, 'Mahila Manoranjan', and *Chand* will guide the discussion:

(i) How did editors describe the editorial goals of their periodicals?
(ii) What was the periodicals' role in prevalent discourses of the time?
(iii) How did the periodicals interact with their readers?
(iv) How did the periodicals position themselves vis-à-vis gender roles?

My discussion of *Stri Darpan* and *Grihalakshmi*, both first published in 1909, is far more elaborate than the discussion of *Arya Mahila*, the columns entitled 'Mahila Manoranjan' in *Madhuri* and *Chand*. This is primarily because the first two periodicals were readily available as bound volumes in the Hindi archives. While there were many missing issues of *Arya Mahila*, I still include it in this study since *Arya Mahila* is a specially interesting case. First published in 1917, it was a women's publishing venture that set out as a religious periodical, but saw itself forced to accommodate the political and social exigencies of the 1920s. Taken together, *Stri Darpan*, *Grihalakshmi*, and *Arya Mahila* provide evidence of a confluence of ideologies that were at times complementary, at times opposed, and at all times intervening in, as well as shaping feminist, domestic, and religious ideologies for women. 'Mahila Manoranjan' in *Madhuri* and *Chand*, both first published in 1922, also fall into the core period that this work seeks to cover. Their slightly different formats add further perspective to the development of women's periodicals from the 1920s to the 1930s. A discussion of two girls' periodicals, *Kanya Manoranjan* and *Kumari Darpan*, published in 1913 and 1916 respectively, follows this chapter. I include these periodicals as they were symbiotically related to women's periodicals.

Stri Darpan, Women's Mirror (1909–28)

One of the earliest Hindi women's periodicals edited by women, *Stri Darpan* (Women's Mirror), was first published in 1909 at the Law Periodical Press in Allahabad. Its chief editor was Rameshwari Nehru, a *zenana*-educated Kashmiri Brahmin from Lahore. After her marriage to Brijlal Nehru, in 1902, Rameshwari came to live amongst the politically affluent Nehru family in Allahabad. With the support of several female members of the Nehru family, she launched *Stri Darpan* and took her first steps in what was to turn into a career as editor, social reformer, and political activist.

From 1923 onward, the periodical was published in the business town Kanpur, at Coronation Press, by Sumati Devi and Phulkumari Mehrotra.[11] In the late 1920s, editorship of the periodical came into the hands of Rajaram Shukla. Shukla had been in charge of readers' submissions since April 1927, when publication was moved from Coronation Press to Eastern Press. In June 1928, Shukla apologized for not having published a pre-announced special issue because of a severe illness.[12] It was perhaps this illness that also forced the editor to discontinue the periodical, as the last available issue of *Stri Darpan* dates June 1928.

Two self-advertisements on the inner cover of *Stri Darpan* in March and October 1914 promote the periodical as affordable and ambitious literature for women:

> *Stri Darpan* is a Hindi monthly, first launched and edited by women on the first day of every month in Prayag [Allahabad]. It contains suitable articles and stories on social reform and other topics composed for women. Women also contribute to the periodical. The editor is *Śrīmatī* Rameshwari Devi Nehru. The manager is *Śrīmatī* Kamla Devi Nehru. The periodical contains approximately seventy-two pages every month. It is well printed on good quality paper and the articles are enjoyable and instructive. The annual subscription rate is only two rupees and four annas. One issue costs four annas. Try a sample copy! Every January and July the volume number changes. The fifth part began in July 1911. Be a subscriber and support women's reforms. *Stri Darpan* has been praised in English and Hindi papers, but it is best to check this out for yourself.[13]

> [*Stri Darpan*:] The first suitable Hindi monthly paper for women and girls. In this paper, articles on dharma, literature, society, reforms, and other topics are written for the most part by women.[14]

The annual subscription rate with postage was two rupees and four annas, which was the average annual price of many periodicals at the time. *Stri Darpan* had approximately 800–1,000 subscribers, according to the quarterly listings of reported newspapers and periodicals published in the *Selections from Indian-Owned Newspapers Published in the United Provinces* (hereafter, *Selections*). The periodical was frequently referred to in the political sections of the *Selections* making references not only to women-related topics such as the role of women in World War I, (discussed in the March 1917 issue), but also to political news of the day, such as indentured labour and constitutional reforms. It is important to note this, since it challenges popular opinions that women's periodicals were not considered political enough for mainstream public discourse.

Stri Darpan gained prominence as the most influential instrument of the women's movement in the Hindi-speaking provinces (Talwar 1989: 207). Also termed a 'social action journal' (Mohan 2002: 250), it was the mouthpiece of the Prayāg Mahilā Samiti (Women's Assembly Allahabad) that Rameshwari Nehru had founded in 1909. The monthly ran fifty-five to sixty pages in length, excluding advertisements. A typical issue was roughly divided into four sections. First, an editorial informed the reader of current events at local, national, and international levels, making special reference to women. Compared with other women's periodicals, editorials in *Stri Darpan* were detailed and covered an exceptionally wide range of topics. A second section consisted of informative texts and essays on a variety of social, cultural, historical, and political topics. Professional writers and eminent public figures—both male and female—contributed to this particular section. A third, literary section consisted of serialized novels,[15] short stories, biographies,[16] poems, and prayers. Miscellaneous items, readers' letters with editor responses, and book reviews constituted the fourth section. Under the editorship of Rameshwari Nehru, men and women contributed in equal shares to the periodical. After it was shifted to Kanpur, contributions by men exceeded those by women. This eventual transfer of authority from women to men, who took the lead in editing and writing for women is a somewhat ironical development and not unique to *Stri Darpan*. But while it is true that men took over the sceptre of the periodical in the 1920s, it is worth mentioning that, by this time, many women editors had acquired leading positions in the anti-colonial struggle and many other women were (physically) involved in non-cooperation movements and other public events. All the Nehru women who were active in nationalist politics continued to publish in *Stri Darpan* and other women's periodicals until the 1930s.

As can be seen in the self-promotion quoted at the beginning of this section, the editor described the periodical as a publishing venture geared towards women. Subscribing to the periodical not only meant supporting the woman's cause, but supporting society at large. The 'mirror', as it was mentioned in its title, not only referred to a mirroring of women's roles and responsibilities in familial, social, and national contexts; in many instances the metaphor also functioned as a window, to use Ramanujan's (1992) artistic play on both terms. From this window as it mirrored details of reality, female readers were able to observe the world and, in a self-reflexive move, also observe themselves, and participate in its making.

An Elite Women's Project

The editorial board of *Stri Darpan* consisted of three eminent women from high-caste, upper-class, and nationalist-political backgrounds: the chief editor was Rameshwari Nehru (1886–1966); Kamla Nehru (1899–1936), whose husband was Jawaharlal Nehru, was the manager; and Roop Kumari Nehru, who edited the children's supplement *Kumari Darpan*, was the daughter of Mohanlal and Kamla Nehru and the niece of Uma, Kamla, and Rameshwari Nehru.[17] The editors were likely to have received financial and ideological support from the politically active and influential Nehru family, even though they never refer to the familial background in their writings. In the 1920s, Jawaharlal Nehru's sisters Sarup/Svarup Kumari (better known by her married name Vijaya Lakshmi Pandit) and Krishna, as well as his sisters-in-law Uma (wife of Shyamlal Nehru) and Rameshwari, his wife Kamla, and his mother Svarup Rani Nehru all became staunch supporters of the nationalist movement under the leadership of Mahatma Gandhi. The Nehru women—most of whom had married into the Nehru family—also had individual political careers. Sarup/Svarup Kumari was cabinet minister, governor, and India's first woman ambassador to Russia, the United States, and Mexico. She was also high commissioner to the United Kingdom and president of the UN General Assembly (Pandit 1981). Uma Nehru pioneered the Indian feminist movement and was an MP. Rameshwari Nehru became known as a Gandhian socialist with a feminist outlook, and social worker. She was member of the Age of Consent Committee in 1926–7 and the women's representative at the Round Table Conference in London in 1930. Furthermore, she participated in the League of Nations convention in Geneva in 1931 and in numerous Harijan campaigns in the 1930s (Paliwal 1986). Shyam Kumari Nehru was a member of the Rajya Sabha. Lado Rani Zutshi, the wife of Ladli Prasad (the first son of Patrani Nehru, sister of Motilal and Nandlal Nehru), along with one of her four daughters, Manmohini Zutshi Sahgal, was active in nationalist politics (Sahgal 1994). Furthermore, Roop Kumari taught at the Crosswaithe Girls' High School in Allahabad (see Figures 2 and 3).

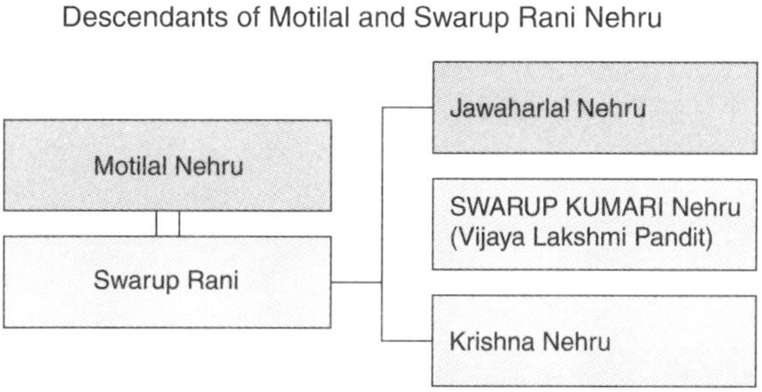

FIGURE 2 Descendants of Motilal and Swarup Nehru. (Names in capital letters denote involvement in *Stri Darpan* and/or the Prayāg Mahilā Samiti.)

It is surprising that the autobiographies of Krishna Nehru-Hutheesingh (1967) and Vijaya Lakshmi Pandit (1981) barely mention the journalistic ventures of their female relatives. Vijaya Lakshmi Pandit has only a short appreciative paragraph on Rameshwari Nehru's efforts as editor of *Stri Darpan*, in which she deems the periodical on par or even superior to its western counterparts:

> My cousin Rameshwari Nehru (Bijju *bhābī*) had started a woman's magazine called *Stree Darpan*, *The Woman's Mirror*, which was the equal in content of any modern woman's magazine published in America or the United Kingdom—probably better, since it dealt with subjects important to the Indian woman such as the need for better education, inheritance, abolition of child marriage, divorce, remarriage of widows, and the right to vote (Pandit 1981: 16).

She makes no direct connection between *Stri Darpan* and the nationalist movement. Elsewhere, she mentions that she published her early writings in Hindi magazines and sporadically contributed to *Stri Darpan* and its supplement *Kumari Darpan* (Pandit 1981: 45). Her first encounters with politics took place at the meetings of the Prayāg Mahilā Samiti. But overall, the biographical information about the Nehru women mostly focuses in nationalist historiographical fashion on their (physical) involvement in the nationalist movement, that is, for example, how they mobilized fellow women, their participation in the salt march, and their imprisonments, and not on their feminist writings, through which

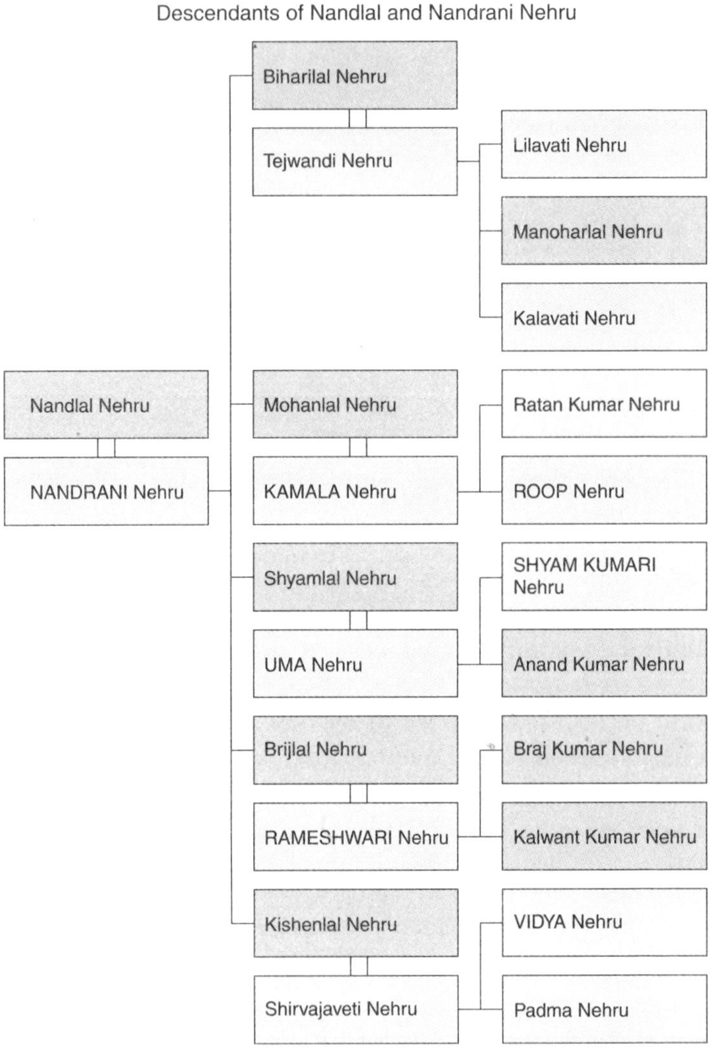

FIGURE 3 Descendants of Nandlal and Nandrani Nehru.[18] (Names in capital letters spread over three generations denote involvement in *Stri Darpan* and/or the Prayāg Mahilā Samiti.)

they were able to give the nationalist movement a different direction. In 1987, the Indian post office issued a commemorative stamp to recognize the achievements of Rameshwari Nehru as *political* activist. Recent scholarship has described Rameshwari Nehru as developing a brand of 'Gandhian feminism' (Sinha 1997). Similarly, Talwar (1989: 226–30) has analysed Uma Nehru's contribution to the feminist movement, arguing that she was perhaps the most progressive of the feminists in the period. He, however, also claims that her literary contributions were more relevant to women's movements abroad and relatively ineffective in the Indian women's movement (Talwar 1989: 229–30). Uma Nehru had published a series of articles about women and civil society in the 1918 issues of *Stri Darpan*, but this series was discontinued after the editors openly refuted her views.[19] A couple of years later, however, the editors once again began publishing Uma Nehru's articles. In the opening paragraph of an article, Uma Nehru notes contently that *Stri Darpan* had changed its outlook, which once again made it possible for her to resume her series:

> In the past few months, [*Stri*] *Darpan* has undergone significant changes. It is as if it has been reborn. Its articles, its opinions, and its core are now much broader in scope and it has acquired a new political dimension. I congratulate *Darpan* on the occasion of this change and am resuming my old series for the benefit of *Darpan*.[20]

The contributions found in *Stri Darpan* offer valuable evidence for an early assertion of women's rights and redefinition of gender roles as articulated within the broader nationalist movement. They also regularly took a stand on mainstream nationalist issues. More than in other women's periodicals, editorials in *Stri Darpan* regularly commented on government bills and on decrees of the Indian National Congress. They did not shy away from analysing and criticizing political matters and decisions. When doing so, positions are clearly identified as editorial comments. The editors did not impose their viewpoints on the readers. In the editorial of the October 1915 issue, as Mohan (2002: 235) has also observed, Rameshwari Nehru announced her wish to promote dialogue by juxtaposing various points of view in essays on society, culture, and politics. The editorials were thus to be understood as just one view amongst many others. Hers was a very conscious move to grant plenty of space for a range of viewpoints.

Stri Darpan was also not a mouthpiece of the Indian National Congress. Of course pro-nationalist concerns ultimately covered the major space in this periodical (which was also the case in many other periodicals); a significant section of feminist contributions, however, covered another mission of the women's periodical in the 1910s and 1920s. This consisted of scrutinizing the causes of women's subjugation and of gender roles more broadly, which meant analysing assumptions about intellectual and emotional dispositions of *both* men and women, along with their implications for spatial reorganization, private and public: the core of these debates revolved around the question what women and men were expected to *be* and *do* in certain spheres and capacities. This scrutinization and analysis, it must be noted, included that which went beyond the nationalist movement.

Many female contributors rejected the relegation of women to a private or spiritual sphere from which they were supposed to represent an essentialized 'Indianness'. *Stri Darpan* reinvestigated gender roles as well as women's responsibilities and proposed a series of different, though not entirely contradictory, approaches to promote the nation's larger cause: self-government. As Tharu and Lalita (1991: 154) have pointed out in connection with women's writings in the nationalist period, 'the writers contested the structures that were shaping their worlds: they tactically redeployed dominant discourse, held on to older strains and recharged them with new meanings and even introduced new issues [...] emphases, [and] orientations'. Such new orientations made women's concerns a national concern. Contributors to women's periodicals also added a social feminist strand to the debates, as the politicization of women's issues meant struggling for women's personal *and* national liberation. Rameshwari Nehru phrased it in her customary straightforward manner: 'if men demand independence from the British they will first have to grant their *dāsīs* independence'.[21] This demand was not antagonistic to nationalist claims, but rather hyphenated the Indian women's movement in its nascent phase with the mainstream nationalist struggle. This stand differed considerably from that of leading political actors in the Hindi public sphere who drew on women's support in the nationalist struggle. *Stri Darpan* resolved the tension between self-sacrifice and self-interest by addressing nationalist *and* feminist issues simultaneously. This predicates my argument that the Indian (elite) women's movement had been initiated in the women's periodical as part of a political agenda in which women's emancipation was considered a precondition for political independence, not a logical consequence thereof.

Rameshwari Nehru was articulate in her demand for political power: 'We need to be given the right to rule alongside doing service, we need to be in a position to give orders alongside receiving them'.[22] More than a stylistic device, her use of the pronoun 'we' further along in her essay suggests that Nehru, speaking on behalf of women, was addressing a community of women beyond those who were elite and upper class. Although I agree with Mohan (2002: 264–5) and Orsini (2002: 265) that, overall, *Stri Darpan* did not pay tribute to the heterogeneity of women's oppression—an exercise that would have required a more thorough analysis of caste, religion, and the economic conditions in society—it needs to be acknowledged that Nehru as editor referred frequently to illiterate and poorly educated, lower-caste and lower-class women. Whereas the suffrage movement of the late 1910s, the legislation for conjugal rights and the act that lifted the ban on widow remarriage all advocated political rights for upper-class and elite women only, *Stri Darpan* also campaigned for the rights of women and men in the lower rungs of society, such as female domestic servants, labourers, and coolies, thus making the category *woman* a central political category that went beyond class and caste exclusions.

In Conversation with Men and Gender

In the editorial comments of the February 1917 issue, Rameshwari Nehru informed readers of *Stri Darpan*'s approaching eighth anniversary. She pointed to the economic hardships that vernacular periodicals had been facing during World War I and she proudly declared that *Stri Darpan* had neither reduced its format nor increased its price, as had been the case with other papers. The editor continued with another concern: men's disapproval of *Stri Darpan*. She reassured readers that there was nothing harmful for women in the periodical. She appealed to men to refrain from confining women to household activities, and asked instead that women be prepared for India's political independence, a goal common to women and men. This, the editor held, was also the major objective of *Stri Darpan*:

> I have been saying it again and again and will repeat it once more: there is *nothing* in *Stri Darpan* that could be harmful to women. [...] *Stri Darpan* wants to develop women in such a way that they too may be prepared to save the honour of their country. Through women our Mother India will again reach its true, rightful, and exalted position in the world where it stood long ago. Until there is room for patriotism in women, men will have difficulty in obtaining self-rule. *Stri Darpan* tries to teach [women] their dharma and will continue

its efforts as long as it exists. [...] I also request our men that they write to us whenever I or my contributors are wrong about any matter. I request that they show us our mistakes, and not disallow their wives our periodical. It is our dharma to teach dharma; it is the dharma of others to lead us to the right path whenever we make mistakes. This will be advantageous for people on *both* sides and the country will progress.[23]

It is very clear that Rameshwari Nehru was keen on soliciting men's approval for *Stri Darpan*. In fact, a few years later, she proudly announced that the periodical had been approved by the communities of women (*strī samāj*) and men (*puruṣ samāj*).[24] She positioned herself as a mediator who was constantly concerned with creating dialogue and encouraging the contribution of various opinions. She believed that opposing viewpoints could generate debates required for society's uplift. She even granted men a certain authority over the periodical by suggesting they detect mistakes by women and lead women on to the right path. In depicting the subcontinent as *Mother India*, Nehru drew on the rhetoric of a mother-centred nationalism with the purpose of stimulating women's active involvement. According to her, the country needed help, not just women; and it was the country's honour that was at stake, not just that of women. The editorial reveals how carefully Rameshwari Nehru countered possible objections to the periodical. Through involving men as readers and as contributors, she sought acceptance and recognition for the periodical.

It is significant that many contributions about gender roles were submitted by male contributors. While the periodical relied on a diversity of women's experiences to break the silence about the quotidian realities of women, analytical essays in *Stri Darpan* often discussed gender roles and responsibilities. In certain contributions, the rhetoric of complementary gender roles was not supported. Authors assuming this position called for the reversal of traditional gender roles. The eminent leftist politician and writer Ramshankar Avasthi, a supporter of the movement for equal rights (*samān adhikār kā andolan*, as he called it), drew a connection between women's inferior status and the patriarchal division of labour. In a contribution to *Stri Darpan* he dismissed all physical and psychological differences in women and men:

This does not make any sense! Neither has God made man strong and sturdy nor woman delicate like a flower. This assumption is especially untrue for men and women of ancient times. At the time of creation, women and men had the same physiology; later—due to the division of labour—men became strong and sturdy and women, due to the type of work they did, stayed behind and were confined to interiors. They became weaker, tender, and gentle. As time passed this gap widened. [...] But because of the peculiar circumstances and because of their degradation, women were forced to subordinate themselves. As they began accepting the authority of men, women's dependence and men's *liberum arbitrium* became the rule. This is how equality was strangled to death. [Women's] dependence stopped the path of progress and this is how women's constitution became weaker and men stronger. Men made laws only according to their needs.[25]

Avasthi identified gender as an artifice of history that had developed into binary categories, equating maleness with such traits as strength, activity and domination, and femaleness with such traits as delicacy, passivity and subordination. Similar to Beauvoir's (1970 [1949]) path-breaking insight in the second half of the twentieth century, thus preceding the debates in *Stri Darpan*, that one is not born 'Woman' but becomes 'Woman' according to cultural norms, Avasthi identified social stratification as preceding gender division.[26] The division of labour had not only made women physically weaker but also led to their subjugation.

Avasthi also envisioned a world in which gender roles were completely reversed. According to him, men ought to experience the oppressions and subjections experienced by women and be confined to the domestic sphere where they would be obliged to perform domestic and menial labour. He described a time when women would supplant men as the 'dominant sex':

The poor men will live a life of dependence. Women will rule over them. They will do menial work in order to provide men with food and clothing. Resistance against such a development will weaken men. They will become delicate, beautiful, and frail. Just like women are considered birthing machines, in the coming age, this condition will be that of men. Today we find female prostitutes in the markets, in the coming age, men will fulfil their *dharmik* duties by working as prostitutes in the markets. The meaning of all this is that the present state of the world will become reversed.[27]

The editor did not agree with Avasthi's dystopian-utopia. To Rameshwari Nehru, the issue was neither about perpetuating oppressive structures nor about reshuffling power relations. She considered Avasthi's depiction harmful to the present state of women's affairs. Problems would not be made better by effectively obliging men to experience the physical pain they had caused women. Instead of simply reversing gender roles, society had to be restructured on the basis of egalitarian principles. In a postscript to Avasthi's article, Nehru held: 'This respectable author has envisioned a time that even the women community would rather not see. Freedom for women cannot mean slavery for men'.[28] The editor certainly did not consider radical ideas to be the most effective tool to overcome women's oppression, even though the issue of gender reversal was often addressed in debates on *purdah* (veil), *lajjā* (shame), and *izzat* (honour), in which women writers in particular held that men should be made to experience life in seclusion.[29] But the literary strategy of gender reversal was detrimental to the woman's cause in the eyes of others.

Another author sanctioned gender reversal if it could be demonstrated that it led to economic improvement and wrote, 'I do not hesitate to go as far as to argue that, God willing, if in a household the woman is more educated and if she as a teacher can earn more than a man, there is no reason for the man to refuse assuming cooking and related responsibilities.'[30]

Such an argument was certainly not representative of women's periodicals in general, but it illustrates the different viewpoints expressed in debates on gender. Another common viewpoint did not favour unlimited independence and equal rights for women but instead suggested a middle-of-the-road path of 'men-controlled independence'.[31] Whatever opinions and demands the writers articulated, traditional images of Indian womanhood (and not those of traditional manhood) remained a common reference point in their articles.

Grihalakshmi, Lakshmi of the Home (1909–29)

Grihalakshmi was first published in 1909 in Allahabad by Pandit Sudarshan Acharya and his wife Śrīmatī Gopaldevi. Along with *Stri Darpan*, the periodical was the earliest (traceable) Hindi periodical with women on the editorial board.[32] *Grihalakshmi* was published by Sudarshan Press, a press committed to the publication of Sanskrit, Hindi, and English books with special emphasis on literature for women.[33] In all likelihood, the press, as its name suggests, belonged to Pandit Sudarshan Acharya. This illustrated monthly was, on average, sixty-four pages in length.[34] It was a two-colour periodical with approximately sixteen contributions and two to three illustrations per issue. The annual subscription rate including postage was two rupees and eight annas.

Grihalakshmi was also one of the most popular women's periodicals: in the first year of its publication, it had the support of 4,000 subscribers. In 1917, there were 2,000 subscribers, a number that fell to 1,000 in the early 1920s, but sprung back to 2,000 by 1924 (*Selections*).[35] From the 1920s, until it ceased publication in 1929, the periodical was edited in Gopaldevi's name by the Hindi writer, publicist, and editor Thakur Śrīnāth Singh (Orsini 2002: 262).

Sculpting the well-educated (*suśikṣitā*) homemaker, the 'Lakshmi of the home', was the editorial objective of *Grihalakshmi*. As the title of the periodical suggests, Lakshmi, the goddess of wealth, was linked to the home, *gṛha*; she brought happiness and prosperity and was also responsible for *creating* the home by virtue of her intelligence and learning. Naming a women's periodical *Grihalakshmi* reflected the debates of the 'different yet dominated discourse' of colonial modernity, including efforts to construct a model woman along the lines of a 'modern, but not Western' woman—a 'modern Lakshmi' so to say (Chatterjee 1986; Chakrabarty 1994). The division of public and private in *Grihalakshmi* was based on a supposed natural gender difference of kind rather than hierarchy, since women and men had different yet equally important responsibilities. The domestic sphere was acknowledged as being as important an area of activity as was the public sphere; in fact, it was often argued that it was more difficult to keep a home in order than it was to rule a country. Gopaldevi also laid out in 'principles of *Grihalakshmi*' that the periodical would keep out of political and religious debates and requested contributors to not submit articles on these topics.[36] A look at the contents, however, indicates that this principle was one which editors and contributors scarcely acknowledged. In spite of the rather clearly set agenda for educated, domestic, middle-class woman's literature, the message delivered in *Grihalakshmi* was far from coherent and not at all disconnected from gender politics. Of course, the periodical aimed at sculpting '*grihalakshmis*', but, as we will see, contributors were not unanimous in their conceptions of ideal womanhood.

The Guardian of the Home

The frontispiece of the 1913 issues pictures the aspirations of the 'modern *Lakshmi*' (see Figure 4). At the centre of the image is a woman comfortably seated on a chair, slightly reclined, her hair hanging loose,

FIGURE 4 *Grihalakshmi* frontispiece (May/June 1913 [Jyeṣṭ 1970])

her body shrouded in what could be either an extravagantly lengthy *lahaṅga* (voluminous skirt) or a sari, her legs crossed, reading. Her appearance is that of an elegant woman. Her surroundings contain patent representations of a modern lifestyle: a room furnished with a chair, a carpet, and a plant. The title of the periodical is printed on a window (or screen), which is flanked by a plant and a pillar to its left and right, respectively. The screen seems to act as a frontier, arguably that between the inner and the outer worlds, or, perhaps it serves as a window, a means to observe, question, negotiate, and eventually also participate in the public. In the drawing, by means of a deft stroke, the outer world penetrates the area in which the woman is sitting. The woman's feet point towards the outside, as if she were soon to arise and step out.

A year later, the frontispiece of *Grihalakshmi* was changed (see Figure 6). In the 1914 issues, the woman is seated on a carpet instead of a chair. Her head is now covered with her sari. She is no longer alone and engaged in her own thoughts, but does embroidery as a teenaged girl, seated beside her, reads a book. A young boy is shown behind them, spinning a top. In the background, a woman is seated on the floor preparing food on a clay stove. Apart from a side table with a book on it, there is no other furniture. The framed picture of a Hindu goddess is hanging on the wall and a sitar is placed next to a pillar in the room. The cover itself has borders of lotus flowers and other ornate patterns into which the title of the periodical is set.

FIGURE 5(a) Reading Women (*Grihalakshmi*, April/May 1913 [Vaiśākh 1970])

FIGURE 5(b) Reading Women (*Madhuri*, April 1923)

Figures 5(a) and (b): Reading women in different poses—lying in the grass or seated on a balustrade. (They also adorned the frontispieces of other periodicals, such as The Indian Ladies' Magazine.*)*[37]

FIGURE 6 *Grihalakshmi* frontispiece (April/May 1914 [Vaiśākh 1971])

In this second frontispiece, the domestic woman is relocated from a 'room of her own' to a common area. She is engaged in a typically Victorian pastime, embroidery, surrounded by her children and near the kitchen. She appears very comfortably established in the domestic sphere and seems capable of overseeing the activities taking place in the kitchen while giving her immediate attention to her children. The living quarter contains a blend of modern and traditional items, whereas the kitchen stove is a traditional one. This is noteworthy because kitchen organization in particular was inextricably linked to the lifestyles of women.[38] Could it be inferred, then, that the change in imagery reflected an attitudinal shift of the periodical? That is, could it be possible that it reflects a willingness to rediscover tradition in a new, modern, but also patriarchal, context?

The change of frontispieces points to the tendency of *Grihalakshmi* to identify itself as a domestic 'ladies' paper' and not one that aspired towards the emancipation of women, an objective that one could much more readily associate with *Stri Darpan*. As a caveat, however, it must be remembered that the frontispiece could not be assumed to reflect the contents of the periodical itself.[39] As in the other women's periodicals, the contents of *Grihalakshmi* were diverse and covered a wide range of topics. Compared to *Stri Darpan* and *Arya Mahila*, though, *Grihalakshmi* granted more extensive space to household affairs as well as to the responsibilities of women as mothers and caretakers within a joint family. This is well reflected in the editorials. While focusing on domestic matters they also negotiate 'modernity' as it entered the domestic sphere and therewith the lives of women.[40]

Each issue of *Grihalakshmi* began with poems on religion, mythology, and patriotism in a variety of genres, such as the *bhajan*, *ğazal*, *qawwalī*, and *dohā*, as well as rhymes and lullabies. The Vaiśākh 1970 (April/May 1913) issue, for example, contained a long poem about the mythological figures Savitri and Satyavan (see Figure 7); a poem on modesty, humility, and politeness (*vinay*); a patriotic religious poem (*bhūmī bhārat*); and a rhyme about a mouse (*khuśāmad līlā*). A second section contained short stories and historical essays, texts on Hindu religious festivals as well as stories, fables, and tales from all over the world (see Table 2.1).

FIGURE 7 Savitri and Satyavan (*Grihalakshmi*, April/May 1913 [Vaiśākh 1970])

TABLE 2.1 *Table of Contents*[41]

	Contents		Page
1.	*Rām Navamī* (poetry)	Śrīyut Mahant Lakshmandas	1
2.	Is this not unjust to the women's *jāti*?	Śrīmatī Kamaladevi	2
3.	Two friends discuss education	Śrīmatī Sundar Rani	10
4.	On child-care	Śrīyut Musiram Adhyapak	17
5.	Child education	Śrīmatī Satyavati	19
6.	The duty of girls towards their parents	Śrīmatī Kripadevi	21
7.	The causes for the fall of *Bhāratvarś*	Śrīyut Baburam Mishra	25
8.	The danger of tobacco	Reprint from *Chikitsak*	29
9.	How to prevent fruits from turning bad	Reprint from *Jayaji Pratap*	31
10.	*Pārvati*	Śrīyut Bhagvandin Pathak	33
11.	Insects from the family of bugs	Śrīyut Lajjashankar Jha	38
12.	The fruits of patience	Śrīyut Jahurabakhsh Adhyapak	44
13.	Hopeless hope (poetry)	Śrīyut Nanhailal Abhir	48

The literary standard of the prose literature varied. Whereas we find contributions by renowned writers such as Girijakumar Ghosh (editor of the *Sammelan Patrika* at the time) and public intellectuals such as Shridhar Pathak, there are as many contributions that rather bluntly promoted a particular moral and paid no attention to style, language, and literary conventions set by acclaimed literary periodicals. The poems and biographical narratives were often accompanied by illustrations or portraits of mythological figures from the Hindu pantheon such as Parvati, Savitri, and Satyavan, and historical figures such as Snehlata Devi (Figure 8) and Joan of Arc (Figure 9). Other illustrations of airplanes, guns, body parts, bugs and dinosaurs, for example, were featured alongside scientific texts.

Figure 8 Snehlata Devi (*Grihalakshmi*, April/May 1914 [Vaiśākh 1971])

Figure 9 Joan of Arc (*Grihalakshmi*, October/November 1913 [Kārtik 1970])

FIGURE 10 British Field Marshal Lord Kitchener and French General Joseph Joffre (*Grihalakshmi*, December/January 1914/1915 [Pauṣ 1971])

Editor–Reader Interaction and Other Dialogues

Male contributors to *Grihalakshmi* outnumbered female contributors significantly. In the first years of publication there were only one to two articles written by women; occasionally women submitted up to a third of an issue's articles. In later years, the number of female authors increased in the fictional section.

More than the other women's periodicals, *Grihalakshmi* reprinted essays from other Hindi periodicals, such as *Vigyan*, *Jayaji Pratap*, *Maryada*, *Sudhakar*, *Hitkarini*, *Navjivan*, and the health periodical *Chikitsak*. Such reprints were for the most part scientific articles, health-care information, and essays on social reform; occasionally there were also reprints in the poetry and fictional sections. What was considered *suitable* information for women could thus very well stem from writings

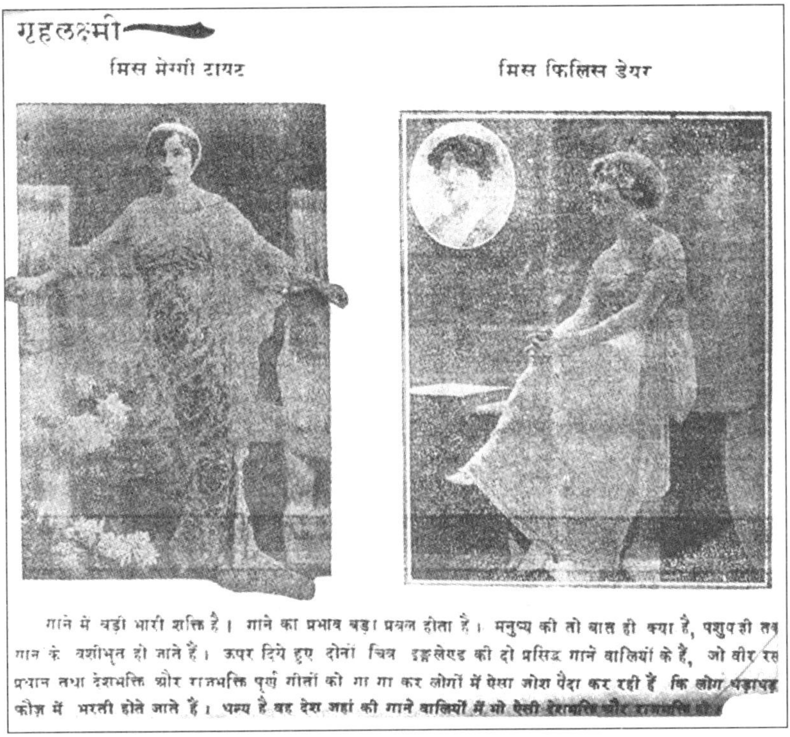

FIGURE 11 Maggie Tait and Phyllis Dyer (*Grihalakshmi*, December/January 1914/1915 [Pauṣ 1971]). 'Singing is overwhelming and powerful. The effect of a song is dramatically potent. Music fascinates not only humans, but also animals. The pictures are of two famous singers from England who, by virtue of their patriotic songs incite the people in such a way that they immediately want to join the army. How fortunate is a country where singers are loyal and patriotic.'

that were originally written for men. While this borrowing could certainly be read as a lack of articles written specifically for women, another plausible explanation would be that separate articles were not considered necessary, as women and men were capable of reading the same articles on certain topics. It would be the periodical *Chand* in the 1920s that would break down the category of the gender-specific *women's* periodical.[42]

गृहलक्ष्मी

वेस्टमिनिस्टर की डचेस

आप वेस्टमिनिस्टर की ठकुराइन (डचेस) हैं। आप घायलों की सेवा करने के लिए बहुत सी अंग्रेज़ी सेविकाओं को साथ लेकर रणभूमि पर गयी हैं। आपके पति वेस्टमिनिस्टर के ड्यूक ने भी रणस्थल में अच्छा नाम कमाया है।

सुदर्शन प्रेस, प्रयाग।

FIGURE 12 The Duchess of Westminster (*Grihalakshmi*, December/January 1914/1915 [Pauṣ 1971]). 'She is the Duchess of Westminster. She has been on the battlefront along with many English women volunteers to treat the wounded. Her husband, the Duke of Westminster, has also gained fame on the battlefield.'

FIGURE 13 Grandmother's story (*Grihalakshmi*, December/January 1913/1914 [Pauṣ 1970])

As against *Stri Darpan* and *Arya Mahila*, *Grihalakshmi* did not contain a regular editorial. The editors also seldom commented on the contributions; not even when they appeared to contradict the periodical's stated ideas about domesticity.[43] Instead, the editorial voice was limited to occasional calls for the submission of recipes, children's photographs, and participation in essay competitions. Yet, from readers' contributions published in *Grihalakshmi*, it appears that the editors were not averse to reader submissions. A contributor named Manorama introduced the story of her life thus:

> Today I come before the readers of *Grihalakshmi* with a domestic incident. The description of the event that I am presenting to the readers took place in my own house. And it is not an exaggeration to say that amongst those who were present to witness the incident, I was most affected. *Grihalakshmi*-reading sisters! My request to you is that you carefully read about this event and that you be so kind to respond to *Grihalakshmi* so that they may print your assessment about who was most guilty in this matter, and about the extent to which I am also at fault.[44]

She concludes her contribution with another call to readers to submit their reactions to her story:

Grihalakshmi-reading sisters! You have now heard the events first hand. Next, I ask that you please suggest a way out of this situation for my own peace of mind. Please also offer your judgement as to who you believe is most at fault and as to what extent you believe I am to blame.[45]

Throughout her article, Manorama calls out to the readers when she sees herself in a dilemma: 'Readers! What was I to do in such a situation? It is of utmost importance in my life to obey the orders of my husband. But how could I have done so in this situation?'[46]

FIGURE 14 Editorial (*Grihalakshmi*, April–May 1913 [Vaiśākh 1970])

The editorial voice was present, if not in formal editorials, in dialogues that were interspersed with implicit and explicit editorial comments: *Grihalakshmi* contained several contributions arranged as dialogues between friends, husband and wife, and mother and daughter. In such dialogues, which very well may have stemmed from traditional oral narrative genres and then set in print (Dalmia 1999: 177), one character either provided instruction to the other or they both engaged in a conversation about a controversial topic.[47] Both sides were always granted sufficient space to present different viewpoints on the subject matter (for example, on the benefits and harms of purdah and education, or on marriage practices, or on home-spun cotton clothes). The women encountered in the contributions were far from being the projected ideal women. Kamla, for example, initially did not accept her husbands' patriotic ideas, but had to be convinced in a series of dialogues to display her patriotism by wearing home-spun cotton saris. At first, she refuses to wear the sari her husband has brought for her and she commands him to exchange it:

> You are unrelentingly nagging. If I don't like it [the sari] you *will* have to go. (She looks at the fabric). Alas, after asking you so often you have brought a sari, but one that I don't like. Neither is the cloth of superior quality, nor does it look good. If I wear such coarse cloth and mingle with people, what will they say?[48]

Granting different points of view adequate space—regardless of whether they were considered cultivated, ignorant, educated, orthodox, or reformed—served the purpose of giving voice to subordinate groups (such as to a wife or daughter in the presence of an authority figure). In a similar light, it could very well be argued that the spirit of this dialogic genre was extended to others to follow suit; readers regularly submitted contributions in reaction to published pieces, thus effectively creating a sort of dialogue between reader and text.

Quotidian life is at the centre of debates in all women's periodicals (as it is in girls' periodicals): an essay, for example, points to the irony that Hindu women bathe publicly in the Ganges but are unable to bring their male in-laws medicine for fear of violating codes of conduct. Many of the contributions in *Grihalakshmi* also called for a redefinition of the concepts of modesty and shame. They did so by offering an open forum for debate. Discussions of the advantages and disadvantages of purdah (veiling in public) and *ghūṅgaṭ* (veiling in front of elder male in-laws), for example, are set in the form of dialogues.[49] The conversation between the two friends, Kamla and Purnavati, is an example of such a debate: Kamla, whose mother has prohibited her outings, is an advocate of purdah. She does not consider the demeaning aspects of the practice and even considers it convenient especially in the hot season that women need not step out of the home. Further, the rather pragmatic Kamla holds, purdah is an ancient custom that must be maintained unconditionally. Purnavati counters with the argument that confinement to the home physically weakens women and their offspring. Moreover, she holds, if purdah was introduced in order to protect Hindu girls from Mughal rulers, this practice was, if nothing else, obsolete.[50] Purnavati, aware of the *high* status of (unveiled) women in western countries, regrets the backward state of women living in purdah in colonial India.

A dialogue on the benefits of education lays arguments from the most common social reformist debates into the mouth of female protagonists. In a conversation between a mother and her daughter, the former asks the latter to focus on her domestic duties. The daughter, in response, calls attention to the importance of education through books and expresses her desire to learn photography with a friend. At this, the mother gets upset and emphasizes the importance of needlework:

Mother: You don't mince matters. You cannot even sew properly. If you knew how to sew you would have long finished [your chores] by now. You don't understand that mothers know very well what their daughters need to learn.

Daughter: Yes, mother, this is true, but I will one day have to learn other things. I have often heard that children are taught essential things from childhood onward. Please be so kind and tell me what I should learn?

Mother: Yes, this is true, but not every human being needs to learn everything. What is important for one may not be important for the other.

Daughter: Why is that, mother?

Mother: The primary goal of education is to prepare a person for the work that he has been set out to accomplish in this world. This work differs between man and woman.[51]

During the course of the conversation, the mother explains that the extent to which women are to be educated depends on their caste and class. In a household such as their own, in which servants were not employed, the mother carries more household responsibilities. For example, clothes would not be sewn by a tailor, but by the mother herself. As for the importance of reading, the mother claims that it is not only important for personal entertainment and enjoyment (*manorañjan*), but also for education. Hence the importance of good books:

Some books impart religious teaching about our Creator as well as His and our responsibilities towards each other, all of which we should always remember. Education in geography is also very important. You may remember when Chameli was ridiculed for suggesting that one had to travel to Lanka by train. [...] Next we will need to know about botany, zoology, and mineralogy because we need to acquire knowledge about many things in our daily lives.[52]

The mother goes on to emphasize the importance of knowing the planets, astronomy and astrology, as well as history, especially that of one's own country. She even recommends English as the lingua franca of people from different regions. The mother attaches importance to handwriting and orderly book-keeping for which arithmetic is also necessary. Neither the mother nor the daughter is depicted as uncouth in this lively conversation. The daughter asks questions and demands explanations, such as why she should bother to learn English if she never intends to live in England. The mother is depicted as the prototypical *Grihalakshmi*; she is educated and yet has not abandoned her traditional values. She is a proponent of modern education, but does not disregard women's domestic responsibilities and religious duties. And, notably, she imparts this education in a simple, standardized Hindi.[53]

Readers of *Grihalakshmi* received a wealth of knowledge pertaining to household affairs, child rearing, nutrition, and healthcare. Besides domestic advice, they were introduced to essays, anecdotes, poems, and fictional literature that contained messages about values and morals on topics such as friendship, respect, modesty, humility, and politeness (*vinay*, *namratā*), effort (*mehnat*, *abhyās*), caution (*sāvdhān*), the art of giving advice, the importance of good company, and the ways to develop a strong personality. Contributions about charity (*paropkār*) appealed to women to take action in whatever capacity they were able: teaching, social and religious reform, or working in factories, widow homes, and orphanages.[54] Everyone, regardless of wealth or reputation could support the country, the author held.[55] An article on friendship held true friendship in higher esteem than it did blood relationships or marital ties, for friendship was reflected as a relationship based on hierarchically equal positions of its constituent members.[56] It is doubtful that women readers cultivated such intimate friendships amongst each other, considering the restrictions placed on their physical movement outside of the domestic sphere. Not all these moral messages were designed exclusively for women; many teachings claimed to be equally important for and applicable to men. Besides contributions on virtuous behaviour, there were those that condemned vices (such as greed, disrespect, jealousy, mistrust, anger, ignorance, and laziness).

A reader of *Grihalakshmi* also learned about the state of society in articles on social reform, the status and position of women, and on women's education. What seems most important is that *Grihalakshmi*, in spite of its often conservative character, exposed readers to information that effectively turned the periodical into a space for critical thought and enabled female readers to develop a critical awareness of their position and role in society. Even a comparison of different scrubbing agents used in India and the west triggered thoughts revolving around customs and habits in the household: 'It is not my intention to suggest that we abandon our old Indian customs in favour of those from the west,' the editors write, 'but it is good for everybody to stay informed about the customs of different countries as sometimes this can be of advantage.[57] This exchange of information took place in a language that was easily accessible to women and adhered to a style that included modes of expression commonly used in women's daily lives.

Arya Mahila, Arya Woman (1917–1940s)

A self-advertisement of *Arya Mahila* (Arya Woman) in a 1923 issue described the periodical and the 'new' woman it had set out to *re*-create:

> The purpose of *Arya Mahila* is the revival of women's dharma, the Arya community and society; the progress of knowledge, arts, crafts, and moral conduct, the reform of fallen customs; the preaching of our ancient ayurvedic knowledge for the benefit of domestic life; the teaching of the sciences of music and cookery in order to realize the ideals established for the dutiful woman's community and in order to serve Arya women's organizations.[58]

Arya Mahila was first published in 1917 at the Śrī Mahāmaṇḍal Bhavan in Benares. The editor of this quarterly periodical, which became a monthly in the 1930s, was Surath Kumari Devi (1866–1936). In the periodical itself she was also addressed as Bharat Dharma Lakshmi Śrīmatī Surath Kumari, OBE, gold medallist of Khairighar, Kheri District, Oudh. She had succeeded to the title of Rani of Khairighar in 1885. Pandit Ramgovind Trivedi Vedantshastri managed the periodical's operations. *Arya Mahila* was the official periodical of the Śrī Ārya Mahilā Hitkārinī Mahāpariśad (Society for the Welfare of Aryan Women), registered in December 1919 under the Act for Registration of Literary, Scientific, and Charitable Societies.[59] The main objective of this welfare organization was to protect *varnāśrama* dharma, the ritually prescribed stages in the life of Hindu men and, I presume, also women. This required the reform of practices that did not conform to the *śāstras* and included religious home education for girls and women, including widows of all ages. This society promoted philanthropic work and established educational and social institutions such as colleges (the Śrī Ārya Mahilā Mahāvidyālaya), widow homes, and a training centre for teachers, preachers, and governesses who were then employed as home educators. The society was also active in the publication of religious and educational literature. In the 1930s, *Arya Mahila* became the school journal of the Ārya Mahilā Vidyālaya.[60] The periodical came free of cost for members of the society. An annual subscription cost six rupees and a single issue two rupees and eight annas, which made *Arya Mahila* an expensive periodical for non-members when compared to other women's periodicals that offered a yearly subscription for approximately the same price as that of a single issue of *Arya Mahila*.

Stri Darpan, in a review of *Arya Mahila*, praised the periodical as the first monthly to provide women a sound religious education in the tradition of *sanātana* dharma. *Stri Darpan* alluded to the goddess-centred nationalism prevalent especially in Bengal, with the goddesses Durga and Kali as the region's major points of religious reference:

> [The periodical] is modelled along the lines of Uma, who is delicate but also capable of wielding great power that can split the heart of the enemy, just as the powerful Durga can do when required. It is going to be the goal of this periodical to make women virtuous like the presiding Mahadevi, as well as powerful and delicate.[61]

The frontispiece of the periodical epitomizes such nationalist rhetoric centring on *shakti*, female power. At the riverside, surrounded by mountains, forests, and a temple, goddess Durga (*Siṅhvāhinī Tṛśūldhāriṇī Durgā*) is seated on a rock, holding a trident. She is clothed auspiciously in a pink sari and her lion is seated next to her.[62] The illustration, titled *Jaganmātā* (world-mother), represents goddess-centred Hindu nationalism. The role model here is not only a strong and religious woman; she is also a goddess.

As a self-proclaimed periodical for the Arya woman, *Arya Mahila* aimed at the revival of eternal dharma (*sanātana* dharma) and the preservation of social order, varnāśrama dharma, with caste as its most important component.[63] The ideology of *Arya Mahila* stood close to the religious and educational ideology of Swami Vivekananda's (1863–1902) reformed Hinduism and his teachings on Hindu Aryan womanhood. The editor of *Arya Mahila*, a disciple of Swami Vivekananda, aimed to re-establish the former ideal state of society, in which women were revered and respected. In the first years of its publication, *Arya Mahila* emphasized a revival of the Hindu cultural heritage and refrained from discussing topics such as reforms for women and their emancipation. *Arya Mahila* was then a part of debates on the rediscovery of an imagined Indian past and the construction of tradition, two ventures in which Indian and British Orientalists had been involved since the nineteenth century. A look at the contents of the 1918 issue supports the claim that the periodical prioritized the revival of an ancient Hindu Aryan social structure rather than the woman question: religious texts and prayers in Hindi, translated from authoritative Sanskrit scriptures, form the core of the contributions to this issue. 'Mother of the world' is a three-page eulogy and prayer that the lord of the world (*jagadguru*) may manifest himself, revive the Arya race, and spread Arya dharma.[64] An article by Swami Vivekananda on the four stages of the life of (male) Brahmins catered more to a male readership than to female readers.[65] The article did not discuss the stages of women's lives, even though such a topic could have been articulated nowhere better than in this periodical. Most of the short stories (some of which were Hindi renderings of Bengali texts) were situated in orthodox religious Brahmin settings. Among the informative texts in the issue there were essays on religious sites (including temple sketches) and a book review of the Orientalist George Grierson's pioneering work on Hindi literature.[66] In the course of just a few years, however, *Arya Mahila* underwent significant restructuring. As I argue, it was the genre of the periodical that made this renewal possible.

It needs to be emphasized that the periodical had never been an exclusively religious periodical: progressive poetry by Upadhyaya Singh 'Hariaudh' had been published in its pages,[67] as had nationalist literary criticism, such as an article by the leftist writer Satyabhakt who called for women's engagement in *sāhitya sevā*, the service of literature.[68] Such contributions were not considered antagonistic to articles that extolled ideals of Aryan womanhood. The initial objective of re-establishing a religious ideal, however, had to heed to pressing socio-political matters as they also bore upon women's lives.

Apnepan[69] and Progress

Arya Mahila was particularly proud of making the concept of self-respect (*apnepan*) a central principle of the periodical. Apnepan even became an indicator of social and individual progress. In emphasizing self-respect, the periodical distanced itself from other periodicals and occasionally also critiqued them for their proximity to western thought. The majority of contributions in *Arya Mahila* were based on the injunctions of the authoritative Sanskrit *Dharmashastras*. Unlike nineteenth-century discourses on social reform, which often made women 'the ground' of tradition (Mani 1989), discourses of the early twentieth century illuminated a new tendency: social reform not only became increasingly concerned with women, but was often promulgated *by* women and catered *to* women. In *Arya Mahila* these strands come together even though they might have been undergirded by patriarchal assumptions on gender roles and responsibilities. Celebrating the sixth anniversary of *Arya Mahila* in 1923, Surath Kumari Devi in her editorial presented women's dharma according to the principles of Arya dharma and the ideals of an imagined Arya womanhood.[70] Her aim was the re-establishment of the supposedly golden Vedic age of worship, ritual purity, and austerity, in which Aryan women were revered and learned. Dharma was to be resurrected by means of education in ancient arts, sciences, and vocational skills. Western formal education was not considered necessary.

This emphasis on religious revival notwithstanding, the editor and contributors repeatedly called for reforms and the participation of women in women's organizations. It is at this juncture that even a periodical such as *Arya Mahila*, which appeared to have a conservative religious and social editorial agenda, acknowledged and accommodated a more proactive take on the woman question and on gender roles. Shivpujan Sahay, for example, who was also an eminent figure in the Hindi world of letters, emphasized sameness, regardless of the physical differences between women and men. In his contribution to *Arya Mahila* he states: 'It is an acknowledged fact that there is no difference between husband and wife. Their bodies are different only in their appearance. But their mind, vitality, heart, soul, worries, ideas, and emotions are all the same.'[71] He called attention to biological difference and even more to the psychological similarities of characteristics in women and men, and argued for women and men's joint mobilization in the cause of nationalism.

Nationalist discourse absorbed traditional concepts of dharma and *seva* (service), giving these concepts new meanings even within a supposedly religious periodical. Though the public in which women were asked to engage was gendered (women could figure only in women's organizations), women's responsibilities were no longer restricted to their traditional responsibilities. They gained significance beyond the concept of the dutiful wife, mother, and householder, acquiring national importance.

From the passage in the opening quote, we can deduce ideological assumptions not only about the content but also about the linguistic stance of *Arya Mahila*. The language of *Arya Mahila* contained a notably high number of words from Sanskrit, so-called *tatsama* words. It is unlikely that women were familiar with such vocabulary unless they had received religious education. The language in *Arya Mahila* was thus far more sophisticated (according to the standards of the Hindi literati) than the language in *Stri Darpan*, except for the articles that *Arya Mahila* reprinted from *Stri Darpan*. In a review of *Arya Mahila*, *Stri Darpan* communicated its support of a periodical catering to Indian women. The language of the periodical, however, was criticized:

> In our opinion, the language of this periodical is too sophisticated. If it were more straightforward, there would be hope that ordinary women could benefit from the periodical. If even a large number of men in this country would not be able to understand the language of *Arya Mahila*, poor women are even more unable to keep pace.[72]

And yet, *Stri Darpan* did not consider *Arya Mahila* detrimental to the project of awakening women. Publications for women were all part of one project catering to different women in society. That *Arya Mahila* happened to be more religiously oriented and had flaws did not diminish its value to the woman's cause.

It must be noted that many Sanskrit-derived words were explained with more common Hindi/Urdu words in the footnotes.[73] The editor's decision to nevertheless use these tatsama words was part of the larger mainstream literary project of Sanskritizing Hindi and purging it of colloquial terms (see Chapter Five). Benares, from where *Arya Mahila* was also published, was a centre for the emergence of Sanskritized Khaṛī Bolī Hindi (King 1994: 30) and it had been primarily through the patronage of Hindu merchants and the aristocracy that vernacular literature emerged in the early nineteenth century (Dalmia 1997: 192). *Arya Mahila* was, thus, also part of the discourse on language and the promotion of a national language. It not only provided information on Arya dharma but promoted what it envisioned as the unifying language of the Indian Aryan (that is, Hindu) nation. But Surath Kumari Devi was also aware that *Arya Mahila* was doomed to failure if it did not cater to its primary readership, that is, women. In a 1923 editorial, she referred to reader complaints about the periodical's lack of contributions relating to women's interests and to the difficulties encountered in comprehending the language.[74] She announced changes in content and language and presented the revised format of the periodical with the hope of increasing the number of subscribers: *Arya Mahila* would henceforth contain seven sections (*stambaddh*): (i) exclusively religious texts; (ii) literary prose and articles on literature, society, and history; (iii) appropriate articles for women (sampling debates on women's education, household matters, child rearing, health, pregnancy, and maternity); (iv) sermons; (v) a rubric on women's awakening (*strī jāgaraṇ*) with appropriate (*upayogī*) essays for women on regional, national, and international news (this section would also reprint articles from other women's periodicals and newspapers); (vi) letters to the editor and book reviews; and (vii) an editorial. A column for girls was planned as well. The editor assured readers that the periodical would switch to a simple and amenable language.[75]

These changes testify to a common trend in the 1920s, in which women's periodicals were developing into socio-political journals with nation-building themes. At first sight it might appear that the new concept of the periodical shifted from religious to social issues with a special emphasis on women. The editor, however, drew links between social reformist, nationalist, religious, and spiritual themes. She drew on the shared network of Hindi publications for women and introduced readers' participation as a constitutive element in her periodical. In addressing the language and comprehensibility of the contributions, she also acknowledged that the formation of a national language had to consider specific readerships. She abandoned a purified Hindi of the Sanskrit-educated (male) Hindu elite in favour of a language that would cater to all prospective citizens, including women. In terms of content, *Arya Mahila* began to reprint an increased number of articles from other periodicals, especially those on the importance of women's education.[76]

'Mahila Manoranjan', Woman's Entertainment, in Madhuri, Sweetness (1922–50)

Madhuri, subtitled 'a monthly illustrated periodical covering different topics and related to literature',[77] was a literary periodical of 110 pages in length. It was published from 1922 to 1950 from the Newal Kishor Press in Lucknow, a traditional centre of Urdu and Persian language and literature.[78] As Stark (2004) has shown, the Indian-owned commercial Newal Kishor Press was not only important for the promotion of Indo-Persian and Urdu literature (as well as government announcements and textbooks for government approved schools in the entire Northwest/United Provinces), it was also vital to the spread of Hindi literature in the second half of the nineteenth century. *Madhuri*, with its focus on questions of literary criticism in prose and poetry, was a central publication in this regard. With this periodical, the Newal Kishor Press patronized Hindi devotional literature and court poetry as well as Hindi translations from Sanskrit texts.

Over the first four years of *Madhuri*'s appearance, Dularelal Bhargava and Rupnarayan Pandey launched and maintained the periodical, after which the editorial board changed frequently. The annual subscription rate was as high as seven rupees and eight annas; a six-month subscription cost four rupees. The number of subscribers to *Madhuri* was high: the *Statement of Newspapers and Periodicals published in the United Provinces* counted 6,000 in 1926, 4,000 in 1930, and 2,000 between 1935 and 1937 (Orsini 2002: 65). Of course, not all these readers were women, but the periodical also addressed women.

Even though *Madhuri* was not a women's periodical per se, I consider it important to include this periodical in my analysis, as it created a place for women writers and readers in its pages. It did so by means of the column 'Mahila Manoranjan' (Woman's Entertainment) that was specifically designed for women. Women writers almost solely published in this woman's column and not in the remaining part of the periodical (the July to December 1925 issues contain one woman poet among thirty-five poems by male poets as well as one prose article written by a woman outside the 'Mahila Manoranjan' column); but even though women readers were conceptualized as a separate readership, they could hardly be barred from reading the other columns of this large literary periodical. The women's column of the periodical, *Mahila Manoranjan*, is useful for analysing the changing perceptions of women's roles as they were laid out in a mainstream literary periodical. It is thus important to consider the women's column as a genre, for by the 1920s all major Hindi periodicals included a special column for women (Orsini 2002: 266).

Madhuri can be translated as 'sweetness' or 'charm'. Its related adjective *mādhurya* is used in the same meaning in poetic literary language. The feminine and poetic connotations of the title are reflected in the design of the periodical. Within the first four years of publication, the inner cover of *Madhuri* changed from flowery ornamentation to elaborate images of gods, goddesses, and women. Drawings (Radha–Krishna, Figure 15), women in romantic and romanticized poses (Figures 17[a] and [b]) were replaced with photographs (a portrait of Sarojini Naidu at her election as the president of the 40th Indian National Congress in 1925 [Figure 16]). One can witness a gradual shift in the design and layout of the periodical's first page. From simple ornamentation (in February 1923 [see Figure 15]), the design (from March 1923–June 1923) changed to images inspired by symbols related to Krishna and the Bhakti movement (peacock, flute, a crown of peacock feathers, Krishna's devotees), and explicit depictions of Radha and Krishna, often in embrace (see Figure 17[a]). Later still (August 1925–December 1925), it changed to images that suggested a more explicit feminine orientation, for example one that included a woman's flowing veil (see Figure 17 [b]).

Madhuri's major goal was the promotion of Hindi literature. The periodical appealed to a variety of literary tastes (*saṅskāras*) and was written in two literary languages, Khaṛī Bolī Hindi and Braj Bhāṣā. It was divided into prose (*gadya*) and poetry (*padya*) sections. The prose section contained columns with scientific information (*vijñān vāṭikā*), collections of essays (*suman sañcay*), songs (*saṅgīt sudhā*), poetry criticism (*kavi carcā*), picture reviews (*citra carcā*), and book reviews (*pustak paricay*). The prose section further contained texts on history, religion, and philosophy (with topics such as idolatry in the Bhagavad Gita, religious disputations, and information on religious festivals and pilgrimage sites). The editorial focused on diverse themes, providing practical advice and relaying international news. Sometimes it consisted solely of satire with illustrations by Rameshwar, who supplied most of the illustrations in the periodical. Readers' contributions on debates in Hindi literature and literary criticism were encouraged.

माधुरी
राधा-कृष्ण
[पं० विष्णुनारायणजी भार्गव की चित्रशाला से]
नित प्रति एकत ही रहत ; बैस, बरन, मन एक ;
चाहियत जुगल किसोर लखि लोचन-जुगल अनेक।
—बिहारी
N. K. Press, Lucknow.

FIGURE 15 Radha–Krishna (*Madhuri*, February 1923)

FIGURE 16 Sarojini Naidu (*Madhuri*, December 1925)

FIGURE 17(a) *Madhuri* first page (*Madhuri*, March 1923)

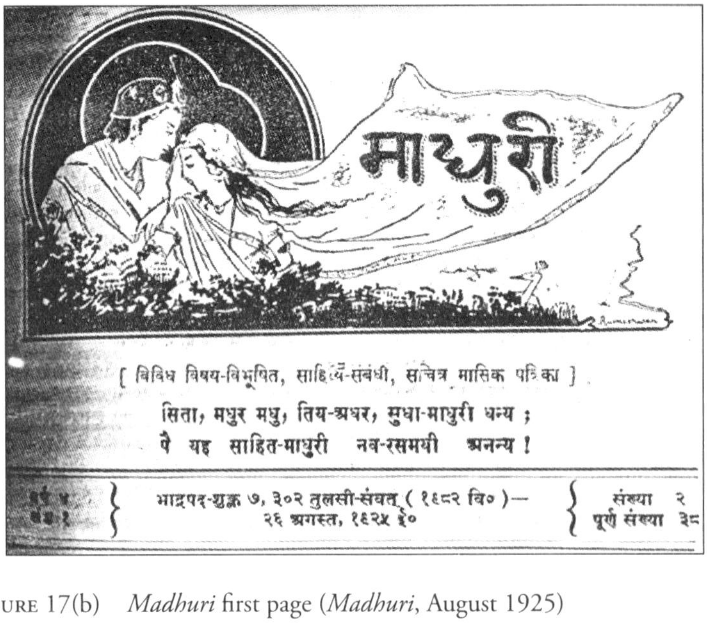

FIGURE 17(b) *Madhuri* first page (*Madhuri*, August 1925)

Integrating Women into Mainstream Periodicals

Madhuri displayed exemplary openness; it took into account all possible literary tastes by offering verse ranging from Braj Bhāṣā poetry to experimental Khaṛī Bolī Hindi verse and by presenting different opinions on a wide range of subject matter (Orsini 1999a: 411). A number of illustrations accompanied the articles. The periodical was almost double the size of women's periodicals. *Madhuri* and women's periodicals shared a number of columns, such as the ones on music, science, social reform, letters to the editors, book reviews, news items, and biographical narratives; the difference being that the women's periodical targeted women in all its columns and not in a specifically designed 'women's entertainment' column.

Among the eminent contributors—of which the majority held academic titles—were the leading writers, literary critics, and editors of the time: Mahavir Prasad Dwivedi, Ramchandra Shukla, Ayodhyasimha Upadhyay 'Hariaudh', Shridhar Pathak, Maithili Sharan Gupta, and Jayshankar Prasad. Some of these celebrities also published original contributions and reprints in women's periodicals, bearing testimony to the shared networks in the Hindi public sphere.

The four-page column 'Mahila Manoranjan' (Woman's Entertainment) was specifically designed for the entertainment (manoranjan) of women. The column was informative as well as instructive given the diversity of information and critical thought presented in it. It also needs to be kept in mind that just as women would have leafed through the entire periodical, it is likely that men alighted on the women's column. 'Mahila Manoranjan' was very informative and covered a wide range of news concerning women: 'Russia's last female ruler', 'London's female teachers', 'Occupations of Japanese women', 'Female police officers', 'Women members of the Legislative Council', 'Women's progress all over the world'—such were the titles of short essays. Some contributions critiqued patriarchy, others promoted *pativratā* (women's devotion to her husband) along with *patnīvratā* (man's devotion to his wife) as an ideal in marriage.[79] The column hosted national and international news on women's topics and provided information on women's daily routines, their political and social struggles, and their achievements in the fields of women's rights. There were accounts of working women in Japan and of the marriage and divorce practices in America and Europe. The August

FIGURE 18(a) 'Mahila Manoranjan' (*Madhuri*, March 1923)

FIGURE 18(b) 'Mahila Manoranjan' (*Madhuri*, August 1925)

and December 1925 issues provide comprehensive documentation of women's educational institutions in British India, such as the Isabella Thoburn College in Lucknow and the Kanya Mahavidyalaya in Jallandhar. The majority of contributions focused on women's education and ways of emancipating them vis-à-vis public roles, but there were also contributions focusing on women's responsibilities as caretakers and mothers. There was a tendency, however, to not only emphasize the importance of education as a means of uplifting women's status, but particularly of promoting women's *economic* independence. Several articles admonished women's economic dependency on male family members and identified it as the major reason for women's subordinate status. Working for an income was thus presented as the means to break the vicious cycle in which women were trapped.

Occasionally, articles prescribed women's roles and responsibilities on the grounds of biology and 'natural' predisposition, but this was certainly only one facet of the contributions to 'Mahila Manoranjan'. The column also addressed different types of obstacles faced by women who wished to engage in the public sphere. Bhagvati Devi, for example, brought to readers' attention the difficulties faced by women writers in finding publishers. She attacked publishing houses for their reluctance to publish women's writings in mainstream periodicals, noting that *Madhuri* was an exception.[80]

A recurrent critique in 'Mahila Manoranjan' was the lack of solidarity in the women's community:

> Seeing another woman, she will ridicule her, seeing abuse, she will abuse even more, and seeing a woman fall, she will kick her once or twice. But I have never come across a woman who will help to relieve the plight of another woman.[81]

Appealing to sisterhood amongst readers, 'Mahila Manoranjan' regularly discussed topics such as women's rights, emancipation, liberation, and education. But the space for demanding women's emancipation and politicization, though a very powerful one when judged upon from the contents of the articles, was restricted to a few pages in each issue. Often these contributions appeared without the disclaimers that preceded many contributions in other women's periodicals. Addressing such topics in a mainstream literary periodical helped to create a critical public discourse on gender issues. In addition to addressing men who were interested in reading the women's column, it also tried to win the favour of men not yet alert to women's issues. The readership was gradually being conceptualized as a composite entity common to women's periodicals as well as to analogous circulatory literature.

Chand, Moon (1922–1940s)

Chand (Moon) was first published in 1922 from Chand Press in Allahabad by Ramrakh Singh Sahgal and his wife Vidyavati Devi. To a substantial extent, the periodical standardized and further developed what the women's periodicals of the 1910s had set out to do: it tendered an even broader format of literary—and socio-politically—informed writings for women, thus remaining oriented towards the gendered audience, while at the same time making the periodical available to the entire middle-class family. In addition to addressing the concerns of women, the periodical promoted itself as overtly nationalist. *Chand* had been such an influential and accomplished periodical of its time that a discussion of it is necessary to complete and conclude this exploration into women's periodicals of the early twentieth century.[82] In arguing that *Chand* represented the pinnacle of the women's periodical, I also aim to support my broader argument that the genre of the women's periodical peaked in popularity in a periodical format such as that of *Chand*.

The objectives of the periodical, as presented in its inaugural editorial of November 1922, focused on addressing social injustice in the context of domesticity:

> To remove social evils such as ignorance among women, the custom of purdah etc.; to acquaint women on a sustained basis with information of use and benefit to them; to equip them with skill and proficiency in essential household tasks or in other words make the Indian woman into an ideal housewife. (As translated in Talwar 1989: 211)

With Sahgal and Vidyavati Devi as its editors for over a decade (1922–33), and Sahgal's brother Nandgopal Sahgal as the manager, the self-proclaimed women's periodical did not revert back to the nineteenth-century tendency of providing traditional suitable literature for women that rendered them the recipients of male solicitude. Instead, *Chand* was 'pushing the boundaries of social criticism and [...] locating women's issues at the core of the nationalist project' (Orsini 1999b: 146–7), a practice, as we have seen, that was also not foreign to *Stri Darpan* and *Grihalakshmi*. While the editorial of *Chand*'s inaugural issue still claimed a certain orientation towards social reform through instruction in domestic skill, it was the 'uncensored flow of information' (Orsini 1999b: 148) offered to the readers that allowed for new understandings of women's roles beyond the domestic domain. Orsini (1999a: 412) analyses the influence of *Chand* as follows:

> It broke the boundaries of (a) 'what women should know' and (b) 'what women should say'. In the first instance, it dedicated more space to news than any other

women's periodical—more than most monthlies in fact. All sorts of political, economic, social and historical topics were presented with no censorship of any kind: scattered among tips on hygiene, such seemingly 'neutral' information carried in fact a much wider and political education than could be achieved through schools by simply exposing women to information they would not encounter elsewhere. Implicit in this uncensored flow of information was the idea—crucial to Habermas' model—that exposure to information itself develops critical attitude and political awareness by making issues public and the concern of each reader.

Such exposure was not entirely novel to the readers of women's periodicals. In a certain sense then, *Chand* fell on fertile ground in the Hindi publishing world; what we may call the new female reader consciousness had already begun to develop a decade ago with periodicals such as *Stri Darpan* and *Grihalakshmi*.[83] Now, women in their role as citizens, and even as emotional beings could be further honed.

Ramrakh Singh Sahgal (1896–1952), a Khatri from Lahore, was well established in the Hindi literary and political sphere prior to launching *Chand* with his wife. His activity in Congress politics informed his new journalistic venture; he aimed to draw women into the nationalist project by redefining the conceptions of seva (service) and dharma (moral duty), and by expanding their scope beyond the private sphere. He had contacts with revolutionist organizations and leaders such as Bhagat Singh and Chandrashekhar Azad (Orsini 1999b: 147; 2002: 267). A shelter, which he had established in Allahabad for mothers and widows seeking refuge, became a meeting place for *female* revolutionaries (Orsini 1999a: 425), and in its miscellaneous section the periodical reported on women who had been incarcerated for the service they had rendered the nation (Thapar-Björkert 2006: 223). Despite its propagandist nature, *Chand* was recommended for use in schools and circulated in public libraries until 1929, when it was banned for serializing a nationalist history of British rule in India by Pandit Sundarlal (Orsini 1999b: 149). Although this did not halt the publication of the periodical, articles were thereafter censored and lawsuits were filed against the periodical under the Press Ordinance of 1930, all of which hurt *Chand* and Sahgal, financially. Sahgal resigned in 1933 to embark on other literary-political ventures and after Navjadiklal Shrivastava's two-year stint as editor, the sceptre was handed over to the long-time contributor and student of Vidyavati Devi, Mahadevi Varma.

She had, by then, risen to fame as poet in the Hindi literary sphere and under her editorship (1935–8), the periodical flourished anew.[84]

Chand had voluminous issues of 100 pages. The language of the periodical could readily be described as amenable and uncomplicated and its style as entertaining (Schomer 1983: 182). As the periodical became financially successful, a smaller Urdu edition of *Chand* was published (Ibid.: 224). This expansion is significant as it speaks to the readerships that were split by the Hindi/Urdu script controversy. No other periodical explicitly addressed either Urdu-reading audiences or, for that sake, Muslim readers. The columns were oriented along those of women's periodicals from the preceding decade and became even more refined and specific. Over the years, there emerged columns titled 'Home-made Remedies' (*gharelū davāeṇ*), 'Jokes' (*cuṭkule*), 'Recipes' (*pāk śikṣā*), 'News from our Colleagues' (*hamāre sahyogī*) [that is, other periodicals in Hindi, Urdu, Bengali, Gujarati, Marathi, English, and Japanese], and spiritual snippets (*śānti kuṭir*) (Orsini 1999b: 147–8, n. 38). Columns featured popular authors such as G.P. Shrivastava and Vishwambharnath Sharma Kaushik, and columns on films (*sinemā aur raṇgmaṇc*), interesting court cases (*dilchasp mukadme*), as well as Urdu verse by 'Bismil' Ilahabadi were novelties on the Hindi literary scene (Ibid.). Occasionally, special issues were printed on topics such as education, child marriage (1922), widows (1923),[85] prostitutes (1927), capital punishment (1928), and the Marwari (1929), Kshatriya, and Rajputana communities. Special issues also featured exclusively female writers (such as in 1923 and 1935–6) as a result of attempts by Sahgal, Vidyavati Devi, and later, Mahadevi Varma, to more actively include women in their publications.[86] Despite their efforts, however, the periodical had difficulty in recruiting female authors. There continued to be a dearth of women writers.

Readers' letters, which had already become popular in the women's periodical, reached their height in *Chand*, where they became essential in claiming a new 'right' for women in distress. They created new space for the expression of women's emotional selves in front of the editors and readers of the periodical. Such letters often questioned traditional assumptions and conceptions of the roles and responsibilities of married women vis-à-vis their husbands and in-laws. Emotional distress was often the result of mismatched marriages (mostly due to age difference), or unkind, uneducated, or uncouth husbands and in-laws, or due to personal unhappiness stemming from a diversity of causes. Women even disclosed in letters their desire to part ways with their husbands for various reasons. Ultimately, it was the prevalence of readers' letters, the epistolary subgenre in *Chand*, that was perhaps most instrumental in the opening up of a space in which women could publicly express their emotional selves.[87]

New Space for the Expression of Feelings and Emotions

Chand's ability to foster relationships amongst women and the periodical can be attributed to its support of a space in which women could express and seek support for their emotional needs. This was important in the process of calling attention to 'tensions between the individual and society' (Orsini 2002: 275), thus providing a space in which individual subjectivity could take centre stage and in which 'social and family norms' (Ibid.) could be presented and renegotiated. In *Chand*—more so than in the periodicals that preceded it—the focus was on institutional, *social* more than political, structures with women as *subjects* and as thinking and feeling entities who engaged in writing as a self-reflexive activity. Their emancipation was seen as intricately linked with the development of individual subjectivity and the editors vigorously followed this line of thought. The public, creative space developed by *Chand* for discussing and debating the nature of female individual subjectivity was consequential in terms of its treatment of women as emotional beings for whom an internal world played very much a part of representing an outer world. In calling attention to the *emotional* (however inconspicuously), *Chand* created significant connections between women of different social status, and featured literature as—to borrow from Orsini—a 'safe place for the triumph of individual feelings' (2002: 289).

The emergence of this space that allowed for individual subjectivity to come to the fore cannot be discussed without mentioning the ideational interpenetration that was encouraged by the periodical format.[88] The juxtaposition of various subgenres allowed the reader to make intuitive and intellectual as well as emotional connections among different subgenres of the periodical. The interpenetration of ideas went far beyond that of propositional content. The format of presentation was intricately linked with the meaning derived from its content. Form combined with content, in addition to the spatio-temporal particularities of the periodical and of the article itself (both in terms of its placement within the journal and in terms of *when* it was being read), *and* of the person interacting with the piece, all constitute a rather entangled web of interaction and impression. This space created by literature, however, and '[literature's] relationship to reality must be understood to be at best oblique ... [l]iterature in this period was "imaginative". New figures and relationships could be imagined while remaining within the boundaries of the verisimilar' (Orsini 2002: 307). Programmes for political mobilization required, to a certain degree, internal consistency in terms of social and emotional underpinnings. Women were to be included, but their entering into the public sphere was not to be and did not occur in a way that could be described as unmediated. Roles would have to be negotiated and renegotiated and, in the case of *Chand*, this was done in the discourse of seva-dharma.

Seva-Dharma and Nationalism

With the proliferation of political publications during the 1920s, *Chand* emerged on the literary scene in the midst of a very distinct climate in the literary sphere (Kumar 2000). And while nationalist sentiment most certainly informed the creation and direction of the periodical, *Chand*'s orientation toward social reform was most definitely aimed at the conditions of women. In this vein, *Chand* reported news that emphasized an awakened female consciousness on both national and international levels. In doing so, it created a sense of community, however imaginary, between and amongst women on a grand scale. More obviously, it integrated women's concerns with nationalist ambitions (Orsini 2002: 267), offering extensive coverage of nationalist leaders, women *satyagrahis*, women's public gatherings, and other political events (Orsini 1999b: 148). Such articles, it must be noted, were also reprinted in *Stri Darpan* and *Grihalakshmi*. But *Chand*'s nationalism was less overt before 1930, communicating its nationalist messages in ways 'furtive, between the lines, hidden in small news items, with most of the emphasis on social reform' (Orsini 2002: 271). During this time, seva-dharma was constantly mentioned in order to address the redefinition of women's roles in the context of nationalism.

The inclusion of concepts of seva (service) and dharma (moral duty) in the discourse of social reform sought to redefine them beyond immediate familial contexts. Popular keywords were used to garner support and service was no longer defined in religious and conjugal contexts alone, but extended on towards respectable service of the society and nation. Women were asked to contribute *more*. The seva-dharma discourse itself almost naturalized female participation in public and rendered somewhat strange the reality that women were *not already* involved in contributing to both society and the nation. Thus writes Sahgal:

The life of a woman is the very image of *seva*. She faithfully serves not only her husband but dutifully serves and nurtures her entire family. [...] Her responsibilities, however, do not lie within the boundaries of her own family, but also exert a significant influence on the society in which she resides; the community is bettered because of her sacrifices. Even in these fallen times, the women's community has made such service its priority; even though she takes care of her children, husband, father, and mother-in-law—and devotes her entire life to them, she has forgotten to serve and exercise her influence on her society. [...] What I wish to say is that our women... often do not understand the essence of seva, and they continue to put their every effort in serving their family alone, effectively neglecting the essence of what it means to participate in seva-dharma.[89]

This excerpt is indicative of a prevalent attitude of the periodical, an orientation that accurately describes *Chand* during the years before its unconcealed nationalist temper. Making reference to female role models of the past (such as Gandhari, Urmila Devi, and Sita), Sahgal reminds readers of the 'fervent sacrifice' and the 'lovely display of the observance of seva-dharma' demonstrated by women in times of 'Bharat's golden age'.[90] He calls attention to the multiple roles and responsibilities of these women, and claims that the virtues associated with the performance thereof are 'innate' in Indian women. Sahgal thus constructs a natural relationship between servitude, morality, and (Indian) womanhood, projecting the image of the *complete* Indian woman as she who relentlessly renounces personal desire and ambition for the sake of her husband, family, society, and nation, and as one who has *always* done so. In the end, it is precisely 'this idiom of service that allowed women to step out of traditional roles and places without losing respectability' (Orsini 2002: 271). It is also worth noting Sahgal's association of the idealized practice of seva-dharma with 'Bharat's golden age', and the presentation of this relationship in the context of prevailing nationalist sentiments.

Importance of Chand in the Hindi Literary Sphere

Thirteen years after the first women-edited Hindi women's periodicals *Stri Darpan* and *Grihalakshmi* were launched, *Chand* was to become the most popular periodical of its time, interlinking literary, women's, and political objectives in its aim to intensify social reform. Ideational boundaries were expanded through exposure to international news and events affecting women, redefining the position of women in light of prevailing nationalist sentiments and aspirations. The production and reproduction of the projected ideal housewife became secondary to the reconstitution of social attitudes toward women (Talwar 1989: 211). This particular orientation was not, however, entirely new. What *was* new was its dedication to inclusivity and, perhaps more importantly, its perspective on the nature of social injustice.

Orsini (2002: 245) has suggested that 'the great popularity of *Chand*, the most prominent Hindi women's journal, which became the most widely read Hindi journal generally' may be attributed to its role in 'raising questions about the family and about women's status in the family from new angles', and in '[arguing] for the need to acknowledge individual emotions as well as duties'. The significance of these consequences cannot be overstated. As a home of 'imaginative' literature, *Chand* managed to create a space in which notions of subjectivity could be considered and questioned. This, given the reach and interactive nature of the periodical format, was quintessential in terms of providing ideational alternatives and perspective in terms of the place of women both at home and in the world.

The general absence of an anti-male attitude (Talwar 1989: 210) calls attention to the absence of an explicit correlation established between *social evils* and patriarchy. Its dedication—one that was much more obvious when the journal was under Sahgal's and Vidyavati Devi's editorship, especially in its formative years—to representing and addressing women beyond the upper, educated classes almost necessitated exposure to the similarities between the life situations of women of different classes, and exposure to relatively open and honest accounts of each other's circumstances and difficulties. Social reform required mobilization, and mobilization required that connections between groups (vertically and horizontally) be established.[91] While this objective could not always be realized within the periodical, the editors published special issues to inform readers about the lives and conditions of a diversity of Indian communities. In this vein, oppression of all kinds was condemned. The open format of the periodical provided space for emotional response. In this way, 'issues like dowry, family oppression, even economic and sexual exploitation, were linked and presented as concerns of all women and of society, not only of an unlucky few' (Orsini 2002: 307). Such new perspectives would inform old ones; interaction with the physical, emotional, intellectual, and even spiritual conditions of other women would affect both social and political attitudes.

Although it never bore comparison with sophisticated literary magazines of the time such as *Saraswati* (Schomer 1983: 182–3), *Chand*, much like *Saraswati* some decades earlier, 'had managed to foster in its relationship a feeling of identification with the journal' (Orsini 2002: 272). In addition, Sahgal and Vidyavati Devi sought to use their periodical to '[foster] a civic and political consciousness for women' (Ibid.: 269). With a perspective on social injustice that did not see as a simple solution the 'uplift of women', *Chand* did not shy away from providing a space in which women's roles and responsibilities could be redefined. The goal was not to 'teach' women, but to educate them in matters historical, socio-political, and domestic. It was perhaps the absence of the moralizing discourse that made *Chand* attractive; women were not seen, however directly or indirectly, to be the cause of the evils that the periodical had initially sought to remove. In fact, it was instrumental in redefining the traditional suitable literature, '[addressing] women as protagonists and active subjects of Indian society and of the movement for national regeneration, not only symbolically, but also as empowered individuals, [m]aking women equally knowledgeable about all sorts of political, economic, social and historical questions, with no censorship', and '[c]arrying news on women satyagrahis and leaders and identifying the journal itself with the nationalist movement' (Ibid.: 268). The influence of *Chand* on the types of literature and knowledge that became 'suitable' for women was significant. And it was with this changing consciousness that women could themselves become more active agents of social change.

In discussing the features of women's periodicals in their early years of publication, I have attempted to create a profile of the women's periodical as it emerged in the Hindi public sphere of the early twentieth century. Journalistic writing became important in the women's periodical because it generated a discursive space of fundamental importance for women of the Indian elite and middle classes. Women's periodicals redefined what was understood as 'suitable' and normative domestic literature for women. Women were no longer addressed as ignorant dependants responsible for the smooth running of the household; they were identified as a female readership requiring a special type of information that would enable them to become involved in national affairs. Women's issues thus became crucial and not incidental in this process of discursive expansion, which is also why women, in their new participatory roles as readers and writers, began to receive attention from the wider Hindi literary sphere.

Women's periodicals were situated in larger discourses on nationalism, language politics, and the woman question. *Stri Darpan* not only created a communicative space for the politically active woman and man, it also circulated news and information for the domestic woman so that she could become part of the public sphere. Even though *Stri Darpan* was a self-proclaimed women's periodical, its readership was not limited to women, as can be seen by the extent to which men were addressed and encouraged to contribute to the periodical. The editor's elite background had an immense impact on the political scope of the periodical. However, the periodical did not promote any single ideological position and it also did not become the mouthpiece of any political party.

Grihalakshmi distinguished itself from *Stri Darpan* and *Arya Mahila* in that it emphasized domestic responsibilities and tasks that women were expected to learn and perform as well as virtues they were expected to possess. Politics, religion, and spirituality were not central to the periodical. However, *Grihalakshmi* was also vital to the women's cause because it acquainted women with dominant debates on the woman question in its news, information, and advice sections. Such information triggered a critical awareness that was vital to the mobilization of Indian women. The editors of *Grihalakshmi* did not explicitly involve male readers to the same extent as those of *Stri Darpan* and *Arya Mahila*; in fact, male authors outnumbered female authors. However, as I will discuss in Chapter Four, the fact that domestic work was treated as a learnable task implied that even men could learn and perform household chores, if it became necessary. In providing advice on domestic issues from such a vantage point, *Grihalakshmi* became an important source for the redefinition of gender roles.

Arya Mahila's primary objective was the revival of Arya dharma. The definition of dharmic tradition, however, was tempered by concerns of national progress and socio-religious reforms. In spite of its claim to retain apnepan (self-respect), *Arya Mahila*, expressly conceived as a religious periodical, was drawn into the larger discourses pertaining to women, social reform, and nationalism. The 1923 editorial revisions ultimately led to a more comprehensible literary style and content revisions established in the idiom of *sahityā sevā*—writing in and as service of literature. Periodicals sculpting the 'new', modern, and traditional *Arya Mahila* and *Grihalakshmi* became part of the larger developments in a nationalist programme. They joined *Stri Darpan* to become part of a wider journalistic network: they reprinted from or quoted each other's contributions and referred to each other whenever discussing issues of shared interest. This happened while traditional female roles were left largely intact. They also challenged patriarchy and older gender roles, sometimes in unintended ways.

Even though the column 'Mahila Manoranjan' and the periodical *Chand* do not fit neatly in the same category as the other women's periodicals (and haven't been granted equal space in these case study analyses), it has been useful to analyse them for the larger argument of this book: a periodical not primarily designed for women was also part of the project of liberating and emancipating women, and a women's periodical such as *Chand* with its focus on social injustice had the potential to act as a national periodical for the citizens of India. Thus, 'Mahila Manoranjan', *Chand*, and other women's periodicals taken together demonstrate that the contributions targeted a community of women without isolating themselves from the imagined community of the nation.

A single periodical issue went through a number of hands in a wide geographical area. All the periodicals from the early decades of the twentieth century provide evidence for this. What must be remembered, however, is that the space provided by these periodicals for women's political and social education, contest, confession, and exploration of hitherto unfamiliar gender roles, though imagined as an emerging physical space for women in the Hindi public, did not readily translate into social realities of the majority of middle-class women (Orsini

1999b: 154). Despite the new roles offered to women and created by women and men writers, these roles added to existing ones, and did not replace them.

Notes

1. In regions such as Bengal and Gujarat, women's periodicals had been published some decades earlier than in the Hindi belt. *Stri Bodh* (Woman's Knowledge) was a journal edited by Gujarati reformers from 1857 onwards. Originally meant for the Parsi community, it was also read by the Hindu and Muslim elite (Shukla 1991). The Marathi journal *Subodh Patrika* (Intelligable Paper) was published from 1877 (Anagol 2005). In Bengal, *Bamabodhini Patrika* (Woman's Paper, 1863) and *Antahpur* (Woman's Quarter, 1898) were popular journals (Borthwick 1984). Stark (2000: 48) has traced references about the supposedly first Hindi women's periodical titled *Sugrihini* (Good Housewife), published from Lahore in Punjab. Jointly edited by Babu Navinchandra Rai and his daughter Hemantkumari Chaudhurani, this periodical (of which no copies can be traced) might have been published as early as 1887 and only for a few years. Two early Urdu periodicals were *Tahzib un-Niswan* (Women's Conduct, 1898) and *Ismat* (1908), published from Lahore and Delhi, respectively. These journals were edited by men or in joint ventures with women. The first Tamil women's periodical edited by women was *Amrita Vacani* (Sweet Voice, 1865).

2. Such titles of Hindi women's periodicals of the early twentieth century emphasize women's identity as female being—as a woman. In contrast, periodicals in Marathi emphasize sisterhood, as the titles of Maharashtrian women's periodicals *Arya Bhagini* (Arya Sister) and *Swadeshbhagini* (Sister of a Self-Ruled Country) suggest (Anagol 2005: 15). Bharatendu Harishchandra introduced his Hindi women's periodical *Balabodhini* (Young Woman, 1874–8) to the readers as their 'younger sister' (Dalmia 2004: 407).

3. Orsini (1999b, 2002), Talwar (1989, 1993), and Mohan (2002, 2005) have developed similar arguments based on their discussions of the women's periodicals *Stri Darpan*, *Grihalakshmi*, *Madhuri*, and *Chand*.

4. Dalmia borrows these terms from Orsini (2004: 435–6). Dalmia (2004: 403) refers to three genres utilized by Bharatendu Harishchandra: the allegorical play, the popular novel, and the women's periodical. Each of them addressed the woman question in different ways, at times excluding certain topics on women in one genre while making them the focus of the other genre. She concludes that the respective genres do not intermix for many decades to come.

5. This codification in print also has roots in colonial efforts to collect information about the colonized country's classical and vernacular languages and, tied into this, about their customs and traditions. From the late eighteenth

century onwards, a diversity of 'grammars, dictionaries, treatises, class books and translations about and from the languages of India' were produced (Cohn 1985: 282). For a list of the leadings texts see Cohn (1985).

6. Amongst our sisters the love for the Hindi language has spread immensely [*Hamārī bahinoṅ meṅ hindī bhāṣā kā prem bhī bahut phailne lagā hai*] (R. Nehru, 1917, '*Sampādakīya: Lekhikāoṅ se prārthnā*' [Editorial: A request to the writers], *Stri Darpan* [December]: 286). This statement nicely shows how the women editors considered it their role to create and spread the Hindi language (see also Chapter Five). Rameshwari Nehru often spoke of the Hindi-speaking women's community (*Hindī bhāṣinī nārīsamāj*), such as in *Stri Darpan* (December 1917): 286.

7. A number of scholars have done so for the British (Armstrong 1987), American (Smith-Rosenberg 1986), and Indian historical (Mukherjee 1994) contexts.

8. Kumar (2000) poses this question about the common grounds of popular and elite literature in the context of novels written by Pandey Bechan Sharma Ugra. These novels found approval from both, popular masses and the elite classes, before attempts to classify literature into high and low as well as popular and elite took sway in the literary sphere.

9. The other three institutions were the Kanyā Mahāvidyālaya in Jallandhar (estd 1896), the Isabella Thoburn School and College in Lucknow (estd in the 1880s) as well as the Indraprastha Girls' High School and College in Delhi (estd 1924).

10. Student publications were often marked as *vidyārthi* (student), an apostrophe that was added to the name of the contributor.

11. Literary activities in Kanpur centred on the Hindi newspaper *Pratap*, edited by Ganesh Shankar Vidyarthi, who was also a regular contributor to *Stri Darpan.*

12. R. Shukla, 1928, '*Sampādakīya*' [Editorial], *Stri Darpan* (June): 871.

13. Strīdarpaṇ ek hindī māsik patr hai jisko striyoṅ ne nikālā hai aur unhīṅ ke prabandh se prayāg se har pahilī tārīkh ko nikaltā hai. Ismeṅ samājik sudhār ādi viṣayoṅ par striyoṅ ke paṛhne yogya kahāniyāṅ aur lekh rahte haiṅ. Striyāṅ bhī ismeṅ lekh likhā kartī haiṅ. Sampādikā Śrīmatī Rameśvarī Devī Nehrū. Mainejar - Śrīmatī Kamlā Devī Nehrū. Ismeṅ lagbhag 72 pṛiṣṭh ke prati mās rahte haiṅ. Kāgaz sundar, lekh rocak, chāpā acchā parantu vārṣik mulya keval 2 I) hai. Ek prati kā mulya I) Namunā maṅgā kar to dekhiye! Har janvarī aur julāī meṅ bhāg badlā jātā hai. Pāṅcvā bhāg julāī 1911 ko ārambh huā. Ghrāhak baṇiye aur striyoṅ kī daśā sudhār meṅ sahāytā kījiye. Aṅgrezī aur hindī patroṅ ne iskī bahut praśaṅsā kī hai, parantu sab se acchā yah hai ki maṅgā kar dekhiye. (*Stri Darpan*, 1914 [March], inner cover)

14. 'Striyoṅ aur laṛkiyoṅ ke paṛhne yogya hindī bhāṣā meṅ pahlā māsik patr. Is patr meṅ dharma, sāhitya, sāmājik, sudhār ādi viṣayoṅ par adhiktar striyoṅ hī ke lekh rahte haiṅ' (*Stri Darpan*, 1914 [October], inner cover).

15. The 1914 issues for example serialized the Bengali historical novel *Rānī Bindumati* by Anadidhan Bandyopadhyay.

16. As early as 1911, *Stri Darpan* published a Hindi translation of a Bengali biographical series on Bengali women.

17. *Kumari Darpan* is discussed in Chapter Three, pp. 103–9.

18. Nandlal Nehru resided in Agra and grew up with his younger brother Motilal Nehru. After Nandlal's death, his widow and five sons moved to the household of Motilal Nehru. Motilal moved the family residence from Agra to Allahabad. The sons of Nandlal Nehru thus grew up in the house of their paternal uncle Motilal Nehru.

19. These three essays were '*Hamāre samāj sudhārak*' (Our social reformers, *Stri Darpan*, March 1918) '*Hamāre sāmājik sāṅce*' (Our social organizations, *Stri Darpan*, April 1918), and '*Hamāre hṛday*' (Our hearts, *Stri Darpan*, May 1918).

20. Ākhirī kuch mās se darpaṇ kī avasthā meṅ ek viśeṣ parivartan dikhāī paṛtā hai, māno isne ek nayā janma liyā ho. Iske lekhoṅ meṅ, iskī dṛiṣṭī meṅ, iske hṛiday meṅ ek prakār kī viśāltā aur iskī nīti meṅ sthirtā dikhāī detī hai. Islie is navīn parivartan par 'darpaṇ' ko hārdik badhāī dete hue ham apnā purānī lekhmālā kī ek laṛī darpaṇ kī sevā meṅ upasthit kartī haiṅ. (Uma Nehru, 1920, '*Hamāre-zevar*' [Our jewellery], Part I, *Stri Darpan* [January]: 5)

21. 'Yadi puruṣ aṅgrezoṅ se svatantratā māṅgte haiṅ to unko pahile apnī dāsiyoṅ ko svatantratā denī paṛegī' (R. Nehru, 1918, '*Sampādakīya: Striyāṅ aur voṭ*' [Editorial: Women and vote], *Stri Darpan* [November]: 225). The word dāsī is mostly translated as servant or slave. It carries a religious-devotional connotation and, in this contribution, is used to describe women's subservient roles in the family.

22. 'Sevā ke sāth hameṅ rājya karne kā adhikār bhī hona cāhiye, ājñapālan karne ke sāth hameṅ ājñā dene kā svatvā bhī milnā cāhiye' (R. Nehru, 1917, '*Strī kā kartavya*' [Women's duty], *Stri Darpan* [July]: 4).

23. Parantu ham yah bahut bār kah cukī haiṅ aur ab phir yah kahtī haiṅ ki strīdarpaṇ meṅ koī aisī bāt nahiṅ rahtī ki jo striyoṅ ke liye hānikārak ho [...] Strīdarpaṇ phir striyoṅ ko vaisā hī banānā cāhtā hai ki jo apne deś kī izzat ko bacāne ke liye svayam bhī taiyār raheṅ. Striyoṅ hī dvārā hamārī bhārat mātā phir ek bār usī uṅce darje par pahuṅcegī ki jis par vah ek samay thī aur jo us kā aslī aur saccā sthān hai. Jab tak striyoṅ meṅ deś bhakti na āvegī tab tak puruṣoṅ ko svarājya kā milnā kaṭhin hai. Strīdarpaṇ striyoṅ ko phir un kā dharm sikhāne kī kośiś kartā hai aur apne jīte jī kartā rahegā. [...] Hamārī bhī apne puruṣoṅ se yahī prārthnā hai ki yadi ham yā hamāre lekhak kisī bāt meṅ galtī karte haiṅ to lekh dvārā ham ko hamārī galtī dikhāveṅ, na yah ki hamāre patr kā apnī striyoṅ meṅ jānā band kar deṅ. Jaisā hamārā dharm hai ki ham auroṅ ko dharm sikhāveṅ vaisā hī auroṅ ka dharm hai ki yadi ham bhūl par hoṅ to ham ko ṭhīk rāste par lāveṅ. Is se donoṅ taraf ke log lābh uṭhāeṅge aur deś kī unnati hogī. (R. Nehru, 1917, '*Sampādakīya*' [Editorial], *Stri Darpan* [February]: 58)

24. R. Nehru, 1920, '*Sampādakīya: Strī Darpaṇ*' [Editorial: *Stri Darpan*], *Stri Darpan* (January): 52.

25. [P]ar hai bilkul thothī bāt! Īśvar ne na to puruṣoṅ ko hī haṭṭā-kaṭṭā banā diyā aur na striyoṅ ko hī baṛā komal—phūl kī tarah. Ādi-yug ke strī-puruṣoṅ ke lie yah siddhānt kārya meṅ nahīṅ lāyā jā saktā. Sṛṣṭī ke yug meṅ strī aur puruṣ ek hī ākār-prakār ke the; bād ko kārya-vibhājan ke anusār puruṣ adhik balī, haṭṭe-kaṭṭe, tathā komaltā-hīn ho gaye aur striyāṅ apne kām ke karte rahne ke kāraṇ pūre vikās ko na pākar kamzor, komal tathā mṛdul hotī gayīṅ. Bhale hī yah antar dhīre dhīre baṛhā ho [...]. Par sthiti aur kuch viśeṣ suvidhāoṅ kī kamī paṛ jāne ke kāraṇ striyoṅ ko dab jānā paṛā. Jab striyoṅ ne puruṣoṅ kī sattā svīkār kar lī tab phir sabhī jagahoṅ meṅ striyoṅ kī paravaśatā aur puruṣoṅ kī svacchandatā mān lī gayī aur is prakār samtā kī hatyā ho gayī. Paradhīntā ne vikās-mārgoṅ ko rok diyā aur is prakār striyāṅ puruṣoṅ se śarīr-bal meṅ kamzor hotī gayī, aur puruṣoṅ ne apne matlab ke adhikār keval puruṣoṅ ke liye hī surakṣit kar diye. (Ramshankar Avasthi, 1920, '*Āgāmī 'strī-śāsan' kī kalpanā*' [The lament of an approaching women's rule], *Stri Darpan* [January]: 2)

26. In Simone de Beauvoir's monograph *The Second Sex* (1970), a social constructivist interpretation of sex and gender roles uncovers processes in which women have been constructed as man's other and reduced to the status of objects. A woman's identity was inextricably linked to a man in her life, hence, she was referred to as the hierarchically inferior *second* sex. Butler (1990: 6, 8) expands on these insights arguing that (i) bodies do not have an existence prior to gender, (ii) that there need not only be two genders, and (iii) that there is no 'mimetic relation of gender to sex whereby gender mirrors sex or is otherwise restricted by it'. Consequently, '*man* and *masculine* might just as easily signify a female body as a male one' and vice versa.

27. Puruṣ becāre parādhīn jīvan meṅ paṛ jāeṅge. Striyāṅ un par huqūmat kareṅgī. Nīc se nīc kām leṅgī aur roṭī kapṛā dekar unkā pālan poṣaṇ kareṅgī. Is vikās ke avarodhan kī avasthā puruṣoṅ ko kamzor banā degī. Ve komal, sundar aur nāzuk hote jāyeṅge. Jis prakār āj kal striyāṅ baccā janne kī maśīneṅ samjhī jātī haiṅ, usī prakār us āgāmī yug meṅ, puruṣoṅ kī hālat hogī. Āj kal ham bāzāroṅ meṅ strī veśyāoṅ ko dekhte haiṅ, us yug meṅ, isī prakār puruṣ bhī ban ban kar veśyā-dharma nivāhne ke lie bāzāroṅ meṅ baiṭhā kareṅge. Tātparya yah hai ki, saṅsār kā vartmān rūp pūrī tarah se palaṭ jāegā. (Ramshankar Avasthi, 1920, '*Āgāmī 'strī-śāsan' kī kalpanā*' [The lament of an approaching women's rule], *Stri Darpan* [January]: 4)

28. 'Lekhak mahāśay ne ek aise yug kā dṛśya dikhāyā hai ki jisko svayam strī samāj lānā nahīṅ cāhtā. Striyoṅ kī svādhīntā ho jāne ke yah matlab nahīṅ ho sakte ki puruṣ parādhīn ho jāveṅ' (R. Nehru, 1920, [Untitled editorial comment], *Stri Darpan* [January]: 4).

29. In 1905, the Bengali author Rokeya Sakhawat Hussain made the bold move of contesting the common narrative of men as protectors and saviours of women. In her utopian fantasy 'Sultana's Dream', the women of 'Ladyland' reigned over the country, whereas men were confined into the *mardāna* (the secluded men's quarters). The story that had originally been published in an English women's periodical was soon translated into Bengali and other vernacular languages (Jahan 1988). *Stri Darpan* carried a similar story about

a society in which women had the say (R. Nehru, 1920, '*Ek sampādikā kā svapna*' [An editor's dream], *Stri Darpan* [May]: 277–83).

30. 'Mai to yahāṅ tak kahne meṅ saṅkoc nahīṅ kartī ki yadi daivāt kisī ghar meṅ strī adhik paṛhī likhī ho aur adhyāpikā ityādi ke rūp meṅ puruṣ kī apekṣā adhik kamā saktī ho to koī kāraṇ nahīṅ ki vahāṅ puruṣ pakāne ityādi kā kām apne na ūpar le leṅ' (Hridaya Mohini, 1917, '*Strī śikṣā par Akbar ke vicār*' [Akbar's thoughts on women's education], *Stri Darpan* [July]: 56).

31. For example, Brahmadin Shaksena, 1914, '*Pativrat dharma aur vartamān śikṣā kram*' [Pativrat dharma and the contemporary system of education], *Stri Darpan* (March): 173–6.

32. As mentioned earlier, there seems to have been an even earlier Hindi women's periodical co-edited by a woman, *Sugrihini* (1887, Lahore), of which no copies can be traced (Stark 2000: 48).

33. Between 1915 and 1950, Sudarshan Acharya and Gopaldevi also edited *Shishu* (Child), a periodical for mothers of infants and young children.

34. During World War I, it cut down on its pages and counted approximately forty pages.

35. These subscription figures are comparable to those of literary journals, such as *Madhuri* and *Saraswati*.

36. Anon., 1913, '*Gṛihalakṣmī* ke niyam' [Principles of *Grihalakshmi*], *Grihalakshmi* (May/June [Jyeṣṭ 1970]), inner cover.

37. The frontispiece of the monthly *Indian Ladies' Magazine* (published in Madras by Kamala Satthianandan from the Methodist Episcopal Press) depicts a woman clothed in a sari, a Victorian blouse and a belt tied around her waist (seen at the India Office Library, London).

38. Krishna Nehru-Hutheesing (1967: 5) describes her home of 1900 as having contained the following: 'a Western and an Indian wing complete with two dining rooms and two kitchens'. The majority of readers of *Grihalakshmi* would not have belonged to similar elite families. The western and Indian inventory of the room depicted on the frontispiece, however, reflect both lifestyles.

39. This disconnect between image and message is also visible in the girls' periodical *Kanya Manoranjan*. See Chapter Three, pp. 117–8.

40. The editorial is translated in full in Part Two, pp. 245–9. Of particular interest are the different mixtures of Indian and western scrubbing agent on pp. 249–50.

41. *Grihalakshmi* (March/April 1917 [Caitṛa 1974]).

42. See the subsection *Chand*, pp. 79–87.

43. An example on where they in fact did comment on a controversial contribution is translated in Part Two, pp. 249–50 and pp. 252–3.

44. Āj maiṅ gṛihalakṣmī kī pāṭhikāoṅ ko sanmukh ek gharāū ghaṭnā lekar upasthit hotī hūṅ. Jis ghaṭnā kā ullekh maiṅ pāṭhikāoṅ ke nikaṭ kar rahī hūṅ vah hī ghar meṅ

ghaṭit huī hai. Aur yah kahnā bhī atyukti nahīṅ hogī ki is ghaṭnā se viśeṣ sambandh rakhne vālī is meṅ maiṅ hī hūṅ. Gṛihalakṣmī paṛhne vālī bahino! Āp logoṅ se ab merī yah prārthnā hai ki āp log nimna likhit ghaṭnā ko dhyān dekar paṛheṅgī aur yadi ho paṛe to gṛihalakṣmī meṅ chapvā kar is viṣay kī sūcnā dene kī kṛipā kareṅgī ki is meṅ sabhoṅ meṅ kinkā doṣ adhik hai aur maiṅ bhī kahāṅ tak doṣī, ṭharāī saktī hūṅ. (Manorama, 1914, '*Ek gharāū ghaṭnā*' [A domestic incident], *Grihalakshmi* [November/December (Mārgśīrṣ 1971)]: 466)

45. Gṛihalakṣmī kī paṛhne vālī bahino! Āp log ab puryokt ghaṭnā ko ādyopānt sun cukīṅ, ab āp logoṅ se merī prārthnā yah hai ki āp log kṛipayā meri citt śānti ke lie koī upāy batāveṅgī, aur yah likhne kī bhī kṛpā kareṅgī ki kaun is meṅ sab se doṣī hai aur maiṅ kahāṅ tak is doṣ kī bhāgī hūṅ. (Ibid.: 470).

46. 'Pāṭhikāo! Maiṅ aisī avasthā meṅ kartī kyā? Patidev kī āgyā mānnā mere jīvan kā ek aṭal siddhānt hai. Is se maiṅ hal kis prakār kar saktī hūṅ?' (Ibid.: 468).

47. Dialogues and conversations were popularly used at the Fort William College not only to teach young British colonial officials vernacular languages, but also to instruct them about the 'manners and customs' of Indians as well as to acquaint them with the 'language of command' in 'master-servant' relationships (Cohn 1985: 306–9).

48. Ai hai, ab to tum baṛe nakhre karne lage. Mere pasand na āyā, to tumheṅ jānā hī paṛegā. (Kapṛe ko dekh kar) Āh, itne dinoṅ ke kahne par to sāṛī lāye, vah bhī aisī, ki mujhe saṅbhale nahīṅ. Na to iskā kapṛā bārīk, aur na dekhne meṅ hī acchī lagtī hai. Bhalā aisā mārkīn sā kapṛā pahin kar kisī ke yahāṅ jāūṅgī, to ve log mujhe kyā kaheṅge? (Anon. [A wellwisher of the country], 1913, '*Svadeśī sāṛī*' [Swadeshi sari], *Grihalakshmi* [September/October (Āśvin 1970): 387)

For a full translation of the dialogue, see Part Two, Box 23, pp. 310–12.

49. Such as Gadadharprasad Jaysaval, 1913, '*Parde kī cāl*' [The custom of veiling], *Grihalakshmi* (April/May [Vaiśākh 1970]) 94–103.

50. Ibid.: 99.

51. Mā: Terī jībh to baṛī caltī hai. Par tū acchā sī bhī to nahīṅ saktī. Jo jāntī hotī to isko kabhī kā sī liyā hotā. Tū nahīṅ jāntī ki mātāeṅ is bāt ko bhalī bhānti jāntī haiṅ ki unkī putriyoṅ ko kyā kyā sīkhnā cāhie.

Beṭī: Hāṅ, mā, bāt to ṭhīk hai; par yah bāteṅ bhī to mujhe kabhī na kabhī sīkhnī haiṅ. Mā, maiṅne bahudhā sunā hai ki bālakoṅ ko āvaśyak bāteṅ bacpan meṅ sugmatā se sikhāyī jā saktī haiṅ. Ab āp kṛipā karke batāiye ki mujhe kyā kyā sīkhnā cāhie.

Mā: Hāṅ, yah to sac hai, parantu har cīz har manuṣya ke lie zarūrī nahīṅ hai. Jo cīzeṅ ek manuṣya ke lie āvaśyak nahīṅ haiṅ ve dūsre ke lie āvaśyak haiṅ.

Beṭī: Kyoṅ mā?

Mā: Kyoṅ ki śikṣā kā pradhān uddeśya yahī hai ki manuṣya ko us pad ke yogya banāve jiske sahāre use saṅsār meṅ nirvāh karna hai. Is viṣay meṅ manuṣya aur strī mātr meṅ bhed hai. (Pyarelal Garg, 1913, '*Kyā kyā sīkhnā cāhie?*' [What all should be learned?], *Grihalakshmi* [May/June (Jyeṣṭ 1970)]: 146)

52. Kuch pustakeṅ to īśvar-sambandhī haiṅ jinse hameṅ yah jñān hotā hai ki hamārā banānevālā kaun hai; uskī aur hamāre kyā kyā karttavya haiṅ; hameṅ use sadā smaraṇ

rakhnā cāhie. Phir bhūgol-śikṣā bhī baṛī āvaśyak hai. Tumheṅ yād hogā ki camelī kī kitnī haṅsī uṛī thī jab usne kahā thā ki laṅkā jāne ke lie rel se yātrā karnī paṛegī. [...] Phir hamko vanaspati, paśuoṅ aur khanij padārthoṅ kā bhī jñān honā cāhie, kyoṅki inmeṅ se bahut sī vastueṅ hamāre upayog meṅ nitya ātī haiṅ. (Ibid.: 148)

53. For a discussion of the language used in this dialogue, see Chapter Five, p. 207.

54. Such as Veniprasad Ara, 1913, '*Paropkār*' [Charity], *Grihalakshmi* (April/May [Vaiśākh 1970]: 82–6). Charity also included forgiveness: Sushila Devi is a widow who forgives her son's murderer (Shaligram, 1913, '*Devi Suśīlā*' [Goddess Sushila], *Grihalakshmi* [September/October (Aśvin 1970)]: 343–52).

55. Veniprasad Ara, 1913, '*Paropkār*' [Charity], *Grihalakshmi* (April/May [Vaiśākh 1970]): 84–5.

56. Veniprasad Ara, 1913, '*Saccī mitratā*' [True friendship], *Grihalakshmi* (April/May [Vaiśākh 1970]): 88–90.

57. 'Merā yah matlab nahīṅ ki ham log apnī purānī hindustānī cāl choṛ kar vilāyatī rīti se kām leṅ. Parantu deś deś kī cāl ḍhāl rīti rivāzoṅ kī jānkārī rakhnā sab ke lie acchā hotā hai aur kabhī na kabhī kām de hī jātā hai' (Gopaldevi, 1913, '*Sampādakīya*' [Editorial], *Grihalakshmi* [April/May (Vaiśākh 1970)]: 112).

58. 'Āryamahilā kā uddeśya nārīdharma, āryajāti aur samāj kā punarunnati, vidyonnati, kalā, śilp, sadācār, kuritiyoṅ kā sudhār, gṛhasth āśram ke upayogī apne prācīn āyurved kā pracār sangīt śāstra, pāk vidya, nārī jāti kī pativratā kā sampādan ārya nārī sabhāoṅ kī sevā ādi karnā hai' (Anon., 1923, [Self-advertisement], *Arya Mahila* [April/May/June/July (Vaiśākh/Jyeṣṭ/Āṣāṛh 1980)]: 380).

59. According to Nita Kumar (1994: 219) the society was established in 1912 as an offshoot of the Bhārat Dharma Mahāmaṇḍal established by Swami Gyananandji. In the 1930s, the Arya Mahila College (which contained a nursery, primary, and secondary educational institutions) was founded by the Śrī Ārya Mahilā Hitkārinī Mahāpariśad and managed by Vidya Devi, a widow from Bihar and regular contributor to *Arya Mahila*.

60. The school was established by Vidya Devi in 1933 as an elementary school and in 1939 higher education was added (Kumar 1994: 220).

61. 'Iskā ādarś ūmā ke samān komal aur samay par mahāśakti uṭhā kar śatru kā hṛday bhed karne vālī durgā ke samān prabalā, naram donoṅ daloṅ kī adhiṣṭhātrī mahādevī ke samān guṇvatī banānā hī is patrikā kā ādarś hogā' (Anon., 1918, '*Samālocanā: Āryā Mahilā*' [Review: *Arya Mahila*], *Stri Darpan* [October]: 224).

62. Unfortunately the poor quality of the periodical issues did not allow for a reproduction of the frontispiece.

63. The term Arya had gained currency in the late eighteenth century when the Orientalist scholars William Jones and H.T. Colebrooke investigated ancient Indian civilization and their languages under the hypothesis of Aryanhood (Chakravarti 1989: 38). It was further popularized in the second half of the nineteenth century, with Max Müller's collation and publication of the Vedas and his usage of the term Arya to denote a racial and linguistic group of Indian and British people. In the nineteenth century, the term Arya was used by social reformers to define a national identity of Indians (Ibid.). In this context, Aryan identity was often conflated with Hindu and even Indian (reformed and/or revived) identity, such as in Swami Dayananda's usage of the term. Debates on Aryan civilization also addressed the condition of Aryan women. A number of Indian and European writers described Aryan women as pious, spiritual, chaste, devoted, nurturing, and educated (Ibid.: 46). Some Hindi writers internalized the self-sacrificial attributes associated with women and engaged with the re-establishment of an Aryan civilization, whereas others contested them and uncovered patriarchal mechanisms that underlay the ancient social structure.

64. Anon. 1918, '*Jaganmātā*' [Mother of the world], *Arya Mahila* (January/February/March/April [Māgh/Phālgun/Caitra 1975]): 215.

65. Swami Vivekananda, 1918, '*Jīvan hiṇḍolā*' [Life's swing], *Arya Mahila* (January/February/March/April [Māgh/Phālgun/Caitra 1975]): 297–301.

66. This was his edited book, *Linguistic Survey of India,* published in Calcutta by the Office of the Superintendent of Government Printing.

67. Upadhyaya Singh 'Hariaudh', 1919/1920, *Arya Mahila* (October/November/December/January [Kārtik/Āgrahāyaṇ/Pauṣ 1976]).

68. Pandit Satyabhakt, 1918, '*Striyāṅ aur sāhitya sevā*' [Women and the service of literature], *Arya Mahila* (April/May/June/July [Vaiśākh/Jyeṣṭ/Āṣāṛh 1975]): 374–7. For a full translation of this essay see Part Two, Box 9, pp. 261–4.

69. *Apnā* is a reflexive possessive pronoun that is generally used as an adjective. Along with the suffix, *-pan*, apnā forms a noun (apnāpan) that can be translated as self-respect. *Arya Mahila* uses the word apnepan, which is not a dictionary entry.

70. See the opening quotation in this section.

71. 'Yah mānī huī bāt hai ki pati aur patnī meṅ kuch bhī bhed nahīṅ hai. Unke bhautik śarīr keval pratyakṣ meṅ do haiṅ. Kintu unke man, prāṇ, hṛday, ātmā, cintā, vicār aur bhāv ādi sārī manovṛttiyāṅ ek hī haiṅ' (Shivpujan Sahay, 1919/1920, '*Pati aur patnī kā paraspar sadbhāv*' [Mutual feelings between husband and wife], *Arya Mahila* [October/November/December/January (Kārtik/Āgrahāyaṇ/Pauṣ 1976)]: 255).

72. 'Hamārī sammati meṅ is patrikā kī bhāṣā bahut ūpar kī or caṛh gayī hai, bhāṣā tanik sīdhī sādhī hotī to sādhāraṇ striyoṅ ko bhī isse lābh milne kī āśā ho saktī. Kyoṅki is deś ke bahutere puruṣ bhī āryamahilā kī bhāṣā bhalī bhānti

nahīṅ samajh sakeṅge, striyāṅ becārī to abhī bahut pīche hī paṛī haiṅ' (Anon., 1918, '*Samālocanā*' [Review], *Stri Darpan* [October]: 224).

73. Some examples of the Sanskritized vocabulary and the word explanations in footnotes are *agocar* (outside) that is explained as *bāhar*; *rahit* (without) explained as *śūnya*; *ke arth* (for, in order to) explained as *ke liye*; and *daurbalya* (weakness) explained as *kamzorī*.

74. Surath Kumari Devi, 1923, '*Sampādakīya*' [Editorial], *Arya Mahila* (April/May/June/July [Vaiśākh/Jyeṣṭ/Āṣāṛh 1980]): 382–4.

75. Ibid.

76. Such as in the issue dated April/May/June/July 1923 (Vaiśākh/Jyeṣṭ/Āṣāṛh 1980).

77. 'Vividh viṣay vibhūṣit, sāhitya-sambandhī, sacitra māsik patrikā.'

78. Literary activity in Lucknow came out of two influential publication houses: Newal Kishor Press and Ganga Pustak Mala.

79. For a full translation of the short story *Patnīvratā*, see Part Two, Box 22, pp. 306–10.

80. Bhagvati Devi, 1925, '*Vartamān paristhiti*' [Contemporary circumstances], *Madhuri* (September): 394–5.

81. 'Ek strī ko dekhkar dūsrī strī haṅsegī, apmān ko dekhkar aur apmān karegī, aur girte ko dekhkar aur do lāteṅ lagāvegī. Parantu yah kabhī na to dekhā na sunā ki ek strī dūsrī strī ko kaṣṭ haṭāne kā udyog kartī aur karātī hai' (Ibid.: 394).

82. While I have also perused *Chand* in Hindi archives, my discussion of the periodical is based primarily on the research done by Schomer (1983), Talwar (1989), and Orsini (1999a, 1999b, 2002). This subsection has been written in collaboration with Balraj Persaud.

83. The new female consciousness encompassed a new female common sense that may be defined as '... untheorised non-homogeneous set of practices and values or beliefs, which are implicit or immanent in the everyday life of groups or social subjects, which contain complex alignments, coherences, conflicts, and contradictions' (Bannerji 1998: 205).

84. Since the time period this book covers ends with 1930, I refrain from discussing the developments of *Chand* under the editors Navjadiklal Shrivastava (1933–5), Mahadevi Varma (1935–8), and Chatursen Shastri (1938–194?). Publication of the periodical ceased in the early 1940s. See Schomer (1983) for a comprehensive discussion of *Chand* under the editorship of Mahadevi Varma.

85. In the special issue dedicated to the condition of widows, Sahgal (1923: 553) and other contributors called for respect and affection towards widows, as well as rights and protection for them. Apart from essays and speeches, the issue contained letters, confessions, and other first-person narratives in biographical and fictional genres. Women's voices, in particular, allowed the

readers to gain insight into the condition of widows from the perspective of the person concerned. In terms of format, many of these special issues were similar, providing an outlet and discussion forum for the readers.

86. This was in line with the objectives of literary associations, such as the Hindī Sāhitya Sammelan, see Chapter Five, pp. 198–9.

87. Orsini (2002: 275) even sees in this 'right to feel' the precursor of the genres of sentimental literature and film.

88. See also Chapter Four for a discussion of how the periodical and its subgenres facilitated the emergence of a new critical discourse on domesticity.

89. Sahgal's essay appeared in *Chand* (1925: 5–8). This extract has been taken from the complete translation of the essay by Balraj Persaud (in Nijhawan 2010: 408).

90. Sahgal's appeals are themselves quite passionate:

> We must inform women that there exists a tremendous difference between one's duty and one's own preferences and desires. We must explain women that being obstacles to the country and society is not seva but selfishness. They should seize every opportunity that presents itself to serve the country. It is a great honour to breathe your last whilst in the service of your country. Women should not be selfish; they should think of others. What beauty is there not in death? What beauty is there not in enduring the anguish of separation? Wherever there is renunciation, wherever there is sacrifice of life, wherever there is a disposition towards sacred service, therein beauty resides. In the protection of the nation, in the salvation of the community, in the deliverance of dharma, of parting with loved ones, in these acts of renunciation of the self lies such sacred magnificence. (trans. by Balṛaj Persaud, in Nijhawan 2010: 411)

91. Orsini (1999b: 307–8) notes, 'after the editor, Sahgal, left and the provocative edge was lost, the issues raised coincided more accurately with the actual readers of the journal, urban, upper or middle caste women on the way to becoming solidly middle class. The claim to represent all women now silently excluded other women subjects.'

3 Girls' Periodicals

So far, I have been discussing women's periodicals that catered towards the domestic woman of the upper and middle classes, but as we have seen, contributions to these periodicals were not limited to domestic affairs. They were also feminist and religious, political and social, moral and popular, and geared towards instruction as well as entertainment. Furthermore, women's periodicals carried topics of interest not only for married and educated women: they were accessible to children, adolescents, the elderly, and men of the joint families, and even of the neighbourhood. With the creation of the female readership, however, attention was now also directed at a different age group—children and girls. Children's, girls', and women's periodicals sometimes had the same orchestrators (*Stri Darpan*'s *Kumari Darpan* and *Grihalakshmi*'s *Shishu*).

Hindi children's periodicals were not the only source of child-rearing advice. An abundance of manuals on child rearing, pre- and post-natal care existed from the late eighteenth century onwards, but the emphasis on children as primary readers was new to the early twentieth century. Addressing this new readership—infants, children, teenagers, and their mothers—the contents of a children's periodicals can roughly be divided into six categories: (i) prayers; (ii) poetry, including rhymes and lullabies; (iii) prose (short stories, tales, serialized novels, and biographies); (iv) moral essays and scientific articles on geography, botany, biology, astrology, music, and domestic science; (v) a riddle section; and (vi) an editorial. They were mostly edited by prominent figures in the Hindi public sphere and printed by publishing houses that were associated with the nationalist project (Chandra 2001). The editors believed that for the purposes of unity in the nationalist project, looking to carve out a national identity not only for families, but also for their children was significant. In this chapter, I argue that children's periodicals gained prominence as national periodicals. *Kumari Darpan* and *Kanya Manoranjan*, the two periodicals discussed in the following, were periodicals that created a sub-category of the female reader by shifting the focus from women in general to girls and young women. They were self-proclaimed young women's (*kumāri*) and girls' (*kanyā*) periodicals, respectively. They complemented two ongoing projects of publishers of women's periodicals: (i) to educate the readers in social and political matters, paying special attention to the woman question, and (ii) to create a level of nationalist awareness in these young women and children and to integrate this awareness into the traditional instruction that focused on their roles as future mothers and even leaders of the nation. Correspondingly, the readers were often addressed as kumārīs, future mothers, and the nation's leaders (*saṇcālak*). In their claim to know what was best for the child and making knowledge available in print, the editors of girls' periodicals *gave* mothers the knowledge required to educate their children. In a contribution to *Kumari Darpan* about geography, B.K. Mitra deplored that mothers were unable to tell children stories about the universe. Addressing children, he holds:

> How often would you have wished to hear stories about all these things? It would have been important to hear these stories from the loving mouths of your mothers but this fortunate day has not come yet. This is why *I* will tell you this story in your own language.[1]

Girls' and children's periodicals thus aimed at filling what was considered to be a void in Hindi literature by providing knowledge to mothers so that they would be able to educate and socialize their children, girls in particular.

Girls' education at home or in schools and the rise of girls' marriage age during the age of consent debates had redefined notions of girlhood that had traditionally abruptly ended with the onset of a girl's menses and her being given away into marriage.[2] Girlhood in the Indian colonial context was therefore defined as a period that could be used to focus on the individual development of girls (Kerkhoff 1995: 121). In the world of print, this meant fostering girls' domestic as well as national capabilities. With the emerging female reader, though, girls and young women were also recognized as economically viable audiences and became a new target in the publishing world (as, too, did the boy child).[3] It has rightly been shown that the projected readership of *children's* periodicals from the early twentieth century were school-aged boys who received supplementary reading by means of periodicals in the Hindi vernacular (Chandra 2007: 295). However, as has been the case with women's periodicals, the genre of the periodical was particularly suited to make its way into an entire joint family and neighbourhood. For readers of all ages—with and without formal education—the periodical with its mix of entertainment and instruction in the form of riddles, recipes, stories, jokes, and games would have been appealing as a genre with both, familiar and new texts that spoke to the diversity of readers. Also, illiterate readers were not barred from the pages of periodicals provided these were read out by other family members.

The contributions in girls' periodicals were not exclusively geared to a gendered reader. At times, gender was even disregarded when texts projected values as equally applicable for girls, boys, women, and men. Chandra, while focusing on periodicals for the male child, even notices the frequency with which female protagonists were 'taking initiatives, wielding guns, [and] plotting escapades' (2007: 311). One can indeed identify a gendered dimension in the discourse on children that prescribed, not surprisingly, domestic responsibilities to girls and not to boys. But the construction of a model of girlhood was only one characteristic of the girls' periodicals.[4] The binding force of nationalism transcended traditional gender divisions and made it possible to focus on the responsibilities of every citizen, regardless of age and social background. The girls' periodicals also appealed to the sense of an imagined community by asking the readers to interact with the periodicals; they were encouraged to try out recipes, games, handcrafts, as well as scientific experiments, and were invited to participate in the riddle or essay contests or to themselves submit riddles and letters to the editor. Once again, the *genre* of the periodical was central to fostering the sense of community amongst children who shared their knowledge and experiences about a particular topic. The possibility of sharing information with fellow-readers beyond the familiar settings, to imagine themselves as part of a larger (national) entity, and even of becoming famous—as I will show in the discussion that follows—constituted a special feature of the periodicals.

KUMARI DARPAN, MAIDEN MIRROR (1916–1920S)

Kumari Darpan (Mirror of the Maiden) was first published in January 1916 in Allahabad. The periodical was distributed as a supplement to *Stri Darpan*, but had its own pagination and was bound in separate biannual volumes. The editors were Rameshwari Nehru (see Figure 19) and Roop Kumari Nehru (after her marriage named Roop Kumari Vancu) who at times jointly and at times alternately edited *Kumari Darpan*. As a supplement of *Stri Darpan*, it continued in the periodical's mission of providing women a forum for publication. Hence, women and girls wrote the bulk of articles in *Kumari Darpan*.

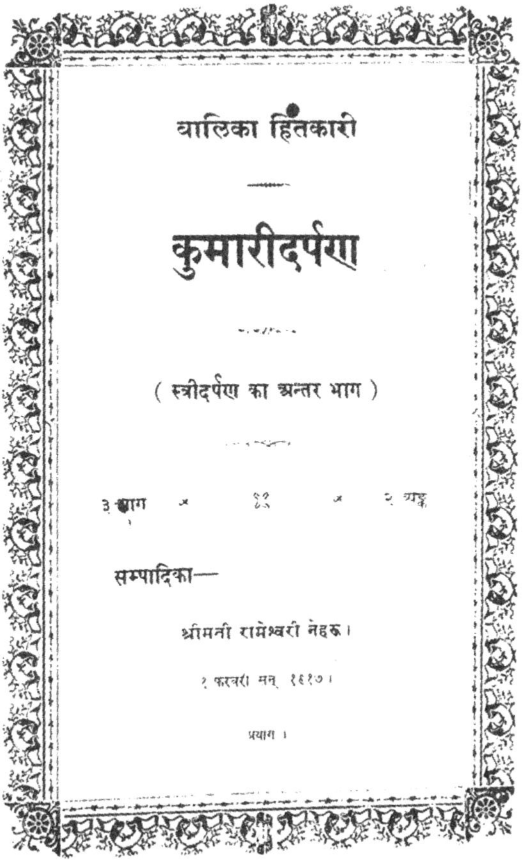

बालिका हितकारी

कुमारीदर्पण

(स्त्रीदर्पण का अन्तर भाग)

३ भाग × [illegible] × २ अङ्क

सम्पादिका—

श्रीमती रामेश्वरी नेहरू।

१ फरवरी सन् १९१७।

प्रयाग।

FIGURE 19 First page of *Kumari Darpan* (*Kumari Darpan*, February 1917)

Each issue was approximately eight to ten pages in length. The periodical carried illustrations and at the end of some articles one inch by one inch separators (see Figure 20) of various images of gods from the Hindu pantheon (Hanuman, Shiva, Saraswati). To a much larger extent than had been the case with women's periodicals, children's periodicals offered children, teenagers, and mothers teachings in the form of stories and essays that carried a moral directed at character development. Most contributors believed that the seeds of national consciousness were sown in the minds of children. Moreover, what was imparted during childhood was essential for adulthood. As such, contributions to this periodical addressed character development for the purposes of creating model citizens.

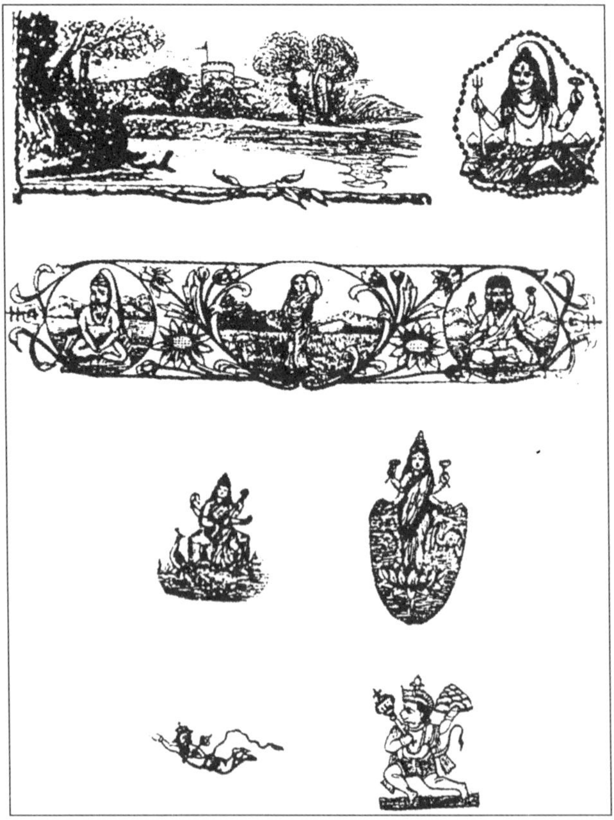

FIGURE 20 Separators in *Kumari Darpan*

Each issue was divided into six sections: (i) prayers; (ii) poems and rhymes; (iii) fiction; (iv) informative texts covering a variety of topics under the heading 'treasure of knowledge' (*gyān bhaṇḍār*); (v) a short editorial; and (vi) riddles.[5]

Prayers

The prayers were directed to devout Hindu girls. Many prayers appealed to god (*prabhu*, *īṣvar*, sometimes to the father, *pitā*) to bestow mercy upon them and free them from the yoke of oppression by granting them education.

Poems and Rhymes

The poetry section covered themes adopted from the daily routine of girls. Some poems were translations of works by European poets such as John Keats. Within the first five years of publication, the number of patriotic poems in *Kumari Darpan* increased significantly. In a social reformist idiom, the prayers and poems called for change through education; girls were in a deep sleep and needed to be awakened. Education was their nutriment. In these poems, patriotic and nationalist idioms often melded with religious ones.

Fiction

The fictional literature section consisted of short stories and serialized novels, in which the reader encountered entertaining literature in Hindi and translations from other Indian vernaculars (mostly Bengali) into Hindi. Translations from English into Hindi were also common, even though the original of a story could be a language other than English, such as Arabic (*The Voyages of Sindabad the Sailor*), German (*Fairy Tales* by the Grimm Brothers), and Danish (*Fairy Tales* by Hans Christian Anderson). Many stories in *Kumari Darpan* extolled the virtues of intelligence and cleverness; others dealt with the lives and routines of married couples and did not shy away from addressing such topics as intimacy and temptations. By way of realist prose, conjugality was discussed in a much more direct and immediate way than in other girls' or even women's periodicals. The writings display consciousness of time and space, they depict realistic characters, occasionally blended with magical realist elements, and protagonists who were able to take their faith into their hands, without showing disregard for the well-being of their community.[6]

Informative Texts

Just like fictional literature, the informative texts in the periodical were aimed at character formation. A large number of contributions condemned greed and revenge. Instead of these traits, others such as generosity, forgiveness, and kindness were presented as exemplary. The often-encountered message was that kindness would reap benefits in the future. People were advised to be generous even if recipients were not 'worthy' of such treatment or even if giving entailed even more personal suffering and sacrifice from the giving side. More than other children's periodicals, *Kumari Darpan* emphasized the development of a rational and scientific consciousness. The informative section contained scientific articles that intended to eradicate superstitious beliefs such as the existence of demons, ghosts, and other supernatural beings (gods from the Hindu pantheon exempted).[7] The readers received information about geography (regions and cultures of the world), meteorology, astronomy (the solar system, stars, eclipses), botany (plants from around the world), zoology (birds and fish from around the world), and health.

Editorials

The editorial was entitled '*Laṛkiyoṅ se bātcīt*' (Conversation with girls). In an informal and conversational tone, it gave information about the periodical's affairs, how articles or riddles were to be submitted, and carried calls for submissions to the periodical. In fact, *Kumari Darpan* urged readers to participate in solving riddles, writing stories, and essay competitions on topics that ranged from the readers' everyday realities to Hindu religious festivals (Holi or Diwali) as they were celebrated in the readers' localities. Furthermore, the editorial section contained minutes of the Kumārī Sabhā (Young Girls' Association) with reprinted speeches from such meetings.[8] Those who wished to contribute to *Kumari Darpan* were requested to write articles on simple topics in a comprehensible language and to submit them with the writer's full name, age, and complete address.

The heightened spirit of nationalist thought and the nationalist movement was also displayed in editorials and news items.[9] Until the mid-1910s, children's periodicals seldom contained discussions regarding the impact of British colonial rule other than in loyalist terms. They refrained from making direct references to oppression and/or colonialism. In 1917, however, *Kumari Darpan* assumed a more explicit and overtly political stance that sought to scrutinize colonial rule. Triggered by the advent of Mahatma Gandhi on the national political stage and his first call for *satyagraha* ('truth-force', expressed through non-cooperation and civil disobedience),[10] Svarup Kumari Nehru in her essay '*Deśbhakti*' (Patriotism) described nationalist developments in India and called upon her readers to practice *deśbhakti*, which literally means devotion to the country:

> Patriotism is to be practiced with the body, the mind and with one's possessions. As for economic wealth, nothing remains in *Bhāratvarṣ*, which is why not everyone can serve *Bhārat* by means of material belongings. But everyone can serve through the body and mind. Whether the person is old, adolescent or a child, rich or poor, it is the dharma of every person [to serve the country]. Whosoever wants to practice true devotion should first make the effort to wear *svadeśi* clothes, eat *svadeśi* food, and advise their friends to do the same.[11]

In Nehru's contribution, the imagination of the nation was linked with personal development and complemented by the various ways in which one could internalize nationalist sensibilities, for example, by way of games, everyday practices, and scientific experiments. The section operated in the idioms of nationalist politics, explicitly critiquing the economic exploitation of India. The broad term dharma provided the moral and religious basis for Nehru's nationalist call, linking religious and nationalist idioms.

Nationalism and social reforms had radically impacted the lives of women. Marriage, for example, was no longer depicted as the only option for girls. This attitude finds articulation in an editorial advice, in which the editors suggest that an unmarried adolescent should be able to decide herself whether she wants to marry the bridegroom her father has chosen for her or whether she prefers to devote her life to social service.[12] At the same time, nationalist discourse made it possible for high-caste and upper-class women to participate in occupations that would have formerly been considered unsuitable or even impossible. If conducted in the service of the nation, social service—which could consist of teaching, preaching, and philanthropic activities—was considered respectable. As an individual gesture of sacrifice for the well-being of society, even unmarried women—as the editors suggested—could devote their lives to the national cause. What had been a new lease on life for aged widows became a valid alternative for women who had not yet fulfilled their duties as wives, mothers, and homemakers. Social service became an equally valid alternative to marriage.

A seemingly small and almost invisible letter column in the editorial could, therefore, turn into a significant component for a reconsideration of the concept of the public. Disclosing and discussing issues that were considered private to a wide male and female readership collapsed the boundaries of public/outer and private/inner spheres as they had been constructed in much of the literature of the nineteenth century. This also raises questions concerning the relationship between the public sphere dominated by male political actors and reformers, and the type of public envisioned by girls' and women's periodicals. There is a paradox to be observed here that does not easily accommodate the distinction between dominant and alternative discourses. It seems that nationalism (retrospectively as a historical event) enabled women to demand rights independently of men. At the same time, nationalism (as a political culture) must be seen as a constraining discourse, where the ideal young woman is one whose duties are bound to the domestic sphere. Alternatively, as suggested in *Stri Darpan*, *Chand*, and *Kumari Darpan*, rights for women were assumed in the form of a double role: whereas women would be required to maintain the home, they would also take on public responsibility.

Riddles

The delightful riddles and questions were, for the most part, submitted by the readers, who often also provided a reward for the first contribution with the correct answer. Such rewards were mostly fictional literature or notebooks. Many riddles consisted of mathematical problem solving. To sample two of them:

(i) A circus company owns animals and birds. Altogether, the company consists of one thousand legs and three hundred and seventy-five heads. How many birds and livestock are there?

(ii) Twenty rotis are to be distributed in such a way that every man gets two and a half rotis, every woman one and a half and every child half a roti. But the rotis are not to be broken apart. Altogether, the men, women, and children count twenty. How many men, women, and children are there?[13]

Other riddles, in verse, described an object that needed to be identified:

(i) A huge tree has large fruits (weighing five *ser*), which are
eaten raw as a vegetable and eaten ripe as sweets

(ii) A lady in green
Her entire body full of color
whosoever wants to be in her company should first color the hands

(iii) One is black, the other white, they serve all purposes
both are sold under the same name
one is expensive, the other cheap[14]

There were no limits to the possibilities of challenging the readers and motivating them to puzzle over a riddle.

(i) Calculation: A man and a woman were walking together. On the way to their destination, they met some women who were picking cotton. The group of women asked the woman passing by about her relationship to the man. The woman replied: His mother in-law and my mother in-law are mother and daughter, now you determine our relationship. Girls, now it is up to you to determine the relationship between the man and the woman.[15]

(ii) On a tree sat fifteen crows. A man shot two of them dead. How many crows remained?[16]

The answer to the final riddle is zero, since all of the crows had flown away after the shot! Whosoever submitted the riddles and their answers was given special mention in the pages of the issue. The solutions and announcements of the winners' names and places of origin were also printed in the subsequent issue. If no one had been able to solve the riddle, it was either printed again or the reward was cancelled.

Mapping Patriotism

Amongst western-educated Indian elites and middle classes, science and reason, among other things, signified education and progress. Reason, as Prakash has stated, became a 'syntax of reform, a map for the rearrangement of culture, a vision for producing Indians as a people with scientific traditions of their own' (1999: 6). Science, Prakash further analyses, 'was safe because it was thought to be nature's self-evident truth, contained in its working, and, unlike faith, free from power' (1999: 67). There existed a crucial link between science, reason, and cultural nationalism in *Kumari Darpan*, which I investigate in the following.

Observing colonial modernity through the scientific writings aimed at children offers a new perspective on how modern thought was communicated in the Hindi public sphere. The informative texts, as I mentioned previously, contained articles that intended to eradicate superstitious beliefs such as the existence of demons, ghosts and other supernatural beings. These texts were not antagonistic to the exciting stories of such otherworldly beings, which were found in the fictional sections of the periodical. In this case, the distinction between informative texts that were based on supposed facts and fictional stories marked as imaginative was well maintained.

I have indicated above that nationalist fervour was on the rise in the poetry and prayer sections of children's periodicals. In addition, scientific articles in *Kumari Darpan* are witness to how the periodical envisioned national culture and how it articulated cultural nationalism. Prakash points to the assumption of Hindu nationalists that a nation not only needed its own literature, history, and culture, but also had to be 'endowed with science, which had become the touchstone of rationality' (1999: 17).[17] The articles on geography in *Kumari Darpan* are a good example of how 'factual knowledge' became a tool to transmit a feeling of national belonging to the readers. In the process, the periodical articles distanced themselves from Puranic conceptions of space and time, a development afloat in colonial geographical texts of the nineteenth century (Goswami 2004: 143) and Hindi textbooks (Prakash 1996). What Chakrabarty (1994: 54) has called the 'awakening to a wider world' that occurred as an imaginative practice before the geopolitical definition of 'India', adequately describes the intent of *Kumari Darpan*'s two-part article on geography. The article, titled '*Brahmāṇḍ Aur Saur Jagat*' [The cosmos and the solar system], intends to awaken the readers' sensibility to the beauty of the world (Part One) and the country (Part Two). Thus, it holds:

Dear children! How pleasing is it to live on this earth. You must have seen its beautiful flowers and fruits, its high mountains and forests and the beauty of its rivers. Some of you might have seen its unfathomable, endless oceans as well as the high mountains with snow-covered peaks even in the summers. You must have seen the moon, the stars, and the sun revolve in all the directions around the sky. How often would you have wished to hear stories about all of these things?[18]

The introductory lines are a general statement about the wonders of the earth, not the country or nation (the Hindi term used is *dhartī* [soil, earth] and not *deś* [country]). After attempting to create appreciation for nature's beauties, the author proceeds to describe 'natural' geographic boundaries of the subcontinent from the Himalayan region in the north down south to the coasts in the east and southwest. In conjuring up an image of India with natural boundaries, feelings for the country as a nation are evoked.

The entrance point to the main part of the article, however, is the sky. What follows is detailed information about outer space: the universe and the solar system, the planets revolving around the sun (they are listed in their Hindi and English names) and the moon. The article describes a model of the solar system and urges the readers to attempt to build a model in their gardens.[19] It explains solar and lunar eclipses, the speed of light, shooting stars, comets, meteors, and the Milky Way. It also explains star constellations and the signs of the zodiac. In fact, the girls are encouraged to locate the constellations in the night sky. It is through this imaginative practice that a new sense of the mother country—and beyond—is planted in the children's minds. The sense of connectedness with other readers stretches out to an even larger space—the universe.

Part Two of the series is concerned with the earth. 'The story of geography' emphasizes the territorial sense of connectedness of the readers.[20] A world map accompanies the article.[21] Hence:

Where is the country in which we live? In which part of the world is it located? Come, let us take a look at the world map. The world consists of different parts. The first part is the African continent, the second is America, and the third Australia. The fourth is Asia and Europe together. Our country, *Hindustān*, which is also called *Hind*, *Bhāratkhaṇḍ*, and *Bhāratvarṣ*, or simply *Bhārat*, is located in South Asia. Asia is the home of many people who populate the land from Asia to Europe. These people are of Aryan origin. Before learning more about the Asian people, we should take a closer look at our country.[22]

The article begins with a definition of the natural geographical boundaries of India: the Himalayas in the north, the southern plains, and the southern plateau. Details about India's major rivers are complemented with agricultural information on the fertile and productive soils of Bengal, Karnataka, and Gujarat. After outlining the geographical boundaries, the author discusses the population of the subcontinent. She distinguishes civilized from uncivilized people and operates in the natural/primitive–cultured/civilized dichotomy of civilizing discourses. Accordingly, Europeans are the most progressive and civilized people in the world whereas Africans, she holds, are primitive people because they lack 'characteristics of civilization', such as an ancient culture, script, and cultivation skills. Equally low in the hierarchy of civilization are Indian aboriginal tribes: the Bhils of the Central Provinces and Rajputana as well as tribes of the Nilgiri Hills.[23] They are considered to be India's original inhabitants, along with the Dravidians, who both were said to have populated the Indian subcontinent before the Aryan migrations. At this point the author uses linguistic terms (Telugu, Tamil, Kannada) to describe Dravidians more precisely. Unlike aboriginal tribes, she holds, Dravidians were civilized people. They fled south as the Aryans began settling in the north-western parts of the subcontinent. Those who remained in the north were employed as servants and eventually came to be known as Shudras. Racial discourse begins to take shape in the pages of children's periodicals. Not only is India mapped in this contribution, the Indian people are being re-mapped as well.

Late nineteenth and early twentieth centuries' scientific discourse on race operated in a framework that was well embedded in the language of colonial ethnography. India's 'Aryanization', characteristic of Orientalist discourse, is also taken up in this contribution. The author describes the Indus valley civilization and praises its knowledge of agriculture, warfare, poetry, and religious scripture. The women of this civilization were responsible for the household and childcare in the joint family. From north-western India, the Aryans spread into the eastern regions (Bengal) and outside the subcontinent to Iran, the Arab countries, and Europe. 'The inhabitants of Europe are for the most part the offspring of the Aryans who travelled west'.[24]

The author holds race as a denominator of supremacy. She establishes a link between Aryan inhabitants of India and Europe (which is also mirrored in her rendering of Asia and Europe as forming the same continent). According to her logic, India was an ancient civilization and Indian Aryans belonged to the 'leading race' of the world. However, she is far from projecting the colonizers as the racial 'other'. She wishes to emphasize that the origins of Aryan civilization spread *from* India. The Indian Aryan identity is projected as a national and hierarchically superior identity, especially when compared to other ethnic/racial formations.

In both articles, race, ethnicity, and territoriality emerge as central denominators of the nation, and nationality is couched in geographical terms. If we relate the article to other patriotic contributions of the periodical (such as some poems and short stories), the point becomes more explicit: factual geographic knowledge of the world is interlinked with cultural knowledge and pride in the Indian (read: Hindu) culture. We find here evidence for what scholars have described as the deep impregnation of national identity in forms of cultural and geographical representation (Goswami 2004; Gupta 2001; Prakash 1996, 1999).

This development intensified in a periodical published more than a decade after *Kumari Darpan* in the mid-1920s, when nationalist campaigns had gained momentum throughout the subcontinent. *Khilauna* (Game) was a children's periodical first published in January 1927 (see Figure 21). In its first year of publication, *Khilauna* consisted of approximately thirteen regular columns of prose and poetry. The periodical was published by Hindi Press in Allahabad, the press that also published textbook materials and was recognized by the United Provinces educational board. *Khilauna* printed an impressive number of 10,000 copies, according to a self-advertisement in the periodical. The first six pages listed quotes from eminent figures of the Hindi literary, political, and educational spheres of Allahabad, Delhi, Gazipur, and Nagpur. Each issue consisted of approximately sixty-four pages and contained up to eight pages of advertisements.

This periodical did not address issues specific to girls and domesticity, but focused on entertainment in the form of games, rhymes, and riddles (see Figure 22). I reference it due to a column that illustrates how the genre of the children's periodical had developed with regard to cultural nationalism and imagined community. *Khilauna* hosted a regular column entitled, '*Deś kī bāt*' (Matters concerning the country). The following quote from this column indicates how patriotism and nationalism were planted into the minds of children through the idea of one origin of Indianness defined as Aryan. In this quote, the linguistic role of Sanskrit conflates with that of ethnic origin.

FIGURE 21 *Khilauna* frontispiece (*Khilauna*, February 1927)

Our country is very big. When we were fewer [in number] we lived in only one place. But slowly, as our brothers and sisters began increasing, they spread to the entire country. There are all sorts of places and areas in our country. Some

FIGURE 22 Children at play (*Khilauna*, January 1927)

are cold, others hot. There are mountains, deserts, fertile and barren regions, in some places it rains more, in others less. As long as we populated one place we had shared customs and traditions, ways of living and modes of conversation. But when we separated, our ways of living, modes of conversation and customs began differing from each other. After a while, people from abroad migrated to our country. They intermixed with us. Their customs and traditions intermingled with ours. This is how different types of people began living in our country, even though they were all the offspring of one mother. On the grounds of these differences, different provinces were formed. Today, there are fourteen provinces in our country. The major provinces are Punjab, the United Provinces, Bengal, Bihar, Bombay, Rajputana, the Central Provinces, and Madras. The Punjabis are strong and simple, those from the United Provinces are very devotional, the Bengalis are fearless and intelligent, the Rajputs are heroic, the Madrasis are simple and the Mahrattas are heroic and clever.[25]

One cannot fail to note the nationalist vigour of this passage. From the geographic and ethnic boundaries and regional particularities of the subcontinent to its exclusively Vedic history and colonization, the article explains to children the cultural diversity of the country. The sense of a diverse 'we', a common history, and a single national language (in spite of the vernacular languages) were projected as the uniting factors of the Indian people. The nationalist tone in *Khilauna* would gradually become combative, such as in the following poem:

> We are heroes, rebels, militant and powerful (1)
> We will be wounded, die in battle and be sacrificed (2)
> We will dedicate, leave behind, and abandon wealth and life (3)
> For the welfare of our own country, our own belief, our own people, and pride (4).[26]

Hindustān, *Bhārat*(*varṣ*/*khand*), and *Āryāvarta* were three terms that described the territory in mind of the contributors to children's periodicals. Another patriotic poem uses these three main terms to describe India. It appeared in the girls' periodical *Kanya Manoranjan*, which will be discussed in the following section:

> Sisters! Dear *Hindustan*
> *Bharat* is our country
> The scriptures describe it as very dear
> *Aryavarta* is our country
> It is our sacred father
> All of you should love it
> And make it a rule
> To serve the country (1)[27]

To describe the territory the poem had in mind, we find the Mughal term connoting the Hindu and Muslim inhabitants of *Hindustān*, along with *Bhārat*(*varṣ*) and *Āryāvarta* each describing not only territorial, but also cultural units. The term *Āryā* in particular established forceful links to the pre-Mughal past by emphasizing an Aryan–Hindu identity (Dalmia 1997: 37). As Dalmia notes, 'Hindustān coalesced only partly with the notion of Bharatvarṣ, which had its own cultural and religious history, just as Hindu, though it coincided with ārya could never have the evocative power of the latter' (1997: 37).

In using all the three distinct terms in the poem, the question of belonging was not clearly defined. I hesitate to speak of an intended confusion and conflation of the principles of Hindu and Indian identity, the way Sarkar (1996: 240) does when noting the usage of the term *mandir* (temple) for post-Independence RSS schools. The equation of national and Hindu identity was certainly one component of women's and children's periodicals, but the inclusive scope of the publishing project should not be underestimated. The allusion to the fatherland, however, reminds of German nationalist discourses during the same time period, which conjured up such very masculine images.

Kanya Manoranjan, Girls' Entertainment (1913–19??)

Kanya Manoranjan (Girls' Entertainment) was first published in October 1913. The editor was Pandit Omkarnath Vajpeyi, who owned the Omkar Press in Allahabad. *Kanya Manoranjan* was an illustrated monthly of thirty to thirty-four pages in length with seventeen to eighteen contributions in each issue.[28] The annual subscription rate was one rupee and four annas, while a single issue cost three annas. Maharani Phulkumari of Dhampur, the Rani of Sherkot, was the main sponsor of *Kanya Manoranjan.* In several self-advertisements, the periodical described itself as a companion for girls and women. It was promoted as the most affordable monthly periodical in India (*Bhāratvarṣ*). The inaugural issue expressed 'the hope that *Kanya Manoranjan* will be beneficial for the community of girls and the world of women all over *Bhārat*'.[29] In all such promotions, the twofold character of the periodical was emphasized: *Kanya Manoranjan* was instructive as well as entertaining—'book of books and game of games'.[30] In the inaugural issue of *Kanya Manoranjan*, Vajpeyi lays out why children are to be conceptualized as an audience different to that addressed in women's periodicals:

> [*Kanya Manoranjan*] has a unique purpose. It is true that many good periodicals for women's education exist. But whosoever knows life will agree that small children, unmarried girls and school children cannot read articles that are designed for the entertainment and instruction of women. This is why a periodical that contains articles and poems for girls is required. We have included suitable pictures. Besides being instructive, we intend to provide entertainment for girls. With the support of our well wishers and readers we will succeed in our goal.[31]

Vajpeyi argued that literature for women was not necessarily suitable for children since entertainment and instruction for the younger generation relied on different parameters. He suggested that children required pedagogical writings specifically designed for them. Vajpeyi specified the audience he had in mind: he distinguished between small children, school children, and girls before singling out girls as the primary audience of his periodical.

FIGURE 23 *Kanya Manoranjan* frontispiece (*Kanya Manoranjan*, October 1913)

The photograph on the frontispiece of *Kanya Manoranjan* depicts five young girls between five and seven years (see Figure 23). They are dressed traditionally in saris, with their heads covered. The attire of the girls, including the sign of modesty expressed by covering their heads, and the earnestness with which four of them were reading a booklet—presumably *Kanya Manoranjan*—does not necessarily correspond to what a reader might have in mind when thinking of a children's periodical. The image conveys seriousness rather than playfulness, as if speaking to future women rather than to children. It would conform more to perceptions of children as undeveloped adults rather than an autonomous stage of childhood. Within the periodical's pages and in the poem underneath the picture, however, a new concept of childhood is visible. The poem on the front cover holds:

> With it the stream of joy flows
> It teaches the knowledge of the arts
> *Kanya Manoranjan* is entertaining
> Look at its threefold benefits.[32]

Although it is true that young girls were trained for their future roles as homemakers, wives, and mothers, they were, however, also treated as children who needed to play and enjoy their childhood (see Figure 24). One advertisement rhyme in *Kanya Manoranjan* held:

> Order *Manoranjan* for us. Read aloud a story from its verses, sing and explain the moral to us, quickly order *Manoranjan* for us. (6)
>
> When I obtain *Manoranjan*, I will play, skip and dance; I will laugh and show it to everyone. I will keep it close to my heart. Quickly order *Manoranjan* for us. (7)
>
> It is better than books. It is full of stories. It has nice pictures. I cannot put it down. Quickly order *Manoranjan* for us. (8)[33]

While being exposed to the playfulness and the happiness that could be derived from the periodical, children were also introduced to their roles and responsibilities towards their families and the nation.[34]

Many articles promoted the periodical as highly valuable for children. Dialogues and poems emphasized the benefits of *Kanya Manoranjan* and the editor recommended the periodical for girls' primary schools. The contributions—prose and poetry—were written in a simple and comprehensible language. In the inaugural issue, the editor thanked a number of periodicals and eminent figures of the Hindi literary sphere

कन्या-मनोरञ्जन
विमला, पन्ना, चन्दा, कुसुम, लल्ला और दुलारी बाग़ में
खेल खेलती हैं।
ओंकार प्रेस, प्रयाग।

FIGURE 24 Girls at play (*Kanya Manoranjan*, November 1913, inner cover)

for their assistance in the making of the periodical.[35] Amongst the regular contributors were well-known figures of the Hindi literary scene such as Girija Kumar Ghosh, Shridhar Pathak, Anadidhan Bandyopadhyay, and the female writer, Bangmahila. The majority of articles were written by men and two to three articles were from female writers.

Each issue began with a prayer column in praise of God (*nāth, prabhu, prānādhār, bhagvān, īśvar*). A drawing showed a girl in prayer, her hands clasped, and her head covered with the end of her sari (see Figure 25, bottom panel). The prayers were set in a humble and modest

FIGURE 25 Illustrations from *Kanya Manoranjan*
Top: Story—Why are you weeping? (*Kanya Manoranjan*, November 1913)
Bottom: Prayer (*Kanya Manoranjan*, December 1913)

tone, emphasizing the trifle of human creatures. They contained requests to protect girls from physical danger, to blanket them from bad influences, to rid them of ignorance and to grant them happiness. They beseeched god to bestow upon them suitable education so that they, by virtue of their intelligence, could spread knowledge all over the country. God was asked to reform society. It is the sacred principle of nationalism, as Sarkar (2001: 250–67) has called it, that shines through in these prayers.

The few scientific texts in each issue concerned topics such as astrology, meteorology, biology, and music, explaining, for example, the organs of the human body, the characteristics of the seasons, or the origin of rain. A regular feature of the periodical was its riddle section. A larger section contained practical information and advice texts on domestic science. Many recommendations regarding cooking and housekeeping were imparted in the form of games.

Approximately three to four stories in each issue were extracts from the epics Mahabharata and Ramayana as well as the *Panchatantra* and *Hitopadesha*, all narrated in Hindi. Parables condemned bad habits and character traits such as pride, greed, and selfishness and instead promoted such traits as hard work, effort, good conduct, and economical time management. Other stories and essays cautioned against trusting strangers and taught the importance of thinking before acting and of carefully choosing one's friends. Nearly every story, including the five to six rhymes (*tukbandiyāṅ*), play rhymes or lullabies in each issue, contained a moral or lesson (see Figure 25, top panel). Usually the good, honest and educated was extolled and projected against the bad, villainous, and ignorant. Many stories validated their moral teaching by claiming the truth of their occurrence. This emphasis on the truth of these stories is an important feature of this and other children's periodicals for the claim of verifiability gave the stories a high degree of authority.[36]

The illustrations on the inner cover of the periodical were accompanied by descriptive text. The pictures or drawings showed Indian personalities such as Swami Vivekananda, Ishvarchandra Vidyasagar (see Figure 26), and Shridhar Pathak, or gods from the Hindu pantheon. Each issue ended with a short editorial consisting of news (*samācār* and *sthānik samācār*) mostly on women's issues, local meetings of women's organizations, and political information specifically written and explained for women and children (such as reports on World War I).

The periodical further promoted books and other periodicals that were considered appropriate for girls and women. Most of the commercial advertisements were from Omkar Press itself. In the advertisement section, the gendered orientation of the periodical becomes visible: of the three-page advertisement of the Omkar Book Depot (see Table 3.1), the following examples give an impression of the way books were advertised. About *Śāntā*, *Kanya Manoranjan* says:

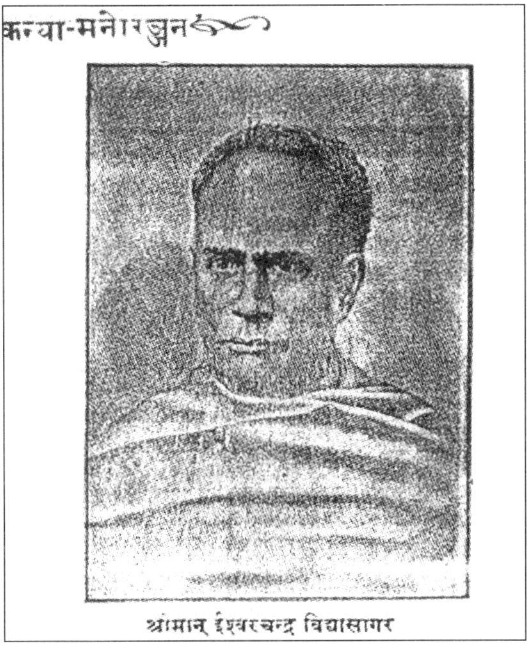

FIGURE 26 The honourable Ishvarchandra Vidyasagar (*Kanya Manoranjan*, December 1913, inner cover)

The second edition of this booklet has been appraised without reservation from renowned newspapers such as *Saraswati*, *Abhyuday*, *Bharatsudashapravartak*, *Bharatmitra*, *Lakshmi*, *Stridarpan*, *Saddharmapracharak*, *Chitramayajagat*, and *Navajivan*. Every household should own at least one copy of this book. In a simple and enjoyable language the author describes the life of an ideal woman. Every girl and newlywed woman who is only slightly educated will be able to understand this book. At several instances there are teachings and advice, all of which are presented in an entertaining way. This book is handed out as an award to students of girls' schools. The deputy inspectors of the educational department have praised it.[37]

The book costs ten annas (eight annas for subscribers of *Kanya Manoranjan*), inclusive of postage. *Lakṣmī*, another booklet, was about a conversation between a married couple, in which the wife proffers matchless advice to improve her husband's business. The fourth edition of *Lakṣmī* promised a 'thrilling lecture'. It would not be put down until finished, the advertisement held; its cost was four annas.

Table 3.1 Advertisement: Books and pamphlets advertised by the Omkar Book Depot (*Kanya Manoranjan*, October 1914: 33)

Kanyāpatradarpaṇ	A booklet for learning the alphabet.
Śiśupālan	A health guide for breast-feeding women.
Kanyā-Sadācār	Essays advising girls about giving speeches and writing essays on topics such as worship, hospitality, obeying parents, modesty, and politeness.
Ishvarchandra Vidyasagar	A biography of Ishvarchandra Vidyasagar.
Bengali textbook	A textbook for home schooling in Bengali language and literature.
Swarṇlatā	A story translated from Bengali into Hindi.
Bhāratīya viduṣī	Biographies of forty learned women (230 pages).[38]
Charitramālā	Biographies on a diversity of personalities from Europe and India including those from Indian mythology, such as Bhishma, Maharana Pratap Singh, Swami Vivekananda, and Herbert Spencer.
Bhūvankumārī	Stories about the amorous escapades of men and women.
Śekhchillī kī kahāniyāṅ	Tall tales about the adventures of a man.

Kanya Manoranjan was also good for surprises as can be seen in the following creative pieces of writing, which is a 'love letter in disguise' (see Box 1, p. 125).

Learning by Playing: The Moral Education of Girls

Kanya Manoranjan sought to enable girls internalize and express—in facets of their everyday lives and routines—the prevailing cultural sentiment of the time. What was vital to this approach was a clear-cut distinction between 'good' and 'bad', as well as 'virtuous' and 'corrupt'. The very first story in the inaugural issue of *Kanya Manoranjan* outlined the kind of qualities and virtues that the periodical would promote in the subsequent issues. The readers were introduced to the sisters Rupvati

Box 1 Letter[39]

—N.N.

Dear Sarla,
The deep love that I have felt for you
is untrue. Now, I feel a disgust for you that
increases with each passing day. The more letters you send to me,
the more I loathe you and
the more I think that I should
loathe you. The truth is that I never wanted to
thank you. In my heart, your sincere letters
are insulting wounds. Don't think that they
confirm your kindness to its full extent.
Truth is that if you do not meet me, well, then
even if we never meet, you will see that I
may be your foe. And you will also see that I do not
respect you. You can trust me that
I am your rival, who never promised that
I will be your friend forever.
When she turned over the letter, she saw the following *dohā*:
Do not weep and lament when you read this letter
Skip every other line and obtain happiness.[40]

and Gunavati. As their names indicate, Gunavati embodies ideal virtues of a woman, while Rupvati is exceptionally beautiful. However, Rupvati is neither intelligent nor modest like her sister. Rupvati is married into a well-to-do family. There she fails to fulfil her household duties and separates from her husband. At the end of the story she is a labourer forced to obtain a living for herself and her child. Her sister Gunavati is studious and successful in school, but her intelligence cannot compensate for her lack of beauty and she is married into a poor family. There she brings happiness and even prosperity to the entire family by virtue of her intelligence and domestic skill. Her children succeed in life. The story concludes:

Dear daughters and sisters! From the story above you learn that good character, knowledge, domestic skill, sweet speech, and compassion are the real jewels for girls, not gold, silver, and precious clothes. If you intend to be loved and happy, then come, eat the delicious fruits of the tree of wisdom and you will be endowed with good character, satisfaction, modesty, hospitability, skilfulness, devotion, and sweet speech. Then you will arrive at the higher stage of another, heavenly world. Remember, virtue, not physical appearance, is venerable in this world.[41]

What distinguished a good girl from a bad girl, virtue from vice and reformed from uncouth was clearly defined in *Kanya Manoranjan*. To convey this message, contrast was commonly used—not only in the prose and poetry sections of children's periodicals, but also in didactic literature of the time as well as in folk and fairy tales (Mukherjee 1994: 24).[42]

The story also deplored that the major part of society still considered appearance more important than education.[43] Reformist literature as well as many periodical contributions claimed that education would effectively make one more beautiful and that nothing could make a girl or women more beautiful than proper education. Many contributions even urged the readers to stop wearing jewellery and to consider education as it was imparted in the children's periodicals to serve as inner and outer adornment.[44]

'Reformed and uncouth' was a poem about the daily routines of two girls.[45] Divided into two sections, the poem begins with a description of dawn. With daybreak, the birds awaken and sing (verse 1). At that very time, Pandits take their baths in the Ganges (verse 2), home-keepers sweep their houses, and daughters tidy up the bedrooms (verses 3 and 4). After outlining these morning activities, the poem describes the morning routine of a girl. First, she combs her hair, oils it, and ties it into a knot (verses 6 and 7). Then she washes herself and her clothes (verse 8). Next, she tidies up the house, gets dressed, prepares food, and serves it to the family. The reader is told how the girl laughs and sings during these activities (verse 11) and how she converses with her parents (verse 13). This first section is subtitled 'reformed' and exalts the archetype of a diligent, clean, and nicely dressed daughter who shows respect for her parents, cares for her siblings, and is devoted to her domestic duties. The second section presents the direct opposite. Subtitled 'uncouth', the reader is introduced to an ill-mannered, immodest, prying, and lazy girl. She is neither versed in suitable Hindi nor is she familiar with etiquette. She misbehaves with her parents, beats her siblings, and whines whenever she is required to perform some task in the household.

She is indifferent toward her personal hygiene, has lice, and wears dirty clothes. Even her parents avoid her company. The poem concludes with the declaration that 'no one will ever marry her'.

The 'reformed girl' and Gunavati in the preceding story are both projected as role models for girls. While it is implied that both girls are educated, the correct performance of (and attitude towards) domestic activities remain at the heart of both contributions. Unlike in domestic manuals for women, housekeeping is presented as a fun activity. This attitude becomes particularly visible in the contributions on cooking.

In the daily routine of girls, cooking was presented as a gateway to fun and recreation (*manorañjan*). It would eventually be promoted as a means to 'nourish the nation'. 'Work games', for example, is a poem bristling with useful advice on cooking and seasoning food.[46] The stanzas discuss the preparation of a nutritious meal including fibre, animal and vegetable protein, root vegetables, and greens. Cooking, which would eventually become one of the central household duties of a married woman, is introduced to the children as an enjoyable activity. It is a game before it turns into a duty. In addition to recipes for nutritious meals, the children are invited to try out recipes for festive activities, such as spongy sugar cake, creative yogurt dishes, special seasonings, and rice pudding.[47] The emphasis on playful, but directed, learning and on learning by doing is central to this periodical.

Another way in which knowledge was imparted to young girls was by means of the doll. 'Girls' games' is a long poem of six stanzas.[48] The tone is instructive: 'I will talk about the dharma of girls, listen what I have to say.'[49] The first stanza discusses the doll's outfit. The reader is told how to weave cloth, apply dye to it, and sew clothes for a doll. Stanza two proceeds with information about designing a home for the doll and the correct performance of domestic duties. In a corner of the room, the doll house should be built with sufficient daylight and air ventilation. The girl is instructed to first build the kitchen, then the altar. She is told how to prepare a proper meal of rice, vegetables, pulses, and grains. After the necessities of food and lodging are taken care of, the girl is told to turn toward interior and exterior designs. She should decorate the house with flowers from the garden and with her own drawings. How pigments are prepared and painting brushes made, is also explained. The poem culminates in the wedding of the doll. The wedding should be celebrated ostentatiously with good food and in accordance to custom and tradition. The friends of the girl should join the wedding procession. The poem issues a final appeal to develop and harbour patience: 'All work requires patience and endurance. Whosoever is impatient will fail.'[50]

In the poem, the reader is given plenty of information about a girl's future role as homemaker. The detailed attention paid to the rooms of the doll house is a direct reference to social reformist discourse on women's ill health being caused by their physical seclusion in dark and poorly ventilated rooms. The doll's sphere of activity is exclusively the domestic realm. The climax of the poem, the wedding of the doll, is a welcome opportunity for the girl to present her 'female' and 'feminine' qualities as cook, host, and artist. Many poems of the periodical thematize the issue of finding an appropriate bridegroom and then culminate in elaborate marriage festivities. This is an expedient and frequently encountered way to prepare the young readers for their future roles as wives, homemakers, and mothers. The doll opens up an entire world of domesticity and adult life. The roles and responsibilities of boys as future men and husbands are not specified, even though boys also listened to *Kanya Manoranjan* stories and were likely to have participated in the 'girls' games' (see for example Figures 22 and 24). Despite the rather clear message of this poem, marriage was not promoted as the only aspiration of girls who were also given the option of becoming social reformers.[51]

Courageous Girls and Intelligent Women

Do you also know the story of such a brave girl? If you have heard of such a story, then send it to us and it will be printed.[52]

Besides the emphasis on housekeeping and education, several contributions in *Kanya Manoranjan* add courage to the list of desirable virtues. Strong women's lives were traditionally narrated in folk and mythological stories, as well as in stories accompanying votive rites and religious festivals. Children's periodicals also carried such popular narratives. In addition, they introduced more realistic stories. 'A thief in the house' is introduced as the true story of a theft that occurred in Kashi (Benares).[53] Jyanvati, a smart and educated woman, notices a thief in her house while in conversation with her mother-in-law. She does not panic, but carries on with her conversation. She begins to tell her mother-in-law about a theft and narrates the section in which the thief is discovered with a loud voice: 'Mother, once there was a thief at our place, but my father caught him by screaming "thief, thief"'.[54] Both the mother-in-law and the thief are under the impression the call for help is part of Jyanvati's story. The men of the neighbourhood, however, hear the screams and rush to help. In the end, the thief is caught. The story concludes as follows:

> Sisters, like Jyanvati you should always be fearless and act with thought. Had Jyanvati screamed out of fear at seeing the thief it would not have been surprising if the thief had killed the mother-in-law and wife or escaped. The mind cannot function in fear; this is why you should always remain fearless.[55]

Jyanvati is introduced to the readers as an exceptional woman. She is not only well accepted by her in-laws; to the women of the entire neighbourhood, her virtues are exemplary. The author informs the reader that Jyanvati earned a good reputation in all of Benares through the above-mentioned occurrence in which she proved her courage and intelligence.

The contributions to *Kanya Manoranjan* repeatedly link girls' and women's courage to intelligence and thoughtfulness but occasionally, even physical endurance falls under this definition. 'Banubai's courage' is reportedly a true story of a seven-year-old Parsi girl named Banubai.[56] Determined to endure the pain for the well-being of her elder sister, Banubai donates a part of her skin so that her sister's burned hand may be treated. Apparently, a part of the story of Banubai was reported in many vernacular newspapers in British India and the government added a biographical account of the girl to textbooks. The author reiterates that girls must be courageous to be remembered all over the world.[57]

Courage and reputation are depicted as desirable virtues: Jyanvati is remembered by the entire city for the courage she displayed in exposing a thief and thus preventing her family from material loss and physical threat. Banubai endured extreme physical pain in order to help a female member of her family. This is a rather unusual example of suffering and sacrifice, which is otherwise mostly depicted in idioms of conjugal or motherly devotion and self-sacrifice. Through the children's periodical, the stories of Jyanvati and Banubai became part of the readers' shared memory. Periodicals were known for publishing acclaimed biographical narratives of mythological and historical Indian women. They also recounted stories of contemporary women (and men) who made individual careers. What is new in the children's periodicals is the appeal to ordinary girls and women to publicize their deeds by submitting true stories of courageous girls. The children's periodicals, therefore, not only offered examples of role models, they encouraged the girl readers to create them. The line between fictional and factional characters as well as the readers themselves blurred—at least such was the case with characters in the pages of the children's periodicals and with those that read them. Henceforth, the readers no longer solely identified and sympathized with the characters of a fictional story, but also with other readers' lives. These new heroines contributed to the changing perceptions of girlhood, womanhood, and citizenship.

There are important links between girls', children's, and women's periodicals: with regard to the targeted readers, the editors of these periodicals assumed a direct correlation between a mother's child-rearing skills and the emergence of future mothers and national leaders, as well as responsible subject-citizens. And with regard to the genre itself, contributions to children's and girls' periodicals, while designed for children, were composed in a way that understood mothers to be their educators. They were thus also a tool for *mothers* to learn what was considered to be significant knowledge. Mothers were not only required to be knowledgeable about pregnancy, infant care, nutrition, hygiene, and general health (information about which was provided in women's periodicals and manuals), they were also expected to teach children etiquette, games, rhymes, songs, and science with the help of children's periodicals. This was to take place in a refined Hindi. *Kumari Darpan*, as supplement of *Stri Darpan*, envisioned national culture and cultural nationalism from the vantage point of young women. The periodical benefitted perhaps most from the nationalist developments of the time that made it possible for women to emerge in the public sphere and acquire respectable responsibilities outside of the domestic sphere. *Kanya Manoranjan* was far more than an 'entertainment' periodical for girls, as its title would suggest. It aimed at teaching girls their future roles in public and private spheres, and used selected genres to convey different messages. Being virtuous, intelligent, and courageous were the new ideals of the time. Their attainment did not come at the expense of respect and obedience towards one's elders.

Unlike the other periodicals discussed in this book, *Kanya Manoranjan* had solely a male publisher and for the most part male contributors. It did, however, share the common goal of other women's, girls', and children's periodicals that made the science of child rearing and child pedagogy a national question. The different subsections in *Kanya Manoranjan* mirror this development: short stories, moral essays, poems, the editorial, and news items, all transmitted values and norms that broadened prevailing discourses on the nation, the family, and children. *Kanya Manoranjan*, as well as *Kumari Darpan* were, thus, also national periodicals geared towards children as the future citizens of India. They both employed the language of social reform when envisioning larger communities of girls and young women that were soon to become citizens of the nation and mothers of future citizens. Within this context, Hindi was projected as the language of progress—a national language in which the future citizens of the nation could be addressed. Central to the contributions in *Kanya Manoranjan* are education and character development. Education is in fact defined as the source of happiness and wealth. Courage, responsibility, and self-determination are also all promoted as valuable virtues. Not all conduct that was promoted in the periodicals was exclusively addressed at a female readership. Kindness, honesty, and forgiveness were presented as universal values that equally pertained to boys and adults. The pedagogical agenda staked out in the Hindi children's periodicals was not simply one of entertaining a new readership with emerging middle-class ideals of childhood; rather, it was a highly political venture dressed in the science of child rearing.

Notes

1. 'Tumhārā kitne hī bār in sab cīzoṅ ke bāre meṅ kahāniyāṅ sunne ko jī cāhtā hogā. Cāhiye to yah thā ki yah kahāniyāṅ tum apnī mātāoṅ ke sneh bhare mukhoṅ se sunte, lekin abhī vah saubhāghya kā kāl nahīṅ āyā isliye maiṅ tumheṅ apnī bhāṣā meṅ vah kahāniyāṅ sunātā hūṅ' (B.K. Mitra, 1917, '*Brahmāṇḍ aur saur jagat*' [The cosmos and the solar system], *Kumari Darpan* [January]: 1).

2. The position of the girl child had become a political topic in the age of consent debates of the late nineteenth century and in the late 1920s. With the rise of the minimum age of marriage from ten to twelve (in 1891) and from twelve to fourteen (in 1929), the stage of girlhood was also extended. Kerkhoff (1995: 113) concludes from this development that amongst many *bhadralok* (upper middle-class) families in Bengal, higher education filled the increasing gap between puberty and marriage.

3. Apart from those women's periodicals with supplements for the young woman (*Stri Darpan*'s *Kumari Darpan*) and the infant child (*Grihalakshmi*'s *Shishu*), or with a special advice section for girls ('Balaprabodh' in *Balabodhini*), periodicals addressed boys and girls explicitly in their titles (such as *Balak*, *Kanya Manoranjan*).

4. As Kerkhoff (1995) has argued in the case of Bengal, it was in girls' schools, where the feminization and nationalization of women's education was enhanced. Institutionalized pedagogy proved instrumental in shaping group boundedness as a 'field above politics'. It also served as a field in which conceptions of girlhood were created often by the teachers of these schools, who were Bengali Hindu and Muslim women as well as missionaries.

5. The 1922 issues of *Kumari Darpan* consisted almost exclusively of riddles and jokes as well as one serialized story.

6. Mukherjee (1994: 3–124) has provided a detailed analysis of early writings in the genre of the novel in which she emphasizes the blending of elements from traditional indigenous narrative traditions and English novels that may have served as models for Indian fiction writing.

7. And yet, the existence of god was thematized in the poem '*Vah kahāṅ*' (Anon., 1917, '*Vah kahāṅ*' [Where is he], *Kumari Darpan* [July]: 2–3). It is set in the form of a conversation between a girl in search of god and a guru who explains that god is omnipresent. The girl exclaims that she has understood that 'in the world, god is in all things and beings' (jag meṅ sab meṅ haiṅ bhagvān) (Ibid.: 3).

8. It is likely that the Kumārī Sabhā was linked to the Prayāg Mahilā Samiti.

9. The minutes of the ninth Kumāri Sabhā meeting listed the singing of the nationalist song '*Vande Mātaram*'. The meeting had focused on the topic of the preservation of one's strength (*śakti*) for the sake of the mother country (*mātṛbhūmi*) (*Kumari Darpan*, 1917 [April]: 28–30).

10. This first call was made by Gandhi in 1917, in Champaran, Bihar.

11. Deśbhakti tan, man aur dhan se honī cāhiye. Dhan to ab bhāratvarṣ meṅ rahā hī nahīṅ, is kāraṇ har ek dhan se bhārat kī sevā nahīṅ kar saktā. Parantu tan aur man se to har ek kar saktā hai. Yadi vah būṛhā, javān yā baccā ho aur cāhe vah amīr ho yā garīb yah har manuṣya kā param dharma hai. Jo aslī bhakti karnā cāhte haiṅ, unko sab se pahile iskā yatna karnā cāhiye ki vah svadeśī vastra pahineṅ aur svadeśī ann khāveṅ aur apne mitroṅ ko bhī yahī upadeś deveṅ. (Svarup Kumari Nehru, 1917, '*Deśbhakti*' [Patriotism], *Kumari Darpan* [October]: 30)

12. R. Nehru and R.K. Vancu, 1922, '*Laṛkiyoṅ se bātcit*' [Conversation with girls], *Kumari Darpan* (May): 39–40. See full translation of the editors' response to a reader's letter in Part Two, Box 3, pp. 249–50, as well as a discussion in Chapter Four, pp. 161–2.

13. (1) Ek sarkas kī kampanī meṅ kuch jānvar aur kuch ciṛiyāṅ haiṅ. Kul gintī ṭāṅgoṅ kī us kampanī meṅ ek hazār hai aur kul gintī siroṅ kī tīn sau pichattar. To batāo ki kitnī ciṛiyāṅ aur kitne caupāye haiṅ?
(2) Bīs roṭī mardoṅ auratoṅ aur baccoṅ meṅ is tarah se taqsīm karnī haiṅ ki har mard ko ḍhāī roṭī aur har aurat ko deṛh roṭī aur har bacce ko ādhī roṭī mile. Lekin roṭī ṭūṭne na pāve. Aur mard auratoṅ aur baccoṅ kī kul tādād 20 hai. To batāo ki mard, aurateṅ aur bacce kitne kitne haiṅ? (*Kumari Darpan*, 1920 [January]: 6)

14. Ek peṛ dhambūsaṛ sā // Phal uskā baṅserī sā // Kaccā vah tarkārī kā // Pakkā lage miṭhāī sā [Ans: Jackfruit].
Ek nār raṅgat kī harī // Sārā badan raṅg meṅ bharī // Jo koī uskī saṅgat kare // Pahile hāth raṅg meṅ bhare [Ans: Henna].
Ek kālī ek gorī nār // Ek hī nām dharā karttār // Donoṅ ek hī nām bikāy // Ek mahaṅgī ek sastī jāy [Ans: Cardamom]. (*Kumari Darpan*, 1917 [October]: 32)

15. Hisāb: Ek ādmī aur ek aurat sāth kahīṅ ko jā rahe the. Rāste meṅ kuch auarateṅ kapās bīn rahīṅ thīṅ, unhoṅne aurat se pūchā, bahin yah ādmī tumhārā kaun hai? Us aurat ne javāb diyā 'bīnan vālī bīno kapās jākī sāsu aur merī sāsu sagī maṅ beṭī hai riśtā tum joṛ lo.' Ab kanyāeṅ batāveṅ ki us mard aur aurat kā riśtā kyā thā [Ans: A woman and her niece's husband]. (*Kumari Darpan*, 1920 [March]: 21)

16. 'Ek peṛ par 15 kaue baiṭhe the. Ek sāhab ne bandūk calā kar do kauoṅ ko mār ḍālā. Kaho to peṛ par kitne kaue bāqī rahe?' (*Kumari Darpan*, 1917 [October]: 29)

17. Prakash's (1999) research investigates how science acquired universal authority effectively gaining ascendancy in the colonies of the British Empire. In the nineteenth century, science occupied a special role in the civilizing mission of British imperialists who sought to modernize India. Hence, modern engineering technologies such as railway tracks, irrigation systems, telegraphs, or allopathic medicine were introduced to the subcontinent.

18. Pyāre bacco! Jis dhartī par ham rahte haiṅ vah kaisī suhāvanī hai. Tum ne is ke sundar sundar phūl phal dekhe hoṅge, is ke ūpar pahāṛ jaṅgal, nadiyoṅ kī śobhā dekhī hogī. Tum meṅ se kisī kisī ne iske athāh samudra bhī dekhe hoṅge ki jinkī hadd dikhāī nahīṅ detī yā aise ūṅce ūṅce pahāṛ bhī dekhe hoṅge jinke sir par garmiyoṅ ke dinoṅ meṅ bhī baraf jamī huī rahtī hai. Tumne iske cāroṅ taraf cānd, sitāre aur sūraj ko phirte hue dekhā hogā. Tumhārā kitne hī bār in sab cīzoṅ ke bāre meṅ kahāniyāṅ sunne ko jī cāhtā hoga. (B.K. Mitra, 1917, '*Brahmāṇḍ aur saur jagat*' [The cosmos and the solar system], *Kumari Darpan* [January]: 1).

19. A ball would represent the sun and in the distance of eighty feet a mustard seed would be placed to represent Mercury (*Budh*). One hundred and forty feet from the sun a pea would represent Venus (*Śukra*), and two hundred feet from the sun would be Earth (in the form of a big pea) and so forth. Note that gardens would have to have been quite large for this model experiment.

20. Prempyari Devi, 1917, '*Bhūgol kī kahānī*' [The story of geography], *Kumari Darpan* (February): 9–13.

21. Nationalism, as inscribed in the object of the map, has also been discussed with regard to the establishment of the *Bharat Mata* temple in early

twentieth-century Benares (Gupta 2001). The temple did not contain any religious icons but 'mapped' the 'divine Mother' and 'divine nation' with a map. In a similar vein, vernacular schools in the United Provinces introduced maps to classes successively by region (with the smallest region being taught to lower-level classes): district maps were taught in class three, provincial maps in class four, the map of India in class five, followed by the map of Asia in class six and the world map in class seven (Goswami 2004: 143). Cartographic knowledge impelled children to envision a larger community beyond their immediate surroundings. Goswami makes an important observation about colonial cartographic sources used as teaching materials, arguing that colonial conceptions were reconfigured to meet nationalist purposes:

> During the last third of the nineteenth century, emergent nationalist discourse transfigured the geographical determinism of official discourse toward a stress on rational, willed agency. Appropriating the cognitive logic of modern maps, especially the unambiguous fixing of people and territory, nationalists forged a practical and visual revaluation of colonial state space as specifically non-national. Baptized with a proper name, *Bharat*, colonial space was reconfigured as national property (2004: 145).

This quote bears even stronger against the background of the following section in the article discussed above.

22. Jis deś meṅ ham log rahte haiṅ vah kahāṅ hai? Duniyāṅ ke kis kone meṅ basā hai? Āo duniyāṅ kā naqśā dekheṅ. Dhartī ke kaī baṛe baṛe ṭukṛe haiṅ. Ek ṭukṛe kā nām afrīkā mahādvīp dūsre kā amerikā mahādvīp tīsre kā āṣṭreliyā aur cauthe meṅ eśiyā yūrop donoṅ mile haiṅ. Hamārā deś hindustān jise hind bhāratkhaṇḍ aur bhāratvarṣ yā keval bhārat bhī kahte haiṅ, eśiyā ke dakṣin meṅ hai. Eśiyā bahut se logoṅ kā ghar hai jo eśiyā hī kyā yūrop tak phaile haiṅ. Yah log ārya jāti ke haiṅ. Eśiyā ke rahnevāloṅ kā vyorā jānne ke pahile, hameṅ apne hī deś ko dhyān se dekhnā cāhiye. (Prempyari Devi, 1917, '*Bhūgol kī kahānī*' [The story of geography], *Kumari Darpan* [February]: 9)

23. Herbert Risley in his early classificatory compilation, *The People of India* (1915: 139), divides different ethnic groups according to 'physical' and 'social' types. He adds proverbs and popular sayings, as well as information on marriage and religious practices of the respective groups. He describes the Bhil as 'animistic tribe outside the bounds of Hinduism' and as 'hunter, blackmailer and highway robber'. It is likely that Prempyari Devi drew on such colonial sources for her article.

24. 'Yūrop ke bāsī adhikāṅś unhīṅ āryoṅ kī santān haiṅ jo paścim kī or gaye the'. (Prempyari Devi, 1917, '*Bhūgol kī kahānī*' [The story of geography], *Kumari Darpan* [February]: 13)

25. Hamārā deś bahut baṛā hai. Jab ham thoṛe the tab ek hī jagah rahte the. Par dhīre dhīre jyūṅ jyūṅ hamāre bhāī bahan baṛhne gaye tyūṅ tyūṅ ve sab sāre deś meṅ phail gaye. Hamāre deś meṅ sab tarah ke sthān haiṅ, koī ṭhaṇḍe haiṅ. Koī garam, koī pahāṛī haiṅ. Koī retī ke, koī upjāū haiṅ, koī baṅjar, kahīṅ varṣā khūb hotī hai aur kahīṅ kam. Jab ham ek jagah rahte the tab rītirivāj, rahansahan, bolcāl ādī meṅ koī bhed na thā. Par jab ham alag alag dūr dūr rahne lage tab hamāre rahansahan, bolcāl aur rasmarivāj

meṅ kuch kuch bhed paṛ gayā. Kuch samay bād bāhar se bhī bahut se log hamāre deś meṅ ākar bas gaye. Ve bhī hamī meṅ mil gaye. Ve apne rītirivāj apne sāth lekar unke rītirivājoṅ meṅ se bahut se hamāre bhāioṅ ne sīkh liye. Is tarah apnī hī mātā kī god meṅ rahte hue bhī tarah tarah ke log hamāre deś meṅ dīkhne lage. Is bhedbhāv ko lekar hī hamāre deś meṅ prānt ban gaye. Yūṅ to hamāre deś meṅ kul 14 prānt haiṅ par mukhya prānt paṅjāb, saṅyuktprānt, baṅgāl, bihār, bambaī, rājputānā, madhyapradeś aur madrās haiṅ. Paṅjābī balvān aur saral hote haiṅ, saṅyuktprāntī dharmaparāyaṇ, baṅgālī nirbal par vidvān, rājpūt vīr, madrāsī sādhe aur marāṭhe bīr tathā catur hote haiṅ. (Shiv, 1927, 'Deś kī bāt' [Matters of the country], *Khilauna* [June]: 190–1)

26. Ham vīr haiṅ, valvīr haiṅ, raṇdhīr haiṅ, balvān (1)
Mar jāṅyage (sic), kaṭ jāṅyage, ho jāṅyage, balidān (2)
Vāreṅge ham, tyāgeṅge ham, choṛeṅge ham, dhanprān (3)
Nij deś hit, nij dharm hit, nij jāti hit, abhimān (4) (Abhichandra, 1927, *Khilauna* [September]: 233)

27. Bahanoṅ! Hindustān dulārā
Bhārat deś hamārā hai
Yah granthoṅ meṅ varṇit pyārā
Āryāvartta hamārā hai
Yahī hamārā pūjya pitā hai
Is se tum sab prem karo
Iskī sevā karne kā hī
Tum sab apnā nem karo (1) (Pandit Thakur Prasad Sharma, 1914, '*Deśprem*', *Kanya Manoranjan* [November]: 39)

28. Between March 1915 and June 1915, the issues were shorter (up to twenty pages). This was likely due to the increase in the price of paper and ink that affected the publishing industry during World War I.

29. 'Āśā hai ki *Kanya Manoranjan* sāre bhārat ke kanyā-maṇḍal tathā strī saṅsār kī sevā meṅ bhalī prakār samarth hoga' (*Kanya Manoranjan*, 1913 [October], back cover).

30. 'Kitāb kī kitāb khilaunā kā khilaunā' (*Kanya Manoranjan*, 1913 [November]: 16).

31. [*Kanya Manoranjan*] kā ek nirālā matlab hai. Yah ṭhīk hai ki strī śikṣā ke bahut se patra haiṅ aur ve baṛī yogyatā se nikāle jā rahe haiṅ. Lekin jin ko saṅsār kā kuch bhī anubhav hai ve jānte haiṅ ki bahut se lekh striyoṅ ke lie upayogī aur manorañjak hote hue bhī nanhīṅ sī bacciyoṅ ke, avivāhit kanyāoṅ ke, kanyāpāṭhaśālā kī bālikāoṅ ke hāth meṅ nahīṅ diye jā sakte haiṅ. Isīse āvaśyaktā huī ki ek aisā patra nikālā jāy jismeṅ bālikāoṅ ke paṛhne ke liye lekh aur kavitāyeṅ raheṅ. Upayogī citroṅ ke diye jāne kā bhī prabandh kiyā gayā hai. Lābhkārī hone ke sāth hī sāth bālikāoṅ kā manovinod bhī ho yahī ham logoṅ kā abhiprāy hai—agar hamāre mitroṅ aur pāṭhakoṅ ne iskī sahāytā meṅ apnā hāth baṛhāyā to ham apne uddeśya kī pūrti kar sakeṅge. (Pandit Omkarnath Vajpeyi, 1913, *Kanya Manoranjan*, [September/October (Āśvin 1970)]: 30)

There follow acknowledgements that thank the magistrate for sparing the periodical the trouble of going through a bail. Further words of thanks are directed at the Maharani Shri Ram Priyaji of Pratapgarh and Rani Hiradevi of

Sherkot as well as to renowned Hindi authors who supported the periodical with their contributions, such as Śridhar Pathak, Girijakumar Ghosh, and Śrimati Bangmahila.

32. Ānand kā śrot (strot) bahā rahā hai.
vidyākalā jñān sikhā rahā hai.
kanyā-manorañjan modkārī.
Dekho ise hai trayatāp hārī.

33. Manorañjan hamko maṅgā do. Usmeṅ paṛh ke kahānī sunā do. Dohoṅ kā paṛh ke mānī batā do. Uske chandoṅ ko gāke sunā do. Manorañjan tum hamko maṅgā do. (6) Jab manorañjan ko pāūṅgī maiṅ. Khelūṅgī kūdūṅgī nācūṅgī maiṅ. Haṅs haṅs ke sabko dikhāūṅgī maiṅ. Chātī se usko lagāūṅgī maiṅ. Manorañjan tum hamko maṅgā do. (7) Sārī kitāboṅ meṅ vah hai kharī. Qisse kahānī haiṅ usmeṅ bharī. Acchī tasvīreṅ haiṅ usmeṅ chapī. Āṅkheṅ haiṅ merī usī meṅ lagī. Manorañjan tum hamko maṅgā do (8) (G.P. Shrivastav, 1914, '*Manorañjan tum ham ko maṅgā do*' [Please order *Manoranjan* for us], *Kanya Manoranjan* [November]: 54–5)

34. This development is not unique to the Indian late-colonial situation. Egyptian children's periodicals also addressed children in the nationalist project (Pollard 1997). The element of obedience, though, does not dominate in *Kanya Manoranjan* and *Kumari Darpan* as it does in the periodicals analysed by Pollard (1997: 183), where children were not only taught to perform their roles as obedient children and trustworthy members of a society, but conceptualized as product if not property of the government.

35. Some of the periodicals mentioned were *Abhyuday*, *Grihalakshmi*, *Maryada*, *Sammelan Patrika*, and *Stri Darpan* in Allahabad; *Pratap* in Kanpur; *Saddharmapracharak* in Delhi; *Balhitaishi* in Meerut; *Arya Mitra* in Agra; and *Hindustan* and the *Dayanand Anglo Vedic College Magazine* in Lahore.

36. Mukherjee (1994: 38–67) has written an insightful chapter on how fiction and fantasy merge with historical facts (and vice-versa) in Indian novels of the late nineteenth century. She writes, '[C]hronicles merge with legend, events lapse into magical happenings, and kings who lived once-upon-a-time cast their spell upon those who ruled at a specific period and over a definite area'.

Fiction was far more than simply a tool used to provide some sort of moral instruction through an entertaining medium. Eliza Haywood, editor of the British *Female Spectator* (1744–6), the earliest woman's essay-periodical edited by a woman, promoted morals and manners primarily through anecdotes that were frequently introduced as 'true stories'. Notwithstanding the fact that the editor herself had been a romance writer and novelist, she was well aware of the potential of fiction as transmitter of reformist thought and vehicle of instruction (Shevelow 1989: 172). Haywood writes:

Nothing indeed is more certain, than that if a gay, thoughtless person takes up a book, which he imagines is composed only for amusement, and before he is aware, happens to meet with some favorite vice of his own, artfully and merrily exposed, he will start at the resemblance of himself, and perhaps be reclaimed by it: whereas he might hear a thousand sermons on the same occasion, without being moved, though ever so learned, or with the greatest grace delivered. (cited in Shevelow 1989: 172)

See also Helsinger (1991) on the imaginative appropriations of historical fiction for nationalist narratives.

37. Yah ādvitīya pustak dūsrī vār chapkar tayyār hai iskī praśaṅsā sarasvatī, abhyuday, bhāratsudaśāpravartak, bhāratmitra, lakṣmī, strīdarpaṇ, saddharmapracārak, citramayajagat, navajīvan ādi hindī ke mukhya mukhya samācārpatroṅ ne muktkaṇṭ se kī hai. Yah pustak pratyek ghar meṅ kam se kam ek prati avaśya rakhnī cāhiye. Ismeṅ granthkār ne ek ādarś strī kā jīvan-caritra kaisī rocak aur saral bhāṣā meṅ dikhāyā hai jise pratyek kanyā tathā nav-vadhū jisne thoṛā bhī paṛhā hai bhalī prakār samajh saktī hai. Ismeṅ sthān sthān par uttam uttam upadeś tathā śikṣāyeṅ baṛī manorañjak rīti par likhī gaī haiṅ. Kanyā-pāṭhśālāoṅ meṅ bahudā ināṃ ke liye maṅgāī jātī hai. Śikṣā vibhāg ke ḍipuṭī inspekṭaroṅ ne iskī baṛī tārīf kī hai. (*Kanya Manoranjan*, 1914 [October]: 33)

38. The advertisement to this booklet emphasized that the book was printed on high quality paper and contained a particularly attractive picture of goddess Saraswati.

39. N.N., 1914, '*Ek patr*' [A letter], *Kanya Manoranjan* (December): 92–3.

40. Pyārī Sarlā,

Vah bhārī prīti jo maiṅ tumse āj paryant rakhtī thī
jhūṭī hai. Ab maiṅ tum se bahut bhārī ghṛṇā rakhtī hūṅ jo
prati din baṛhtī jātī hai. Jitne hī tum patr bhejtī ho
utnī hī tum mujh ko ghṛṇit pratīt hotī ho aur
utnā hī adhik mere citt meṅ ātā hai ki maiṅ tumko
ghṛṇā karūṅ. Satya jāno maiṅ kabhī nahīṅ cāhtī ki tum ko
dhanyavād dūṅ. Tumhāre gūṛh patroṅ ne mere hṛday meṅ
ghāv kar diye haiṅ. Yah mat samajhnā ki unhoṅne
tumhārī sajjantā ko pūrṇ rīti se aṅkit kar diyā hai
satya to yoṅ hai ki jo tum mujh se na milo to hī bhalā hai
jo maiṅ aur tum kabhī milīṅ to dekhogī maiṅ tumhārī kaisī
śatru hūṅ. Aur tum yah bhī dekhogī ki tumhārī kaisī be
ādar kartī hūṅ. Tum viśvās rakkho maiṅ tumhārī vahī
dveṣī hūṅ jisne tum ko yah vacan kabhī nahīṅ diyā yā ki
saccī sakhī vicitr jīvan paryant banī rahūṅgī.

Parantu jab patr ko pīche lauṭ kar dekhā to usmeṅ yah dohā likhā thā:
Paṛhata patra mati roiyo, sakhī kiyo kā hāi
Paṅkti dūsrī choṛike, paṛhata hiyo harṣāī.

41. Śikṣā: Pyārī putriyoṅ tathā bahinoṅ! Ūpar kī kahānī se tumko yah śikṣā miltī hai ki striyoṅ ke lie śīl, vidyā, kām kāj meṅ caturāī, madhurbhāṣaṇ aur dayā dān ādi bhūṣaṇ haiṅ, naki keval sone cāndī ke gahne aur bahumūlya vastra. Is lie yadi tum sab kī pyārī bankar sukhī honā cāhtī ho, to āo, is vidyā rūpī kalpavṛkṣ ke śīl, santoṣ, vinay, atithi sevā, kārya kuśaltā, īśvarbhakti, miṣṭ-bhāṣaṇ ādi svādiṣṭ phal khāo aur parlok meṅ

uttam gati ko prāpt karo. Yād rakkho, saṅsār meṅ guṇ hī pūjya hotā hai na ki rūp. Islie apne kaṇṭh meṅ ūpar batāye hue guṇoṅ kī mālā pahin kar guṇvati ban jāo. (Dipachand Parvar, 1913, '*Rūpvati aur Guṇvatī*' [Rupvati and Gunavati], *Kanya Manoranjan* [October]: 4)

42. Both Nazir Ahmed (1903) in his didactic Urdu novel *Mirat ul-urus* (first published in 1869) and Pandit Gauri Datt (1870) in the Hindi novel *Devrānī jethānī kī kahānī* used a pair of female characters who were direct opposites of each other. As A.S. Kalsi (1990) has argued, *Mirat ul-urus* served as a model novel for many Hindi books to follow.

43. There were many stories in women's and girls' periodicals that thematized the difficulties of poor families in finding bridegrooms for their educated daughters. Brajrani Devi's '*Khoṭā sonā*' (1925) ('Adulterated gold', *Stri Darpan* [January]: 9–16), for example, is about a couple seeking a bridegroom for their fourteen-year-old daughter, Sarla. No family, however, is willing to waive the dowry. Finally, a young, well-educated neighbour suggests that they contact his well-educated college friend. The continuation of this serialized story was not available in the archives.

44. Women's and children's periodicals cautioned the readers against wearing excessive amounts of jewellery and overtly fashionable clothes. According to many writers, spending time on matters of outer appearance not only spoiled women and children, but made them prone to abduction. This attitude towards jewellery is a precursor to nationalist campaigns that called upon women to donate their jewellery for the benefit of the nationalist struggle (M. Jain, 1914/1915, '*Gahnā gale kī phāṅsī: Mātāoṅ kī mūrkhtā*' [Jewellery, death by hanging: The folly of mothers], *Grihalakshmi* [December/January (Pauṣ 1971)]: 512–14) was a reprint of a number of quotes from *Sri Venkateswar Samachar* about instances in which children and women wearing excessive jewellery had been abducted and murdered. Notably, *Grihalakshmi* occasionally contained advertisements for jewellery stores. In the 1920s, the relationship between jewellery and women's identity formation once again gained attention in the serialized essay '*Hamāre zewar*' (1920) by Uma Nehru ('Our jewellery', *Stri Darpan* [January]: 5–11 and *Stri Darpan* [March]: 144–52) and in '*Gahno se hānī*' (1920) by Shivrajpati Kaul ('The harms of jewellery', *Stri Darpan* [May]: 268–73). In the latter, a woman makes her child wear jewellery at a wedding festivity against the will of her husband. The child is abducted and killed. All the images of women in *Stri Darpan* depict women wearing a reasonable amount of jewellery (such as in *Stri Darpan*, September 1925, inner cover).

45. N.N., 1913, '*Sudhar aur phūhaṛ*', *Kanya Manoranjan* (November): 53–4.

46. Mohandevi, 1913, '*Kām ke khel*' [Work games], *Kanya Manoranjan* (October): 13.

47. Such as in Pandit Mahadev Bhatt, 1915, '*Pāk-vidyā*' [The art of cooking], *Kanya Manoranjan* (January): 121.

48. P.N. Dwivedi, 1914, '*Laṛkiyoṅ ke khel*' [Girls' games], *Kanya Manoranjan* (December): 71–4.

49. Kanyā kā maiṅ dharma batāūṅ, sun lo jo maiṅ tumheṅ sikhāūṅ (*Kanya Manoranjan*, December 1914: 71). The section is barely readable in the print copy. Since the verb tenses are in the subjunctive, the passage could also read 'if you would like me to teach about the dharma of girls, then listen what I have to say.

50. 'Sabhī kām dhairyya se hotā. Jo akulātā sohai khotā' (P.N. Dwivedi, 1914, *Kanya Manoranjan* [December]: 74).

51. See discussion in Chapter Four, pp. 161–2 and full translation in Part Two, Box 3, pp. 249–50.

52. 'Kya, tumko bhī kisī aisī bahādur laṛkī kī kahānī yād hai? Aisī kahānī sunī ho to likh bhejho. Vah chāp dī jāyegī' (Girija Kumar Ghosh, 1913, '*Bahādur laṛkī*' [The brave girl], *Kanya Manoranjan* [October]: 29).

53. Anadidhan Bandyopadhyay, 1913, '*Ghar meṅ cor—Ek saccī kahānī*' [A thief in the house— a true story], *Kanya Manoranjan* (November): 34–5.

54. 'Ammā, ek bār hamāre yahāṅ ek cor āyā thā magar hamāre pitā ne use pakaṛ liyā aur phir "cor cor" kar ke cillāne lage' (Ibid.: 34).

55. 'Bahinoṅ tum ko bhī cāhiye jñānvatī kī tarah tum bhī sadā niḍar hokar caturāī se kām lo yadi jñānvatī cor ko dekh kar ḍar kar cillā detī to ajab nahīṅ vah cor sās aur bahū donoṅ ko mār detā yā bhāg jātā. Ḍar se buddhi bigaṛ jātī hai isliye tum ko sadā niḍar rahnā cāhiye' (Ibid.: 35). For a full translation of this story see Part Two, Box 19, pp. 293–4.

56. Sandalaji Nagar, 1913, '*Bānūbāī kā sāhas*' [Banubai's courage], *Kanya Manoranjan* (November): 56–7.

57. 'Yadi tum meṅ sāhas nahīṅ to tum aise kām nahīṅ kar sakogī jismeṅ tumārā [*sic*] nām saṅsār meṅ banā rahe' (Ibid.: 56).

4 Genre and Domesticity

Nineteenth-century social reformers, in their attempt to generate an idiom of domesticity, often projected the home as an inner, autonomous sphere that was not subject to colonial surveillance and interference. More than that, they were concerned about protecting the home from the supposedly hostile influence of the public world (Sarkar 1992, 2001). The assumption of social reformers and, in the latter half of the nineteenth century, nationalists, that the domestic sphere could guard its autonomy when responding to colonial challenges ultimately had consequences for the role of women within the home. Advice texts projected the home as a place of peace and tranquillity, placing the responsibility of its creation in the hands of women. According to texts such as *Strīśikṣā* (Women's education, 1871), *Putrīśikṣopakārīgranth* (A treatise on the education and social duties of women, 1872), and *Nārīsudaśāpravartak* (Education, moral, and physical training of women, 1893–5), all published out of Allahabad with copies in the thousands, it was the duty of women to maintain and restore peace and harmony by virtue of their patience and compliance, especially in mismatched marriages where quarrels occurred frequently. The majority of social reformers and nationalists defined the ideal Hindu woman as entirely committed to her domestic role: as a skilful homemaker, she guaranteed the seamless functioning of domestic affairs. This task included her various roles as the woman in the household who oversaw domestic personnel; as the nurturing and educated mother who raised the children; and as the devoted wife and companion who stood at the side of her husband at all times. In addition, women epitomized the purity (*pavitratā*) of the home and were often elevated to the status of goddesses. An array of reformist literature on domestic and religious affairs written by men for women equipped married women with the necessary instructions on how to perform these roles.[1] Such texts also made their way into women's periodicals.

Treating each variety of text—advice texts, fiction, poetry, essays, and speeches—as its own subgenre, I suggest that an intertextual reading thereof illustrates the degree to which spatial orientation (of each article as situated in the periodical) may have influenced received meanings (see also Preface, pp. xvi–xvii).[2] The presence of the various subgenres found in women's periodicals made for a different reading experience because of the readers' and writers' interactions with other genres in the same periodical. These subgenres informed each other, both within a single periodical, as well as between women's periodicals, thus creating the intertextual linkages in this new literary public of which women's periodicals had become a part. Moreover, the combination of different subgenres was central to the literary shift of domestic advice *for* women to a refashioning of the entire domestic sphere and public world for both, women and men.

Advice texts, for example, contained very particular messages for women readers. However, when published among other varieties of texts and genres, as was the case in women's periodicals, these texts facilitated the emergence of a critical public discourse on domesticity. The subservient and self-sacrificial domestic woman was but one model to which the Indian woman reader could aspire, and this same reader would also encounter texts that called for education and emancipation. Advice texts adhered to a longstanding tradition of (patriarchal) writing of a different sort for women (as laid out in the subsection Gṛhalakṣmī and Pativratā: of Faithful and Devoted Women as well as the first half of the subsection 'Suśikṣitā—How Women Learn Domesticity'), whereas essays and fiction on topics revolving around domesticity allowed for new definitions of dharma, *sevā*, and traditional roles, offering fresh models for women's roles as wives and mothers (as illustrated in the second half of the subsection 'Suśikṣitā—How Women Learn Domesticity', as well as the subsection, 'Personal Fulfilment in the Absence of the Beloved: Suhāg under Threat'). Speeches, on the other hand, were feminist in the broadest sense, as will be seen in the subsection 'Home Rule for Women: A Nationalist Demand'.

Also significant are the comments that were interspersed in advice and fiction: counterpoints, disclaimers, and footnotes all suggest that the subgenres within the women's periodical were no longer as fixed, stable, and pre-defined as they had been some decades earlier.

I describe advice texts as a subgenre, the production of which is embedded within patriarchal social structures, but also as one that was being interrogated even as it was being employed. In many cases, it was the inclusion of editorial and authorial commentaries that were often interspersed within each that facilitated such interrogation: raising questions pertaining to notions of justice and to the investigation of women's living conditions, as well as looking to encourage women to aspire to changing their own lives or those of other women, when deemed necessary. Such comments often appeared in as seemingly an inconsequential way as a disclaimer, footnote, or the publication of a reader's response. In their own ways, all appealed to women to reconsider issues pertaining to their lives. Throughout this chapter, I will flag particular comments that demonstrate the nature of these statements, judgements, reflections, opinions, and questions such as the following:

> Now please, you tell whether the women who are adorned with the power of shaking the whole world should be called weak or strong and whether it is important to reform their condition or not. Who should decide about this, you or I?[3]
>
> This is what I have had to say. It is now up to you to reflect on the value that emerges from it.[4]

Five genres are of particular interest in the following discussion: advice texts, fiction, poetry, essays, and speeches. They span from the years 1911 to 1927, a period in which women's responsibilities were increasingly being conceptualized in mainstream nationalist and emerging feminist idioms. We witness a discourse on women's roles in the family and nation that operated within, but also questioned traditional concepts of femininity. Fiction and poetry often depicted ideal, sometimes normative, and also very real quotidian circumstances and conditions of women. They considered it particularly important that women be strong and courageous. Essays were always interrogative and discursive. Speeches were perhaps the most forthright commentaries of all in women's periodicals: they were critical and often revisited 'patriarchy' in light of new demands for women's emancipation. Frequently turning from one genre to another in the context of thematic discussions, I wish to demonstrate how these different genres facilitated a flexible discourse that moved—in the first instance—in normative, imaginative, and supposedly real worlds simultaneously, and—in the second instance—among the genres of the periodicals themselves; that is, how each text interacted with—and thus shed new light on—other texts in terms of scope, topic, and message.

While I give concrete examples of new definitions of gender and women's responsibilities in women's periodicals and the anxieties that surrounded notions of change in Part Two of this book, it is my aim to show in this chapter how new ideas about women engaged notions of subjectivity and agency—an engagement that was almost absent in the writings of male social reformers—particularly in the discourse of domesticity and its relationship with that of nationalism. I will argue that the Hindi woman's periodical offered a new forum to negotiate and redefine nationalist ideas on domestic women in the context of modernity. Literary discourses, it will be seen, facilitated the early nationalist endeavour to regulate the domestic sphere:[5] while writings retained domesticity as the central marker of upper and middle-class women's identities and aspirations, the scope of women's self-sacrifice was extended toward the *nation*. Besides treating the public and the private as distinct spheres to which women had access, the 'home' became metonymic for the 'nation'. Amidst nationalist sentiment, domestic matters and the importance of women as skilful attendants in homemaking and nation-building were thoroughly debated. In this chapter, I will read women's periodicals 'vertically' (see Chapter One, p. 24): as a discursive sphere of change, a site where gender roles—as defined and reinforced by women themselves, by Indian men, and by the colonial government—were contested, but also confirmed, and where a socially accessible and respectable place was also demarcated for women who were not, or no longer, married.

That said, one could not readily determine any single ideal that was being promoted for the domestic middle-class woman in the women's periodicals. The woman question remained an important site of debate, if not for male nationalist politicians of the late nineteenth century, as Chatterjee (1989; 1993: 117) has argued, then at least for the contributors to women's periodicals (Dalmia 2003; Orsini 2002) and to other Hindi literary genres (Dalmia 2003; Gupta 2001). Furthermore, by debating women's issues as an essential part of nationalist, especially Hindu revivalist, discourse (Gupta 2001; Sarkar 2001; Sen 1993; Visweswaran 1996), it was no longer viable to keep the woman question—and therewith the very women upon whom consent to reforms was contingent—out of political discourse.[6] Demands for the continuance of reforms for upper, middle, and low-class women were expressed in the vernacular. These demands now also included calls for the political education and emancipation of women.

Toward Old, New, and Better Domesticity

In women's periodicals and domestic manuals, writers as well as institutions circulated their old and new ideas about how the domestic sphere was to be organized and refashioned to meet the nationalist demands of the early twentieth century. These debates concerning domesticity rode on a wave of what Chatterjee (1993) has called the *new* patriarchy of the late nineteenth century and what Walsh (1997) has juxtaposed to an orthodox patriarchy rooted in authoritative Sanskrit scriptures. Dalmia (2003) has approached the literary debates on domesticity in the spirit of a third idiom that is described as the reinvention of patriarchal tradition. All these forms of patriarchy—new, orthodox, and reinvented—were of avail to the writers and readers of domestic advice texts in women's periodicals, and while it was rarely the case that writers would entirely break with traditional patriarchal frameworks, it is important to point out that such frameworks did undergo critical investigations. This was especially true when it came to descriptions and definitions of gender roles in women's periodicals (Dalmia 2004: 426).[7]

A large part of domestic advice in Hindi women's periodicals is presented in the tradition of earlier social reformist women's literature. Whereas such writings on women's roles advocate women's obedience and subservience to the family, there were also a number of publications in women's periodicals that straddled conceptions of 'old' and 'new' literature for women, all with the purpose of defining 'better' and 'truer' womanhood. Dalmia (1999: 175), in her literary analysis of the novel *Parīkṣā Guru* (1882), has therefore suggested reading the notion of change not in the binary of old and new but to distinguish between old and true (*saccī*). This distinction better captures how writers sought to transform those traditional elements that were considered useful for modern society and the modernization of tradition (Dalmia 1997). Hindi women's periodicals sought new truths, *saccī śikṣā* (true education), for example, that would be valid for the modern times. They used terminologies, such as *purānā* (old), *nayā* (new), and the English word 'modern', and were even more explicit about that to which and to whom they were referring to when mentioning *purāne feśan vāle log* (old-fashioned people), *purāne zamāne/samay vāle log* (people from the olden times), or *purāne vicāroṅ vāle log* (people with old-fashioned opinions).

An example of such a straddling of old and new with the aim of entering into something that was considered 'better' is visible in the conceptions of the 'home' as delineated in women's periodicals: the home was not only constructed as a refuge from a dangerous public world and as a sentimental and emotional space (Bannerji 1992: 7); it could itself be a sphere of exploitation and suffering.[8] In such a case, women were forced to find shelter outside of the home. Even a periodical catering to a domestic ideal such as *Grihalakshmi* did not deny that the home bore potential threats and that the dangers (often resulting from greed and jealousy) emanating from its male and female members could turn young and newly wedded women into victims.

While advice texts maintained the notion of two existing distinct and generally gendered spheres of public and private, fiction, in ascribing to women protagonists a new agency, participated in the discourse of redefining conceptions of public and private. In a large number of fictional stories, we encounter women who were forced to step out of the domestic sphere into a world hostile to women. Women's emergence in the public sphere was legitimized not only as an alternative to pathological domestic conditions but also as a new form of nationalist patriarchy (Chatterjee 1993: 129–30; Walsh 1997: 643–4); even though women were able to survive in the public sphere, almost all fictional characters aspired to conjugal happiness and gave up their independent lifestyles once they were in a position to resume their roles as homemakers (see the stories of Kishori and Sushila on pp. 154–5).

In this regard, reformist literature—mostly written by men—underscored processes of regulation, normativization, and normalization (Chakrabarty 1994; Walsh 1997; Sangari 1999). Chakrabarty (1994: 53) has argued that reforms to the domestic sphere, as they were promoted through print, penetrated the relatively autonomous domains of women. This statement requires attention: literary discourses facilitated the early nationalist endeavour to regulate the domestic sphere—and thus middle-class culture—according to patriarchal ideas. But literature, in that context, served more purposes: it provided diverse reading materials for women and girls. The framework for education despite its reformist character mostly remained traditional and intended to turn women into efficient and cultured wives, mothers, and homemakers, rather than into emancipated and independent individuals. Indian women were considered to be guardians of the home: it lay in their hands to protect the home from outer influences and it was for them to turn it into a spiritual sanctuary. But how do contributors to women's periodicals tackle normative literary models? What are the premises that underlie a supposedly natural division of social space, in which even female literary voices relegated women to the interior and entrusted men the care of public affairs?

By the early twentieth century, the assumption that women were exclusively guardians of the home had also become common sense for a large number of educated middle-class women protagonists: 'The brilliance of the rose lies within the garden. If the rose leaves the garden, its fragrance and beauty will vanish. Similarly, a woman's honour is preserved at home. It is not suitable for her to go outside. People will laugh.'[9]

The quotation, taken from a dialogue between a married couple, was made by a married woman and written by a female contributor. The husband, who has adopted a European lifestyle in this story, has rented a buggy and wishes to take his wife with him for an outing. She hesitates and points to the concept of *lajja* (shame): it would not be suitable that she frequent the public world of men. An argument begins, in which the wife voices her discomfort with promenading in public. In the end, the wife's vision of womanhood and respectability, expressed through the metaphor of the rose, wins over her husband's progressive views and western definitions of prestige, gentlemanliness, and Victorian lady-like behaviour. She prefers to exhibit her husband's socio-economic status within the domestic sphere rather than in public.

Why is the wife adamant about remaining loyal to cultural values that may be deemed parochial and why is the re-inscription of patriarchy not an exception, but *prevalent* in early twentieth-century writings on domesticity? Walsh (1997: 646), in her reading of Bengali domestic manuals written by women, suggests that internalizing and thus representing a patriarchal point of view, may be read as more than simply 'false consciousness' of women, or as a strategy to survive in a male world, or even as an emphasis on femininity. Rather, she suggests that it be read as 'evidence of a choice'. Though Walsh's claim that women (and men) voluntarily rewrite patriarchy may at some points be too reductive, it must be acknowledged that while reproducing patriarchal discourses, writers also challenged that which was deemed to be appropriate for women. Their language could confirm traditionally accepted notions of duty and self-sacrifice, notwithstanding notions of individuality and choice. However, even though some contributions perpetuated parochial and constricting ideals of traditional Indian womanhood, the literary and generic openness of periodicals made it also possible for new models to emerge. There were writers who suggested that education could change a woman's character for the better and that women could become the architects of conjugal happiness. Even widowed women, who suffered a social death along with the death of their husband, could make new sense of their lives according to many such writings. Women were no longer reduced to displaying middle-class values. At the heart of writings in women's periodicals stood the discussion of a diversity of values and their implications for the readers of the periodical.

In the following, I explore the idioms that mark the new discourse on domesticity, calling attention to the debates around women's traditional roles in various literary genres: roles as wives, mothers, and householders, as well as the place of widows in society. Whereas the writings that addressed domesticity as its primary objective retained domesticity as the central marker of upper and middle-class women's identities and aspirations, women's roles were no longer solely legitimized on grounds of self-sacrifice—as epitomized in the Hindu mythological figures Sita, Savitri, Gandhari, Urmila, and Sulochana—but on grounds of patriotism, love, responsibility, and happiness.

Gṛhalakṣmī[10] and Pativratā[11]: Of Faithful and Devoted Women

The majority of advice texts in women's periodicals reiterated, among other things, a historical legacy with a supposedly authoritative Sanskrit genealogy. Particularly common was the emphasis on *strī* dharma, woman's moral duty, that is, her devotion and servitude to her husband.[12] The advice text '*Striyoṅ kā mukhya dharmma—pātivrat*' (Chastity and loyalty, the prime dharma of women; translated in Part Two, Box 7, pp. 255–7) holds in this regard:

Generally, women are primarily devoted to all earthly customs–dharma, karma, and vrata [ritual fasting]. But according to the principles of the shastric texts and the sayings of sages and wise men there is no dharma for a woman other than her husband, because the word pati in itself means nurturer, progenitor, and destiny. It is written in the shastra that a woman's God is none other than her husband. Brahma, Vishnu, and Mahesh, all dwell within the husband's body. [...] The happiness of a woman who is not dear to her husband is of no use. Eating, drinking, sleeping, and pleasure, in short, life becomes useless because a woman who does not love her husband is born into the world without a cause.[13]

In a hardly legible disclaimer to the section, the author retracted her recommendations suggesting that women also make decisions on their own. The editor in a footnote to the text also reminded readers that the recommendation that worship of the husband was more important than bathing was not to be taken literally.

With increased emphasis being placed on the domestic sphere, *strī* dharma also included the provision that women create the home and make it a peaceful, tranquil, and orderly place. As the guardian of the home, Bandyopadhyay held in a text titled '*Strī prabhāv*' (The impact of women; translated in Part Two, Box 16, pp. 279–81),

It is the dharma of a woman to keep the home organized and tranquil for her master. If he cannot rest at home, the home is of no avail to him. He is required to work hard outside of the home and thus desires peace at home. Our women should pay special attention to this. Mostly, when men come home exhausted after a difficult workday, they must deal with quarrelling rather than being greeted by the comfort of a fan and instead of enjoying sherbet they are forced to listen to grievances.[14]

According to a contribution entitled 'Women's duty', yet another typical advice text (and title) in women's periodicals, there existed three prime (*mukhya*) and moral (*dharmik*) duties: child-rearing, household management, and *pātivrat* dharma (devotion to the husband).[15] Although listed last, *pātivrat* dharma was described as duty above all the other duties. Nothing could be achieved without devotion to a husband, the article held. Women should demonstrate their *pativratā* dharma not only by bodily servitude but also through conviction, deeds, and intellect:

Women's prime duty is to guard *pātivrat* dharma. Women who are unable to take care of this duty cannot fulfil either of the other duties. They will not be able to take proper care of their children and their children will not be able to progress. In the past, women who exemplified this dharma bore brave heirs like Rama and Krishna. If women become *pativratās* in body and mind, it would be no surprise if their offspring could quickly become saviours of Bharat.[16]

The second most important duty pertained to childrearing, where the female readers were cautioned against entrusting their children to lower-class women.

Women should not leave their children with nurse-maids or servants. Doing so spoils children. An ignorant midwife will not impart to a child the education and good teaching in the way of an educated mother. The child will, in this case, be in bad company. Another thing necessary for children is that mothers do not leave them in bad company; because a child will adopt the modes of behaviour prevalent in his surroundings. One should keep the child under one's own care.[17]

The message of the advice text is conveyed in rather blunt terms. It depicts servants as rustic and as bad company for a middle-class child. Women's third most important duty revolved around the management of household chores, which also includes the daily interactions between domestic women and male as well as female servants.[18]

A mistress' prime duty is the organization of the home. If a home is not properly organized, much harm is caused. It is a housewife's dharma to first serve meals to pregnant women, then to the sick, and then to children. After that, she should serve guests and male family members, then daughters-in-law as well as midwives and servants. After all that is done, she should eat. At night, she should go to bed last. Before going to bed, she should take a lamp and walk through the entire house. She should check that all doors are closed and that nothing has been left outside. She should do this herself and not trust anyone else.[19]

Even though domestic servants were instrumental in terms of performing the household tasks of upper- and middle-class women, the married wife was not to trust them with major responsibilities. She alone was in-charge of the family members' well-being and safety, and she fostered a sober work ethic and accounted for the correct managing of daily affairs. This is how the article describes an ideal morning routine of such women:

A housewife should be the first to wake up in the morning and wash herself, then wake up the midwives and servants. After waking up the daughters-in-law and the daughters, she should read a little and then serve all of them breakfast. She should make arrangements to begin work in the kitchen. After serving meals to everyone she should rest.[20]

The passage outlines a daily morning routine that not only regulates the duties of a woman, distinguishing between the lady's and domestic worker's responsibilities, but even how she is to spend her leisure time and when she is to rest. The time for reading was between the short span of waking up the family and serving its members breakfast. The content of the reading material is not dwelt upon; it is however unquestionable that reading should not interfere with the housework. Whilst education through books could hone a capacity for the completion of domestic chores, housework was given priority over knowledge acquired through books. While the domestic woman of the upper ranks was, according to the texts, mostly freed from the menial tasks of the household, she was to manage the household and execute orders throughout the day.[21] An important component of the discourse on domesticity in women's periodicals was advice directed at men:

There are many fools that don't realize how they hurt their Lakshmis with a few loveless and harsh words. It is absolutely necessary to avoid hatred and ignorance. A wise man once said, 'When I see a man of irascible temper, I pity his wife and when I see a happy person I am delighted at the sight of his happiness as well as that of his wife and his relatives'.

It is the hope that the men of irascible temper will change their temperament upon reading this article and that their wives will use their good influence to reform them.[22]

Nowadays it appears that people are astir and that in most papers and periodicals articles are being published about the need for women to be faithful and devoted, about their responsibilities towards their husbands, their dharma, their quotidian lives and their conduct with their husbands. With regret I must say that I have not seen a paper or periodical published on the responsibilities of husbands towards their wives. Whilst an article entitled 'men's treatment of women' was published in *Grihalakshmi* (Āṣāṛh 1971) by a gentleman named 'Gupta', the article was not satisfying because, apart from one perspective, there was no other advice for men to understand and learn about their dharma. Reflecting on this, I decided to write this article. It is my hope that gentlemen readers will be able to get some instruction from it and make my efforts fruitful.[23]

Such statements about men's responsibilities were frequently encountered in women's periodicals. They added a dimension to prescriptive literature that was not often found in monographic advice literature (see for example, Box 22, pp. 306–10).

Another characteristic of texts on women's household responsibilities as propounded in women's periodicals are references to western women. Compared to the discourse on women in Bengal, where modern, often western, women were rejected as a model for Indian women (Sarkar 2001: 35), Hindi women's periodicals showed a more benevolent attitude towards British women. Rather than condemning certain stereotypes attributed to the emancipated western woman, *Stri Darpan* emphasized the commonalities between Indian and British women when it came to their sense of responsibility. The 'myth' of British women is the theme of the article '*Inglenḍ kī bahū aur beṭiāṅ*'.[24] The author's aim is to rectify general Indian public opinion on the duties and responsibilities of 'European ladies'. The lives of England's married women does not solely consist of leisure and enjoyment. On the contrary, he argues, English women accomplish as much housework as Indian women.[25]

Other articles talked about laziness as the worst of vices and breeding ground of bad habits: 'England's well-off women do not waste their free time in idleness. They spend their time in support of a welfare organization. They consider it their duty to help in this way. They have no hesitation in doing so. Cleaning and tidying up the house is the work of servants; well-off women do not consider this their job.'[26] Whether or not the English routine as it is described in the article is intended to serve as a model for Indian women is left open. As Bannerji (1992: 24) has observed in the writings of Bengali women, 'Western educated and economically active women stand as examples of the capabilities of all women, but not as their invariable ideal expressions'. The same, I would suggest, holds true for western women. The texts do not call for emulation but intend to bring awareness to a 'global community' of domestic women (Walsh 2004). They do so by providing 'truthful accounts'—unravelling myths and prejudices—about the lives of women in Europe, America, and Asia.

While the quotes admittedly come from rather normative and reformist sources, all with the purpose of creating the modern, responsible and—whenever necessary—self-reliant woman, men's roles and responsibilities were not left unexamined. Women were often asked to make individual decisions and to themselves decide when to follow traditional values and when to reject them as corrupted or false. Of course, writers considered it their responsibility to guide women in the deliberation. Hence, they offered upper- and middle-class women manifold ways to lead their lives. Agency was but ultimately located in the domestic woman's ability to learn from the texts to which she was exposed.

Suśikṣitā[27]—How Women Learn Domesticity

Despite the anxiety involved in discussing conjugality (Ray 1994), domesticity (Roy 1995), and modern education (Talwar 1989), according to women's periodicals, conjugal happiness was to be based on a combination of knowledge, *true* love, and *patisevā* (service towards the husband), as well as skill. In this context, education was considered to be important as a means to transform ignorant and superstitious women into modern domestic housewives and into partners who were capable of conversing about public matters. There was general agreement that ignorance caused the decline of families. *Grihalakshmi* contained myriad stories and essays on women's suffering caused by the lack of education. Unable to read, for example, women were deceived in public by random people, religious figures, and even by fellow women. As dialogues repeatedly revealed, ignorance was also described as anti-nationalist and un-patriotic. Education, thus, not only referred to domestic skill, but also to the demonstration of patriotic behaviour, which included an understanding of the significance of wearing home-spun cotton,[28] boycotting foreign produce, and educating other female family members who may have been illiterate by reading to them. More so, even a woman's happiness was contingent on education, writers held. The suggestion that knowledge of domestic (and other related) skills and duties could be accessed through literary texts and was not innate in a woman's being, was crucial to new definitions of gender roles in women's periodicals. A woman was capable of learning domestic chores and codes of conduct, and women's periodicals set out to convince her to do so for the sake of her own happiness, as well as that of her husband and the family, and even the nation.

'*Nārīcaryā*' is an unsigned essay about the conduct and daily routine of women.[29] Central to the essay is the importance of suitable education for women:[30] 'Only an appropriately educated woman can quench the thirst and remedy the pain of the household, which is burning in the heat of illness, sorrow, plight, and poverty. [...] A man who has obtained such a woman is blessed. For him, heaven could not be better.'[31]

Unlike other regions, such as Bengal and Punjab, where debates surrounding the type of education, be it in English or modern, traditional, religious, caste-based, or a blend of different types, caused ideological splits amongst reform organizations (Borthwick 1984; Kishwar 1986), such debates did not cause the same uproar in Hindi women's periodicals, not even in religiously-oriented periodicals such as *Arya Mahila*. By the early twentieth century there existed general agreement that girls and women required a blend of modern western and traditional Indian forms of education (hence subjects such as English and science were studied alongside religion) and, furthermore, that education was to attend to women's and girls' gendered and class-based needs (hence subjects such as domestic science). With regard to the duration, education up to matriculation was commonly accepted, especially amongst those groups in society that customarily gave their daughters away in marriage when they had reached their mid-teens and not with the onset of their menses. This extended period of girlhood made higher education for girls easier to access (Kerkhoff 1995).

The common belief that a woman had not only the capability, but also the responsibility to keep the household free from misfortune and social ills is frequently articulated in the context of education. The educated woman was responsible for the family's health and good spirits. Seen in this light, the importance of education contradicted various oft-encountered assumptions, specifically the one that educated women posed a threat to the spiritual purity of their families. Such women were often described as rebellious and prone to widowhood. In women's periodicals, however, an educated woman was never considered dangerous but was described as particularly well suited to protect and nurture the family. Education enabled fictional characters to discover their 'true selves' in order to become what a modern egalitarian society expected them to be: responsible citizens as well as happy and contented individuals. This was also an essential asset for men: as fathers they were responsible for the education of their daughters, as brothers, they were to tutor their sisters, and as husbands they were to respect their wives.[32] Such were the new expectations of the time. Writers agreed that since women lacked constitutional rights, the initiative to educate women required male support. There were also demands by both women and men that men be respectful of women. In a reader's response to the contribution '*Pativratādharmma*' that had described women's roles in a derogatory way, the male writer declared emphatically, 'First we must become men!'[33] Girija Kumar Ghosh voiced a similar critique of men's cavalier behaviour and mental incompetence in a poem of 1911 titled '*Puruṣ caritra*':[34] 'Men are fundamentally unwise, / of bad conduct, sinful and arrogant. / Man's mind is filled with sins / and they don't even feel ashamed of themselves.'[35]

In the decade to come, the certainty that men were incapable of instigating change alone produced new types of writings that rigorously investigated gender roles. Before I turn to this development by looking more closely at fiction and (reprinted) speeches in women's periodicals, I will consider passages in women's periodicals that describe the making of well-maintained homes, which were projected as the precondition for political self-government.

Kishori is a beautiful girl married to Vireshwar.[36] After their marriage, it is learned that she is not educated and is oblivious to all codes of conduct. She misbehaves before her in-laws and does not display dilligence in overseeing the management of household affairs. One day, her husband suggests that she learn the basic skills of reading and writing: 'Take a look at some books, I will teach you how to read and write. "Cast off illiteracy and educate yourself, this is the vow of an auspicious woman". Kishori! Wisdom is a beautiful jewel, unequalled in the world.'[37]

After a couple of months, Kishori becomes enthusiastic about books, monthly periodicals, and newspapers:

> Now, Kishori reads good books day and night and learns about her dharma and karma. After a few days, wisdom has turned that very Kishori—whose ruthlessness and uncivilized behaviour has been brought to the reader's attention in great detail—into such a modest and virtuous woman whose qualities are unequalled. Day and night she cares for her in-laws and her husband. She cares for the household even better than many women would today.[38]

In the story, education revolves around the maintenance of the home and the performance of religious duties. Servitude and dedication are extolled and the literature read by Kishori is considered the cause for her change of character. Other effects of education come to the fore in the story 'Sushila'.[39] Sushila is the daughter of a doctor trained in both ayurvedic and allopathic methods. After her marriage to Amolchandra, a medical student, it is learned that Sushila can neither read nor write nor maintain the household. Amolchandra and his sister-in-law Vidya Sundari proceed to educate the young bride. Sushila develops into a model woman:

> Sushila is no longer the Sushila of old. Now, she is truly the wife of a doctor. After hard work for three years she has come to master Hindi. Since last year, Amolchandra has been teaching her elementary English and introduced her to the basics of medicine. [...] Sushila has a daily schedule and performs every task that is required accordingly. This is why she still finds time to read and write, even given her housework, her service to her husband and the medical attention she sometimes gives to other women. Right now, Sushila is reading a daily and a monthly paper, doing some homeschooling on her own and even studying Sanskrit.[40]

Due to the joint effort of her husband and sister-in-law, Sushila has not only become a perfect householder and wife (appropriate to the status and position of her husband), she even provides women medical treatment and still manages to further her education in Sanskrit and Hindi. The story proudly asserts that Sushila even reads canonical literature such as Mahavir Prasad Dwivedi's Hindi rendition of the Mahabharata. The household is presented as a model household (*ādarś gṛhasth*) with Sushila as the model woman. Her transformation from an uncouth and ignorant woman to an intelligent and educated one who also contributes to the husband's career as his medical assistant and as a devoted and modest housewife is given expression as a new norm for modern upper- and middle-class women. Kishori and Sushila both receive praise for services rendered to others as well as for their acquired language and literary skills.

Both stories describe a young generation of the educated middle class. They depict the older generation as indifferent towards women's education and holding old-fashioned views (*purāne vicāroṅ vāle*, *purāne feśan vāle*). The parents of the protagonists even *pretended* that their daughters were educated when seeking suitors. Sushila's father, himself a doctor, has neither educated his wife nor his daughter, and purposely marries Sushila to the nephew of an opponent of social reform (*jinke vicār sudhārakdal ke vicāroṅ se nahīṅ milteṅ*). In both stories, education has transformed men and women of the younger generation. Education is equipped with the transformative power to cause a change of character amongst illiterate women within a matter of months—an encouraging promise for less-educated women who heard these stories, as well as a call to literate family members to also educate women and girls.

Besides introducing this new class of heroines in fictional pieces, the periodicals also got down to the nitty-gritty of modern education. The editors of all women's periodicals supported education for girls and women, yet, opponents of women's education were likely to argue that modern education was incompatible with traditional values. Proponents of modern education countered this postulation (and addressed the fear that accompanied it) by claiming that women had to first develop a sense of individuality. Without this, they would merely perform their duties as puppets, which was not beneficial to the society. Most of the stories and essays emphasized that a woman's intelligence and sense of responsibility would not make her rebellious and disobedient.

'Shyama' is the story of a girl educated up to the seventh grade in the Lucknow English School.[41] She breaks the ties to her family as she falls in love with Jackson (formerly known as Jai Krishan), a Christian convert. Impressed by Christianity and western culture, she does everything to imitate his lifestyle. But Shyama contracts smallpox and is abandoned by Jackson. From her deathbed she writes a letter of apology to her parents, in which she requests that they have her story published in a periodical so that a large readership can learn of her faults. The editor, though, notes in a footnote that it would be a fallacy to draw a connection between western education and Shyama's death:

> It seems that the esteemed author suggests that English education has led to Shyama's downfall, but this is not correct. To be righteous and to be spoiled is a question of man's and woman's nature. There is no such education that teaches one to disobey one's parents. There are also Hindu girls who disobey orders without having received English education. One cannot blame their education or religion.[42]

Many contributors also claimed that if men did not forget their familial and social duties after receiving a western education, there was no reason to believe that women would abandon them. Suitable education was defined as broad and inclusive in scope. It could incorporate modern science and English literature, as well as teach women traditional values, religious duties, and the management of household chores. The stories all emphasize the potential of literature (in Hindi and other Indian vernaculars, English, and Sanskrit) as a transmitter of socio-political and cultural knowledge. Once women developed a sense for reading, uplift would not be long in coming.

Personal Fulfilment in the Absence of the Beloved: Suhāg under Threat

The concept of *suhāg* (conjugal happiness) was popular in oral and literary discourses. To live in suhāg was the ideal of every woman. One can call into question the degree to which such happiness was 'personal', given that it was contingent on the happiness of a woman's husband and in-laws. In this way, *suhāg* was debated in essays, dialogues, and fictional literature.

'*Kālī mem*' (The black/dark madam), a term generally used to describe Indian women who imitated western women, was the title of a story set in a conversation between two young women and an anglicized woman, simply named *Kālī* mem.[43] The latter criticized the concept of *suhāg* as being rooted in patriarchal power structures. The setting of the story is a household into which the *Kālī* mem has been invited to sing devotional songs (bhajans). After the performance, she engages in a discussion with the daughter and daughter-in-law of the house. She dismisses the practice of wearing excessive jewellery and holds purdah responsible for a woman's ill health and lack of individuality. On the concept of *suhāg*, she says:

> *Suhāg*, what a misconception this is. I insist that a Hindustani woman lacks common sense and—chanting the words of *suhāg*—blindly surrenders her personal freedom to her husband. A husband means everything to her. Listen to what I have to say about this issue: a man is nothing. I do not care for men. I care for personal freedom.[44]

The *Kālī* mem rejects marriage as an institution and does not have a very high opinion of men. To her, women's independence is not compatible with marriage. This radical tone was unusual in women's periodicals, as was the use of derogatory language. The message of the story as it developed was not to be mistaken: Indian women who imitated western women in attire and behaviour while disregarding their own cultural background were condemnable. The *Kālī* mem is clearly depicted as what may be perceived of as an independent and emancipated woman. Her appearance is rather frightening: 'The madam was pitch-black, pot-bellied, and plump. It seemed as if a sheet were draped over her entire body. Her hammer nose was squeezed from the weight of her glasses. Looking at her, she was so 'beautiful' that a person would certainly faint from fear when meeting her in the dark.'[45]

The *Kālī* mem represents a negative stereotype of the westernized woman. While the story may certainly be read as a parody—after all it was written by the famous humour writer G.P. Srivastava—what is striking is the aversion to the ideas and appearance of the modern woman: the girls in the story describe her as mother of the demon Ravana and as Tarka Devi, the demon who intended to kill the god Krishna through poisoned breast milk. This is one of the few stories in which the liberation and emancipation of a woman effectively disposes her of motherly qualities. It leads to the mockery of the *Kālī* mem who represents emancipation in its worst incarnation. She even makes a fool of herself in her attempt to show the girls early morning exercises as she trips, stumbling over her long skirt, falls down the stairs, and is attacked by a dog. In the course of defending herself, she confounds grammatical articles, a common grammatical mistake among Hindi-speaking Bengalis, which can only be conveyed in the original Hindi: '*Badan meṅ bahot furtī ātā hai, kabhī bīmārī nahīṅ hota hai, tākat khūb hotā hai, samjhī?*'[46]

If this was a critique of westernized (not western) women, with many allusions to the anglicized Bengali *bībī*, who abandoned the traditional virtues of Indian womanhood, then the following examples taken from the fictional sections of *Grihalakshmi* are examples of the *changing* concepts of *suhāg*. '*Ādarś pati prem*' is the story of Vimla, whose husband has been the victim of a conspiracy and is imprisoned. Vimla refuses the help of a man who offers 'protection'.[47] She rejects his sexual advances and repeatedly emphasizes devotion to her husband. She travels from Benares to Calcutta, where she gains a reputation as a Sanskrit scholar and ayurvedic physician. She heals the wife of an officer who, as a gesture of gratitude, offers help in releasing her husband from prison. At the end of the story the couple reunites and returns to Benares.

In a similar vein, Malti, who is wandering in the forest in search of her husband, succeeds in protecting herself from several men who look to take advantage of her state as a single, seemingly defenceless, woman.[48] Towards the end of the story, two male adolescents reunite her with her husband. Malti is overjoyed. She exclaims: 'Lord, god has reunited us after so many days. Who knows how much trouble you had to endure.'[49]

There are several common features in the storylines of Malti and Vimla. They are depicted as women without joint families, whose responsibility it would have been to protect them in the absence of their husbands. Instead, both women are exposed to dangerous situations through encounters with strangers. They remain steadfast in their faithfulness to their husbands, rejecting sexual advances and proposals for marriage as well as enticing material gains. Vimla even manages to enter the traditional male domain of Sanskrit learning. However, in both stories, men not only pose a threat to the two women, but also are responsible for re-establishing *suhāg*. This reunion is the culmination point in both stories. Vimla immediately abandons her profession in order to return home with her husband. Both women adhere unconditionally to the principle of *pātivrat* dharma. At the same time, they have demonstrated strength of character and have proven that they are able to survive in a hostile environment and protect themselves from men.

Some stories went so far as to legitimate murder as a tool of self-defense for women. '*Vīrāṅganā-Rūp Kumārī*' was the story of Roop Kumari, the devoted wife of Dharma Singh.[50] During her husband's absence his supposed friend Bhagwat Das, who had been asked to protect Roop Kumari, threatens to take the life of her child if she does not comply with his sexual demands. The story devotes much space to depicting Roop Kumari's physical struggle against the advances. As Bhagwat Das finally manages to enter the room in which she has locked herself, she stabs him to death. The story concludes: 'The heroism, with which Roop Kumari killed the wicked and evil Bhagwat Das to protect her chastity, was not punishable under the laws of the state. From that moment on, the reputation of the faithful Roop Kumari became known through all of *Bhāratvarṣ*.'[51]

At times, women's periodicals highlighted the courage displayed by female friends in securing a young woman's suhāg. '*Ādarś sakhī*', is a story about the planned wedding between sixteen-year-old Kamla and Yugal Kishor, a drunkard, libertine, and widower aged sixty.[52] Kamla's stepbrother and her father, who was also a widower, both greedy for the money that Yugal Kishor had promised them, had arranged the match. As the only one who stands by her, Kamla's friend Sheila objects to the marriage, at first in an unsuccessful attempt to have Kamla's father revoke his decision by appealing to his common sense. She then arranges a suitable match for Kamla: Kamalnayan Babu, a responsible twenty-five-year-old graduate of the medical school in Lucknow. Kamalnayan and

Sheila succeed in their plan to have Yugal Kishor arrested for adultery. It is the law in Benares that brings about the turn in the story: at the end, Kamla and Kamalnayan are married.

Throughout the story, Sheila is Kamla's only hope. Sheila, about whom we do not receive any background information, is depicted as a strong woman and devoted friend, ready to fight for justice and for the happiness of Kamla. She is forced to confront Kamla's male family members, and by the story's end, even Kamla's father, who had initially abused and insulted her, asks for her forgiveness: 'My dear daughter. Whatever I have said to you, I ask you to forgive me. Sheila! I will always be indebted to you. Daughter, I have done you injustice. I was unable to see your virtues. Will you forgive me for this glaring mistake of mine?'[53] In this story, men are not concerned about women's happiness. It is a strong-willed, virtuous, young woman who has a profound impact on her girlfriend's life. At the end of the story, the author calls on readers to consider it their dharma to be good friends and to fight injustice and corrupt customs: 'It is my hope that you have learned from Sheila's conduct and that you will always maintain pure, truthful, and loving relationships with your friends. If you ever see a friend of yours being married to a dishonourable man, you should try to save her to the best of your abilities and not abandon her.'[54]

This appeal to women to not passively accept decisions made on their behalves is also a recurrent theme in periodicals for children and young girls (see Chapter Three, pp. 107–8). For this, girls' and women's courage was frequently linked to intelligence and thoughtfulness. Courage and the maintenance of an unsoiled reputation became desirable virtues, which could even protect from mismatched marriages. Stories such as that of Sheila also informed readers that conjugal happiness was under threat in the colonial public sphere, in which importunate demands were made to Indian women. It was, therefore, the responsibility of women to do what was in their power to restore and maintain *suhāg* for the sake of *both* marriage partners. In this case, a woman's role as the proverbial architect of household happiness was extended: not only was she required to serve her husband to his content, she was now asked to act as a responsible and reliable member of a society of women. In the remainder of this section, I discuss how fictional literature tackled situations in which a woman was unable to live in *suhāg* because she was widowed.

One possibility for a widow was to commit herself to nationalist activities. The story 'Sushila' bears several similarities to the stories of Vimla and Malti, except that in the case of Sushila, the husband of the protagonist dies, leaving behind his wife, their four children, and his mother.[55] Sushila is left with the responsibility of earning money to feed the family. The story is set in a working-class milieu and Sushila takes up employment in a cloth mill. There, she is harassed by her male supervisor and she quits the job in order to avoid further sexual advances. Desperate to find employment, she hears of Mahatma Gandhi's svadeshi-campaign and decides to support the movement. Ultimately, it is the *charkha* (spinning wheel) that emerges as Sushila's saviour. Some volunteers bestow Sushila and her mother-in-law with a spinning wheel and teach them how to spin cotton:

> From that day on, both began to spin cotton and the house quickly became filled with happiness and peace. Whenever Sushila finds time she gently promotes the practice of spinning cloth amongst her neighbours. As a consequence, spinning wheels have found their way into many homes and a large number of women have begun regarding Sushila with great respect.[56]

The spinning wheel rapidly changes Sushila's fortune. Her new activity is not only regarded as respectable, it also supports her family as well as the nationalist non-cooperation movement. As it is evident in this story, and many other stories, remarriage was not an option for the protagonist. Instead, nationalist urgencies led to new roles for widows that went beyond those found in social reformist discourse. The spinning wheel as a Gandhian saviour motif was one way of establishing social and national roles for women. Other fields of occupation lay within social and educational institutions established for girls and women, such as widow homes and schools.

In depicting the lives of widows in service of society, the institution of marriage for once became a peripheral matter in women's periodicals. Such was the case not only for widows: the supplement to *Stri Darpan* for the girl and young woman, *Kumari Darpan*, contained an editorial advice section in which the editors suggested that an unmarried adolescent should be able to decide herself whether she wants to marry the bridegroom her father has chosen for her or whether she prefers to devote her life to social service, thus suggesting that marriage was not the only option for girls. This suggestion was in response to a letter to the editor, in which a twenty-one-year-old woman wrote about her intention to marry a married man.[57] Her parents objected to the marriage. The wife of the married husband had agreed to a divorce. The woman sought advice from the editors, whose response was printed along with the reader's letter. The editors' response took several turns: first, Nehru and Vancu (in 1922 Kumari Darpan was jointly edited by Rameshwari Nehru and Roop Kumari Vancu [nee Nehru]) defined and praised the institution of marriage as a sacrament. They emphasized the importance of love and partnership in a relationship stressing that a marriage was intended to last a lifetime. Consequently, second marriages were objectionable. The editors, however, also doubted the sincerity of the husband, suggesting that he might one day also abandon the reader: 'How can one trust that such an unstable man will not decide to marry yet another woman in addition to the one with whom he is living?'[58] The editors also sympathized with the position of the parents, who out of love for their daughter objected to the union. What were possible alternatives for the girl? The editors had several suggestions:

> There remains your question whether or not to marry at all and whether to marry the man whom your father has chosen for you. You will first have to settle in your mind whether you at all wish to marry and whether you think that the groom your father has chosen is suitable, educated, and a gentleman. If yes, go ahead and marry him. Forget about the married man. If you do not want to marry right now, then wait for a couple of years. There is no hurry. Tell your father that you will not marry right now. The future will bring a solution and it is not a problem to decide to remain unmarried. Marriage is not the sole purpose in the life of a woman. Spend your time in the service of society.[59]

The reader's letter alongwith the editor' response pose an important counterpoint to the otherwise abundant articles on marital life and the rewards of marriage as found in women's and girls' periodicals. The editors suggest that the woman carefully weighs her *options* before confronting her father with her own decision. They emphasize that *she* has the right to judge whether the bridegroom that her father has chosen for her is suitable. The editors even suggest that the girl—already aged twenty-one—wait a couple of years before stepping into marital life.

In terms of the scope of action available to high-caste and upper-class women, nationalist discourse made it possible to offer formerly unthinkable possibilities. If conducted in the service of the nation, social service was considered respectable. As an individual gesture of sacrifice for the well-being of society, even young unmarried women—as the editors suggest—could devote their lives to the nationalist cause. What had been suggested as a way to renew life for aged widows now was a viable option for women who had not yet fulfilled their duties as wife, mother, and homemaker.

A seemingly small and almost inconspicuous letter column, it can be seen, was entirely capable of challenging prevailing conceptions of the public: revealing matters that were considered private to a wide male and female readership collapsed boundaries of 'public/outer' and 'private/inner' spheres as they had been constructed in much of the literature of the nineteenth century. By the early twentieth century, letters in periodicals were part of a new style of writing in which women articulated a hitherto solely privately expressed perception of femininity including the 'right to feel'. Orsini (2002: 284), in her exploration of women's expressive modes (subtitled 'the right to feel'), posits that the combination of fictional and real occurrences (as expressed in readers' letters), as well as instruction and entertainment made it possible to reconsider model roles for women.[60] Such reconsiderations were abundant in the different sections of women's periodicals.

Home Rule for Women: A Nationalist Demand

In the following poem about the political awakening of women, author Matadin Shukla requests that women consider service to the country (*deś sevā*) as part of their personal responsibility. He phrased his appeal in idioms of domesticity, asserting that women needed to first awaken and recognize the fallen state of society and women's deplorable condition therein; second, they were to become allies of men and mobilize to serve their motherland. Their confinement to the domestic realm was disparaged, even though it could have been read as the fulfilment of a patriotic duty in and of itself.

> Wake up women, the morning is upon us
> Awaken your senses
> Look at the birds, they will teach you
> Leave the ignorance caused by sleep behind and
> Familiarize yourself with politics and dharma
> Consider the condition of the fallen country as your domestic work
>
> A man may be wise, yet he cannot achieve anything alone
> He will always await your support

Just like the cart cannot move with one single wheel
One person alone cannot maintain the ties that bind society and the home

Men are not without fault, however, you must also participate
Born a human being will you die due to the sins of others?
Are you ready to endure the troubles of the world for the sake of your motherland
Or will you live cooking, sleeping, in worldly enjoyments and in fear?[61]

A new emphasis was placed on women's interventions as advocates of social reform and nationalism. Such an alignment of social and political concerns has been described as a new form of women's political agency that sought to establish a collective political identity of women.[62] While Sinha focuses on women's political achievements in the late 1920s, as women were articulating a language of individual rights, her interpretation of historical events also holds true for the late 1910s, as Hindi women's periodicals had already begun to articulate a gendered imagined community. The political activities of women in the nationalist movement could, of course, be seen as the consequence of personal choices made by women who wished to engage in the public sphere; but they could also be seen as the result of a new sense of obligation for women to become socially active (Sarkar 1989: 231). This calls attention to the question of the, at once, enabling and restraining aspects of nationalist discourse. On the one hand, the nationalist movement offered new and socially accepted roles for women that were not solely defined in a domestic paradigm and in relationship to other (male) family members. On the other hand, it may be argued that women could not be truly liberated by nationalist discourse because male hegemony continued to prevail. Mohandas Karamchand Gandhi, for example, repeatedly clarified in his speeches that women who engaged in the nationalist struggle were not to break away from their domestic duties.

The contributions discussed so far have illustrated how women's periodicals carried forward, but also refashioned debates of the nineteenth century on domesticity and conjugality. To an increasing extent, literary engagements with topics such as education and the status of widows (including remarriage) took on a tone that claimed to be nationalist while also not shying away from identifying patriarchy and tradition as causes for the subjection of women. An investigation of tradition was vital to the self-fashioning of women. Many contributors held that it was patriarchy or 'man's tradition' (*puruṣ samāj*, *puruṣ jāti* or *puruṣ gaṇ kī paramparā*) that kept women in a state of dependency. Consequently, a periodical contributor named Miss R.P. Pal, a Bengali member of the Brahmo Samaj, argued that women had to go beyond working toward reforming (*sudhār karnā*) oppressive customs and evil practices that had been tolerated and even extolled by society, seeking instead to destroy them (*nāś karnā*):

I will say that women need to be prepared to destroy the present misery that Indian women have had to endure far too long in the name of tradition. We speak with great pride about our past and tell great stories about it. We say that in those times our position was the best in the world. Some eminent people even boast about our present state. It is possible that in some respect our status is and has been a good one. But the situation of Indian women is steadily worsening, and every Indian citizen should feel ashamed.[63]

Pal severely criticized those who turned to the past and romanticized it without confronting the injustices of the present. She urged her readership to understand that arguments about a supposedly golden Vedic past reinforced the grounds for, rather than undermine, the subordination and exploitation of women. According to her, women possessed the capacity to intervene in such debates and thereby put an end to the plight of their fellow women. Pal was precise in her critique of the deployment of authoritative Hindu religious scriptures to systematically oppress women:

Keeping Indian women in the pit of ignorance and dependency in the name of tradition is legitimated by the ancient *Dharmashastras*. Those shastras that keep Indian devis in a state of ignorance and slavery have ruined the future generations of women and there is no use singing and eulogizing the shastras that were recited in ancient times. They very well depict god in the highest stage, but consider the following: how can a nation that keeps its women in such injustice, ignorance, and dependence please god? Our men may eulogize the very same shastras that have legitimized keeping women and Shudras in bondage and these men may be pleased to narrate such religious-moral works; but there is no reason why women should be prepared to join them in doing so.[64]

Pal urged women to not join in men's eulogies of the shastras. Her religious inquiry into causes for women's subordination was accompanied by a political inquiry that I will later turn to.

For the most part, women writers were aware of their limits. It was seldom possible and not even absolutely desirable to aspire to leading positions in politics; however, nationalist rhetoric was effective in redistributing responsibility and modifying power arrangements within the household. In order to support the claim that women were political subjects, periodical contributors investigated the differences between women and men, as well as the gendered division of their spheres. They redefined the basic assumptions and terms on which public and private spheres were founded. Integral to this mode of reasoning was the question of the ideological premises upon which gender roles were predicated. Women's periodicals explicitly problematized issues of governance. In fact, nationalist public debates were appropriated into a supposedly domestic context of the women's periodical. The political term 'Home Rule', for example, had been employed to articulate the nationalist demand of self-rule. Pal, in her usage of 'home rule', refigured the term in order to stake a claim in favour of women's emancipation and empowerment. The term home rule was based on the Irish Home Rule Movement and used by Annie Besant in 1916 to describe the activities of the Indian Home Rule leagues set up to spread the idea of political self-rule. A few years after the foundation of the Home Rule leagues, Besant distanced herself from the movement and founded the National Home Rule League (1919) that demanded Dominion Home Rule for British India. In her speech, Pal used the English term, explained it in the Hindi '*ghar kā śāsan*', and applied it to a domestic context. National institutions set up by men throughout the country to promote Home Rule had achieved nothing to improve the situation, according to Pal. In order to successfully achieve political change, she suggested that women as mothers, wives, and sisters wield the proverbial sceptre (at home). Referring to the Home Rule Movement of the late 1910s, she held,

> I believe that if you people really want the country to progress, then you should first give women 'home rule'. [...] From the husband to the servants and beyond, women should rule over it all. The husband should not make decisions regarding the house or public affairs without consulting his wife and he should always take her along. The origins of charity lie at home. It is at the time to realize this principle.[65]

According to Pal, Home Rule—as the term suggests—should begin at home. With women as rulers of the home, men would be better guided. '*Gṛhasth śāsan*' (House/Home rule) was often the title of contributions about the challenges and responsibilities of ruling the home.[66] Women's agency was then defined in direct relationship to men who required women's co-operation and support. At a later point in the speech, Pal collapsed traditional conceptions of gender roles, arguing that men, too, had domestic obligations, and that women had the responsibility to participate in political affairs:

Just like men-folk enjoy great freedom to travel all over the country to promote welfare, woman should have at least the same freedom. She should be given this independence so that among us the devis may be prepared to at least promote patriotism and pride in the country. [...] I believe that just as women are responsible for the organization of the household, men should feel equally responsible for it. Furthermore, the path that is opened for men to serve society after being educated should also be accessible to women.[67]

Pal clearly emphasized the shared responsibilities of women and men in both spheres. What is remarkable about this position is not only women's role as patriotic preachers, but the proposition that men be assigned a new responsibility in the home. Eminent figures of the Hindi literati clearly opposed such a viewpoint. Dwivedi for example, disapprovingly wrote in an essay:

If some law-knowing woman tells her husband, 'Listen, your rights and mine are equal, I am free and so are you. One day I'll cook and clean the house, and one day you. One day I'll take care of you, one day you of me.' Or suppose she says, 'I refuse to produce a child'; tell me what would such freedom result in? (cited in Gupta 2001: 126).

It is important to clarify that Pal did not simply extend the scope of the woman's role alone, but that she *reassigned* responsibilities to women and men on the assumption that neither cultural nor biological differences legitimized an absolute gendered division of responsibilities. Shared responsibilities could be predicated on the equality of sexes. This idea collapsed the partly Victorian-derived ideal of partnership that saw women as the companions of men, but that also divided the responsibilities of women and men along gender lines.

The concept of Home Rule was also addressed in a poem that a reader submitted to *Stri Darpan*. 'You want home rule?' was a poem explicitly directed at a male readership in the familiar rather than formal mode of address (employing the pronoun *tum*, and not the customary *āp*).[68] Jyandevi scornfully denounced men for not having eradicated various social ills. She questioned the legitimacy of the male-dominated INC and the demand for Home Rule in light of the fact that none of the male members were willing to change their attitudes towards the social and political status of women. She suggested that men lacked the will to instigate *real* change and spent time only discussing matters behind closed doors.

Both the essay and the poem used nationalist idioms to argue that real Home Rule had to begin where women were situated. Before political Home Rule could be achieved, the home itself had to be 'cleaned up' and become socially just. Pal assigned women an active role in domestic and public politics, and Jyandevi pointed her finger at men's incapacity for reforming society. Both authors thus broadened the meaning of Home Rule so that it served social feminist interests. This did not entail women abandoning their domestic responsibilities. On the contrary, we see in the term 'Home Rule' an intended double meaning, representing yet another example of how closely the domestic was tied to ideas pertaining to the national, as well as how political terminologies were redeployed in the context of a woman's public sphere.

Some contributors to women's periodicals explicitly saw women as political actors. As one contributor of *Stri Darpan* put it:

> Now the women community is ready to state 'Great Men, well done, we salute you.' Until now you have been very selfish. You have enslaved us and made us do menial work. Are we not the offspring of India? Are we not destined to serve our Mother India? What do we lack? Are we not part of human kind, or do we lack intellectual and physical power? Is that it, you selfish men! You have not granted us the time to do significant work. You have deceived us, but this game is over now. We are not only women, we are also members and citizens of Indian society. Just like every woman has duties towards her family, she has, even more, duties towards society.[69]

A cascade of rhetorical questions articulates the author Hridaya Mohini's anger against men. She goes on to criticize the hypocrisy and double moral standard of social reformers who, in her point of view, educated women, but did not liberate them: Why do you need to show yourselves in *public*? / Learn how to read and write, but remain gods in the house only. / We will place you in a nook and worship you. / If you can enjoy sitting at home, the master's governor will feel less grief.[70]

Like other periodical contributors who looked to establish new frameworks in which public and private spheres were understood and distinguished, Mohini contested the gendered division of public and private spheres.[71] By positing that women could be meaningful actors in the political arena, she extended women's responsibilities to include those beyond the domestic sphere. A century after the pioneers of social reform movements had given the woman question public attention by raising issues about upper-class marriage practices and widowhood, women also considered it their responsibility to follow in the footsteps of reformers such as Ram Mohan Roy and Ishwarchandra Vidyasagar, who are also often referred to as the pioneers of the women's movement. New to the discourse that continued to operate in the idioms of *sevā* and dharma was that women's responsibilities no longer solely revolved around husband, children, extended family, and household.

Mohini linked the glorification of women to their marginalization: thus her witty suggestion that men 'enjoy' the 'honour' of being worshiped. Her discontent with life in domestic confinement was also directed at those who granted girls and women the opportunity to obtain education, but at the same time kept them under rigorous familial supervision. In her text, she undauntedly addressed men with the informal second-person pronoun tum rather than the formal *āp*.

The deification of women, many contributors held, ruled out any possibility of their participating role in public. Tamallata Vasu in the women's column of *Madhuri* criticized the two extreme positions that were assigned to women: either they were elevated into the divine position of a goddess or degraded as inferior human beings. But according to her, 'A woman's place is neither above the head nor below the feet. A woman's place is in the heart.'[72] In this essay she criticized the deification of women as a strategic device employed by men in order to perpetuate the oppression of women. She also criticized the commodification of women, particularly newly wedded ones. For Vasu, the religious significance of a marriage ritual lost all meaning when regarded in terms of the daily exploitation to which women were subjected by her in-laws. Vasu ended with a call that men should recognize the unjust treatment of women and that women should find ways to prove that they are worth more than being servants.

The explicit feminine mode of writing that appealed to women's role as the nurturer is characteristic not only of occasional contributors who might have been ordinary housewives.[73] Female politicians, too, emphasized motherhood and religious purity in an explicitly feminine mode to appeal to a large community of women. We have seen in Chapters Two and Three (pp. 44–5, 102) how some contributors argued that gender roles were to be collapsed entirely, with men and women sharing responsibilities in public and private spheres. Some contributors maintained hierarchical frameworks in their commentaries, according to which women were to overtake the (supposedly superior) roles of men in order to prove that they could be even more successful. Most common, though, was the egalitarian and complementary approach to gender roles, often expressed in the metaphor of the cart that cannot move without two wheels, woman and man each symbolizing one such wheel. From such a perspective, the primary duties of the household and of childcare were assigned to women, but it was also made possible for them to physically step out of the interior in times of need and as long as domestic duties were not neglected. These gender redefinitions, reversals, and subversions also intersected within one and the same contribution, as in one to *Stri Darpan*, wherein the writer discussed the topic of women's responsibility in politics in the rhetoric of men's failure. This was a radical approach to the subject matter for it proclaimed that women were more capable than men and able to overtake traditional male roles in order to accomplish political demands that were pending.

> Men are tired of constantly complaining over years. They have not been able to achieve anything. They keep demanding alms from the government, they ask for several rights but are unsuccessful. Sisters, show them that it is possible to accomplish what they have not been able to achieve until now. Give them the reason to say 'what we have not been able to achieve has been accomplished by our mothers and sisters'.[74]

This passage was authored by none other than the eminent politician and poet Sarojini Naidu (1879–1949). As one of the first Indian women who had received her education in England, Naidu pioneered women's emergence in mainstream politics. She was involved in major political campaigns on widow remarriage, women's education, and women's franchise, and in 1914 had become a staunch supporter of Mahatma Gandhi. By 1916, Naidu claimed to speak for all Indian women, consistently pointing towards women's abilities. She was critical of all comparisons to western feminism, referring to pre-colonial indigenous traditions and emphasizing the physical and spiritual power of motherhood. To mark one highlight of her political career, in 1925 she was elected president of the Indian National Congress (Kumar 1993: 56–7).

Being well aware that women were forced to endure massive oppression, Naidu was convinced that they carried a special responsibility for the uplift of society and the creation of the Indian nation. She believed that women—as mothers and wives—could supplant men as political and public leaders and successfully campaign for legislative changes before the government.[75] Addressing the topic of *deś sevā* in front of the Women's Assembly in Allahabad (Prayag Mahila Samiti) in early 1917, she employed a rather unconventional image of imprisonment: 'Your men are enslaved. They are caught in the chains of bondage. Their hands are in cuffs and their feet in fetters. The keys are in your hands, but you are not using them. You are capable of breaking the chains, but you are not doing so. You can free them, but you are not.'[76]

Rather than evoking the more common image of women as hostages, Naidu used an image that elevated women to the status of guards of the proverbial prison with men as its prisoners. The common image of imprisonment appeared often in the pages of *Stri Darpan*. Rameshwari Nehru, for example, used the image of the female prisoner restrained by the four walls of her home, her energy wasted, and time squandered on menial tasks such as cleaning dishes. With such an attitude of women as domestic servants, she held, men would never be able to accomplish their project.[77] Uma Nehru, too, in the style of her contemporary Mahadevi Varma often used the images of chains and fetters to describe the bondage of women (Talwar 1989; Varma 2000).

Naidu appealed to women to pursue those tasks that men had not been able to achieve because they were entangled in a web of power relations. She made the bold move of juxtaposing women's energy and capacity with men's weakness and dependence. She did not operate within the binary of colonial masculinity and native effeminacy that the feminist historian Mrinalini Sinha (1995) has identified in her research on colonial and nationalist politics in late nineteenth-century India; however, she operated in the discourse of effeminacy described by Sinha, positing men as weak, incapable and in need of support. If men dominated women and were in turn dominated by colonial rule, Naidu implied that women's role was to free men and therewith the nation. She did not spell this out explicitly, but left it to her listeners to draw this conclusion. This is in fact the point Rameshwari Nehru emphasized first in her introduction to Sarojini Naidu's speech: 'Even after hearing your speech, our weak brothers remain unprepared to undertake a movement in the manner you [Sarojini Naidu] have suggested'.[78]

What crystallizes from the passage is Naidu's evaluation of colonial discourse in terms of the paralysing impact it had on Indian men. In her view, women were required to perform a double task when taking over a field of activity traditionally ascribed to men. Her narrative turned the passive virtues of obedience, sacrifice, docility, and modesty into agency and salvation. As we will see in the following, however, she also reverted to the earlier practice of evoking women's self-sacrificial virtues by referring to the mythology of ideal womanhood.

Naidu considered it rare, difficult and not necessarily desirable for women to aspire to leading positions in politics. Instead, women needed to recognize their *own* strength. This strength was rooted in their capacity of reproduction and their supposed natural mothering instincts. Naidu reminded women that all of them had a home from where they could contribute to the welfare of the country by educating children, removing the sorrow of the unhappy and helping those in need. That was how they could serve the country and fulfil their dharma (*Stri Darpan*, February 1917: 61). This part of the speech went hand in hand with social reformers' and nationalist politicians' ideas about women's roles and responsibilities. Naidu, who had demanded earlier that women assume various roles of men, tempered her radicalism by harkening back to virtuous and heroic mythological figures, a prominent practice amongst those advocating a return to a golden Vedic past: 'Like Sita, you [women] should bear the pain and share man's plight. Like Savitri you should fight against Yamaraj and save your men's lives.'[79] She then promoted the ideal of responsible motherhood with educated, sensible, and truly loving mothers:

> Like me, you all are also mothers. We all know the love of a mother very well. There is no one amongst us, whose heart is not filled with the love for a child. A mother's love is endless. Which mother does not herself experience pain upon seeing her child suffer? What is the use of this love alone? As long as you cannot tell your children, I am your best friend and as long as you cannot teach them the importance of self-confidence, and make them understand their faults when they have erred ... to lead them on to the right path whenever they have gone astray—until then, our love will remain fruitless.[80]

Naidu's speech took many unexpected turns. On the one hand, she urged women to shoulder the responsibilities of men with idioms of self-empowerment; on the other hand, she called on women to serve the nation in their self-sacrificial function as responsible mothers. It is perhaps because of this seeming paradox that Forbes (1998: 158–9) describes Naidu's ideology as social feminism so closely linked to nationalist ideology that it impeded the emergence of a radical feminist critique of gender roles. The mobilization of women is articulated in the discourse of dharma. And yet, in invoking the names of Sita and Savitri, Naidu was subverting terms of nationalist discourse in that she emphasized goddesses' and mothers' strength, will, and capacity to act, not necessarily their purity, submission, or obedience. Bannerji (1992: 14) has described a similar reshuffling of concepts of self-sacrifice and selflessness in the writings of Bengali women who rejected mythological images as patriarchal ways of oppression: 'Women [...] stressed the need to go forward with the enlightened male section of their class, rather than to retreat into the past. This, however, did not signal the end but rather an augmentation of a gender struggle'. Naidu also negotiated and redefined gender roles for the sake of national liberation without losing sight of women's empowerment. The language was still that of social reforms, except that now men—and not women—were the ones who needed help.

As women's roles and responsibilities were increasingly defined in larger political contexts, traditional images of womanhood, earlier characterized by sacred and glorified but submissive traits, underwent critical and creative investigation. Maintenance of the home, healthy family relationships, personal happiness, and good standards of education became dominant issues in women's periodicals of the early twentieth century. At the same time, women and men reinforced patriarchal norms by emphasizing the importance of women's exceptional devotion, self-sacrifice, and selflessness. Some advocated constricting codes of conduct, whereas others refigured traditional conceptions of femininity. In the negotiation of these two positions, fraught with tension as it was, contributors shifted emphasis from discourses about honour and tradition to the practical implications of virtue for 'real' women and their quotidian lives. Even though upper-middle class women's access to the public sphere and the degree to which they could pursue and attain economic independence remained restricted, the power of the texts at work gained momentum in public discourse of the early twentieth century.

New concepts concerning individuality were also gaining prominence in essays, autobiographies, short stories, poems, and advice texts in women's periodicals. This is not to say that similar concepts did not exist in pre-colonial India. In a colonial environment, however, they acquired new meaning as they encountered western liberal-democratic concepts of free will and personhood—key concepts that constituted the modern subject. Women writers distanced themselves from representations of women as religious and national icons. Instead they emphasized the lives of 'real women' with which the readers could identify. The new representations of, and for, women, also claimed to be *ideal*—as the prevalent use of the word *ādarś* (model/ideal) suggests. These models, though, were far from being propagated and discussed from the vantage point of a homogenous ideology. They may rather be described as a search for new role models for a society, in which women were no longer marionettes performing domesticity to please others. Now, women aspired to their own larger objectives with society and the nation in mind.

Women's periodicals emphasized women's determination, strength, and self-reliance. Against this background, passive and submissive traits such as obedience, servitude, and self-sacrifice—which remained central to the image of Indian womanhood—intersected with another, oft-forgotten, heroic Indian woman: (i) a *pativratā* was also a strong woman able to stand on her own feet; (ii) a woman could be devoted to her husband and family, but also to society; (iii) traits such as self-sacrifice, devotion, and obedience were not adverse to independence of mind.

Women's periodicals also refuted assumptions that had become common sense for many middle-class Indians, such as the assumption that western women were inherently rebellious, sexually liberal, and self-indulgent. The goal was to emphasize similarities in the lives of Indian and western women. What was, however, severely criticized was the blind imitation of western habits, especially when they entailed the abandonment of traditional Indian cultural and religious values, as in the case of the *Kālī* mem. Such discourse reconfigured notions of participation outside the household in a way that suited the nationalist sentiment of the time—that is, in a 'uniquely' Indian way. Public service did not automatically entail the loss of shame and modesty, as many opponents of women's emergence in public believed.

Whereas nineteenth century social reformers and colonial legislators had reinstituted rather than challenged patriarchal definitions of women's roles, a new generation of male and female nationalists—amongst them many contributors to women's periodicals—scrutinized the origins of gender discrimination in theory and practice. The political culture, along with Mahatma Gandhi's expressed support of women's participation in the nationalist movement, enabled women, with elite women taking the lead, to step on the political platform physically and to participate in the non cooperation and civil disobedience movements of the second and third decades of the twentieth century, leading up to Indian Independence. As a result of historical conditions, women campaigned in their neighbourhoods to spread the message of *satyagraha*, they engaged in spinning cotton and wearing *khadi* ('home'-spun cotton), picketed liquor and foreign textile shops, boycotted British manufactures, and even went to prison (Sarkar 1989).

However, women's periodicals did not break entirely with the traditional roles of women; neither did the liberation of women lead to their political emancipation. Some scholars have concluded that nationalist activities, as they were laid out for women, made them the 'tools' or 'puppets' of male nationalist leaders (Agnew 1979: 61), and were not meant for permanent changes to women's customary role (Sarkar 1989: 241).[81] Efforts to politicize women were justified in the name of dharma and women's engagement in the national cause was framed in idioms of religiosity. Such an assumption would also hold that the politicization of women was not a logical consequence of women's emancipation. Forbes (1988: 54–5) concludes that 'the structures developed to mobilize women for the protest movement proved inadequate to the tasks of politicizing women, ensuring continued participation, or acting as channels for the expression of their interests'.[82]

Yet, women's periodicals envisioned the Indian nation as one that also granted rights to oppressed groups in society, including women. Individual contributions voiced discontent regarding the outcome of social reforms as well as the '(male) nationalist resolution' of the woman question that relegated women's issues to institutions like the National Social Conference or tied them into the nationalist agenda of restoring 'Indian' culture. They criticized the unfinished project of social reform by exposing how oppressive patriarchal structures continued to permeate society. They rejected the notion that women should be shunted into a private or spiritual sphere from which they were expected to safeguard an essentialized Indianness. Instead, they redefined gender roles as well as women's responsibilities and proposed *different*, sometimes contradictory, approaches to promote the nation's larger cause—self-government. Eventually, in women's periodicals, a movement was launched that encompassed regional boundaries and linked nationalist to feminist demands. Affinities with Gandhian efforts to politicize the domestic sphere and enable women to interact in public can thus be found even in the 1910s.

Contributions to women's periodicals also suggest that women participated in political discourses without being fully determined by them. They subverted and re-deployed the terms of these discourses, interacted with traditional images of common mythological figures (such as Sita or Savitri), and appealed to the ideal of motherhood. It is no surprise that many contributions emphasized women's reproductive potential as well as their role as mothers. Those contributions that had outlined uncommon fields of activity for women were most likely to at least mention women's traditional domestic and nurturing roles. The affirmative stance toward the domestic sphere as a place for Indian women might be understood as a recognition of a certain reality of the 'women on the ground'; one might also argue, however, that it was a rhetorical device not to appear threatening when staking out new arenas for women or voicing a critique of patriarchal structures. Contributors also repeatedly said that raising consciousness would lead to widespread awareness amongst the readers of women's periodicals. Once patriarchal practices were exposed, men themselves would see the need to end the oppression of women.

Notes

1. Early advice literature had for the most part adopted a perspective that emerged from women's social realities. In the preface to the Urdu novel *Mirat ul Urus* (The Bride's Mirror, 1868), for example, the author Nazir Ahmad (1903: 2) announced that he had combined religious knowledge and moral instruction in a way that would suit the intellectual capacities and everyday realities of his female readership. The protagonists were two Muslim sisters with starkly contrasting dispositions and levels of intelligence, one virtuous and

intelligent, the other rustic and ignorant. With the novel, the author intended to prepare readers for their domestic roles after marriage. This type of writing was also prevalent in women's periodicals.

2. Because of the situation of these texts in periodicals, they can be differentiated from the immensely popular and widely circulated advice texts in both Hindi and Bengali, as discussed in the scholarly works of Banerjee (1996, 2004), Bannerji (1991, 1992), Chakrabarty (1994), Roy (1995), Sangari (1999), and Walsh (1997, 2004). While the presented content might resemble each other, it is the context that makes for the difference.

3. 'Āp hī svayam dekhiye ki sāresaṅsār ko hilā ḍālne vālī śakti so vibhūṣit striyāṅ 'ablā' kahlāne yogya haiṅ athvā 'sablā' aur in kī daśā sudhārne āvaśyak hai athvā nahīṅ. In kā phaislā kaun kare ham yā āp?' (Radha Krishna Jhingaran, 1917, '*Ablā yā sablā*' [Weak or strong], *Stri Darpan* [March]: 136).

4. 'Bas mujhe itnā hī kahnā thā, is kā sār kyā niklā, āp khud vicāreṅ' (Kamta Prasad Vidyarthi, 1917, '*Bhūt nahīṅ billī—galp nahīṅ saccī ghaṭnā hai*' [Not a ghost, but a cat—not a story, but a true incident], *Stri Darpan* [March]: 51).

5. See Chakrabarty 1994; Walsh 1997; Sangari 1999.

6. Tanika Sarkar's (2001) observation of the gendered relationship of nationalism and middle-class formation is mainly concerned with the figure of the Hindu wife, who is granted a large measure of self-determination and responsibility in the domestic sphere, while retaining her purity and chastity. I have gathered much information from scholarship on Bengali discourses on domesticity of the nineteenth century, while I also wish to point out new developments in the Hindi discourse on domesticity and nationalism of the early twentieth century. Hindi writings also attempted to define an autonomous Hindu sphere, untouched by colonialism, and also placing emphasis on the *new* domesticity that was nationalist in outlook. Furthermore, respectability and status were no longer immediately contingent on caste and could be acquired through certain conduct, education, and lifestyle (Banerjee 2004: 5). Women in the United Provinces were actively involved in the Hindi literary discourse, just as Bengali women were in the Bengali literary discourse (Bannerji 1991; Borthwick 1984; Walsh 1997, 2004). The interfaces of public and private, however, are much more explicit in the United Provinces than in nineteenth-century Bengal. While women may have accepted their traditionally assigned roles, and even insisted on them, they also sought to redefine their role as homemakers, wives, mothers, and citizens. Bannerji (1991) used the term 'fashioning a self', while referring to this development in the title of her article on Bengali educational proposals. In the pages of Hindi women's periodicals, women assigned themselves responsibility for the household and wrote about domestic affairs self-reliantly and with confidence. Women's strength and devotion as wife and homemaker in particular stood at the centre of such

writings. In this regard, nationalism was an enabling component allowing writers to reflect on how women could contribute to nationalist politics from within the domestic sphere, but also through engaging in the public sphere.

7. Shevelow, who makes a similar observation with regard to the British single-essay periodical *Visiter* (1723–4), notes how this women's periodical established ways of debating women's duties and rights and how this new focus, in turn, gave the domestic sphere public importance. This, Shevelow holds, can be attributed to the fact that *women* were the editors of domestic periodicals:

> When women editors, writing through female personae, became the producers and controlling figures of the women's periodical, they established a new authority of women writers to pronounce upon women's topics. Thus they brought a new editorial perspective to the periodical discourse about women which refigured, but did not fundamentally alter, the way in which femininity was being written in the popular periodical. (1989: 166–7)

8. In Bengal, threats to the home as safe haven were publicly debated after the death of eleven-year-old Phulmonee in 1890. Phulmonee had died after having been forced to engage in sexual intercourse with (and by) her husband who was then in his thirties. The rape of Phulmonee was widely debated in the media. Ultimately, the public uproar pressured the colonial government to reassess the age of consent for Indian girls (Sarkar 2001: 191–225).

9. 'Gulāb kī āb bāg hī meṅ hai. Bāhar jāne meṅ na usmeṅ vah sugandh rahtī hai na saundarya. Isī tarah aurat kī izzat ghar baiṭhe hī hai. Use bāhar kī hokar rahnā acchā nahīṅ. Jo dekhegā haṅsegā' (Jyampyari Seth, 1920, '*Pardā*' [The veil], *Stri Darpan* [March]: 165).

10. The *Lakshmi* (Goddess of Wealth) of the Home.

11. The Faithful and Virtuous Wife.

12. The words for responsibility and duty used in the Hindi original texts are, besides dharma, *kartavya*, *uttardāyitva*, and *adhīn*.

13. Prāyaḥ sāṅsārik sab ācār dharma karma vrata ādi meṅ striyoṅ ko mukhya śraddhā hotī hai, par sab śāstroṅ kā aur ṛṣī muniyoṅ kā mat aur siddhānt yahī hai ki strī ko pati se baṛh kar aur koī dharma nahīṅ hai. Kyoṅki pati śabd kā arth pālan karne vālā, mūl aur gati hai. Śāstra meṅ likhā hai striyoṅ kā devtā keval pati hai. Brahmā, viṣṇu, maheś sab pati ke aṅg meṅ nivās karte haiṅ. [...] Jo strī pati kī pyārī nahīṅ hai, uske sab saubhāgya vyarth haiṅ. Uskā khānā pīnā sonā, śṛṅgār karnā varañc jīnā tak [not readable] hai, kyoṅki, - jo apne pati se prem nahīṅ kartī vah saṅsār meṅ vyarth hī janmī hai. (Ambikaprasad Shukla, 1913, '*Striyoṅ kā mukhya dharma—pātivrat*' [Chastity and loyalty, the prime dharma of women], *Grihalakshmi* [September/October (Aśvin 1970)]: 361–2)

14. Anadidhan Bandyopadhyay, 1913, '*Strī prabhāv*' [The impact of women], *Grihalakshmi* (September/October [Aśvin 1970]): 385–6.

15. Indumati Sharma, 1923, '*Strī kartavya*' [Women's duty], *Madhuri* (July): 683–4.

16. Striyoṅ kā mukhya kartavya hai pātivratdharma kā pālan. Jo striyāṅ is kartavya kā pālan nahīṅ kar saktīṅ, ve kisī kartavya kā pālan nahīṅ kar saktīṅ aur na unke bacconṅ kā pālan hī ṭhīk tarah se ho saktā hai. Na unke bacce hī sudhar sake haiṅ. Pahle striyāṅ jab pativratā hotī thī, unke laṛke rām kṛṣṇa ke samān vīr tathā svanām-dhanya hote the. Agar phir bhī striyāṅ vaisī hī man-vāṇī-kāyā se pūrṇ pativratā hoṅ, to koī āścarya nahīṅ ki unkī santān thoṛe hī dinoṅ meṅ bhārat kā uddhār kar le. (Ibid.)

17. Striyoṅ ko apne bacconṅ ko dāī-naukaroṅ ke ūpar nahīṅ choṛnā cāhiye. Aisā karne se bacce bigaṛ jāte haiṅ. Mūrkh dāī bacconṅ ko paṛhī mātā ke samān ucc śikṣā tathā acche upadeś nahīṅ degī. Is tarah laṛkā bure ādarś kā ho jāegā. Ek bāt bacconṅ ke liye yah bhī āvaśyak hai ki unheṅ bure saṅg meṅ na paṛne diyā jāy; kyoṅki baccā jaisā saṅg meṅ rahega, vaisā hī uskā ādarś hoga. Unko apnī hī dekh-bhāl meṅ rakhnā cāhiye. (Ibid.: 683)

Contributors who supported this opinion also provided citations from western pedagogues or Greek political philosophers. *Stri Darpan* quoted the Greek saying 'let your child be educated by a slave and you will have two slaves instead of one (Ambika Prasad Pandey, '*Ghar aur mātā*' [The home and the mother], *Stri Darpan* [October]: 242).

18. Servants were not endowed with much agency in Hindi writings, unlike in Bengali personal narratives, where authors would frequently describe the ambiguous power of servants in a home, and sometimes even voiced their debt and gratitude to servants (Banerjee 2004: 127–8). In the Hindi context, only a mother was supposedly able to raise a child. If a substitute proved unavoidable, an educated midwife was an option. Female relatives were not mentioned in the context of child-rearing. Banerjee (1996: 6) also notes the strident condemnation of entrusting children to nurse-maids in the Bengali context. She points to the seeming paradox of protecting children from the bad company of nurse-maids and housewives' maternal attitude towards maids who were treated as family members despite constant efforts from the Bengali middle class to distinguish themselves from their lower-class counterparts. Such a cross-caste and class notion of belonging is not visible in the Hindi periodicals, where servants hardly even find mention.

19. Swāminī kā pradhān kartavya ghar kā prabandh karnā hai. Ghar kā prabandh ṭhīk na rahne se hāni hotī hai. Svāminī kā dharma hai ki sab se pahle garbhavatī strī ko khilāve, phir bīmāroṅ ko, tab bacconṅ ko. Uske bād atithiyoṅ tathā ghar ke puruṣoṅ ko khilāve. Phir bahuoṅ tathā dāī-naukaroṅ ko khilākar ant meṅ svayam khāe. Rāt ko sab ke ant meṅ āp sonā cāhiye. Sone ke pahle sāre ghar meṅ rośnī lekar ghūm lenā cāhiye. Dekh le ki kahīṅ koī kiṅcāṛ to nahīṅ khulā hai, yā koī vastu to bāhar nahīṅ paṛī hai. (Indumati Sharma, 1923, '*Strī kartavya*' [Women's duty], *Madhuri* [July]: 683)

20. 'Svāminī ko, sabere, sab se pahle uṭhkar nitya-karm karne ke bād ghar ke dāī-naukaroṅ ko jagānā cāhiye. Phir bahū beṭiyāṅ ko jagākar kuch thoṛā-sā paṛhe. Uske bād sab ko jal-pān karākar rasoī kā prabandh kare. Phir sab ko khilākar ārām kare' (Ibid.).

21. From this article it remains unclear whether the woman or the servants cook. Cooking was a much-discussed topic in women's periodicals (such as in *Stri Darpan*, July 1916, September 1916, April 1917). See also Part Two, Box 11, pp. 267–9).

Women were responsible for food preparation because of the importance ascribed to food for a healthy body and mind. Even in the contemporary fashionable world, authors held, food stood at the centre of women's responsibilities. The essays however also made concessions: if it was too tiring to prepare food on the traditional stove (*cūlhā*), a coal oven (*aṅgrezī cūlhā*) could be used (Satyavati Devi, 1917, '*Striyoṅ apne hāth se bhojan kyoṅ banāveṅ*' [Why women should prepare the food with their own hands], *Stri Darpan* [April]: 221–4; for a full translation see Part Two, Box 11, pp. 267–9). In *Grihalakshmi*, the readers were reminded of the sacredness of food preparation in a 'world of fashion and modern education' (N.N., 1913, '*Striyoṅ ko apne hāth se bhojan banānā cāhiye*' [Women should prepare food with their own hands], *Grihalakshmi* [September/October (Aśvin 1970)]: 389–90). Proper food, the essay held, would keep the family members healthy and spare them medical expenditures.

22. Bahut mūṛh aise haiṅ, jo nahīṅ jānte ki thoṛe se apriya aur kaṭhor vacanoṅ se apnī lakṣmī ko kitnā kaṣṭ pahuṅcātā hai. Yah sab dveṣ aur agyāntā ke bhāv ke dūr karne kī atyant āvaśyaktā hai. Ek vidvān kahā kartā thā, ki jab maiṅ kisī puruṣ ko ciṛciṛā mizāz ko dekhtā hūṅ to mujhe uskī patnī par dayā ātī hai aur jab maiṅ kisī ko prasanncit dekhtā hūṅ to maiṅ uske bandhu bāndhav aur uskī strī ke anand ko smaraṇ karke khuś ho jātā hūṅ.

For a full translation, see Part Two, Box 16, pp. 279–81.

Āśā hai, is lekh ko paṛh kar ciṛciṛe mizāz puruṣ apne mizāz ko sudhāreṅge aur unkī striyāṅ unko sudhārne meṅ apnā prabhāv ḍāleṅge. (Anadidhan Bandyopadhyay, 1913, '*Strī prabhāv*' [The impact of women], *Grihalakshmi* [September/October (Āśvin 1970)]: 386)

23. Ājkal bahudhā dekhne meṅ ātā hai ki manuṣya isī bāt kī baṛī dhūm macā rahe haiṅ aur bahudhā patr, patrikāoṅ meṅ bhī yahī lekh adhiktar nikalte haiṅ ki striyoṅ ko pativratā hona cāhie. Unkā pati ke prati yah kartavya hai; unkā yah dharm hai; unheṅ is bhāṅti rahnā cāhie tathā is bhāṅti pati ke sāth bartāv karnā cāhie. Kintu khed kā viṣay hai ki hamne kisī patr, patrikā ko yah chāpte nahīṅ dekhā ki pati kā patnī ke prati kyā kartavya hai? Yadyapi āṣāṛh 1971 ke gṛihalakṣmī ke aṅk meṅ 'gupt' mahāśay dvārā 'patnī ke prati pati kā bartāv' is śīrṣak kā ek lekh prakāśit kiyā gayā thā, kintu vah lekh bhī kuch santoṣ janak pratīt nahīṅ huā - kāraṅ ki usmeṅ ek dṛiṣṭānt ke atirikt koī anya upadeś nahīṅ diyā gayā, jisse puruṣ apne dharm ko samajhte aur use kuch śikṣā grahaṇ karte. Ataeva isī bāt ko soc kar maiṅ ne is lekh ko āpke sammukh upasthit karne kā vicār kiyā hai. Āśā kartā hūṅ, āp sab pāṭhak mahāśay isse kuch śikṣā grahaṇ kar avaśya hī mere pariśram ko saphal kareṅge. (Vidyarthi Banvarilal Gupta, 1917, '*Pati kā patnī ke prati kartavya*' [A husband's duty towards his wife], *Grihalakshmi* [August/September (Bhādrapad 1974)]: 212)

For a full translation, see Part Two, Box 8, pp. 257–61.

24. Dhaniram Bihari, 1917, '*Ingleṇḍ kī bahū aur beṭiāṅ*' [England's wives and daughters], *Stri Darpan* (May): 231–2.

25. 'Jitnā ki hindustān kī bahū beṭiyāṅ kām kartī haiṅ, iṇgleṇḍ kī bahū beṭiyāṅ bhī utnā hī kām kartī haiṅ' (Ibid.: 231).

26. Ingleṇḍ kī dhanvān striyāṅ apne fursat kā samay ālas meṅ nahīṅ vyatīt kartīn. Ve apnā samay kisī upayukt saṅsthā kī madad karne meṅ lagātī haiṅ. Aisī sahāyat karnā vah apnā karttavya samajhtī haiṅ. Aisā karne meṅ unko saṅkoc nahī hotā. Ghar kī cīzoṅ ko sāf karke ṭhīk ḍhaṅg se rakhnā yah naukaroṅ kā kām hai, aisā vahāṅ kī dhanvān striyāṅ tak nahīṅ samajhtīṅ. (Ganpatrao Devsakar, 1913, '*Iṅglenḍ kī striyāṅ*' [England's women], *Grihalakshmi* [September/October (Aśvin 1970)]: 366)

27. Suitable education.

28. See Anon. [A well-wisher of the country], 1913, '*Svadeśī sāṛī*' [Swadeshi sari], *Grihalakshmi* [September/October (Aśvin 1970)]: 387–9; for full translation, see Part Two, Box 23, pp. 310–12.

29. N.N., 1913, '*Nārīcaryā*' [The conduct of women, Part I], *Grihalakshmi* (April/May [Vaiśākh 1970]): 104–7; N.N., 1913, '*Nārīcaryā*' [The conduct of women, Part II], *Grihalakshmi* (May/June [Jyeṣṭ 1970]): 159–62.

30. *Suśikṣitā* is a gendered term that is frequently used to describe suitable literature for women.

31. 'Rog, śok, dukh, daridratā ityādi tāpoṅ se jalte hue gṛhasth kī ek mātra suśikṣitā nārī hī ās kī pyās miṭānevālī aur pīṛā kī auṣadhi hotī hai. [...] Jo manuṣya aisī strī pātā hai, vahī sukhī hai. Uske liye svarg bhī koī vastu nahīṅ hai' (N.N., 1913, '*Nārīcaryā*' [The conduct of women, Part I], *Grihalakshmi* [April/May (Vaiśākh 1970)]: 104).

32. Anadidhan Bandyopadhyay, 1913, '*Strī prabhāv*' [The impact of women], *Grihalakshmi* [September/October (Aśvin 1970)]: 386.

33. 'Pahile ham ko ādmī banna cāhiye' (Mannan Dwivedi Gajapuri, 1911,'*Hindī Samāj meṅ Striyāṅ*' [Women in the Hindi society], *Stri Darpan* [December]: 342).

34. Girija Kumar Ghosh, 1911, '*Puruṣ caritra*' [The character of men], *Stri Darpan* (December): 363.

35. 'Re re, puruṣ adham ajñānī / Durācār, pāpī, abhimānī. / Pāp bharā hai tere man meṅ. / Lajjā hai vahīṅ tere man meṅ (Ibid.).

36. Shyama Charan Varma, 1917, 'Kiśorī' [Kishori], *Grihalakshmi* (May/June [Jyeṣṭ 1974]): 114–8.

37. 'Tum kuch kitābeṅ dekhā karo, maiṅ tumheṅ paṛhnā likhnā sikhāūṅgā. Tajo avidyā sīkho vidyā, yah hai śubh strī kā nem. Kiśorī! Vidyā aisā sundar ratna hai jiskā mol saṅsār meṅ nahīṅ (Ibid.: 117).

38. Ab to kiśorī rāt-din acchī acchī pustakeṅ paṛhne aur apne dharm-karm ko samajhne lagī. Thoṛe dinoṅ meṅ vidyā ke prabhāv se vahī kiśorī, jiskī niṭhurtā aur asabhyatā ke viṣay meṅ hamko itnī der tak pāṭhikāoṅ ko apnī or dhyān dilānā paṛā, aisī suśīl aur guṇvatī ho gayī ki jiskā udāharaṇ milnā asambhav hai. Rāt din sās-sasur, pati

ityādi kī sevā meṅ lagī rahtī. Grihasthī kā prabandh aisā uttam karne lagī, jaisā āj kal kī striyāṅ śāyad hī koī kartī hoṅ. (Ibid.)

39. Anon. [A reader], 1917, '*Suśīlā*' [Sushila], *Grihalakshmi* (May/June [Jyeṣṭ 1974]): 119–27.

40. Suśīlā pahilī sī suśīlā nahīṅ rahī. Ab vah sacmuc ḍākṭarnī ban gayī hai. Ghar par tīn varṣ barābar pariśram kar usne hindī kī acchī yogyatā prāpt kar lī hai aur pichle ek varṣ meṅ amolcandra ne usko aṅgrezī kā sādhāraṇ jñān karā ḍākṭarī ke prayojanīya niyamoṅ kī bhī sādhāraṇ śikṣā dī hai. [...] Suśīlā ne ek samay-vibhāg banā liyā hai aur sāre kārya usī ke anukūl kartī hai—isī kāraṇ bhojanālay sambandhī kārya, pati dev kī sevā sambandhī kārya aur strīrogiyoṅ kī cikitsā ityādi karne par bhī use kuch samay likhne paṛhne ke lie bac rahta hai—is samay meṅ suśīlā ek dainik māsik patra paṛhtī hai, svādhyāy kartī hai aur kuch saṅskṛt bhāṣā kā bhī abhyās kartī hai. (Ibid.: 126–7)

41. Ganesh Prasad Mehrotra, 1917, '*Śyāmā*' [Shyama], *Stri Darpan* (August): 86–101.

42. Lekhak mahāśay kā vicār yah mālūm hotā hai ki aṅgrezī bhāṣā ke paṛhne se śyāmā kī yah durdaśā huī parantu yah ṭhīk nahīṅ hai. Strī yā puruṣ kā sambhalnā, bigaṛnā us ke svabhāv kī bāt hotī hai koī śikṣā aisī nahīṅ jo mātā pitā kī ājñāpālan karnā na sikhātī ho. Dekhā gayā hai ki hindū laṛkiyāṅ bhī aisī nikal jātī haiṅ jo binā aṅgrezī paṛhe baṛoṅ kī ājñā kā ullaṅghan kartī hoṅ kintu yah un ke dharm yā śikṣā kā doṣ nahīṅ hotā. (Ibid.: 101)

43. G.P. Shrivastav, 1913/1914, '*Kālī mem*' [The black madam], *Grihalakshmi* (December/January [Pauṣ 1970]): 515–9.

44. 'Chiḥ sohāg kis ciṛiyāṅ kā nām hai. Yahī to bolā ham, ki hindustānī aurat akil kī andhī sohāg sohāg bol ke apnī sab āzādī apne mard ko de detī haiṅ. Mard ko apnā sab kuch samajhtī haiṅ. Dekho, kaisā be samajh bāt. Mard kuch nahīṅ haiṅ. Ham log mard kī parvāh nahīṅ kartī, āzādī kī parvāh kartī hai' (Ibid.: 517).

45. 'Mem sāhab kauā sī kālī, tond kī bhārī, bilkul beḍhaṅgī. Magar sāyā kā gilāf tamām badan par caṛhā huā hai. Aur pakauṛī sī nāk ainak kī kamānī se khūb kasī huī thī. Dekhne meṅ aisī khūbsūrat thīṅ ki agar rāt ko sāmne ā jātī, to ādmī māre ḍar ke behoś to zarūr ho jāye (Ibid.:515).

46. 'It activates the body. One never falls sick. One gains strength. Do you understand?' (Ibid.: 518).

47. Lakshminarayan Gupta, 1914/1915, '*Ādarś pati prem*' [The ideal love towards a husband], *Grihalakshmi* (December/January [Pauṣ 1971]): 523–6.

48. Vidyarthi Purandas 'Abhir', 1914, '*Pativratā Māltī*' [Malti, the faithful woman], *Grihalakshmi* (June/July [Āṣāṛh 1971]): 138–43.

49. 'Nāth! Īśvar ne kitne divas bād āj ham logoṅ ko milāyā hai. Na jāne āpko kitnī taklīpheṅ sahan karnī paṛī hoṅgī' (Ibid.: 143).

50. Dakorvasi Vaishnav Devadas Dev Sagar, 1917, '*Vīrāṅganā-rūp kumārī*' [Roop Kumari, the heroine], *Stri Darpan* (August): 72–7.

51. 'Rūp kumārī ne apne satītva rakṣā ke liye jaisī vīrtā ke sāth duṣṭ durācārī bhagvat dās kā saṅhār kiyā us ke nimitt rājya ke niyamānusār vah nirdoṣ ṭhahrāī

gaī. Us samay se is satī rūp kumārī kī kīrti kaumudī adyāpi paryant bhāratvarṣ bhar meṅ prakhyāt hai' (Ibid.: 77).

52. Gulabdevi Chaturvedi, 1918, '*Ādarś sakhī*' [The model friend], *Stri Darpan* (July): 9–18; for a full translation see Part Two, Box 13, pp. 274–7.

53. 'Maiṅne jo kuch tujhse kahī sunā ho, use kṣamā karo. Śīlā! Tumhāre is upkār ke lie maiṅ sadaiv tumhārā ṛṇī rahūṅgā. Beṭī! Maiṅne tumhārā baṛā apmān kiyā hai. Maiṅ tumhāre guṇoṅ ko na pahicān sakā thā. Kyā tum mujhe is bhārī aprādh ke lie kṣmā na karogī?' (Ibid.: 17).

54. 'Āśā hai ki āp śīlā ke vyavhār par avaśya dhyān deṅgī aur apnī sakhiyoṅ ke sāth sadā nirmal śuddh prem rakheṅgī, aur yadi kisī sakhī kā vivāh kisī durācārī ke sāth hotā huā dekheṅ to uskī rakṣā karne kā bharsak yatna karne se mukh na moṛeṅgī' (Ibid.: 18).

55. Chaturbhuj Ji Divaniya, 1927, '*Suśīlā*' [Sushila], *Stri Darpan* (January): 7–16.

56. 'Usī din se ve donoṅ carkhā calāne lagīṅ aur ghar meṅ usī din se sukh aur śānti kā sāmrājya chā gayā. Suśīlā jab mauqā pātī apne paṛos kī striyoṅ se bhī carkhā kātne kī prārthnā kiyā kartī jiske phal svarūp bahut gharoṅ meṅ carkhe calne lage. Aur adhikāṅś aurateṅ suśīlā ko baṛī ādar kī dṛṣṭi se dekhne lagīṅ' (Ibid.: 16). For a full translation of this short story, see Sneha Desai in Nijhawan 2010: 411–8.

57. R. Nehru and R.K. Vancu, 1922, '*Laṛkiyoṅ se bātcit*' [Conversation with girls], *Kumari Darpan* (May): 39–40; for a full translation see Part Two, Box 3, pp. 249–50.

58. 'Aise asthir puruṣ kā kyā bharosā ki ek strī rahte hue bhī dūsrī se vyāh karnā cāhe?' (Ibid.: 39).

59. Ab rahā tumhārā yah praśna ki tum janma bhar kvārī raho yā pitā ke ḍhūṇḍe hue var se vivāh kar lo. Is praśna kā uttar tum apne man se pūcho yadi tum vivāh karnā cāhtī ho aur yah samajhtī ho ki tumhāre pitā kā ḍhūṇḍā huā var yogya, śikṣit aur bhalemānas hai to tum avaśya śādī kar lo. Us vivāhit yuvak kā xyāl to bilkul hī tyāg do. Yadi abhī tum vivāh na karnā cāho to do ek varṣ ṭhahar jāo koī jaldī nahīṅ hai, apne pitā se kah do ki tum abhī śādī nahīṅ karogī āyandā dekhā jāvegā. Aur yadi tum kvārī hī rahnā cāho to bhī kuch harz nahīṅ. Strī kā ek mātra lakṣya vivāh nahīṅ hai. Koī paropkār kā kām uṭhā lo aur usī meṅ samay bitāyā karo. (Ibid.: 40)

60. Sreenivas (2003: 59) takes this observation even further and speaks of a 'paradigm of emotion' in Tamil women's periodicals, in which women writers raised issues around love, affection, and pleasure, facilitating radical critiques of women's oppression, as well as the emergence of new images of women. While such a discourse is certainly also visible in Hindi women's periodicals, Hindi writers drew on many more ways of addressing social injustice. Appealing to a rational consciousness, for example, was at least as important as touching the emotional consciousness of readers.

61. Uṭho bhaginiyo! Huā saverā, ab to tanik cet jāo. Pakṣī tumheṅ sīkh dete haiṅ, ṭuk to dhyān idhar lāo. Nidrā rūp mūrkhtā tyāgo, nīti, dharma nij apnāo. Bigaṛe hue deś ko ghar kā kāj samajhkar banvāo. (1)

Gyānī bhī ho puruṣ akele, kām nahīṅ kar sakte haiṅ. Ve sarvadā tumhārā āśraya pāne ko muṅh takte haiṅ. Jaise ek cakr ke dvārā, nahīṅ kabhī rath caltā hai. Tyoṅhī ghar samāj kā nātā, nahīṅ akele paltā hai. (2)

Yadyapi ve nirdoṣī na hoṅ, par tum ko bhī kuch karnā hai. Mānuṣ tan pākar kyā tum ko pāp parāyaṇ marnā hai? Matṛ-bhūmī ke liye jagat meṅ nānā saṅkaṭ sahnā hai? Athvā bhojan, nīnd, viṣay, bhaya ādi hī meṅ rahnī hai! (5) (Matadin Shukla, 1917, '*Mahilāoṅ se nivedan*' [A plea to women], *Stri Darpan* [March]: 132).

For a full translation, see Part Two, Box 24, pp. 313–14.

62. Sinha (2006: 10) develops this line of thought with regard to the controversy following a publication titled *Mother India* (1927), written by American journalist Katherine Mayo.

63. Yah maiṅ kahūṅgi ki jin paramparā gat vicāroṅ ke kāraṇ bhāratiya striyoṅ ko vartamān durdaśā meṅ ānā paṛa hai un vicāroṅ ko nāś karne meṅ unheṅ avaśya tatpār ho jānā cāhiye. Apne bhūtkāl ke viṣay meṅ ham baṛe abhimān ke sāth baṛī baṛī bāteṅ banāte haiṅ aur kahte haiṅ ki us yug meṅ hamārī daśā sāre samsār se acchī thī. Kuch mahāśaya to aise haiṅ ki jo apne vartamān samay ke viṣay meṅ ḍīṅg mārā karte haiṅ. Sambhav hai, kaī bātoṅ meṅ hamārī daśā prācīn kāl meṅ aur āj kal bhī acchī ho, parantu bhāratīya striyoṅ kī to aisī durdaśā ho rahī hai ki uske liye pratyek bhāratīya santān ko lajjā ānī cāhiye. (R.P. Pal, 1917, '*Striyoṅ ko pahile hom rūl dījiye*' [First give women 'home rule'], *Stri Darpan* [February]: 73)

This reprinted speech was initially delivered at a Brahmo Samaj meeting of women. The text was rendered and annotated by Satyavati Devi and Lakshmi Devi Vajpeyi. They introduce Pal's contribution as 'important to know about for every single woman and man in India' (Ibid.: 72).

64. Jin rūṛhiyoṅ ke kāraṇ bhāratīya striyāṅ sadaiva ajñān aur parādhīntā ke gart meṅ paṛī rahtī haiṅ un rūṛhiyoṅ ke liye prācīn dharmaśāstroṅ ke pramāṇ dikhāye jāte haiṅ. Jin śāstroṅ ne bhāratīya deviyoṅ ko ajñānāndhkār aur dāsya paṅk meṅ saṛāne kī vyavasthā dekar apnī bhāvī santān ko satyānāś kar diyā hai aur aise śāstra jis samay race gaye, un śāstroṅ aur us samay kī baṛāī gāne meṅ āj koī lābh nahīṅ hai. Un śāstroṅ ne īśvar kā cāhe jaisā ujval svarūp dikhlāyā ho; parantu āp acchī tarah dhyān meṅ rakkhem ki jo rāṣṭra apnī deviyoṅ ko atyācār aur anyāy se, ajñān aur parādhīntā meṅ, rakhtā hai us par īśvar kī prasanntā bhī kaise ho saktī hai? Striyoṅ ko aur śūdroṅ ko gulāmī meṅ rakhne kī jin śāstroṅ ne ājñā dī hai, hamāre puruṣ log unkī mahīmā gāyā kareṅ aur aise dharma granthoṅ kī racnā par man hī man mugdh huā kareṅ; par koī kāraṇ nahīṅ hai ki striyāṅ bhī unke sāth vaisā hī karne ko taiyār ho (Ibid.: 73).

65. Hamārā yah spaṣṭ kathan hai ki yadi āp sab log deś kī saccī unnati karnā cāhte haiṅ to striyoṅ ko 'hom rūl' pahile dījiye. [...] apne pati se lekar aur naukar paryant, sab par striyoṅ kā śāsan rahnā cāhiye. Pati ko cāhiye ki binā patnī kī sammati ke koī bhī garhasthya yā sārvajanik kārya na kare, patnī ko sāth lekar cale. 'Paropkār kā prārambh ghar se hī hotā hai', is kathan ko caritārtha karne kā samay yahī hai (Ibid.: 75).

66. Such as *Grihalakshmi* (October/November 1913 [Kārtik 1970]): 427–30.

67. Jis prakār puruṣ svatantratā pūrvak deś hit meṅ bhāg le saktā hai usī prakār strī bhī le sake, itnī svatantratā use denī cāhiye kam se kam strī jāti meṅ svadeś prem aur svadeśābhimān jāgṛit karnevālī deviyāṅ ham meṅ taiyār honī cāhiye. [...] Maiṅ to samajhtī hūṅ ki gṛha prabandh kā uttardāyitva jaisā striyoṅ par hai vaisā hi puruṣoṅ par bhī rahnā cāhiye, tathā vidyā prāpt kar sarvajanik samāj sevā karne kā mārg jis prakār puruṣoṅ ke liye khulā hai usi prakār striyoṅ ke liye bhī khulā rahnā cāhiye. (R.P. Pal, 1917, '*Striyoṅ ko pahile hom rūl dījiye*' [First give women 'home rule'], *Stri Darpan* [February]: 75–6)

68. Jyandevi, 1918, '*Kyā homrūl loge?*' [You want home rule?], *Stri Darpan* (December): 288; for a full translation see Part Two, Box 25, pp. 314–15.

69. Ab strī jātī bhī yah kahne ko taiyār ho gaī hai ki mahāpuruṣ tum dhanya ho tumheṅ bhī dūr hī se namaskār hai, tum ne ab tak baṛī svārthanā se kām kiyā. Ham ko apnā dās banākar rakkhā, apne nīc karma karvāye, kyā ham bhāratīya santān nahīṅ? Kyā bhārat mātā kī sevā hamāre bhāgya meṅ nahīṅ vadī hai? Ham meṅ kyā nyūntā hai. Ham manuṣya jāti meṅ se nahīṅ ki ham meṅ mānsik tathā śarīrik śaktiyāṅ nahīṅ? Phir kyā bas yahī ki svārthī puruṣo! Tum ne ham ko kuch ucc kārya karne kā avakāś hī nahīṅ diyā. Bahut dhokhā diyā kintu bas ab tumhārī dāl na galegī, ham keval striyāṅ hī nahīṅ haiṅ kintu bhāratīya samāj kī sadasya tathā nāgarik bhī haiṅ. Jis prakār pratyek strī kā kuṭumb kī or kartavya hai usī tarah us se kahīṅ adhik kartavya samāj kī or bhī hai. (Hridaya Mohini, 1917, '*Strī śikṣā par Akbar ke vicār*' [Akbar's thoughts on women's education], *Stri Darpan* [July]: 55)

Sections of this reader's response to a parochial poem on women's education that had been published in *Grihalakshmi* are also discussed in Talwar (1989: 221–2; 1993).

70. 'Pablik meṅ kyā zarūr ki jākar tane raho. Paṛh likh ke apne ghar hī meṅ raho. Tum ko biṭhā ke tāq pai pūjā kareṅge ham. Bhogo jo ghar meṅ baiṭh; na lāṭoṅ ko hove gam' (Hridaya Mohini, 1917, '*Strī śikṣā par Akbar ke vicār*' [Akbar's thoughts on women's education], *Stri Darpan* [July]: 54).

71. It is typical that she used the English loan word, as a Hindi equivalent that was able to semantically convey the meaning of 'public' did not exist (Orsini 1999a: 409). Hindi words were either *sarkārī* (for governmental institutions), *jāti* or *sarvasādharan*. Orsini (Ibid.) suggests that 'community' is a more appropriate translation of these terms.

72. 'Strī kā sthān sir ke ūpar nahīṅ hai, pairoṅ ke nīce bhī nahīṅ hai—hṛday ke bhītar hai' (Tamallata Vasu, 1923, '*Strī kā sthān*' [The place of women], *Madhuri* [January]: 91).

73. I use this term in distinction to expressly female and feminist perspectives in writing as Moi (1989) has categorized them: 'feminist' is an explicitly political label, whereas 'femaleness' is a matter of biological disposition. Consequently, not all females are feminists and feminists need not necessarily be female. Besides the political and biological labels, a third category is that of

'femininity'. Femininity is defined on grounds of cultural and social norms. Patriarchal ideologies, however, hardly distinguish 'feminine' and 'femaleness', and as a consequence, women tend to be essentialized on grounds of femininity and femaleness.

74. Mard to āj varṣoṅ se cillāte cillāte thak gaye unke kiye to koī kām hotā nahīṅ. Vah sarkār se bār bār bhīk māṅgte rahte haiṅ ki hameṅ yah haq do hameṅ vah haq do lekin vah unko miltā nahīṅ. Bahinoṅ tum vah kām karke dikhā do ki jo un se ab tak nahīṅ huā. Tum un ko yah kahne kā mauqā do ki jo kām ham se nahīṅ huā hamārī māeṅ, aur bahinoṅ ne kar dikhāyā. (R. Nehru, 1917, '*Sampādakīya: Śrīmatī Sarojinī Devī Naiḍū kā vyākhyān*' [Editorial: The speech of Sarojini Devi Naidu], *Stri Darpan* [February]: 62)

75. The demand for women's suffrage was such a campaign that she would be leading successfully a few months after this speech was published.

76. 'Tumhāre mard gulām haiṅ, vah gulāmī kī zañjīroṅ se jakṛe hue haiṅ, unke hāthoṅ meṅ gulāmī kī hathkaṛiyāṅ aur pairoṅ me beṛiyāṅ paṛī haiṅ. Us kī kuñjī tumhāre hāth meṅ hai lekin tum use kholtī nahīṅ. Tum unheṅ āzād banā saktī ho lekin banātī nahīṅ' (R. Nehru, 1917, '*Sampādakīya: Śrīmatī Sarojinī Devī Naiḍū kā vyākhyān*' [Editorial: The speech of Mrs Sarojini Devi Naidu], *Stri Darpan* [February]: 62).

77. 'Strī jāti ko cārdivāroṅ meṅ qaid rakhne aur un kā bal keval cauke bartan meṅ xarc karne se hamāre puruṣgaṇ svayam kām pūrā nahīṅ kar sakte' (Ibid.: 58).

78. 'Jis prakār kā andolan honā cāhiye us prakār kā karne ke vāste āp ke vyākhyān sunkar bhī hamāre nirbal bhāī taiyār nahīṅ hūe' (Ibid.: 61).

79. 'Jāo, sītā kī tarah tum bhī duḥkh saho apne mardoṅ kā hāth baṭāo. Jāo tum bhī sāvitrī kī tarah yamrāj se laṛkar apne mardoṅ kī zindagī bacāo' (Ibid.: 62).

80. Āp sab bhī māeṅ haiṅ aur maiṅ bhī māṅ hūṅ. Ham log sab māṅ kī mohabbat ko acchī tarah jānte haiṅ. Ham meṅ se kisī kā kalejā apne bacce kī mohabbat se nahīṅ bharā hai. Apne bacce ke dukh se kis māṅ ke dil meṅ dard nahīṅ huā hai. Kis kā jigar apne bacce ke dard se nahīṅ phāṭā hai lekin siraf is gaṅvāru mohabbat se kyā fāydā? Jab tak ki āp apne bacce ko yah nā kah sakeṅ ki maiṅ terī duniyāṅ meṅ sab se baṛi dost hūṅ. Us ko apne meṅ bhaṛosa karnā nā sikhā sakeṅ, us se yah nā kah sakeṅ ki tū bhūlega to maiṅ tujhe batāūṅgā. ... tū kurah jāega to maiṅ tujhe sīdhe rāste par lāūṅgī tab tak ham apnī mohabbat ka acchā vyavhār nahīṅ kar saktīṅ (Ibid.: 62).

81. The tendency to relegate women to the domestic sphere after times of crises is also visible in other literary genres. In the novels of the Bengali author Bankim Chandra Chattopadhyay the female characters emerge into the political arena in the name of nationalism but willingly return to the interior spheres after the political crisis is solved (Sarkar 2001).

82. Majumdar (2002: 20) has summarized the two strains of research, which ask 'whether the past produced the disadvantages that women had to overcome

in order to be fully participating citizens, or [whether it was] a resource that made Indian women specially suited to participation in national life, whether as virtuous mothers and wives at home or as dutiful members of the public sphere'. Majumdar posits that the issue should not be treated in the form of an either/or proposition, which forecloses the possibility of both statements being reasonable.

5 Hindi and the Question of Comprehensibility

The emergence of new literary genres in Hindi from the mid-nineteenth century was linked to three broader developments in the sphere of language politics at the time: the creation of modern Hindi as a print language, the projection of Hindi as the national language of the nation-to-be, and the creation of a literary canon in modern Hindi that, as Hindi writers and intellectuals envisioned it, would eventually be recognized as a national canon. This large-scale literary and nationalist project involved a number of Hindi writers who were willing to participate in the 'service of literature' (*sāhitya sevā*). As Dalmia (1997: 147) argues, it was the emerging middle class in the second half of the nineteenth century—with Bharatendu Harishchandra playing a leading role as their non-Brahmin spokesperson—that claimed an official and national status for Hindi.[1]

Some decades later, as Orsini (2002: 4) has observed, it were still the 'higher and middle castes, of once-diverse linguistic competencies that compacted around Khaṛī Bolī Hindi. They produced the first wave of activism and created institutional spaces for Hindi in the form of periodicals, literary and public associations, and textbook writing'. Among them, as I have shown in this study of women's, girls', and children's periodicals, were also women editors and writers. They shared the belief of the literati that Hindi, with its increasing prevalence and authority in the politically dominant north had the potential to rise from the status of a vernacular to that of a national language. But their main concern—and this is where their opinion differed from that of the mainstream male advocates of Hindi—was the degree to which the projected national language was *accessible* to the middle-class readers. All involved in the project were quick to realize that the term Hindi was used for many *regional variants* (*bolīs*) and that it did not stand for *one* language. While women editors also believed that a certain measure of standardization was necessary in order to advance Hindi as the national language, this was not to take place at the expense of comprehensibility: it was essential to the editors that women comprehend the texts that were written for them.

Standardizing and codifying Hindi as a print language was indeed a complicated matter. Who had the authority to lead such an undertaking and whose responsibility was it to participate therein? Nationalist historiography of Hindi has drawn a curtain over the literary diversity in the Hindi public sphere at the turn of the century (Orsini 2002: 31). What has therefore often remained unnoticed is that literary diversity was also created in women's periodicals. An investigation of such periodicals reveals that editors and writers were still vague about the place of writings *by* and *for* women in the established literary sphere. They had, however, little doubt that women bore the responsibility to participate in nationalist writing. The writer Pandit Satyabhakt wrote in *Arya Mahila* in 1918 about the importance of engaged writers—female and male—who would wield their pens in social-reformist and nationalist endeavours:

> The service of literature is one of the best and meritorious tasks of humankind. Social work, teaching, moral-religious education, and the promotion of equity and moral conduct are considered personal adornments. Those involved in such activities are described as charitable and noble, and are respected and venerated by the people at large; the same holds true for those involved in the service of literature. The service of literature immensely benefits humankind. Through literature, people enhance their knowledge and intellect, and their hearts fill with joy. This is why a servant of literature is highly respected in the world. He holds an important and revered position. People consider him to be the leader of the nation. One's character is enhanced through the service of literature. Because of this, man considers it very important to support such a project and he creates the very best of books and volumes for the benefit of the country and for his own personal happiness.
>
> Today it is mostly men who take on the service of literature. They are the ones who compose various kinds of books and essays. They edit periodicals and papers and they are the ones who organize associations and societies to discuss

literature. Only recently have women begun to participate in this activity, but now, they are also part of this noble task and their involvement is increasing steadily.[2]

In highlighting the importance of creating literature in Hindi, Satyabhakt was not only referring to the editors, publishers, and authors of literary and political periodicals, but also to those actors involved in the making of women's, girls', and children's periodicals. The latter, as I show in this chapter, reconciled two objectives with regard to standardizing Hindi as the national language: (i) to retain the flexibility of the Hindi lexicon (which included Urdu words and only a reasonable number of Sanskrit loanwords) for the sake of comprehensibility, and (ii) to pay allegiance to the linguistic and literary expectations of the Hindi literati and their project of creating modern standard Hindi. Meeting these two objectives simultaneously was not impossible. It did however entail an interrogation of the mainstream nationalist agenda of developing not only a *standardized*, but a *Sanskritized* form of Hindi. Women's and girls' periodicals demonstrated this possibility: their conciliatory move accorded well with the Hindi literati who readily acknowledged that literature had to be simple in style and lexicon in order to be comprehensible to middle-class women and girls.

In this chapter I discuss the ways women's periodicals sought to develop a language for women while paying allegiance to the linguistic conventions set forth by the Hindi literati. While I have already discussed the emergence of the women's periodical as a literary genre as well as the creation of the woman reader, I now intend to analyse the language politics that manifested itself in the periodicals. What factors determined the choice of language of female and male contributors in the aftermath of the Hindi/Urdu language and script controversy and how did contributors take part in the language debates? To what extent did they use Persian, Arabic, and Sanskrit loanwords in their contributions? How did the language of these periodicals differ from the Hindi of literary periodicals and texts that later came to be considered part of the modern Hindi canon? In this context it is important to differentiate the multiple identities of Hindi that have been conceptualized in the frameworks of (i) the Sanskritized 'Hindi' that Rai (2001: 122) uses with quotation marks to allude to the language's 'Sanskritic usurper', as well as (ii) the many *standardized* variants of Hindi, as they were described by Kellogg (1893 [1876]: 67) in the late nineteenth century.[3]

When considering these questions around Hindi it needs to be kept in mind that Khaṛī Bolī Hindi (modern standard Hindi) was not the mother tongue of middle-class women. They may have been cognate learners of Hindi and formally educated in this language; but their domestic language was Hindi in its many regional variations (bolī). By exposing women to Hindi in a standardized and reasonably Sanskritized form, women's periodicals became part of yet another nationalist venture: apart from their role as social, educational, and political mobilizers, they acquired linguistic importance. In order to focus on this aspect, this chapter makes use of extensive quotations in the Hindi original to illustrate linguistic idiosyncracies employed in women's periodicals. These quotations thus serve two purposes: thematically, they demonstrate contributors' opinions about the exigencies towards a *national* language. Linguistically, they offer those readers proficient in Hindi and/or Urdu the evidence of what was then believed to be a credible version of it. My syntactical, lexicographical, and etymological analyses are based on this usage of Hindi. Apart from their content, the original quotes are analysed etymologically in the light of four categories: (i) *tatsama* loanwords of Sanskrit origin, (ii) *tadbhava* words that were borrowed from Sanskrit, but had undergone phonetic changes (this category of words is not highlighted in the citations as I consider it a constitutive part of the lingua franca of the readers), (iii) Persian loanwords, and (iv) Arabic loanwords. I often subsume categories three and four under the term Urdu since contributions to the periodicals were not heavily Persianized or Arabicized. While the reader will also find a few English words in the quotes, it must be noted that English was the least likely to be used in women's periodicals. When speaking about Hindi, I specify whether I am referring to:

(i) Khaṛī Bolī Hindi as a composite language suitable for standardization, by all means, with Urdu vocabulary as well as few tatsama (Sanskritized) words
(ii) a Hindi *bolī* (a dialect with full-fledged grammar, but one that was not considered suitable for standardization)
(iii) Sanskritized and standardized Khaṛī Bolī Hindi (with tatsama and tadbhava words, and without Urdu words).

I make reference to the language of children's periodicals for comparative purposes: women's periodicals occupied a special position with regard to language politics because of their focus on remaining intelligible, whereas the editorials of children's, and also often girls', periodicals followed the mainstream nationalist agenda of promoting a Sanskritized Khaṛī Bolī Hindi. It needs to be clarified that this was not always the case for the actual contributions, which were closely oriented to a spoken idiom and did not necessarily purge Urdu words deliberately. I conclude that women's and children's periodicals promoted Khaṛī Bolī Hindi and Sanskritized Khaṛī Bolī Hindi, respectively. Throughout the early twentieth century, however, the definition of standardized Khaṛī Bolī Hindi was open to broad interpretation.

Identifying etymologies has not always been as straightforward as the current practice of dipping into a dictionary or encyclopedia would suggest. While I have consulted the dictionaries compiled by Kellogg (1876 [1893]), Turner (1966), and McGregor (2004), I also relied on mainstream literature of the early twentieth century, canonical writing in particular, to get a sense of the language *as used* by the Hindi literati. I begin the chapter with citations from the major male literary figures Bharatendu Harishchandra and Mahavir Prasad Dwivedi, and another public persona, Pandit Satyabhakt, all of whom published in women's periodicals. Their Hindi is a Sanskritized Khaṛī Bolī Hindi that for the most part dispensed with Urdu words. Following this thematic and linguistic analysis are examples authored by editors and contributors that display a diversity of Hindi variants.

To a Hindi linguist, my linguistic analysis might not seem complete. I have for the most part not classified individual words (nouns, conjunctions, postpositions, and adverbs in particular) that I have identified as part of the basic 'Hindustani' vocabulary of the readers and I have made this decision based on the language of literature of the early twentieth century as published in women's periodicals and other literature for women (pamphlets, manuals, novels). This is a slippery slope, but it needs to be remembered that the differentiation of Hindi and Urdu is in itself based on a construct and that clear-cut differentiations are not necessarily more accurate when seen from a *socio*-linguistic perspective. Orsini's (2002: 43) usage of the concept of literary *saṅskāra*, 'a taste, an inclination *and* its source', has been useful to show that readers were familiar with various literary traditions, which could be 'inherited from one's family, local traditions and tastes, or [acquired] through education and contact with the outer world and with literary trends' (Ibid.). In inquiring into the language of women's periodicals that had a variety of literary tastes to offer, I wish to open a debate on how the language in women's periodicals informed and was formed by literary developments.

In the late nineteenth century, as the Hindi public was in the early stages of its formation, two pioneers of Hindi, Bharatendu Harishchandra (1850–1885) and Mahavir Prasad Dwivedi (1864–1938), campaigned for the advancement of the Hindi language and literature. The eponyms of the two literary periods (*kāl* or *yug*), Bharatendu kāl (1868–93) and Dwivedi kāl (1893–1916), were well aware that the regional variations of Hindi were numerous and that one single, standardized form of Hindi (the envisioned Khaṛī Bolī Hindi) did not exist. In the 1880s, Harishchandra declared in a tract titled *Hindī Bhāṣā* (*Hindi Language*, published posthumously in 1893) that despite his attempts to establish Hindi as the national language of India, the language as he envisioned it was not in use in everyday situations. Hindi, Harishchandra (1893: 1) conceded, was not the native language of a particular territory; it had travelled to the North-Western Provinces with merchant migrants from the western parts of the subcontinent:

> Languages have three sections, that is, the language spoken at home, the language of poetry, and the written language. It cannot be ascertained what the language spoken in the homes of the north-west provinces is, since in the province of Delhi as well as in other cities, no one speaks Hindi at home besides the Khatris and the Panchahi [western] Agravals, so much so that after every *kos* [mile] the language changes.[4]

As for the written language, Harishchandra had this to say about the language dispute between Hindi and Urdu that had held sway in the nineteenth century (and that would not come to a close until the middle of the twentieth century):[5] 'The third section of language is the written language about which there is dispute. While one says that it should contain Urdu words, another says it should contain Sanskrit words, and all opine according to their own tastes, which is why, at this moment, no [standard] language can take form.'[6]

As a preliminary stage in the standardization process, Harishchandra (1893: 12–13), in his anthropological desire to document the prose language of the late nineteenth century, identified nine variations of Hindi:

(i) Hindi with many Sanskrit words (also called 'Pandit Hindi');
(ii) Hindi with less Sanskrit words;
(iii) *Śuddh* (pure, cleansed) Hindi (also called 'Munshi Hindi'), which was considered to be colloquial Hindi[7];
(iv) Hindi that was not loaded with any loanwords (and that also contained Urdu words);
(v) Hindi with Persian and Arabic loanwords (also called 'Maulvi Hindi' or 'Muslim Hindi');
(vi) Hindi from Calcutta (also called 'Eurasian Hindi') with many English loanwords and expressions;
(vii) Hindi spoken in the Eastern regions (the '*deśbhāṣā* of Kashi' [language of Benares]);
(viii) Hindi spoken by the less-educated (*arddhśikṣit*) residents of Kashi;
(ix) Hindi spoken by the people of the south.

These were the popular terms used in language debates in the decades that followed, including those debates that featured women writers. Taken together, this collection of variants indicates that Hindi was seen as an umbrella term under which a diversity of variations, including Urdu, were subsumed (Orsini 2002: 132). The boundaries of classification, however, were porous. The majority of contributions to women's periodicals several decades later fell into the variants that Harishchandra described under (i) to (iv), namely, Hindi with a different proportion of tatsama, tadbhava, and Urdu words, whereas the variants (v) to (ix) were not encountered. The language Harishchandra himself used in his tract was Sanskritized Khaṛī Bolī Hindi (variant number i). Below, once again, is the quotation from the opening paragraph of his tract, this time in the original Hindi, wherein one is able to recognize that the majority of his vocabulary consisted of tatsama words (Urdu words were not used; tatsama words are indicated in italics):

> *Bhāṣāoṅ* ke tīn *vibhāg* haiṅ *yathā* ghar meṅ bolne kī *bhāṣā*, *kavitā* kī *bhāṣā* aur likhne kī *bhāṣā*. Ab *paścimottardeś* meṅ ghar meṅ bolne kī *bhāṣā* kaun hai yah *niścay* nahīṅ hotā kyauṅki dillī *prānt* ke *vā anya nagaroṅ* meṅ bhī khatriyoṅ *vā* pachāṅhoṅ agarvāloṅ *vā* aur pachāhoṅ jātiyoṅ ke *atirikt* ghar meṅ hindī koī nahīṅ bolte *baraṅc* yahāṅ to kos kos par *bhāṣā* badaltī hai.[8]

In inquiring about the *domestic* role of Hindi, Harishchandra presaged a concern central to the contributors to women's periodicals: 'the language spoken at home' (*ghar meṅ bolne kī bhāṣā*). Women's periodicals explicitly addressed questions about language and communication in editorials and essays. The actual language used in individual contributions best reveals what language was considered appropriate to address women readers. Most of the contributions were not written in Sanskritized, Khaṛī Bolī Hindi. Such was the case for various reasons: first, the parameters of this language as it was undergoing standardization were still in flux, even among literary connoisseurs. Second, the audiences that the periodicals addressed would not be able to understand the language. Even Bharatendu Harishchandra, as founder and editor of the women's periodical *Balabodhini* (1874–78), had avoided excessive usage of Sanskritized words and made use of colloquialisms, aiming at a lively style.[9]

Editorial Agendas and Language Politics

While the idea of modern Hindi as the language of the public sphere had still been under negotiation in Harishchandra's times, in the early twentieth-century Hindi was undergoing lexicographical scrutiny and standardization for its increased usage as a print language. Anderson's (1983: 36) seminal work on 'print capitalism' and its power to bring about 'imagined communities' holds that it was the process of reorganizing methods of producing and disseminating printed literature that rapidly growing numbers of people began to think about themselves and relate to each other in new ways. Print capitalism and print technology triggered the creation of print vernaculars, which in turn created 'unified fields of exchange and communication' (Ibid.: 44). Through print vernaculars, Anderson has shown, people were able to comprehend and communicate with fellow readers. They shared information that went beyond their locality, oral language, religion, and age. Women's periodicals, however, complicated the notion of a fixed and stable language in that they defied what the Hindi literati defined as print vernacular (Orsini 2002: 12).[10] Their contributions thus show that processes of national imagining through language were much more fractured and contested than Anderson's model allows. While the power of the print media was crucial for the participation of women in the public sphere, it is also true that the contributors did not adhere to set standards of one single print vernacular. Many ordinary readers and contributors even expanded the concept of print language.

The editor, literary critic, and writer Mahavir Prasad Dwivedi put the responsibility of creating a national language in the hands of contemporary writers of modern Hindi. Following the example of his predecessor Harishchandra, Dwivedi urged the young, predominantly male, writers under his patronage to produce Hindi literature in a language that was instructive and capable of expressing complex thought. The results are to be found in the literary periodical *Saraswati* (1900–75, Allahabad). As the fastidious 'editor-arbiter' (Orsini 2002: 54) of *Saraswati* between 1903 and 1920, Dwivedi worked relentlessly towards the cause of Hindi. His initial objective had been to create a language that had the potential of serving as the language of public discourse and of becoming the universal mother tongue of people in the Hindi-speaking provinces.

One can discern a similar attempt in women's periodicals, where the objective was to create another tongue for those segments of society that had up to that date been excluded from the Hindi public. Women advocates of Hindi extended Dwivedi's call and considered it important for women to write in an explicitly feminine idiom (see p. 212). Furthermore, Hindi was envisioned as a language comprehended in all of India and not just in the Hindi belt. To what extent did literary periodicals such as *Saraswati* and the *Nagari Pracharini Sabha Patrika* with their clear expectations of Hindi style and lexicon differ from the women's periodicals *Stri Darpan*, *Grihalakshmi*, *Arya Mahila*, and *Chand*? Dwivedi, in his effort to establish standardized Hindi as the language of prose, poetry, and public affairs, wrote most of the articles of his periodical himself and rigorously edited those of other contributors. The editorial guidelines of the *Nagari Pracharini Sabha Patrika* from the outset would not accept contributions that used extensive Sanskrit, Arabic, and Persian lexicon (Orsini 2002: 53). Women editors such as Rameshwari Nehru of *Stri Darpan*, Surath Kumari Devi of *Arya Mahila*, and Mahadevi Varma of *Chand* were also in search of a Hindi standard, but their periodicals sought to maintain the flexibility of Hindi. As they saw it, Hindi was to become a means to circulate socio-political news, disseminate scientific knowledge, and even to communicate personal matters. The editors of women's periodicals did not edit the contributions so that they would conform to one single literary standard—apart from Mahadevi Varma (Schomer 1983: 225). In *Stri Darpan*, *Grihalakshmi*, *Arya Mahila*, as well as *Kumari Darpan* and *Kanya Manoranjan* of the 1910s and 1920s, Hindi remained flexible while acquiring a certain measure of standardization.

Dwivedi (1995: 120–1) noted in 1911 at the annual meeting of the Hindī Sāhitya Sammelan that there existed different literary registers of Hindi that were applied according to subject matter and target audiences. The language of his own contribution is Sanskritized Kharī Bolī Hindi. This is of course no contradiction, as he was addressing an educated audience of public intellectuals. While he did discuss the question of literature for women, his text was not intended to serve as such. I analyse it to give the reader a better understanding of a Sanskritized Kharī Bolī Hindi text of the early twentieth century (tatsama words are indicated in italics and Urdu words are in boldface).

Viṣay ke *anusār bhāṣā* meṅ bahut kuch *bhed* ho saktā hai. Jaisā *viṣay* ho, aur jis *śreṇī* ke *pāṭhakoṅ* ke lie *pustak* likhī gaī ho, *tadanusār* hī *bhāṣā* kā *prayog* honā cāhie. **Baccoṅ** aur *sādhāraṇ* janoṅ ke lie likhī gaī *pustakoṅ* meṅ *saral bhāṣā* likhī jānī cāhie. *Prauṛh* aur *viśeṣ śikṣit janoṅ* ke lie *pariṣkṛt* aur *ālaṅkārik bhāṣā* likhī jā saktī hai. *Vaijñānik granthoṅ* meṅ *pāribhāṣik śabdoṅ* kā *prayog* karnā paṛtā hai. *Ataeva* unmeṅ kuch na kuch *kliṣṭatā* ā hī jātī hai. Vah *anivārya* hai. Maiṅ to *saral bhāṣā* ke *lekhak* hī ko bahut baṛā *lekhak* samajhtā hūṅ. Likhne kā **matlab** auroṅ par apne man ke *bhāv prakaṭ* karnā hai. Jiskā *manobhāv* jitne hī *adhik* log samajh sakeṅge uskā *prayatna* aur *pariśram* utnā hī *adhik saphal* huā samjhā jāygā. [...]

Ataeva apnī *sāmājik*, *naitik*, *dhārmmik ādi* har **tarah** kī *unnati* ke lie sab *viṣayoṅ* kī acchī acchī *pustakoṅ* kī hindī meṅ baṛī hī *āvaśyaktā* hai. Hindī meṅ islie ki yahī hamārī *mātṛbhāṣā* hai. Isī *bhāṣā* meṅ dī gaī *śikṣā* se *samāj* kā *sarvādhik aṅś lābh* uṭhā saktā hai. Isī *bhāṣā* meṅ *vitaraṇ* kiye gaye *jñān* kā *prakāś* gāṅv-gāṅv, ghar-ghar, pahuṅc saktā hai. Yahī hamārī *bhāṣā* hai; yahī hamārī mātāoṅ kī *bhāṣā* hai; yahī hamārī *bahanoṅ* kī *bhāṣā* hai; yahī hamāre **baccoṅ** kī *bhāṣā* hai. Aṅgrezī yā *anya* kisī *bhāṣā* meṅ dī gaī *śikṣā* se jitnā *lābh* pahuṅc saktā hai usse *saiṅkṛoṅ gunā adhik lābh mātṛbhāṣā* meṅ dī gaī *śikṣā* se pahuṅc saktā hai.

[Depending on the subject matter there can be many differences in the written language. The language should be chosen according to the subject matter and the audience for whom the book has been written. Books that address children and simple people should use a simple language. For mature people and those with special education, books can be written in a purified and elaborate (*parikṛṣṭ aur ālaṅkārik*) language. In scientific works, technical words must be used. Consequently, there will be difficulties (in comprehension). These are unavoidable. Personally, I consider those who write in a simple language to be great writers. The meaning of writing is to convey one's mindset to others. The more people understand the literary manifestations of a writer, the more will his effort and hard work be considered successful. [...]

This is why it is indispensable for our socio-political, spiritual, and other progress to be able to draw on good books on all subjects in Hindi. They must be in Hindi, because this is our mother tongue. From the education imparted in this language most sections of a society can benefit. The light of knowledge imparted in this language can spread in each village and reach every house. This is our language; this is the language of our mothers; this is the language of our sisters; this is the language of our children. There will be a hundred times more benefit through education imparted in the mother tongue than through education imparted in English or in other languages.]

Dwivedi was keen to expand the readership of Hindi and thus expand the Hindi public sphere. To this end, Hindi had to retain flexibility besides being standardized—at least for audiences that were considered to be less 'mature'. Dwivedi himself had written a Hindi primer in 'everyday language' (*rozmarrā kī bolī*) for the Indian Press, which typified colloquial Hindi/Urdu and could be printed in either script (Orsini 2002: 99–100). Even in the citation above, Dwivedi used three common Urdu words (*baccā*, *matlab*, and *tarah*), which were not replaced with tatsama equivalents such as *bālak*, *abhiprāy*, and *prakār*. His rhetorical use of an inclusive 'our' described Hindi also as the mother tongue of the female population and children. The importance of creating awareness and a genuine and enthusiastic appreciation for the mother tongue amongst women was expressed in many publications and speeches of the time. This was intensified by the personification of Hindi as Mother Hindi (Gupta 2001: 105–6) and Hindu wife (King 1994: 135) by leading figures of the Hindi literati. The speech of one proponent of women's involvement in the spread of Hindi literature was reprinted in *Stri Darpan* in 1920. Rameshprasad had initially spoken at the tenth meeting of the Hindī Sāhitya Sammelan in what can be identified as Sanskritized Khaṛī Bolī Hindi purged of Urdu words (tatsama words are in italics):

Hindī *pracār* kā *kārya* tab tak *adhūrā* hī hogā, jab tak ki hamārī *parṇkuṭīroṅ* meṅ bās karnevālī bahinoṅ se lekar, *rājprasād* meṅ vicarnevālī bahinoṅ ke *hṛday* meṅ *mātṛ-bhāṣā* ke *prem* kī *jyoti prajvalit* na kar dī jāygī. *Santoṣ* kā *viṣay* hai ki *gat* tīn *sammelanoṅ* meṅ *mahilāoṅ* ne apne *saral evam sārgarbhit bhāṣaoṅ* se yah *siddh* kar diyā hai, ki ve apne bhāiyoṅ kā *rāṣṭrabhāṣā* ke *uddhār* meṅ hāth baṭāne ke lie *utkaṇṭhit* haiṅ [...] *Mātṛbhāṣā* kī *upādhi* to *mātā* kī hai. [...] Jab *mātā mātṛ-bhāṣā* jāntī hī na ho to *anurāg* kaise *sambhav* ho saktā hai?

[The propagation of Hindi will remain incomplete as long as the flame of love for the mother tongue is not afire in the hearts of all our sisters—from those who live in odorous huts up to those who live in palaces. It is a matter of satisfaction that at the past three meetings of the Hindī Sāhitya Sammelan women have proved *in their simple and meaningful language* that they are eager to join men to promote the national language. [...] A mother tongue enjoys the status of a mother. [...] If a mother does not know the mother tongue, how can there be love?][11]

An appeal to motherhood was used to argue for a common language of women across class, caste and rural–urban divides. It was readily accepted that women's language was simple rather than sophisticated. More important than a high register was *sāhitya sevā*—to write in order to impart knowledge for social progress. Yet, Dwivedi and his cohort, along with the contributors to periodicals, were also in the midst of an ideological debate on the scope of a national language. While Hindi was intended to be the language of communication, Dwivedi, like Harishchandra before him, eventually shifted the focus of his attention from comprehensibility to the question of Hindi etymology. Up to that point he would have been in agreement with the language of women's periodicals even though he might have called it immature and not suitable for inclusion in a national literary canon. According to his agenda, however, it was imperative that Hindi grammar, lexicography, syntax, and style undergo standardization. Hindi also had to be purged of words of Perso-Arabic origin and from colloquialisms. This development went hand in hand with the introduction of tatsama words. All members of the affluent Hindi literati, including the editors of women's and children's periodicals, agreed at least theoretically with the first statement: modern Hindi required more 'originally Hindi' words, which according to their perception were derived from Sanskrit. There arose, however, debates about the meaning and extent of 'purification' that involved women's periodicals. Could the Hindi of the women's periodicals be purged of Urdu words if such words were part of the common vocabulary of many readers? Most women's periodicals tackled the question of supposed purity versus comprehensibility in a conciliatory manner.

The quote by Satyabhakt at the beginning of the chapter vividly describes the idea of a public engaged with writing in Hindi. This public also included women. Satyabhakt's essay was published in *Arya Mahila*, a periodical that had originally favoured Sanskritized Khaṛī Bolī Hindi before orienting its language towards a more accommodating Khaṛī Bolī Hindi. Whether the average woman reader understood the Sanskritized

Kharī Bolī Hindi of Satyabhakt's speech is debatable. This is not to say that she had never encountered Sanskritized Hindi. Other (oral and written) genres available to her, such as articles and texts offering advice on household management and religious tracts, also used tatsama words similar to the ones used by Satyabhakt. Orsini (2002: 44–5) describes familiarity with different literary genres as a trait of the time: Brahmin families would be better versed in Sanskrit knowledge traditions, whereas Kayasths would be more familiar with the Urdu *saṅskāra* of poetry and secular prose. Literary Kharī Bolī Hindi was *but one* new literary taste that was produced and disseminated through printed literature and formal education (Orsini 2002: 45–6). Women were thus also likely to carry several linguistic repertoires: vocabulary on moral conduct (such as the words, *sadācār*, *bhūṣaṇ*, *svarūp*, *pālan*, *paropkārī*, *sajjan*, *ādar-sammān*, *śraddhā*) and social reform (such as the words, *sāhitya*, *sevā*, *śikṣā*, *pracār*, *upadeś*, *sunīti*, *buddhi*) were likely to have been known to the readers. The words indicated in italics from the citation of Satyabhakt from the beginning of the chapter, however, were tatsama words that were rarely encountered in the new literature for women:

> *Saṅsār* meṅ *manuṣya* ke karne *yogya* jo *śreṣṭ* aur *praśaṅsā* ke *yogya kārya* samjhe jāte haiṅ, sāhitya-sevā bhī unmeṅse ek hai. Jis prakār samāj-sevā karnā, śikṣā-pracār karnā, dharmopadeś denā, sunīti, sadācār pracār karnā ādi kārya *manuṣya* ke bhūṣaṇ-svarūp samjho jāte haiṅ, unkā pālan karnevālā sab logoṅ dvārā baṛā paropkārī *tathā* sajjan samjhā jātā hai, *sarvasādhāraṇ* uskā ādar-sammān aur śraddhā-bhakti karte haiṅ, vahī daśā sāhitya seviyoṅkī bhī hai. Isse bhī *mānav* samājkā amit upkār hotā hai, manuṣyoṅko jñānkī vṛiddhi hotī hai, buddhi baṛhtī hai, citt ānandse *paripūraṇ* ho jātā hai. Isīliye *saṅsār* meṅ sāhitya-sevakkā baṛā sammān hai.[12]

Moreover, the contribution did not contain a single word of Perso-Arabic origin. This is perhaps the most striking difference of Satyabhakt's contribution when compared to those of women writers. The choice of words by Rameshwari Nehru, for example, displays a high number of Urdu words next to tatsama and tadbhava words. She also uses phrases that consist of both, Persian or Arabic and Sanskrit loanwords, such as *deś kī izzat* (*deś* being of Sanskrit origin and *izzat* of Persian descent) and *aslī aur saccā* (*aslī* being of Arabic origin and *saccā* of Sanskrit descent).[13] Considering her educational background—she had received *zenana* (home) education in Lahore prior to coming to Allahabad—it is no surprise that she regularly used Urdu vocabulary in her contributions.

The following quote by Nehru speaking about men's approval of her periodical shows how 'seamlessly' she welded registers (tatsama words are italicized and words of Urdu origin are indicated in boldface).

Parantu ham yah bahut bār kah cukī haiṅ aur ab phir yah kahtī haiṅ ki strīdarpaṇ meṅ koī aisī bāt nahiṅ rahtī ki jo *striyoṅ* ke liye *hānikārak* ho [...] Strīdarpaṇ phir *striyoṅ* ko vaisā hī banānā cāhtā hai ki jo apne *deś* kī **izzat** ko bacāne ke liye *svayam* bhī **taiyār** raheṅ. *Striyoṅ* hī *dvārā* hamārī *bhārat mātā* phir ek bār usī uṅce **darje** par pahuṅcegī ki jis par vah ek *samay* thī aur jo us kā **aslī** aur *saccā* **sthān** hai. Jab tak *striyoṅ* meṅ *deś bhakti* na āvegī tab tak puruṣoṅ ko *svarājya* kā milnā *kaṭhin* hai. Strīdarpaṇ *striyoṅ* ko phir un kā *dharm* sikhāne kī **kośiś** kartā hai aur apne jīte jī kartā rahegā. [...] Hamārī bhī apne *puruṣoṅ* se yahī *prārthnā* hai ki *yadi* ham yā hamāre *lekhak* kisī bāt meṅ **galtī** karte haiṅ to *lekh dvārā* ham ko hamārī **galtī** dikhāveṅ, na yah ki hamāre *patr* kā apnī *striyoṅ* meṅ jānā band kar deṅ. Jaisā hamārā *dharm* hai ki ham auroṅ ko *dharm* sikhāveṅ vaisā hī auroṅ ka *dharm* hai ki *yadi* ham *bhūl* par hoṅ to ham ko ṭhīk **rāste** par lāveṅ. Is se donoṅ **taraf** ke log *lābh* uṭhāeṅge aur *deś* kī *unnati* hogī.[14]

In women's periodicals, the issue was not so much that of replacing a supposedly uncouth language, but that of finding a balance between *erudite* Hindi, a language that Rameshwari Nehru described as *paṇḍitaū* and Harishchandra called language with many Sanskrit (tatsama) words (variant i), and *composite* Hindi that consisted of a mix of tadbhava and Urdu words. Nehru's editorial reconciled Sanskritized and composite Hindi, as did the majority of contributions in women's periodicals.[15] While this language variant does not 'fit' any of the linguistic variants established by Harishchandra (it perhaps falls somewhere in between that possessing fewer Sanskrit words [variant ii] and that possessing fewer loanwords [variant iv]), I wish to stress that this Hindi variant, as it drew on Urdu and tatsama words simultaneously, may have been neither more nor less 'natural' or 'artificial' than other variants, if our benchmark was the quotidian language of the domestic sphere. Furthermore, in this language variant there are no signs that specific words from the spectrum of Hindi variations had been avoided or purged. This also meant that linguistically versatile writers such as Rameshwari Nehru were opposed to re-lexification—that is the replacement of Urdu words with tatsama equivalents or vice-versa. Stark (1995: 203), in her analysis of Hindi novels by Muslim writers, has termed this lexicographical borrowing natural bridging (*natürlicher*

Brückenschlag) and I concur with her evaluation as it is especially in the language describing quotidian situations in women's periodicals that Urdu variants for Hindi words were commonly used.[16]

In contrast, the editorial of the girls' periodical *Kanya Manoranjan* hardly reflected a language that was closer to the spoken language of children (as learned from mothers or as spoken in the domestic sphere). Tatsama and tadbhava words were much more common than were Urdu words, which made the language resemble the Sanskritized Kharī Bolī Hindi of textbooks as they were written from the mid-nineteenth century onwards (King 1994: 103). As many contributions in children's (read: boys') periodicals came from a surplus of textbook writings (Chandra 2007: 295), the language was accordingly Sanskritized.[17] In the following quote from the editorial of the girls' periodical *Kanya Manoranjan*, which also seems to have been orienting itself towards the language of textbooks, tatsama words are italicized and Urdu words are in boldface:

> *Kanyā manorañjan* kā ek *mukhya uddeśya* hai. Iskā ek *nirālā* **matlab** hai. Yah **ṭhīk** hai ki *strī śikṣā* ke bahut se patr haiṅ aur ve baṛī *yogyatā* se nikāle jā rahe haiṅ. **Lekin** jin ko *saṅsār* kā kuch bhī *anubhav* hai ve jānte haiṅ ki bahut se *lekh striyoṅ* ke lie *upayogī* aur *manorañjak* hote hue bhī nanhīṅ sī **bacciyoṅ** ke, *avivāhit kanyāoṅ* ke, *kanyāpāṭhaśālā* kī *bālikāoṅ* ke hāth meṅ nahīṅ diye jā sakte haiṅ. Isīse *āvaśyaktā* huī ki ek aisā *patr* nikālā jāy jismeṅ *bālikāoṅ* ke paṛhne ke liye *lekh* aur *kavitāyeṅ* raheṅ. *Upayogī citroṅ* ke diye jāne kā bhī *prabandh* kiyā gayā hai. *Lābhkārī* hone ke sāth hī sāth *bālikāoṅ* kā *manovinod* bhī ho yahī ham logoṅ kā *abhiprāy* hai—**agar** hamāre *mitroṅ* aur *pāṭhakoṅ* ne iskī *sahāytā* meṅ apnā hāth baṛhāyā to ham apne *uddeśya* kī *pūrti* kar sakeṅge.[18]
>
> *Āśā* hai ki *kanyā manorañjan* sāre *bhārat* ke *kanyā-maṇḍal tathā strī saṅsār* kī *sevā* meṅ *bhalī prakār samarth* hoga.[19]

This Sanskritization was very similar to that found in Hindi textbooks, even though it also needs to be noted that the paragraph was not *systematically* purged of Urdu words (*lekin*, *baccā*, and *agar* are favoured over *parantu*, *bālak*, and *yadi*). In several instances, Urdu words (such as *bahut* or *ṭhīk*) are not avoided in favour of tatsama words. The paragraph even contains words of tatsama/tadbhava origin that are used alongside Urdu words with the same meaning (*tathā* and *aur*, *abhiprāy* and *matlab*).

This Sanskritized and yet negotiable lexicon notwithstanding, there was a visible divide between the language promoted in the *editorials* of girls' periodicals and that of other contributions. The contributions retained the complexity and fluidity of Hindi rather than promoting one single style, despite the fact that the editorial and reprints from textbooks and periodicals for boys were written in Sanskritized Khaṛī Bolī Hindi.[20] Such contributions impacted the language skills of women as well, since articles were often read *to* the children. In doing so, mothers learned the new language of the envisioned nation. I read the introduction of Sanskrit-derived vocabulary *along with* common Urdu words as a move of the editors to familiarize women and children with the envisioned national language without compromising comprehensibility. Another example for such a promotion of composite Hindi is the following citation from an essay on geography published in the periodical for girls and young women, *Kumari Darpan* (tatsama words are italicized and words of Perso-Arabic origin are in boldface):

Pyāre **bacco**! Jis *dhartī* par ham rahte haiṅ vah kaisī *suhāvanī* hai. Tum ne is ke *sundar sundar phūl* phal dekhe hoṅge, is ke ūpar pahāṛ jaṅgal, *nadiyoṅ* kī *śobhā* dekhī hogī. Tum meṅ se kisī kisī ne iske *athāh samudra* bhī dekhe hoṅge ki jinkī **hadd** dikhāī nahīṅ detī yā aise ūṅce ūṅce pahāṛ bhī dekhe hoṅge jinke sir par **garmiyoṅ** ke dinoṅ meṅ bhī baraf jamī huī rahtī hai. Tumne iske cāroṅ **taraf** cānd, **sitāre** aur sūraj ko phirte hue dekhā hogā. Tumhārā kitne hī bār in sab **cīzoṅ** ke bāre meṅ *kahāniyāṅ* sunne ko jī cāhtā hoga. Cāhiye to yah thā ki yah *kahāniyāṅ* tum apnī mātāoṅ ke *sneh* bhare *mukhoṅ* se sunte, **lekin** abhī vah *saubhāghya* kā kāl nahīṅ āyā isliye maiṅ tumheṅ apnī *bhāṣā* meṅ vah *kahāniyāṅ* sunātā hūṅ.[21]

The choice of language was a political one, but comprehensibility and room for the improvement of vocabulary as well as a sophisticated grammar (frequent use of the presumptive mood) were equally important to women's, girls', and children's periodicals. Tatsama words such as *suhāvanī*, *athāh*, *sneh*, and *mukh* indicate a heavily Sanskritized vocabulary. And yet, the introduction of these words may also be read as a move to encourage the expansion of 'Hindi' vocabulary. A tatsama phrase such as '*sneh bhare mukhoṅ*' is 'seamlessly' followed by the Urdu conjunction *lekin* (and not the tatsama *parantu*). In the same manner, the Urdu *hadd* is not replaced with the tatsama *sīmā*. In the long run, however, the search for *one* lexicon for women and men from the different Indian provinces intensified and women's periodicals did not remain unaffected by this development.

Quotidian Hindi

According to the most influential proponents of Hindi, the language required a genealogy that was distinct from other vernaculars. This was considered necessary in order to claim for it the status of a national language and to avoid historical overlaps with Urdu, the vernacular projected as the language of Muslims. To Dalmia (1997: 150), this nationalization of Hindi is an expression of a 'third idiom' that emerged out of the colonial encounter and debates on tradition and modernity:

The concretization of the notion of Hindi as a national language in the modern context could be viewed as the third idiom, which was then projected backwards, as if through the ages there had been a consistent and linear development in the language and literature of the Hindus. Here the comparative science of languages was of much help, since it served to establish clearly the ancient lineage of Hindi as an Indo-Aryan language and connect the literature which it claimed as its own with classical Sanskrit. The exercise needed to coin a contemporary Hindu idiom called for some effort. Once it began to take shape, however, this modern idiom was an important identity marker, connected as it was to the constitution of the cultural-religious, as well as to the political identity of the Hindus in north India, an identity which had emancipatory functions when pitted against the British, but which could as well become insular when turned against the Muslims, as was increasingly to become the case.

In his later life, Harishchandra retracted on his original proposition that Hindi could contain words of Perso-Arabic origin. This position was retained by the Hindi literati till well into the early twentieth century. But in women's periodicals, depending on the regional background of the contributors, Hindi and Urdu vocabulary was endorsed. Sarojini Naidu, for example, a prominent contributor to *Stri Darpan*, had grown up in Hyderabad, and the Dakkhanī Hindi of the south she used contained many Perso-Arabic words. I quote from her reprinted speech with the majority of Urdu words indicated in boldface and the few tadbhava and tatsama words in italics:

Īśvar ne ham ko jo kuch diyā hai, **ilm**, **aql**, **sehat**, **himmat**, vah sab isliye dī hai ki ham us ko auroṅ ko bāṅṭeṅ aur unko is se **fāydā** uṭhāne deṅ. Ham parameśvar kī **taraf** se in sab **sifatoṅ** ko *keval* rakhne vāle haiṅ. Abhī hamārī presīḍent sāhabā [Rameshwari Nehru] ne kahā hai ki ek pahiye se gāṛī nahī cal saktī lekin ham to āj saiṅkṛoṅ *varṣoṅ* se ek hī pahiye se gāṛī calā rahī haiṅ usī kā **natījā** yah hai ki jab aur **mulkoṅ** meṅ log **taraqqī** ke airoplenoṅ par jā rahe haiṅ tab ham **hindostānī** log ek hī pahiye par cal rahe haiṅ. [...] Purāne **zamāne** meṅ **hindostān** kī **bībiyāṅ** aisī na thīṅ. Us **zamāne** meṅ jab ki ham **duniyāṅ** ko **aqal** sikhāte the hamārī **auratoṅ** kā **tarz** kuch aur hī thā. Jāo sītā **kī tarah** tum bhī duḥx[22] saho apne **mardoṅ** kā hāth baṭāo.[23]

Other Urdu words Naidu used in her speech were *mohabbat*, *dost*, *kī vajah*, *bevaqūf*, *kośiś*, *ummīd*, and *hāsil*. These words were juxtaposed with tatsama equivalents (*pyār*, *mitr*, *ke kāraṇ*, *mūrkh*, *prayatna*, *āśā*, and *prāpt*) from other contributions of the periodical issue. Despite the increased use of Urdu words, Naidu opted for the tatsama words *keval* and *varṣ* instead of the equivalent Urdu words *sirf* and *sāl*. Of particular interest is her use of Hindo*stān* (with the nominal suffix from Persian), rather than either Hindu*sthān* (with the Sanskrit nominal suffix) or Bhārat—the latter being favoured in girls' and children's periodicals. The term Hindostān points to the inclusive conception of a territory with Hindu and Muslim inhabitants rather than to an exclusionary Hindu-Arya India.

Naidu's speech made use of a lexicon that was readily available to the women readers. It was published as part of the editorial by Rameshwari Nehru and next to essays (such as reprints from mainstream periodicals) in Sanskritized Khaṛī Bolī Hindi. It was the diversity of contributions in women's periodicals that allowed for the promotion of a language that had the potential to connect female audiences.

I now turn to a selection of contributions that were deliberately written in a simple language and syntax. Short sentences, questions, simple idiomatic expressions, and spoken speech characterized the dialogic endeavour of such texts in which readers were directly addressed. In order to replicate the essence, if you will, of spoken language and to enhance some phonetic appeal, the contributions made frequent use of phrasal reduplications and enclitics. They were mostly set in a simple, but also flexible syntax that did not necessarily adhere to the standard subject–object–verb arrangement. The texts were always divided into paragraphs. The sentences contained western punctuation marks such as colons, semicolons, parentheses, interrogation, and exclamation marks alongside the single punctuation mark of the Nāgarī script (*virām*). All these were new features of Hindi print language.[24] Unlike the language I quoted in the last section, the following dialogue between a mother and her daughter had neither extensive use of tatsama words nor words of Arabic and Persian origin. It falls into what Harishchandra had categorized as language that was not specifically oriented towards any loanwords and that also contained Urdu words (variant iv):

Beṭī: Hāṅ, mujhe **yād** hai jab ek bhale **ādmī** hamāre yahāṅ madrās se āye the to ve hindī meṅ nahīṅ bol sakte the, aur na unkī *bhāṣā* ham samajh sakte the; phir unhoṅne aṅgrezī meṅ bātcīt kī thī jisko āp aur pitā jī ne bhalī bhānti samajh lī thī. Mera jī bahut cāhtā thā ki maiṅ bhī kuch samjhūṅ, par kuch na samajh sakī.

Mā: Acchā, tum aṅgrezī paṛhne kā bhī *lābh* jān gayī na? Iskā paṛh lenā acchā hai, *yadi* samay mile.[25]

In the dialogue that follows, the mother has the tendency to use a reasonable number of tatsama words (*parantu*, *sadā*, *paśu*, *avakāś*, *nitya*) when explaining to her daughter the necessity of education, insinuating that the modern woman knew Sanskritized Khaṛī Bolī Hindi. This does not render the dialogue incomprehensible, as the daughter skilfully repeats the statements of the mother in a more comprehensible language.

Like dialogues, speeches (republished in periodicals) also attempted to create dialogue with readers by conveying messages through a language that came close to a spoken form. Fiction, when written by prominent authors was stylistically more sophisticated, whereas the style of lay writers was rather simple. Articles and essays came close to Khaṛī Bolī Hindi (with varying amounts of tatsama as well as Urdu words) or drew on different registers in the same contribution. While sentence structure and lexicon could be more complex, the tone of such contributions was instructional and geared toward making a topic accessible.

Definite conclusions about the politics underlying the language choice of Sarojini Naidu as well as that adopted by editors of girls', children's and women's periodicals would require a much deeper investigation of Hindi language and literature of the time than I could possibly offer here. I am interested in identifying the *diversity* of Hindi prose language as represented in women's periodicals. For this, it is also necessary to think along the lines of Stark's (1995: 200–13) analysis of Hindi novels by Muslim writers in post-colonial India, in which she argues that the choice of words along with the lexical welding of registers also depended on subject matter as well as on a given author's personal preferences.[26] We have seen with the examples of Sarojini Naidu, Pandit Satyabhakt, Rameshwari Nehru as well as the earlier proponents of Hindi, Bharatendu Harishchandra and Mahavir Prasad Dwivedi, that language choice was determined by audience, ideology, and personal preference, as well as linguistic and cultural backgrounds. In a time when the standardization and codification of Hindi was still in full operation, Hindi variants ranging from Sanskritized Khaṛī Bolī Hindi to Khaṛī Bolī Hindi containing Perso-Arabic words were widely in use. Contributors to women's periodicals came from different regional and educational backgrounds and correspondingly chose from different literary registers depending on the subject matter, literary genre, literary taste (*saṅskāra*), and target audience. These variants of Hindi redirected the expectations of the nationalist Hindi elite toward the necessities of finding an adequate voice for a dispersed community of Indian women.

In terms of orthography, apart from slight inconsistencies, women's periodicals maintained the general standard common for literary periodicals. One of the inconsistencies lay in the spelling of two connected vowels, *uā* (as in *huā*) and *ie* (as in *ke lie*) that were also spelled *uvā* (as in *huvā*) and *iye* (as in *ke liye*) (see topic number nine in the call for papers from the Hindī Sāhitya Sammelan, Part Two, Box 4, pp. 250–1). Another spelling inconsistency was the conjunctive participle *kar* that occasionally appeared as *ke*. In one contribution, however, the orthography remained consistent apart from occasional typographical mistakes.

Occasionally, the Sanskrit *visarg* (ḥ) and *halant* (्) were used. Loan-phonemes from Urdu (क़, ख़, ग़, ज़, फ़) were frequently used, but not always fully distinguished as such. Many writers drew on the Nāgarī phonemes that came closest to the Urdu ones and thus refrained from using the dot marking the characters as loan-phonemes (क़ spelled as क, ख़ spelled as ख, ग़ spelled as ग, ज़ spelled as ज, and फ़ spelled as फ). Postpositions and the marker of the perfective tenses with transitive verbs (ने) were often directly attached to the preceding word.

Grammatical and orthographical 'mistakes' also became a stylistic device to indicate different speech genres. Children, for example, spoke differently, which was reflected in the spelling of words (underlined in the following citation). The introductory paragraph (that sets the stage for the grandmother's story that follows), describes children gathering around their maternal grandmother. The language is amenable and hardly contains tatsama words (marked in italics). The lone Urdu word is in boldface.

Rāt kā *samay* thā. Abhī nau bhī nahīṅ baje the ki sab **baccoṅ** khā pī kar *taiyyār* ho gaye aur sab ke sab nānī ke pās jā pahuṅce - koī god meṅ baiṭhā, koī pās hī nānī ko ghuṭnoṅ par sir rakh kar leṭ gayā. Koī gale meṅ jā lipaṭā aur lage sab ke sab *kolāhal* macāne, 'nānī, *kahānī* sunāo! Nānī, *kahānī* sunāo.' Ek bolā, 'ambī chuneṅge', dūsre ne kahā, 'ambī', tīsrā bolā, 'nānī baut [instead of 'bahut'] din ho gaye, āj to kai [instead of 'kah'] de'.[27]

Non-native speakers of Hindi were likely to make certain kinds of errors, such as spelling mistakes, the confusion of grammatical gender, the inability to use the *ne*-construction in the perfect tenses and mistakes in subject–verb agreement. In the following citation, in which the grammatical and spelling errors are underlined, the Bengali madam sounds as if on the wrong track: 'Ham **sādī** nahīṅ **kiyā**. Bahot sāhab log hamāre yahāṅ āyā. Ham sab ko bol diyā ki ham **sādī** nahīṅ karne cāhtī.'[28] [...] 'Suno, suno! Dharm kī bāt suno. Isse tum *akil* hoga. Phir tum bhī hamāre **māfik** rahne sakogī. Tum log jo **jevar** banvātā hai. Kuch **fāydā** nahīṅ.'[29] Regardless of the 'mistakes', the above passage deferred from replacements of *śādī*, *muāfiq*, *zevar*, *fāydā*, with tatsama words such as *vivah*, *anukūl*, *ābhūṣaṇ*, and *lābh*.

In fiction, a servant's speech, though very rare, was written in a rural dialect. Even more rarely were entire stories written in a regional dialect such as Awadhi, Chattisgarhi, and Etawah.[30] The same holds true for stories that contained abusive and obscene language, or a language that was condemned by the literati as the uncouth language of women.[31] The following citation is a rather impolite introduction to the Bengali madam by a woman and her sister-in-law. It is one of the very few instances, in which obscenities are used (underlined):

> Bhāvaj: Bhābī, ā gayī vah.
> Nand: Kaun, rāvan kī ammā?
> Bhāvaj: Hāṅ hāṅ, calo, zarī der cuhal rahegī.
> Nand: Cūlhe meṅ jāy aisī cuhal, hameṅ to us muṇḍīkāṭī kī bāteṅ zarā bhī nahīṅ bhātīṅ.
> Bhāvaj: Acchā calo to, āj maiṅ bhī muṅh-toṛ javāb dūṅgī.[32]

Tension between a husband and his wife could be expressed as in the following statement of a husband who is rather impatient when presenting a sari to his wife:

> Kiśorcandra ne apnī patnī kamlā se kahā—'Sunojī! Abhī acchā hai. Acchī tarah dekh lo. Yah sāṛī pasand hai, yā nahīṅ? Āj kal mujhko bār bār bazār ko yahāṅ dauṛne kī fursat nahīṅ hai. Pīche zyādā caṛ caṛ karogī, to acchā nahīṅ hogā.'[33]

His wife sounds poised:

Kamlā: Eh he, ab to tum baṛe nakhre karne lage. Mere pasand na āyī, to tumheṅ jānā hī paṛegā. (Kapṛe ko dekh kar) Hāy itne dinoṅ ke kahne par to sāṛī lāye, vah bhī aisī, jo mujhse saṅbhle nahīṅ. Na to iskā kapṛā bārīk, aur na dekhne meṅ hī acchī lagtī hai. Bhalā aisā mārkīn sā kapṛā pahin kar kisī ke yahāṅ jāūṅgī, to ve log mujhe kyā kaheṅgī?[34]

With these examples from different contributions to women's periodicals, I intend to ground my argument that the language in the Hindi women's periodicals was for the most part an amenable composite Hindi written in the Nāgarī script. Even *Arya Mahila*, which at first used much Sanskritized vocabulary and had at first eliminated Perso-Arabic and Urdu vocabulary from its pages or relegated them to footnotes to explain tatsama substitutions, announced after some years that it would switch to a simple and amenable language.

Citations in Sanskrit and English were translated into Hindi in the footnotes or within the text. English words were used in a Hindi text if a proper Hindi term was lacking or uncommon (for example, university, public, style, volunteer, deputation, president, proofs), but contributors mostly tried to find Hindi synonyms for English words (such as *lahaṅgā* for skirt) and sometimes also English synonyms for Persian words (such as petition for *darkhāst*). Sometimes, the English was kept in parentheses. Words of Perso-Arabic origin were sometimes hyphenated with the corresponding Hindi word (*bandīgṛh-kārāgar*), be it to explain a word or to offer a synonym to broaden the vocabulary of the readers. In contributions (essays and fiction) that recounted legislative matters, Hindi women's periodicals drew on words from Persian administrative and legislative language and often explained supposedly complicated terms. We also find several translations of articles in European languages, Sanskrit, and Indian vernaculars into Hindi.

Sāhitya Sevā as National Service to Literature by Women

Considering that many proponents of Hindi pointed to the importance of creating appropriate literature for women, it is worth exploring the significance of this literature published in women's periodicals for the Hindi literary canon. Not only were literary texts reprinted in women's periodicals from mainstream periodicals and thus disseminated to a new readership, they were often first published in women's periodicals before being published a second time in a monograph or anthology, such as the serialized novels of Rameshwari Nehru (*Jale dev kā punarjāgaraṇ*) in *Stri Darpan* and Premchand (*Nirmalā*) in *Chand*, or short stories by many Hindi writers. In this section, I investigate debates in women's periodicals that highlighted women's participation in the production of Hindi literature. I have devoted a considerable amount of space to the discussion of the role of women's periodicals in the social, educational, and political mobilization of women. Now I ask whether it is justifiable to consider contributions to women's periodicals as part of the creation of a national literary canon in Hindi.

Contributors to women's periodicals and women speakers at public literary events were not only attentive to their own use of language, they also explicitly addressed the necessity of projecting Hindi as a national language along with a national literary canon. The language of women who spoke at literary events and then published their speeches differed from the flexible colloquial Hindi that readers otherwise encountered in women's periodicals: women speakers were much more likely to address their mostly male audiences in the literary Hindi promoted by the influential literati-cum-politicians. This literary Hindi then also found entry into women's periodicals.[35] The Bengali woman writer Balaji, for example, evaluated the state of Hindi literature for women in a contribution that had initially been written for a panel on suitable women's literature at the annual meeting of the Hindī Sāhitya Sammelan in Indore (1918).[36] At this meeting that counted an impressive 700 women participants and that was chaired by Mohandas Karamchand Gandhi (Talwar 1989: 210), Balaji expounded the importance of literature for social uplift. She spoke in Sanskritized Khaṛī Bolī Hindi (tatsama words are in italics and the lone Urdu word is in boldface):

Sāhitya kī *unnati samāj* kī *unnati* aur uske *vyaktiyoṅ* ke *mānasik vikās* par *nirbhar* hai. *Itihās* batlātā hai ki kisī *deś* ke *vāsiyoṅ* ke *vicāroṅ*, *bhāvoṅ*, *ruciyoṅ* aur *āvaśyaktāoṅ* ke *parivartan* ke sāth sāth vahāṅ ke *sāhitya* meṅ bhī *parivartan* hotā jātā hai. *Striyoṅ* ke *yogya sāhitya* kā *praśna* hamāre *deś* ke liye **bilkul** nayā hai.

[The progress of literature is linked to the progress of society and the mental development of its members. History tells us that a change in the thoughts, ideas, interests, and needs of the residents of a country also has an impact on their literature. The issue of suitable literature for women is completely new to our country.][37]

The point Balaji wished to make in her speech was that women required a literary forum. To her, literature was the reflection of a *nation*'s soul, which was why it was inevitable and timely to discuss literature suitable for women in the national language at a national literature gathering (tatsama words are italicized):

Sāhitya rāṣṭrīya ātmā kā *pratibimb* hai. [...] *Ataeva rāṣṭrīya bhāṣā* aur *rāṣṭrīya sāhitya-sammelan* meṅ *striyoṅ* ke *yogya sāhitya* kī *carcā* honā *atyant upayukt* aur *samayānukūl* hai.

[Literature is the reflection of the nation's soul. [...] Thus, it is both appropriate and most pressing that we discuss suitable literature for women at a national language and literary convention.][38]

Balaji, who was speaking at the most influential and renowned literary convention of the times, appreciated the fact that an increasing number of printing presses and publication houses in British-Indian cities such as Allahabad, Bombay, and Agra, as well as in the princely states, were specializing in literature for women; but Balaji's main demand was directed at women as writers: they were asked to produce literature for women.

As I have shown at the beginning of this chapter, Pandit Satyabhakt voiced a similar claim to that of Balaji when defining *sāhitya sevā* as a patriotic activity for women. Calling on women to engage in literary activities, he held in Sanskritized Khaṛī Bolī Hindi (tatsama words are italicized):

Jñān-prapti kī *pradhān-kāraṇarūpiṇī sāhitya-sevā* to *strī* aur *puruṣ* - donoṅ ko *karaṇīya* hai [...] *Sāhitya-sevā* jaise *pavitra kārya*kī or abhī *yuktprades*kī *striyoṅ*kā *dhyān* bahut hī kam gayā hai. *Hindībhāṣābhāṣī prāntoṅ*kī *striyoṅ* ko bhī *sāhitya-sevā*kā *kārya* karke *hindībhāṣākī śrīvṛddhi* karnī cāhiye. *Āśā* hai, kuch *samay*meṅ yah *prades* bhī is *prakār* pichṛe hue nahīṅ raheṅge aur yahāṅ bhī *anya* prāntoṅke *samān sulekhikāeṅ utpann* ho kar *mātṛbhāṣā* kī *sevā* kartī huī *sarvasādhāraṇ* ko *lābhānvit* kareṅge.

[Both, women and men should engage in the prime cause of service towards literature, which will lead to knowledge. The women of the United Provinces have not yet devoted much attention to the sacred work of the service of literature. The women of the Hindi-speaking provinces should also engage in the service of literature and should add to the prosperity of the Hindi language. Let us hope that after some time this province will no longer lag behind and that just as in other provinces (such as Bengal, Gujarat, Maharashtra), capable women writers will serve the mother tongue for the benefit of the people at large.][39]

Assigning literary responsibilities to women was new in Hindi. Before women began editing women's periodicals, the (male) Hindi literati had taken the responsibility of producing literature for women. *Feminine writing*, in Balaji's words, 'from the eyes and feelings of a woman' would shed new light on 'the consideration and interpretation of Indian glory, the Indian heart, Indian nature and Indian ideals, Indian life and society' (tatsama words are italicized): '*Bhāratīya pratibhā* aur *bhāratīya hṛday*, *bhāratīya prakṛti* aur *bhāratīya ādarś*, *bhāratīya jīvan* aur *bhāratīya samāj* kī *vyākhyā* aur *mīmāṅsā nārī-netroṅ* aur *nārī-bhāvoṅ dvārā* abhī tak *lekhvaddh* nahīṅ huī hai.'[40] Balaji made this statement in Sanskritized Khaṛī Bolī Hindi without using a single word from the Urdu vocabulary.

Balaji and Satyabhakt, besides promoting suitable literature *for* women, also placed emphasis on the importance of literature created *by* women. Such claims were repeated at several occasions later in the 1920s and 1930s. Mahadevi Varma during her editorship of *Chand* (1935–8), made it one of her objectives to encourage women writers to join the literary scene by contributing short stories, novels, drama, poetry, and critical essays (Schomer 1983: 227–8). Women's periodicals and women's columns, in which women could publish and share their knowledge with fellow-women, were particularly useful to this project. As for the themes of women's literature, Balaji suggested that they include not only fiction, but literature in the broadest sense that included educational texts on astrology, philosophy, history, sociology, and specific women's issues.

To further institutionalize female authorship as a practice, she called for the introduction of literary awards. In demanding institutional recognition for women's writings by the most important literary organizations, the Nāgarī Pracārinī Sabhā and the Hindī Sāhitya Sammelan, Balaji attempted to draw women into a gendered literary establishment. The winning essays were regularly published in women's periodicals.

Her last claim was also directed towards the objective of recognition: women's literature required institutional support, as well as the support of eminent male writers. Balaji was well aware of the power of institutional networks in promoting Hindi language and literature. 'Normative institutions' (Orsini 1999a: 413), however, such as the Nāgarī Pracāriṇī Sabhā or the Hindī Sāhitya Sammelan, promoted a type of Hindi that was Sanskritized and not necessarily close to the spoken language of the common people. The point Balaji emphasized was the comprehensibility of literature for women. How did she reconcile the seeming divergence between mainstream literary expectations and the importance of using language registers that were not considered suitable for entry into the national literary canon?

Balaji's emphasis that women write literature for women also implied that female authors would best be able to create a link between the literary standard that the male literati sought to create and what could be called women's lingua franca. Her recommendations regarding the language of women's literature concurred with claims of Hindi proponents who advocated a suitable Hindi for women. Books for women were to be written in a simple and comprehensible (*saral aur subodh*) language fit to enhance instruction and impart useful knowledge (*śikṣāprad aur upayogī jñān ke baṛhānevāle*). The topics of the books were to be in accord with the background of Indian women (*strī-samāj aur sthiti ke anukūl hoṅ*) and not derived from European or American contexts. It was thus also important to write genuinely Hindi literature rather than merely publish translations from western literature. Balaji also asked that literature for women be made affordable.

As the citations have indicated, the language Balaji used in her speech at the Hindī Sāhitya Sammelan was far from simple and comprehensible. It conformed to standards set by the Hindi literati, who were among her audiences, but hardly considered the 700 female participants present at this gathering. But this was not the language that she recommended for the production of Hindi literature for women (which was much unlike Gandhi's use of Hindustani in his address at the same literary gathering). Balaji herself was also not a native Hindi speaker, but a cognate learner of Hindi. Important to remember is that regardless of her own preferences or those of the literati at the Hindī Sāhitya Sammelan, *women's periodicals* did not exclusively promote Sanskritized Khaṛī Bolī Hindi. On the contrary, the majority of publications were written in a language that was simple and easily understood (*saral aur subodh*) in the way that Balaji, Satyabhakt, Dwivedi, and other proponents of female writers wished it to be. The *literature* produced in this language, however, would not find entry into the national literary canon of the time. What defined this canon remained diffuse well into the 1930s, when the editor of *Saraswati*, Devidatt Shukla, admonished that there still existed no national canon of Hindi (Orsini 2002: 361). This notwithstanding, the writings under investigation here are testimony to the creation of a canon for women (also read by men) that emerged out of women's periodicals and other publication genres and that was publicized in the book advertisements published in women's periodicals.

With debates surrounding the suitability of literature for women underway, women's periodicals contained many reviews of new and established Hindi publications (also see the advertisements translated in Part Two, Box 30–1, pp. 320–1). Such books were assessed according to the language, content and educational value for women and girls. Hindi had become the medium of primary instruction in Benares and Allahabad in 1825 (Vedalankar 1969: 139) and the urgent need for textbooks was expressed on several occasions. This might not have immediately impacted the female population as the number of school-going girls remained low in the early twentieth century. The editors of women's periodicals, however, considered it their responsibility to inform the readers about books that used Hindi as the language of instruction. In the section that advertised books, the editor of *Grihalakshmi* highlighted the importance of textbooks in Hindi as follows: 'It is very important to have such [text]books in Hindi. [...] There exist numerous works in English on this topic but only a few are written in Hindi and even those are not very good.'[41] The original Hindi was in a welded register, in which the *tatsama pustak* (book) was given preference over the Arabic *kitāb* (book), but the Persian *zarūrī* (necessity) was used instead of the *tatsama āvaśyaktā* (necessity) (tatsama words are italicized and the single Urdu word is in boldface): 'Aisī *pustakeṅ* kā hindī meṅ honā bahut **zarūrī** hai. [...] Aṅgrezī meṅ to is *viṣay* par bahut baṛe baṛe *granth* haiṅ par hindī meṅ bahut kam haiṅ aur jo haiṅ ve bhī bahut acche ḍhaṅg se nahīṅ likhe gaye.'[42]

Translations (from English) were not necessarily disapproved of as long as they were written in what was considered to be 'proper' Hindi. In a book review in *Stri Darpan*, the editor admonished the unrefined language of a book as follows: 'The book is a good one, but the language should have been more refined and there remain too many formal and orthographic mistakes.'[43] The Hindi original was in an equal mix of tatsama words (italicized) and Urdu words (in bold), and even one English word (underlined): 'Pustak apne ḍhaṅg kī acchī hai, *parantu bhāṣā* kuch *adhiktar mārjit* honī cāhie thī aur **hijje** tathā <u>prūf</u> dekhne kī **ğaltiyāṅ** bahut rah gayī haiṅ.'[44]

The importance that the language of books be accessible to their readers was expressed in a book review of children's lullabies (*Śiśulorī*; for a full translation see Part Two, Box 31, p. 321). The editor held:

> But in our opinion it would have been better if the language had been more simple and colloquial so that children would be able to understand it without help. At some places, the words are too difficult.
>
> [*Parantu* hamārī *sammati* meṅ śiśuoṅ ko binā *sahāytā* ke samajh meṅ ā jāne *yogya adhiktar saral* aur *bolcāl* kī *bhāṣā* hotī to acchā hotā. Jahāṅ tahāṅ kuch *śabd kaṭhin* ho gaye haiṅ.][45]

Despite the critique voiced about the children's book, the language of this review also bordered on incomprehensibility for the average reader.

From Regional to National Debates about Hindi

Many proponents of Hindi as a national language conceded that Hindi was not the mother tongue of the common people in the United Provinces. It was imperative, however, that the *idea* of a national language was promoted by all means. In the late 1920s, the children's periodical *Khilauna* (Toy, 1926–60) introduced the concept of a national language to children:

> In Punjab one speaks Punjabi and one speaks Hindi in the United Provinces, Central Provinces, and Bihar, Bengali in Bengal, Tamil and Telugu in Madras and Marathi and Gujarati in Bombay. Hindi is a language that can be understood by everyone. Once upon a time, Sanskrit was the only language in all of *Bhāratvarṣ*. [...] Today, Hindi is Bhārat's national language. The language that can be understood and that is spoken in all parts of the country is called the national language. Through the national language, all brothers and sisters of a country are united. In *Bhāratvarṣ*, Hindi is this language.[46]

Despite the acknowledgement of Indian vernaculars, Hindi was elevated to the language 'understood by everyone' partly through establishing a genealogy with the projected 'mother of all languages', Sanskrit. The quote also indicates that the emphasis had shifted from finding one standardized version of Hindi to spreading Kharī Bolī Hindi as a unifying language of *Bhāratvarṣ*, which included the connotation of *Hindu* India.

But unlike the editor of *Khilauna*, who quite conspicuously supported the view that only Hindi had the capacity to serve as India's national language (*rāṣṭra bhāṣā*), the editor of *Stri Darpan* put such a resolution up for debate: 'Is it really Hindi that is suitable as the national language?', asked the editorial in July 1918.[47] Surely, the editor reasoned, a nation required its national language, but the question about the lingua franca was certainly more complicated. People in different regions spoke in different vernaculars and the editor reminded the readers that this also held true for Hindi in its variants that were spread over a number of provinces. Rameshwari Nehru referred to a speech delivered by the president of the Bengali Office of the National Language Association in Calcutta, calling for an opinion poll in the United Provinces on Hindi as the national language. Nehru saw this as an opportunity to encourage readers to share their opinions about Hindi as a national language.[48] A few months later, in October 1918, the periodical's focus shifted to the disconnect between Sanskritized Khaṛī Bolī Hindi as it was envisioned to transcend regional boundaries and regional variants of Hindi, the so-called *bolīs*:

Hindi should be the national language. By now, almost everyone agrees with this statement. The people of one province should be able to communicate with people of other provinces in one language that is proper Hindi. But which dialect of the Hindi language should be the national language and which dialect will be able to fulfil the requirements? People have started posing this question in many ways. Bengalis, Maharashtrians, and some other people, too, will easily be able to learn Sanskritized Hindi. If they are confronted with Hindi containing many Urdu words, they will understand less and whatever little love they will have developed towards Hindi will vanish. In a similar manner, the people of Punjab and many from the United Provinces who till today think they are showing love for their mother tongue Hindi are, in reality, speaking Urdu instead of Persian. They will either hate erudite (*panditaū*) Hindi or will not be able to understand it. The result will be that the national language will consist of two versions, one Muslim Hindi and the other erudite (*panditaū*) Hindi.

[Hindī ko *rāṣṭra-bhāṣā* banānā cāhiye yahī *sammati* is *samay* lagbhag sabhī logoṅ kī hai. Ek *prānt* ke rahnevāle dūsre *prāntoṅ* ke sāth *sahaj* meṅ apne *manobhāv prakāśit* kar sake iske lie ek *mātr* hindī *bhāṣā* hī *upayukt* pāyī gayī hai. *Parantu* hindī *bhāṣā* kī kaun sī bolī *rāṣṭra-bhāṣā* ban kar kām acchī **tarah** kar saktī hai? Yah *praśna* bhī *bahudhā* logoṅ ke man meṅ uṭhne lagā hai. Baṅgālī log, mahārāṣṭravāle, *tathā* kuch aur log bhī samskṛt milī huī hindī hī ko *sahaj* meṅ jaldī sīkh sakte haiṅ. Unke sāmne urdū milī huī hindī bolī jāyegī to ve kam samjheṅge, aur hindī kī or unkā jo kuch thoṛā bahut *prem* jagāyā jā rahā, sab bekām ho jāyegā. Isī *prakār* paṅjāb ke *sajjanoṅ* aur *yukt prānt* ke bhī bahutere logoṅ ko jo ab tak *mātṛbhāṣā* hindī se dikhāvaṭī *prembhāv* rakhte haiṅ aur asal meṅ fārsī kī toṛ urdū hī kām lene ko taiyār haiṅ; paṇḍitaū hindī se *ghṛṇā* hogī, yānī ve aisī hindī ko samajh na sakeṅge. Isse phal yah nikalegā ki *rāṣṭra-bhāṣā* ke do *svarūp* bane raheṅge, ek musalmānī hindī, dūsrī paṇḍitaū hindī.][49]

It is clear from this passage that the idea of a national language met with concrete challenges posed by regional variations of Hindi and ideas about standardization. Following the British example, the editor argued for a single literary and print language that was also the lingua franca of the people. She was anxious about two languages (Sanskritized and Persianized Hindi) opposing one another, effectively undermining the idea and purpose of a national language. The original Hindi of her contribution that appeared as political commentary had also shifted towards a Kharī Bolī Hindi with less Urdu words than was otherwise the case in her writing.

The question of language had not emerged out of a vacuum. Orientalist philological discourses on new Indo-Aryan languages had identified a number of Indian vernaculars as having descended from Sanskrit and as sharing a common grammar and etymology (Shackle & Snell 1990: 1). Amongst the vernaculars were Hindi, Bengali, Punjabi, and also Urdu. Based on this knowledge, Rameshwari Nehru, like colonial linguists, asserted that the common Sanskrit basis would help non-Hindi native speakers become accustomed to Hindi. She was also caught in the larger debate concerning linguistic, cultural, and regional nationalism. The recognition of the country's linguistic diversity and the acknowledgement that Hindi contained many words of Perso-Arabic descent (especially in the Punjab and parts of the North-Western Provinces) despite its origins in Sanskrit, drew heavily on Mahatma Gandhi's conviction that Hindi, Urdu, and Hindustani were one and the same language. Rameshwari Nehru concurred with him in the assumption that Indians were capable of being multilingual and that they had the responsibility of learning several Indian vernaculars. To both, (Rameshwari) Nehru and Gandhi, Hindi was the only language suited to serve as the national language and as the language of the people. Learning Hindi was in fact considered easier than learning English because of Hindi's cognate similarities with languages such as Gujarati, Bengali, Marathi, and Tamil. Gandhi, like Rameshwari Nehru, highlighted the shared Sanskritic tradition of Dravidian and Indo-Aryan languages. But Gandhi levelled his argument at the English language and he defined Hindi as Hindustani, which was closer to Urdu than to Sanskritized Khaṛī Bolī Hindi. Rameshwari Nehru, on the other hand, focused on lexicographical practicalities. For this reason she switched camps from Gandhi's views to that of the more conservative Hindi literati, effectively dispensing with her earlier view that Hindi remain—above all—accessible, and instead suggesting that Sanskrit be the shared basis of all vernaculars (including those of the south).

Nehru never demonstrated a clear position toward English. For nationalist politicians like Gandhi, English was a contested language of communication in the Indian public sphere (this issue was especially burning in the south where Gandhi campaigned in favour of Hindi rather than English). Women's periodicals give mention to neither the role of English as a rival language, nor the Hindi/Urdu language and script controversy despite the fact that it remained a prevailing topic throughout the nationalist struggle. In these periodicals English was rarely used; with regard to the script, Nāgarī was so well established as to need no further discussion.[50]

Both Gandhi and (Rameshwari) Nehru entrusted the actual work of entrenching Hindi to experts; that is, the Hindi literati in service of literature as well as teachers, who were given the authority to set new standards. Gandhi (1965: 16–17) demanded good teachers, and 'a handy book sort of a "Hindi Teacher"' that met the needs of speakers of other vernaculars who wished to learn Hindi. He also called for grammar books and that Hindi be used in national councils. Rameshwari Nehru asked the intelligentsia to produce texts which would reconcile Sanskritized and composite Khaṛī Bolī Hindi, producing a body of 'model' writings that would act as a middle-of-the-road vernacular (in the fashion of the Progressive Writer's Association some decades later). These writings would also override the divisive textbook writing of Pandits and Maulavis that had become prevalent since the second half of the nineteenth century. According to Rameshwari Nehru, whose own language was beginning to shift from composite towards Sanskritized Khaṛī Bolī Hindi, this would be a long process (tatsama words are italicized, Urdu words are in boldface, and the single English word is underlined):

[*V*]*idvadsamāj* ko cāhiye ki ve bīcobīc meṅ ek **rāh** nikāl kar caleṅ jisse unke *lekhoṅ* ko *ādarś* mān kar donoṅ or ke *rāṣṭra-bhāṣā premī* log donoṅ hī sṭāiloṅ ko dhīre dhīre samajhne aur usse kām lene kā *abhyās* kiyā kareṅ. Hindī *bhāṣā* kā *vistār* itnā lambā cauṛā hai ki kabhī kisī *samay* meṅ iskā ek *mātr rūp* ban jānā *asambhav* hai. Is lie dūsre *prānt*vāloṅ ko kuch na kuch *kaṭhināiyoṅ* kā sāmnā karnā hī paṛegā. *Parantu* hamko *āśā* hai ki 10–20 *varṣoṅ* meṅ yah *kaṭhināī* bhī bahut ghaṭ jāvegī, *yadyapi* sab **jagah** ek hī *prakār* kī hindī kā *pracār* bhī nahīṅ dekhne milegā. Jis *prānt* kī *mātṛbhāṣā* hindī hai (*yānī yukt prānt* kī), vahāṅ bhī bahutere log abhī tak *śuddh* Hindī ko bhalī bhānti nahīṅ samajh sakte. Gandhī jī jaise *mahānubhāv* log urdū hindī ko ek hī mānne lage haiṅ. Aisā hī mān lenā ṭhīk bhī hai. Tab bhī *anya prānt*vāloṅ ko apnī or milā lene ke lie hamko kuch na kuch *svārthatyāg* karnā hī paṛegā, aur *kaṭhin paṇḍitaū* hindī yā maulavī hindī par aṛe rahnā *ucit* na hoga.[51]

[T]he learned society needs to find a compromise. They need to create model texts, from which the proponents of both 'national languages' [Sanskritized and composite Hindi] may appreciate and make use of both *styles*. Hindi has such a broad range that it is impossible to create one single form thereof. That is why those from other provinces will encounter difficulties. But we hope that in ten to twenty years, these difficulties will be overcome even though one single form of Hindi will not be found everywhere. Even in a province that calls Hindi its mother tongue (like the United Provinces), people still cannot properly understand *śuddh* Hindi. People like respected Gandhiji consider Urdu and Hindi one and the same. This assumption is acceptable. Nevertheless, we must not be selfish. We must include people from other provinces as well. It will not be good to insist on erudite Hindi or Maulavi Hindi.

The long-term project laid out by Rameshwari Nehru required that speakers of Hindi as a second language, as well as native Hindi speakers, learn standardized Hindi. It is likely that she considered her editorials with the increased number of tatsama words as such a middle-of-the-road vernacular. She also agreed with the Gandhian scheme of a national language that could be called Hindustani (Hindi and Urdu as the lingua franca of Hindus and Muslims without too many loanwords from Sanskrit, Persian, or Arabic). At the same time, she distinguished her opinion from that of Gandhi when emphasizing the importance of standardization with vocabulary based on tatsama words. Introducing tatsama words was thus not only a means of purification and establishment of a Hindi genealogy distinct from Urdu; from the perspective of women editors it was necessary in order to construct a common basis with other Indian vernaculars (Barannikov 1936: 390).[52] Gandhi (1965: 15) demanded that Hindus and Muslims each learn some Persian and Sanskrit vocabulary, an exchange which he felt would 'enrich and strengthen the Islamic language and provide a very fruitful means for bringing Hindus and Muslims closer together'. Rameshwari Nehru, however, pointed to the status of Sanskrit as the mother of Dravidian and Indo-Aryan languages in her demand for an increased use of Sanskrit vocabulary.

While it is true that Rameshwari Nehru aimed to put into effect her idea of Hindi as a national language through Sanskritized writings in her editorials, she at the same time had inclinations towards Urdu vocabulary. This can be best illustrated through her treatment of contributors and subscribers from Punjab: from its inception, *Stri Darpan* regularly reported socio-political and educational developments in Punjab, a focus that was hardly coincidental. In the late nineteenth and early twentieth centuries, an upsurge of reformist writings in which the issue of language ideology featured centrally emerged from the province. Controversies about language were evident in the opposing claims of Singh Sabha and Arya Samaj reformers, the former striving for a standardized Punjabi that would be closely identified with the Sikh tradition, whereas the latter championed what they called their 'original' Hindi mother tongue. *Stri Darpan*, operating out of the Hindi heartland, supported the Arya Samaj movement.

A report in *Stri Darpan* about the thirty-forth meeting of the Indian National Congress in Amritsar also addressed the question of the Nāgarī script in Punjab. The author Jagdishprasad Mishra deplored the fact that Gurmukhi and Urdu were progressing in Punjab, whereas Hindi and with it the Hindu dharma were being left behind. His language included many tatsama words (in italics), but it was not purged of Persian and Arabic words (in bold):

Yadi thoṛe din aur aisī hī *daśā* rahī *to* **yād** rakhie ki paṅjāb *deś* meṅ hindū bhāī apnī *mātṛbhāṣā* ko **bilkul** hī bhūl jāyeṅge. Kyoṅki āj paṅjāb *prānt* se hindūoṅ ke jitne *samācārpatr* nikal rahe haiṅ, ve cāhe ārya-samāj ke hoṅ, yā dharm-samāj ke hoṅ, sab urdū se bhar rahe haiṅ aur urdū bībī kī *sevā* kar rahe haiṅ. *Samast saṅsār* meṅ hindū hī ek aisī jāti hai ki jo apnī *mātṛ-bhāṣā* ko choṛ kar *anya bhāṣāoṅ* kī *unnati* kar rahī hai. Yahī *kāraṇ* hai ki hindū jāti dharm se korī kī korī rah kar *nāstik* ban rahī hai.[53]

[If this continues any longer, remember that our Hindu brothers in Punjab will completely forget their mother tongue, because all the newspapers that are being published in Punjab today, including those of the Arya Samaj and the Dharma Samaj, are full of Urdu words and are serving Lady Urdu. The Hindu *jāti* is the only one in the world that would leave their own language behind in order to develop other languages. This is the reason why Hindus are forgetting about their religion and turning towards atheism.]

Hindi and the Nāgarī script were the subject of debate in the Punjab since the 1860s as a response and contribution to the Hindi/Urdu language and script controversy.[54] The author called for a purification of the language used by Hindu reformist organizations so that the nation could progress in the literary field. He also conceptualized Hindi as the language of all Hindus when claiming (in Sanskritized Khaṛī Bolī Hindi) that 'as long as Hindi is not promoted all over India, the Hindu *jāti* will never be able to mount the summit of prosperity' [Jab tak *sampūrṇ bhāratvarṣ* meṅ *mātṛbhāṣā* kā pūrā pūrā *pracār* na hogā, tab tak hindū jāti *unnati* ke *śikhar* par kabhī *ārūṛh* nahīṅ ho sakegī].[55]

There existed a number of Hindi periodicals in the Punjab, which included women's periodicals. *Jyoti* is of particular interest here because it specifically addressed the Punjabi Hindu community. This monthly periodical was first edited in 1920 by Vidyavati Seth from Lahore with patronage from the Raja of Baroda. It promoted a diversity of publications in Hindi on religious, scientific, and philosophical topics,[56] among them were Hindi translations of works in English written by eminent scholars as well as Hindi children's literature. Noteworthy was the fact that reviewers recommended books written in a simple language (*saral bhāṣā*), which at the same time fostered 'pride in Hindu and Arya dharma' (*hindū vā āryya dharmm abhimānī*). This periodical devoted much space to the promotion of Hindi literature in its editorials and advertisements. One recurrent critique held that Punjabi Hindus lacked their 'own' language and were thus unable to progress. An opinion piece on the Hindī Sāhitya Sammelan and the spread of Hindi, for example, deplored that Punjab did not have its own language (that is, a certain form of Hindi) and could thus not flourish intellectually.[57] Punjabi Hindus had neglected their culture and language by not fostering Sanskrit and Hindi. Now, 'Punjab is in search of a Bankim' (p. 431), such was the conclusion of the editor, referring to the renowned Bengali author Bankimchandra Chattopadhyay.

As mentioned above, *Stri Darpan* supported the Arya Samaj movement from the very heartland of the Hindi-speaking area. The editors appealed to Punjabi writers to publish in Hindi. An editorial of 1920 proudly introduced Amichand, a Punjabi writer who would from then onward regularly publish social reformist poems and songs in Hindi. Such contributions were encouraged even if they were not in the 'pure' Hindi that Rameshwari Nehru, for example, used to introduce the author (tatsama words are italicized):

Āp panjāb *prānt* ke rahnevāle haiṅ, isī liye āpkī *bhāṣā* kahīṅ kahīṅ kuch *asādhāraṇ* jacegī. *Parantu* āpke panjāb-*nivāsī* hone hī ke *kāraṇ* ham in *kavitāoṅ* ko chāpnā ucit samajhtī haiṅ. Panjāb meṅ hindī kā *pracār* bahut kam pāyā jātā hai, *parantu* āp jaise *utsāhī lekhakoṅ* ke *lekh* hindī *patroṅ* meṅ *prakāśit* hote raheṅge to dūsre panjābī bhāiyoṅ kā bhī *utsāh* baṛhegā aur dinodin hindī likhne paṛhne meṅ unkī *ruci* baṛhegī.[58]

[You live in Punjab, which is why your language appears sometimes unusual. But because of your Punjabi origins, we consider it appropriate to publish your poems. In Punjab there is very little public exposure given to Hindi, but if articles continue to be published in Hindi periodicals from enthusiastic writers like you, our Punjabi brothers will be inspired and their interest in reading and writing Hindi will increase day by day.]

As Rameshwari Nehru indicated, *Stri Darpan* was ready to make concessions regarding the 'quality' of Hindi if this was likely to increase the (male?) Hindi readership in Punjab. She also announced the publication of a series of poems in 'pure' (*ṭheṭh*) Punjabi, 'especially for the pleasure of Punjabi subscribers to *Stri Darpan*'.[59] What was considered harmful to the unity of the national language by some advocates of 'pure Hindi' (because it did not enhance the standardization and purification of Hindi) was being recognized by *Stri Darpan* as a way to foster linguistic diversity and literary tastes (*saṅskāras*) in the Hindi public sphere. Her proclivity for Sanskritized Hindi as it was now manifesting itself in her editorials thus bowed given the linguistic background of writers from Punjab.

The Hindi/Urdu language and script controversy of the second half of the nineteenth century had revolved around the genealogies of Urdu and Hindi, as well as the official status of these vernaculars. Language and script were not only standardized, but constituted a literary claim with widespread political implications. In this process, the instrumentalization of language became a central means to emphasize difference between Hindus and Muslims (Dalmia 1997: 223). If we read the language controversy through the lens of women's periodicals that were published a few decades after the beginnings of the Hindi movement in the 1860s, some of the issues that had defined the controversy had already been resolved: women's periodicals did not problematize the question of script, since Nāgarī had meanwhile been accepted as the only script of Hindi women's periodicals. Debates concerning questions of lexicography, however, continued. The editors prioritized comprehension over sophistication, while this priority did not necessarily reflect the language they themselves used in editorials. Compared to the language of mainstream literary journals the individual contributions avoided excessive Sanskritized vocabulary (tatsama) and favoured a language that was refined and standardized according to the periodicals' expectations. Important was a simple syntax and accessible vocabulary including words of Perso-Arabic origin. Thus while editorials showed a clear tendency towards Sanskritized Kharī Bolī Hindi and the promotion of the mainstream literary ideology, when it came down to the nitty-gritty, the majority of contributions, especially those by ordinary writers, were written without many tatsama words.

The periodicals also were forced to deal with regional variations of Hindi. Because a number of contributors hailed from the different Hindi-speaking provinces as well as from regions outside of the Hindi belt, concessions were made with regard to Hindi vocabulary. While a literary periodical such as *Saraswati* paved the way for the standardization of what is today known as modern Sanskritized Kharī Bolī Hindi, women's periodicals encouraged contributions from non-native speakers of Hindi, such as from Punjab or Bengal. They did not correct grammatical mistakes in the way that it would have been done in *Saraswati* in order to maintain a certain standardized language and literary standard.[60] As the agendas of women's and children's periodicals were also guided by their readers, these periodicals remained outside the fold of the mainstream literary canon of their time. Women's and children's periodicals nevertheless provide an excellent example of the way new audiences were introduced *in* Hindi to the public discourse *on* Hindi. Such periodicals broadened the definition of literary Hindi in that they considered their contributions as written in the national language which for them coincided with the projected language of communication. Unlike women's periodicals, children's periodicals promoted Sanskritized Khaṛī Bolī Hindi as the language to discuss even simple topics. But Sanskritized Hindi and comprehensibility were not always antagonistic to each other. Neither were tatsama words and Urdu words in the same contribution considered inconsistent. Rather, different lexicons enriched the vocabulary and general knowledge of women and a new generation of Hindi readers, namely, children.

Further, the Hindi that was publicly being promoted in women's periodicals, took account of the regional dialects of the Hindi *bolīs*. Ultimately, however, it is apparent that women's periodicals were in search of a middle-of-the-road vernacular that was understood by all Indians and reasonably Sanskritized. They thus participated in the nationalist discourse on language and literature in a spirit of conciliation and compromise with the needs of the female readership placed at centre stage while acknowledging the diverging positions of both public authorities: Mahavir Prasad Dwivedi and Mahatma Gandhi.

Protecting composite Hindi from delexification remains a mission up to the present day. Rai (2001) is a proponent of a Hindi containing Urdu words as it builds on the popular heritage of the people from the Hindi belt. To him, it is the hybrid and heteroglot character of Hindi that makes the language suitable as a national language, precisely because it is accessible to the Indian people at large and not restricted to a small elite. Turning native speakers of variations of Hindi into second-language learners of Sanskritized Hindi is to Rai (2001: 105) a theft of a person's mother tongue. Women's periodicals, as we have seen, also resisted this transformation of Hindi in its various incarnations into one single language.

Notes

1. Other proponents of the idea of a national language were missionaries and textbook authors. Both explicitly addressed a Hindu audience in *Hinduī* written in the Nāgarī script. The Christian Gospel was printed in *Hinduī*, as were numerous tracts and textbooks published out of Benares, Allahabad, Calcutta, and Agra in the early nineteenth century. These writings also played a key role in the formation of modern Hindi as a print language (Dalmia 1997: 169). Dalmia (1997: 173) comments on the activities of such tract societies: 'the policy, however, was not simply to translate, but to set the texts in an Indian context. The texts were written by missionaries but their work

was corrected by native speakers'. Some of these translations—proof-read by prominent figures of the Hindi literati—acquired the status of model texts for the Hindi literary canon.

2. Pandit Satyabhakt, 1918, '*Striyāṅ aur sāhitya sevā*' [Women and the service of literature], *Arya Mahila* (AprilMay/June/July [Vaiśākh/Jyeṣṭ/Āṣāṛh 1975]): 374–7. For a full translation, see Part Two, Box 9, pp. 261–4.

3. Kellogg (1893: 67) in the revised edition of his Hindi grammar, replaced the term standard Hindi with 'high Hindi' in order to avoid 'misapprehensions to the relation of this dialect to others'. Also see Kellogg's detailed elaborations on Hindi *bolīs* (1893: xix, 65).

4. This passage has been translated by Dalmia (2003: 4). In an orientalist account of the development of Khaṛī Bolī, Bailey (1936) also presumes that Khaṛī Bolī was not a rural, 'rustic' dialect, but a literary one—and the predecessor to modern Hindi—that developed from a north-western Punjabi dialect. There were two varieties of Khaṛī Bolī, which shared a common grammatical base but were distinct in script: Khaṛī Bolī Hindi written in the Nāgari script and Khaṛī Bolī Urdu in the Nastālīq script (King 1994: 199). Gupta (2001: 203–13) and Rai (2001: 95) have presented a gendered reading of the language debate, suggesting that the question of language became a debate around masculinity. As the Hindi may suggest, the adjective *khaṛā* (standing, erect) stood not only for 'standard', but also for 'erect and masculine'.

5. In producing and translating literature to teach employees of the East India Company, the Fort William College (estd. 1800) also had a huge impact on language politics in the northern plains. The Fort William College gave formal recognition to Hindi in 1825 and granted the vernacular place in the department of Hindustani (Urdu) (King 1994: 27). The boundaries between languages, however, were in flux, which led to Hindustani texts being printed in the Nāgarī script. The Hindustani department also hired a Nāgarī script teacher (King 1994: 27), but clearly, Urdu was favoured over any form of Hindi within the department. During the course of the nineteenth century, what was once considered a composite language spoken by Hindu and Muslim populations of northern India was effectively divided into two culturally and religiously distinct markers with their own individual scripts: Hindi was institutionalized as the language of the Hindus, and Urdu was identified as the language of the Muslim population. In their efforts to identify the various vernaculars of the British Indian Provinces, colonial institutions such as the Fort William College produced an abundance of grammars, dictionaries, and compendiums to better understand the linguistic diversity of the subcontinent. Most notable is George A. Grierson's *Linguistic Survey of India*, a work in eleven volumes listing different language families of the subcontinent and providing language specimens. A review of this work is in *Arya Mahila* (April/May/June/July 1918 [Vaiśākh/Jyeṣṭ/Āṣāṛh 1975]). Other important works are John Borthwick Gilchrist's

Grammar of the Hindustani Language (1796), *The Oriental Linguist* (1798), and *Hindoostanee Philology: Comprising a Dictionary of English and Hindoostanee; with a grammatical introduction* (1810). For a list of publications from the Fort William College, see Vedalankar (1969: Appendix II). The publications were also used as textbook materials in government-sponsored schools.

6. 'Bhāṣā kā tīsrā aṅg likhne kī bhāṣā hai aur is meṅ baṛā jhagṛā hai. Koī kahte haiṅ ki urdū śabd milne cāhie koī kahtā hai saṅskṛt śabd hone cāhie aur apnī apnī ruci ke anusār sab likhte haiṅ aur is ke hetu koī bhāṣā abhī niścit nahīṅ ho saktī' (Harishchandra 1893: 12).

7. See for example Ayodhya Prasad Khatri to whom Munshi Hindi was the 'authentic' Hindi, also known as the Hindustani promoted in the Agra and Delhi schools (King 1994: 30; Rai 2001: 85). In later usage of the term, *śuddh* Hindi was to describe Sanskritized Hindi.

8. Harishchandra (1893: 1). The English translation of this paragraph is on p. 193.

9. His standard, however, could not be implemented consistently in the periodical (Dalmia 2004: 408–9).

10. This was also true for Urdu women's periodicals, which retained a conversational style in the vernacular Urdu/Hindustani and included tadbhava words, colloquialisms, and idioms of a so-called women's language (Minault 1998: 15–6).

11. Rameshprasad, 1920, '*Daśam hīndī sāhitya sammelan meṅ striyāṅ*' [Women at the tenth meeting of the Hindī Sāhitya Sammelan], *Stri Darpan* (May): 283–5, emphasis added.

12. Pandit Satyabhakt, 1918, '*Striyāṅ aur sāhitya sevā*' [Women and the service of literature], *Arya Mahila* (April/May/June/July [Vaiśākh/Jyeṣṭ/Āṣāṛh 1975]): 374. The translation of this opening paragraph is on in Part Two, Box 9, pp. 261–4.

13. Alternating Hindi and Urdu words within one phrase was a stylistic device also used in the second half of the twentieth century by Hindi writers with backgrounds and linguistic sensibilities in both, Hindi and Urdu, such as Rahi Masum Raza, Nafis Afridi, Abdul Bismillah, and Badiuzzaman (Stark 1995: 203).

14. R. Nehru, 1917, '*Sampādakīya: Strī Darpaṇ*' [Editorial: *Stri Darpan*], *Stri Darpan* (February): 58. For the English translation see pp. 45–6.

15. Stark (1995: 201) makes a similar observation with regard to the Hindi writer Badiuzzaman whose Hindi novels contain a majority of Urdu words along with tatsama vocabulary. She does not describe this language as alienated or estranged, but as one of the many variations of Hindi.

16. This was even the case in medieval Hindi literature: Kellogg (1893 [1876]: xiv) notes that words of Arabic and Persian origin were not considered foreign to Hindi.

17. While school-going children were addressed in Sanskritized Kharī Bolī Hindi, the language of the textbooks in the Hindi belt was not as rigorously 'purified' as it was in the Punjab (Orsini 2002: 100). Primers of the early twentieth century promoted by the Arya Samaj through the Gurukul Press used exclusively a high register that was difficult to understand even for children familiar with Arya Samaj literature (Ibid.: 114–5). This high register was created by replacing words of Perso-Arabic origin with Sanskrit loanwords.

18. *Kanya Manoranjan* (September/October 1913 [Āśvin 1970]): 30; see translation in p. 117.

19. Slogan printed on the back cover of *Kanya Manoranjan*. It is the hope that *Kanya Manoranjan* will be of good use for the well-being of the girls' and women's societies all over India.

20. Such was the case not only in the Hindi belt: in Punjab, the Arya Samaj promoted a so-called Arya language for its textbook materials. The publications however consisted of a blend of Sanskritized Hindi and Punjabi as well as colloquial Urdu (Kishwar 1986: 12). In the second half of the nineteenth century, a pioneer of Hindi in Punjab had already made concessions regarding the choice of language for the instruction of girls. Following the advice of his friends that he should pay more attention to the comprehensibility of his textbooks, Babu Navinchandra Rai included Urdu instead of tatsama words in his Hindi writings (Stark 2000: 46–7).

21. B.K. Mitra, 1917, '*Brahmāṇḍ aur saur jagat*' [The cosmos and the solar system], *Kumari Darpan* (January): 1. This passage is translated in Chapter Three, pp. 110–11.

22. Using the Sanskrit *visarg* along with the Arabic phoneme (kh) in a tatsama word is a typographical error (the correct spelling is *du:kh*).

23. All that god has given us, wisdom, common sense, health and courage, has been given so that we may share it amongst others and thus benefit. We are just guarding these god-given qualities. Our respected president has just said that a cart cannot move with one single wheel; but we are moving the cart since hundreds of years with just one wheel. The consequence is that while people of other countries are travelling in airplanes, we Hindustani people are moving on one wheel. [...] Hindustan's wives were not that way in the olden day. At that time when we were teaching the world wisdom, the manners of our women were different. Like Sita you should bear the sorrow and share men's plight (R. Nehru, 1917, '*Sampādakīya: Śrīmatī Sarojinī Devī Naiḍū kā vyākhyān*' [Editorial: The speech of Śrīmatī Sarojini Devi Naidu], *Stri Darpan* [February]: 61–3).

24. John Borthwick Gilchrist, professor and head of the Hindustani department at Fort William College, is said to have introduced punctuation marks into Hindi in the early nineteenth century.

25. Daughter: Yes, I remember when a kind gentleman came to us from Madras. Neither could he speak Hindi nor could we understand his language, so he spoke English and you and father were able to properly understand him. How I wished I would have also been able to understand him.
Mother: So, you have also understood the benefits of learning English, haven't you? It is good to study it when there is time (Pyarelal Garg, 1913, '*Kyā kyā sīkhnā cāhiye?*' [What all should be learned], *Grihalakshmi* [May/June (Jyeṣṭ 1970)]: 149).

26. King (1994: 31) makes the same observation of writers in the nineteenth century.

27. Night had arrived. The clock had not yet struck nine and all of the children had eaten and came to their grandmother. One sat on her lap, another placed the head on grandmother's knees and lied down, and yet another embraced her. They exclaimed in unison: 'Grandmother, tell us a story! A story, grandmother.' One said 'I choose Ambi', the other said, 'Ambi', and the third said, 'Grandmother, it has been so many days, tell it today' (Pushpavati, 1917, '*Nānī kī kahānī*' [Grandmother's stories], *Grihalakshmi* [May/June (Jyeṣṭ 1974)]: 103).

28. 'I won't marry. Many men have proposed. I told them all that I do not wish to marry' (G.P. Shrivastav, 1913/1914, '*Kālī mem*' [The black madam], *Grihalakshmi* [December/January (Pauṣ 1970)]: 517).

29. 'Listen to this! Listen to this religious matter, it will make you complete. You will then also be able to agree with me. You people who have jewellery made. This is of no use' (Ibid.: 516). An edited paragraph could look similar to the following one (with the corrected passages underlined):

Hamne śādī nahīṁ kī. Bahut sāhab log hamāre yahāṁ āye. Hamne sab ko bol diyā ki ham śādī nahīṁ karne cāhtīṁ. [...] 'Suno, suno! Dharm kī bāt suno. Isse tum akhil hogī. Phir tum bhī hamāre muāfiq rahne sakogī. Tum log jo zevar banvāte hai. Kuch fāydā nahīṁ.

30. Such as Awadhi in *Kanya Manoranjan* (Gangaram, 1914, '*Lālā aur cor*' [Lala and the thief], *Kanya Manoranjan* [November]: 46), Chattisgarhi in *Stri Darpan* (Vishnukumari Shrivastav 'Manju', 1928, '*Sukhiyā kā vyāh*' [Sukhiya's marriage], *Stri Darpan* [June]: 819–24), and Etawah in *Kumari Darpan* (Phulkumari Mehrotra, 1925, '*Zevar kī cāh*' [The desire for jewellery], *Kumari Darpan* [July]: 50–1).

31. So far, I have suggested that the Hindi literati was sympathetic and understanding towards a language that was accessible to women, but in cases as the one refered to here, the literati was dismissive of explicitly 'uncouth' language.

32. Sister: Sister-in-law, she has arrived.
Sister-in-law: Who? [The demon] Ravana's mother?
Sister: Yes, come on, we'll have some fun for a little while.

Sister-in-law: Such kind of fun belongs in the oven. I have no interest in what this slut has to say. (*Kālī mem*' [The black madam], *Grihalakshmi* [December/January (Pauṣ 1970)]: 515)

33. 'Kishorchandra said to his wife Kamla, "Listen, is this fine? Look properly. Do you like this sari or not? Nowadays, I don't have the time to keep running to the market. If you complain later, it will be of no avail"' (Anon. [A well-wisher of the country], 1913, '*Svadeśī sāṛī*' [Swadeshi sari], *Grihalakshmi* [September/October (Āśvin 1970)]: 387).

34. Wow, now you are nagging. If I don't like it you will have to go. (She looks at the fabric). Alas, after asking you for so many days you have brought a sari, but one that I don't like. Neither is the cloth fine nor does it look good. If I wear such a coarse cloth and mingle with people, what will they say? (Ibid.).

35. The language that women used to address female audiences remained colloquial and flexible (see the speech of Sarojini Naidu, pp. 204–5).

36. Despite my attempts, I have not been able to gather any biographical information about Balaji who might as well have been one of the readers who had responded to the call of papers for the Hindī Sāhitya Sammelan as published in *Stri Darpan*. In spite of her key role at the Hindī Sāhitya Sammelan, Balaji does not seem to have published in literary journals such as *Saraswati* the way other Bengali women writers of her time did. I thank Sujata Mody for giving me this information.

37. Balaji, 1918, '*Hindī meṅ striyoṅ ke yogya sāhitya*' [Suitable literature for women in Hindi], *Stri Darpan* (November): 243. For a full translation of this essay see Nijhawan (2010: 388–94).

38. Ibid.: 244.

39. Pandit Satyabhakt, 1918, '*Striyāṅ aur sāhitya sevā*' [Women and the service of literature], *Arya Mahila* (April/May/June/July [Vaiśākh/Jyeṣṭ/Āṣāṛh 1975]: 375–6). For a full translation, see Part Two, Box 9, pp. 261–4. Also note the inconsistencies in spelling postpositions (as separate words appended to the words they follow).

40. Balaji, 1918, '*Hindī meṅ striyoṅ ke yogya sāhitya*' [Suitable literature for women in Hindi]), *Stri Darpan* (November): 246.

41. *Grihalakshmi* (September/October 1917 [Āśvin 1974]): 290.

42. Ibid.

43. Anon., 1920, '*Pustakālocanā*' [Book review], *Stri Darpan* (January): 51.

44. Ibid.

45. Anon., 1918, '*Samālocanā*' [Review], *Stri Darpan* (September): 168.

46. Paṅjāb meṅ paṅjābī bolī jātī hai aur yukt prānt, madhyapradeś aur bihār meṅ hindī, baṅgāl meṅ baṅgālī, madrās meṅ tāmil tilagu aur bambaī meṅ marāṭhī tathā gujarātī. Hindī aisī bhāṣā hai jise sab samajh sakte haiṅ. Kisī zamāne meṅ saṅskṛt sāre bhāratvarṣ kī ek bhāṣā thī. [...] Ājkal hindī bhārat kī rāṣṭrabhāṣā hai. Jo bhāṣā sāre deś meṅ samjhī aur bolī jā saktī hai use rāṣṭrabhāṣā kahte haiṅ. Uske dvārā deś ke sab bhāī

bahanoṅ meṅ ektā rahtī hai. Bhāratvarṣ meṅ aisī bhāṣā hindī hī hai. (Shiv, 1927, '*Deś kī bāt*' [Matters of the country], *Khilauna* [June]: 190–1)

47. 'Kyā hindī hī rāṣṭra bhāṣā banne kī yogyatā rakhtī hai?' (R. Nehru, 1918, '*Sampādakīya: rāṣṭra-bhāṣā Hindī*' [Editorial: Hindi, the national language], *Stri Darpan* [July]: 6).

48. She did so in Sanskritized Khaṛī Bolī Hindi without Urdu words (tatsama words are italicized): 'Acchī bāt hai, hamārī bhī apne *pāṭhak pāṭhikāoṅ* se *prārthnā* hai ki ve *śīghra* is *viṣay* meṅ hamāre pās apnī *sammati* bhej dene kī *kṛpā* kareṅ' (Ibid.). I have been unable to locate the responses in the subsequent issues.

49. R. Nehru, 1918, '*Sampādakīya: rāṣṭra-bhāṣā Hindī*' [Editorial: Hindi, the national language], *Stri Darpan* (October): 169–70. Tatsama words are italicized; Urdu words are in bold.

50. *Chand*, however, published an Urdu edition in the 1930s (Schomer 1983: 224).

51. R. Nehru, 1918, '*Sampādakīya: rāṣṭra-bhāṣā Hindī*' [Editorial: Hindi, the national language], *Stri Darpan* (October): 170.

52. Sanskritization was also observed in Dravidian languages of the south, as well as Bengali, Gujarati, and (Arya Samaj) Punjabi. The extent to which loanwords from Persian and Arabic were replaced with tatsama words varied (Rai 2001: 55, 77).

53. Jagdishprasad Mishra, 1920, '*Pañjāb prānt meṅ devanāgarī kī āvaśyaktā*' [The necessity of Deva Nāgarī in Punjab], *Stri Darpan* (April): 197.

54. Babu Navinchandra Rai of Lahore published the Hindi periodical *Jyanpradayini Patrika* (Periodical for the Increase of Knowledge), a bilingual in Hindi and Urdu as early as as 1866/7. It dropped its Urdu sections in 1868 (Stark 2000: 39).

55. Jagdishprasad Mishra, 1920, '*Pañjāb prānt meṅ devanāgarī kī āvaśyaktā*' [The necessity of Deva Nāgarī in Punjab], *Stri Darpan* (April): 198.

56. For example, see *Jyoti*, December 1921: 396.

57. Vidyavati Seth, 1921, '*Vicār pravāh: Hindī Sāhitya Sammelan*', *Jyoti* (November/December [Mārgśīrṣ 1978]): 431.

58. R. Nehru, 1920, Untitled editorial comment, *Stri Darpan* (February): 113.

59. Ibid.: 114.

60. Occasionally, contributors to women's periodicals apologized at the beginning of their articles for possible mistakes (for example, incorrect choice of grammatical gender and/or case).

6 Conclusion

If it is generally true that writing is an exercise in self-representation and self-transformation (Foucault 1997), Hindi women's periodicals are an example of how questions of representation and transformation were generated through a collective effort of publishing in the Hindi literary world of the early twentieth century. At once self-revelatory (writing as a mirror and means of seeing) and self-consciously public, the contributors' self-reflexivity produced new role models for women and men that absorbed nationalist demands of the time.

Hindi women's periodicals effectively confronted mainstream and male-dominated political discourse. Their contributors, women and men alike, carved out new individual, social, *and political*, as well as linguistic identities and staked a claim on the nation's imagined future, keying the readers into a nationalist struggle that was already invested with a historical consciousness that penetrated deep into the past. By the 1930s, women's periodicals helped to institutionalize a broad journalistic network of editors and writers who played a major role in nation building before and after Independence. Girls' and children's periodicals also articulated a new language of politicization and emancipation for the citizen-subject-to-be.

Drawing on my initial encounter with the Hindi literary archives, I began by asking in this work in what ways the women's periodicals were to be considered 'real literature'. I have demonstrated that literary tastes, styles, and the creative exploration of different literary genres were constitutive of the periodicals, notwithstanding limitations in literary scope, if compared with mainstream Hindi literary publications. Not only did periodical editors, readers, and writers engage with an expanding body of fictional writing; by experimenting with what the women's periodical as a genre had to offer, they played an important role in community formation. The different texts encountered in the periodical—essays, biographies, poetry, fiction, letters to the editor, advice—made it possible to evolve a particular ('female') consciousness for married and unmarried women, as well as girls in particular, through a diversity of genres.

Through the interactions with mainstream political, colonial, and literary discourses, from which at those times many of the writers were physically excluded, women's and girls' periodicals formed a discursive field of relations in which different political, historical, and religious texts reached the dispersed readership in domestic settings. Women's and girls' periodicals also became a site of exposing and questioning ideologies. They offered themselves to go beyond existing literary conventions and to create new literary frameworks. The combination of exhortatory and fictional sections in the periodical genre, for example, was central to the occurring literary shift of domestic advice for women to a refashioning of the domestic sphere and public world created by women and men. The home and the world, as the novel of the same name by Rabindranath Tagore (2005 [1916]) suggests, were inextricably linked in literary and political discourses. In a similar way, experimentations with the letter genre made women's private concerns public. A community of readers became part of these developments.

Print media constituted a new communicative medium with far-reaching implications for the way in which the Indian public sphere was shaped, even if this happened in close interaction with more traditional forms of cultural performances glossed under the rubric of public arena (Freitag 1991). The vernacular press not only intensified reporting about nationalist developments, which reached literate and illiterate audiences throughout the Indian subcontinent; print media also had a constitutive effect on women's and girls' identity discourses. The texts analysed in this book illustrate that despite nationalism's stronghold on the woman question, the contributors to women's and girls' periodicals entertained a more differentiated understanding of female roles in society. Joining the effort to mobilize women for the Indian independence struggle, they at the same time subverted the predominant 'discourse of women's salvation' that had informed social-reformist writings (speaking *for* woman, defining what was good for her) and the nationalist agenda (woman as emblematic of tradition). In the periodicals, we find the pointed rhetoric of shame and blame to be directed at those who were held responsible for the plight of women as well as the appeal to common sense and sympathy for those in need. Most important was the plea that women awaken and liberate themselves. Women, in their writings, collapsed gender roles and notions of gendered spaces in order to emerge in a political sphere, sometimes even in order to save men. This action, however, could be considered compatible with other domestic responsibilities of women in their roles as mothers and wives.

Hindi women's periodicals were widely read even beyond the Hindi-speaking belt. The editors applauded submissions in Hindi by non-professional authors, especially by women or by people from regions outside the United Provinces. Their contributions were read as a sign of their love for the Hindi language; as complementing the existing literary canon, and not a distortion thereof. Hindi as it was envisioned in the women's periodicals linked the language of women to the public sphere, thus creating a Hindi that might not have found entry to the national literary canon, but that was equally formative for the development of Hindi as a national language and, even more so, the lingua franca. The Hindi literati's efforts to fashion a new collective identity by standardizing and nationalizing language and literature is thus only one side of the story of the Hindi movement.

The women's periodicals mirrored its middle-class-readers' and contributors' endeavour to distinguish themselves from members of folk and rural communities, lower classes, and different religious communities. This is most visible not in what was present in women's periodicals, but rather in that which was absent: texts on sexuality or obscenity were virtually absent, distinguishing the periodicals from commercially popular but licentious literature and romances. Even the fictional sections that depicted everyday life realities of women did not depict scenes in which women interacted with people from the service sector (such as washer-men and women, sweepers, greengrocers and street vendors), who were marked through gender, class, and religious associations. Muslim culture and Muslim authors were virtually absent from the women's periodicals' fictional sections, as was news coverage on social reform that pertained specifically to Muslim communities and the establishment of educational institutions explicitly marked as Islamic, even though the political sections in women's periodicals recognized, and also problematized, the vexed issue of religious identity and communalism. Despite this absence, it must be noted that the women's periodicals also did not emphasize the readers' Hindu identity. Neither was the Muslim woman (or man) projected or even discriminated against as the inferior 'other', as was the case in other popular Hindi literature at the time that used gendered imagery as a critical marker to emphasize superiority over Muslims (Gupta 2001). In this sense, we can say that gender trumped communalist discourses, but notions of sisterhood were by default Hindu.

Many contributors had recognized the empowering potential of nationalism as a political movement. They were appreciative of women's new politicized roles that ranged from performing the domestic duties of the reformed mother, wife, and householder, to employment in the public sphere as teachers, publicists, directors of social institutions, politicians, writers, and editors. Even though the 'ideal' woman of the middle-class imagination may have been a domestic one, alternatives to conjugal life were normalized in women's periodicals. Many contributors, though supportive of the nationalist movement, also came to the conclusion that social reforms propelled by men required a new, feminist, orientation. Hence, the oft-encountered demand by nationalist politicians that women sacrifice their individuality for the well-being of the family, society, and nation underwent a critical investigation. Central to the women's periodicals was the question how women as individuals *and* members of a political community could live meaningful lives as women and citizens.

After Indian Independence, the majority of Indian women's periodicals lost their provocative tone, as well as innovative literary writing and became exclusively domestic in scope (Orsini 1999b: 137). The majority of mainstream women's periodicals today conform to patriarchal desires of domesticity and global beauty ideals of middle-class culture. A global orientation towards consumerism, fashion, body-cult, and middle-class culture has set a new trend in women's periodicals, which are increasingly also being published in English.[1] Gender identities are thus still being staked out in different ways, sometimes orientated more internationally and at other times locally, and still, in some instances, adhering to ideologies projected as ancient and traditional. There also exist a few vernacular women's periodicals that follow the trajectory of women's periodicals from the early twentieth century, attempting to stake a feminist-nationalist identity that aligns political and social demands. They incorporate features of the global women's movement as well as the immediate concerns of Indian rural and urban women in a rather critical fashion. With the advent of representations of women's activism on the World Wide Web, new forms of dissemination into a virtual world have emerged. The accessibility to such information for a selected audience in the western world expresses a new form of connectedness and community formation that may or may not remain in touch with respective local realities. Of course this interaction poses a whole new set of questions concerning women's social and political mobilization.

Note

1. Such periodicals can be bought at newspaper stands, as can *Grihalakshmi*, a 'new' Hindi women's journal, or publications of the Gita Press that recuperate 'traditional' ideals of Indian womanhood.

Part Two

A Reader

In what follows, I describe the genres featured within the pages of women's periodicals. For this purpose, I have selected a number of examples from a pool of texts from different women's periodicals.

FIGURE 27(a) *Jyoti* frontispiece (*Jyoti*, January 1922)

FIGURE 27(b) *Jyoti* frontispiece (*Jyoti*, September 1922)

Figures 27 (a) and (b): Frontispieces of Jyoti *in January 1922 and September 1922, respectively. Women's periodicals were open to constant revision and experimentation.* Jyoti *changed its frontispiece within months.*

FIGURE 28(a) *Grihalakshmi* frontispiece (*Grihalakshmi*, May/June 1913 [Jyeṣṭ 1970])

FIGURE 28(b) *Grihalakshmi* frontispiece (*Grihalakshmi*, April/May 1914 [Vaiśākh 1971])

Figures 28 (a) and (b): Frontispieces of Grihalakshmi *in Jyeṣṭ 1970 (May/June 1913) and in Vaiśākh 1971 (April/May 1914).* Grihalakshmi *changed its frontispiece within months from the depiction of the individually reading woman to that of the mother surrounded by children and householder (for a discussion see pp. 49–54).*

Each periodical issue was written for a specific span of time (most commonly fortnightly, monthly, or tri-monthly), which was the most significant characteristic of the genre. It generally appeared as a handy booklet, measuring approximately four inches by six inches, printed on good quality paper. Women's periodicals differed in quality and durability from pamphlets and manuals that were lithographed (and not printed) on much thinner paper. Still, they were affordable for the growing number of the upper and middle classes.[1]

Generally, a monthly periodical issue (*aṇk*) was part of a volume (*bhāg*) that consisted of six consecutive months. Accordingly, the issues were collected, bound, and numbered in a six-month span and supplied with a table of contents. The periodicals that I have consulted follow this structure rather meticulously. They rely upon two calendars, the Gregorian and the Vikram Samvat calendar, the latter following a hybrid soli-lunar system beginning with the coronation of King Vikramaditya as emperor of Ujjain in the year 57 BCE. Arguably, the periodicals that focused on traditional, religious, and spiritual aspects chose the indigenous calendar (*Arya Mahila*, *Grihalakshmi*, *Vanita Vinod*), whereas those that claimed to have a more western-oriented outlook chose the Gregorian calendar (*Stri Darpan*, *Kumari Darpan*, *Chand*).[2] Some periodicals listed the dates of both calendars (*Jyoti*, *Madhuri*, *Kanya Manoranjan*). The periodicals were said to have appeared on either the first or the fifteenth day of the month and they were distributed by mail. Subscription rates generally included postal delivery.

Hindi women's periodicals carried many regular features and columns, which can be arranged into ten main divisions. This categorization is not exhaustive. It stems from arrangements within the women's periodicals and the special rubrics in the index of the bound volumes that were added at some later point.[3] As periodical columns were being created and tested out, those that first appeared as loose articles could be turned into a regularly appearing literary category. Such is the case for columns on music, recipes, and essays on social awakening. Amongst the regular and most frequent columns were the following ten: (i) editorials with news items and commentary, (ii) readers' letters, (iii) reviews of books, manuals, and periodicals, (iv) essays, that are subdivided into essays on social reform and nationalism featuring in particular the woman question as well as essays on virtue and morality, (v) reprinted speeches, (vi) advice texts on the proper management of the home and family care (including cooking, health, and hygiene), (vii) (auto)biographical accounts, (viii) fiction, (ix) poetry, and (x) advertisements. All contributions were in Hindi. They had either been primary publications or were reprinted from other sources such as periodicals and advice manuals. There were also translations from English and other Indian languages, especially in the prose and poetry sections. In the following pages, I describe each column and provide examples translated directly from the original sources.

Editorials and Readers' Letters

The editorial was titled *sampādakīya* (editorial) or *ṭippaniyāṅ* (notes). It appeared under different sub-titles, such as *sampādakīya vicār* (editorial commentary), *sūcnā* ([editorial] news), *samācār* (news), *cune huye samācār* (selected news), *naī bāteṅ* (curiosities), *tāze hāl* (current news), *sāhitya kṣetra* (literary field [but mostly consisting of scientific news]), noṭs (notes), and *phuṭkar samācār* (miscellaneous items). Book reviews (*samālocanā*), letters to the editor (*ciṭṭhī patrī*), and a rubric under which women's graduates and donors were acknowledged and obituaries were announced (*badhāī*) were either part of the editorial or appeared in separate columns. The editorial was found at the beginning or at the end of each periodical issue.

The editorials covered topics directed specifically at women. This could be news, essays, and opinion pieces about individual women's achievements in society and politics and about the establishments and accomplishments of women's organizations in the locality, in different provinces and around the world. The editorials also drew their information from other mainstream periodicals when discussing topics around social reform and nationalism. They often reprinted speeches delivered by women at public events as well as letters addressed to the readers of the periodical. Apart from news and commentary, editorial matters were also handled in this section.

Without downplaying the authoritative role of an editor in the making and shaping of a periodical, it needs to be pointed out that many editors conceptualized women's periodicals as a discursive field and broke down the hierarchal distance between readers, writers, and the editor. Considering the diversity of the contributions within one editorial framework, it can be inferred that the editors neither dictated nor eliminated content that did not correspond to one single editorial opinion or even literary style. On the contrary, they encouraged readers' participation and involvement in the shaping of the periodical by inviting them to share opinions even when these were controversial or poorly written, to participate in essay competitions, to submit articles, to contribute to special issues, as well as to send in suggestions regarding the format of the periodical and other types of comments and news.

A 'typical' editorial as it covered topics related to domesticity in its diverse manifestations is that of *Grihalakshmi* (Box 2, pp. 245–9). A demonstration of the editorial voice is the editors' response to a letter from 'an unmarried young woman' who is in love with a married man (Box 3, pp. 249–50; see the discussion of this response in Chapter Four, pp. 161–3). Another editorial lists the topics of the annual convention of the Hindī Sāhitya Sammelan along with a call for papers (Box 4, pp. 250–1).

Box 2 Editorial[4]

Today, the editor of *Grihalakshmi* places a request before her sisters and hopes that they all will heed to it. Papers and periodicals generally publish photographs of women and men. It is the editor's opinion that *Grihalakshmi* should carry photographs of the future generation. If all sisters send in *photos* of their little boys and girls, these photographs will be published in *Grihalakshmi*. If possible, a few matters should be kept in mind at the time of sending the *photo*. At the time of taking the photograph, much jewellery should not be worn. It is by now well known that the natural beauty bestowed upon us by god is not increased by jewellery and expensive clothes, but diminished. Children appear beautiful and adorned in their natural state as in no other state. Along with the *photo* there should be mention of the child's name, age and the names of mother or father. I am fully convinced that everyone will be pleased upon seeing the photographs of these delicate and pure beauties and I am full of hope that from amongst these children there will be some worthy and dutiful ones who will bring glory and splendour to their families. And the day will come when their photographs will be published in papers all over India. When this comes true, the first image that was published in *Grihalakshmi* will become very important. It is my hope that my fellow sisters—if it is not too inconvenient—will soon heed my request.

***

(Contd)

Śrīkhaṇḍ[5] is the name of a sweet dish that is prepared in all parts of *Bhāratvarṣ*. Will one of our sisters who is well-versed in the art of cooking be so kind and send us the recipe for preparing *śrīkhaṇḍ*? The recipe that reaches us first will be published in *Grihalakshmi*.

***

We wish to hand out awards to the female readers of *Grihalakshmi* who have submitted articles and who are between the ages of ten and sixteen. Girls tell stories in many ways. They should send their very best story in neat handwriting, single sided and with wide margins to us. The best story will receive a sari worth four rupees as a present. If the girl prefers cash, she will be sent a money order of four rupees. The article should arrive before 13 July. It should be sent to our address.

Editor, Essay Award Bureau
Grihalakshmi Office
Allahabad

***

Many articles of women (and also of men) reach us in such clumsy handwriting that they are not legible. This is why those who wish to get published in *Grihalakshmi* should heed the following advice:

1. The characters should be clear and not too small.
2. Between the lines there should be space of a finger's breadth.
3. The page should be written on single side, not on both sides.

***

In a previous issue of *Grihalakshmi*, there was an article by [Mrs] 'Chauban' titled 'The fate of sensuous women and the supreme husband'. In this article 'Chauban-ji complains that everyone suggests that women should accept their dependency upon men and that they should make it the highest principle for a woman to become a *pativratā* [a faithful and devoted wife], but that nobody makes even a sound upon seeing the daily atrocities inflicted upon women by men. We have received several submissions in response to this article claiming that upon reading Chauban-ji's article, the minds of less-educated and less-intelligent women will become even more uncertain. There is not sufficient space to print all these response-articles in our small *Grihalakshmi*, which is why we are offering our readers our own commentary on this matter.

The *shastras* have instructions for women's righteous behaviour before men, just as they lay out instructions for men's responsibilities in front of women. There are women who have been educated and stop adhering to

(Contd)

the orders of their husbands, just as nowadays there are men who have turned arrogant from their education and forgotten the wisdom of the home or never even learnt about it. They follow the western example and are forgetting their own customs and dharma. Uneducated men or men who don't know anything about their dharma inflict random atrocities upon their women. All the vices and bad practices that are nowadays to be observed in our society are not injunctions from the shastras. But there is certainly agreement that as a boy with lack of knowledge is dependent on his parents and a people is dependent on the king there is something good about a woman being dependent on a man. When the child has received education, when he matures and brings honour to the family and country, everyone will sing his praise. In the same manner the glory of women will be freely sung, once women perform noteworthy deeds. No woman of any country has acquired the reputation of being a more faithful and devoted woman as our Indian women have. We wish that the high status and pride of our Hindu women may never be broken. Woman and man, both have to be determined to abide by their dharma. Respect is obtained only from righteousness. But if any woman or man forgets about the ideal, and does not live up to dharma and instead breaks into unlawfulness, what should be done? Society will never take an unjust person as an ideal and will never show respect towards him, but only blame. This is the blame that Chauban-ji has for unrighteous men; in our understanding her aim is not about making men dependent or not. True, the worry that uneducated women may misinterpret her article, is not without reason.

***

The topic of women's education is very important. For *Bhāratvarṣ* only Indian education will be suitable. The bad practices that have nowadays befallen the country come from ignorance of our dharma. To avoid ignorance, please read about dharma. Women should adhere to their dharma and men should live up to their responsibilities. Both wheels of the cart need to function properly, otherwise one will be in brilliant and splendid condition [lit. purified] and the other will remain under the dark veil of ignorance. Then, yes then, nothing will ever be achieved.

***

Here, whenever Chaitu's mother cleans the pots, she uses ash and dirt. This is the custom of old India and it is possible that throughout India, pots are cleaned with this precious mixture. But the west is well civilized, all there is new and magnificent; all customs there are modern and the

(Contd)

mixtures for cleaning pots are also remarkable. Ash and dirt do not cost any money, but if it has to be western scrubbing agent for brass and copper pots, high expenses occur. Listen, here is the composition of 'globe polish', the name of the western mixture at the price of two pennies per tin:

An eggshell full of turpentine
An eggshell full of ammonium chloride
An eggshell full of paraffin

Mix these all and store them in a bottle with a wide bottleneck. It is applied on to the pots with a piece of flannel. After rubbing the mixture on to the pots it is polished with a soft cloth. That's it; the pots are clean in an instant without any hassle.

(***)

Apply kerosene on to rusty iron-pots and, after a while, scrub them in the Indian manner with ash. The rust will come off and the iron will be clean again. We have tried it out and it works.

(***)

But this is not the English way of cleaning iron and tin pots. Over there, the following mixture is used for heavy metal and tin pots:

Half a *ser*[6] soft soap
Half a ser sparkling sand—(cream-coloured or silver)
Half a ser whitening
One and a half ser water

All is mixed and boiled over fire in a pot, then, before it sticks to the pot it can be used at its best. Such pots can also be cleaned with baking soda and hot water, but baking soda is not recommended for enamel pots.

***

It is not my intention to suggest that we abandon our old Indian customs in favour of those from the west. Our old Indian customs are very good and even Chaitu's mother who chatters much is very good; may the ash of our clay ovens remain changeless and immortal. But it is good for everybody to stay informed about the customs of different countries as sometimes this can be of advantage. Just as English *grihalakshmi*s make use of baking soda, potash, or alkali, our ash also contains the qualities of potash and alkali. In our country, our old customs are very beneficial. Western pots are often too sensitive for Chaitu's mother. She cannot appreciate them well enough as they will break once she takes them into her hands. In this manner, her ways of cleaning are different. And the west also does not

(Contd)

know untouchability. Over there, pots need not be cleaned a second time after being brought into the cooking area.

***

Speaking of untouchability another thought has come to my mind regarding different and distinct customs of India. There is plenty of water in Bengal. Over there, the pots are kept like ducks in water. Describing it in this manner is not improper. Pots are soaked in lakes before being cleaned. But there is water shortage in Rajputana. There, we encounter the custom of cleaning without water (*sukhmaṇjan*). Cleaning with water is considered impure and the pots are cleaned by scrubbing ash and sand on to them. Restrictions around purity vary in the different regions of India: what might be considered impure by some might precisely be considered pure by the inhabitants of another province. Man is the slave of his customs and habits.

Box 3 Conversation with Girls[7]

'An unmarried young woman' aged twenty-one intends to marry a married man. His wife agrees to this new relationship, but the girl's parents strongly object. This is why the girl is asking for our advice on what to do.

First of all, we are of the opinion that no man has the right to marry a second time as long as his first wife is alive. A marriage, in our opinion, is when a man and a woman who are in love agree to spend life with all its challenges together; it is not to satisfy one's desire. This is why it is not acceptable to exchange one woman for another. This would render us alike with animals. Second, if that man no longer loves his first wife and has instead fallen in love with you, there is no guarantee that a couple of years into the marriage he will still love you. Who can trust such an irresolute man who wants to marry another woman while his first woman is yet alive?

Your father has understood the problem and wants to prevent that this happens to you. No parent would want to see her/his child in distress. They have experience of life; they have seen the world and know that young people, deluded by the idea of love, do things that they regret once they come back to their senses. Keep in mind that those who are trying to stop you are doing this for your sake. Consider all of this and abandon your idea of marrying this married man. [...]

(Contd)

There remains your question whether or not to marry at all, and whether to marry the man whom your father has chosen for you. You will first have to settle in your mind whether you at all wish to marry and whether you think that the groom your father has chosen is suitable, educated and a gentleman. If yes, go ahead and marry him. Forget about the married man. If you do not want to marry right now, then wait for a couple of years. There is no hurry. Tell your father that you will not marry right now. The future will bring a solution and if you wish to remain unmarried there is no harm in that either. Marriage is not the sole purpose in the life of a woman. Spend your time in the service of society. Do contemplate upon marrying or not marrying, but forget about marrying the married man.

Do write us when you have come to a decision about what to do.

Box 4 Editorial: Important Information[8]

Topics of the eighth Hindī Sāhitya Sammelan and a call for papers:

1. Retrospective of the Hindi world of literature in the past eight years.
2. The impact of English literature on Hindi literature.
3. Suitable literature for women in the Hindi language.
4. Suitable literature for children in the Hindi language.
5. Old and contemporary poetry in Hindi and literary criticism.
6. Secondary and higher education in the Hindi language.
7. The need for shared scientific and technical terms in the Indian languages.
8. Findings from the search for an Indian history.
9. Orthography in the Deva Nāgarī script: Thoughts on standardization of words such as *gaī* and *gayī, gae* and *gaye, huā* and *huyā, liye* and *lie, cahie* and *cahiye, nae* and *naye*.
10. The present state of Hindi in the Indian heartland.
11. Hindi in the princely states.
12. The need for Hindi universities.
13. Duties of the speakers of regional languages towards the promotion of Hindi as a national language.
14. Ways to promote the national language Hindi in Bengal, Madras, Maharashtra, Gujarat, and other provinces.
15. Political literature in Hindi.
16. Scientific literature in Hindi.

(Contd)

17. Spiritual literature in Hindi.
18. Is Urdu a language different from Hindi?
19. The old educational system in India.
20. Political administration in old India.
21. Sūrdās.
22. Keśavadās.
23. Bīhārīlāl.
24. The language of the Buddhist era.
25. The rise of mathematics of the old Bhārat dwellers and its didactic methods.
26. Indian and western drama.
27. Philosophical animism and Dr Yosh's invention.

Readers' letters published in women's periodicals attest to new ways of written expression. For one, they enabled readers to share their opinions on contributions from previous issues, which allowed for lively discussion. In the *ciṭṭhī patrī* (letters) columns of *Stri Darpan*, *Kumari Darpan*, *Grihalakshmi*, and *Chand*, married and unmarried women took readers into confidence about their personal plights. They were aware of the intricacies of this column as they were sharing confidential issues with a large audience, including men. Such letters were not always personally signed; it was common to use pseudonyms such as 'unfortunate girl' (*abhāgin kumārī*), 'patriot' (*deśbhakt*), or 'well wisher' (*deśhitaiśī*). The letters were about love and conjugality, which made it necessary for the editors to address questions of illegitimate love relationships, inter-caste marriage, divorce, and even suicidal thoughts. They not only provided a platform on which women could express their feelings, worries, and doubts (Orsini 2002: 274), but were also used to contest social taboos. The anticipatory and responsive facet of genre production that Bakhtin (1986) has pointed to in his discussion of speech genres is thus also worth considering with regard to a seemingly small and unpretentious column such as the letter column in women's periodicals, for it was at such places that women incorporated and created new ways of literary expression.[9]

As Shevelow (1989: 43) has shown with regard to British periodicals, audience engagement represented 'an attempt [of the editors] to establish a continuity between readers' lives and the medium of print, between extra-textual experience and textual expression'. In this sense, readers' letters provided individual feedback for the editors and other readers. Of course it is not absolutely certain that readers' contributions were written by the female readers of the periodicals and not by the editorial team or female impersonators. Dalmia (1997: 262) has shown that the editorial board lead by Bharatendu Harishchandra in the late nineteenth century composed many such contributions as a means of continuing debates on a particular topic. Whether or not such was the case for women's periodicals of the early twentieth century, there are some points to be made when considering the authenticity of readers' letters: they represent a variety of opinions and cover a multiplicity of topics that fulfilled the purpose of triggering debate.

Readers' submissions were mostly signed and sometimes included the author's mailing address in anticipation of responses from other readers who wished to continue the discussion beyond the pages of the periodical. Also, the editors at times distanced themselves from the reader's submissions, stating that these did not necessarily reflect their opinions. This also held true for other submissions, which could be tagged with a footnote from the editors, such as a story in which a girl abandons her culture and religion as she falls in love with a Christian convert. The editor comments that it would be a fallacy to draw a connection between western education and the girl's death.[10]

Box 5 (pp. 252–3) is the opening paragraph of a reader's response to an essay that had appeared in a previous issue of the periodical. Box 6 (p. 253) is a reader's response to a reader's response about the supposed misinterpretation of a poem.

Box 5 Conjugal Love[11]

In the previous issue of *Stri Darpan* I read an essay titled '*Stri Dharma*'. There is no need to repeat the arguments of the essay as the readers will have very well understood them.

Now, I want to offer a response titled 'Conjugal Love' to the readers. It is my hope that the respected editor will grant the essay place in some corner of her periodical and thus fulfil my effort. I am not a writer and I have no accomplished writing skills; however, I have a certain objective that I am

(Contd)

placing in front of the reader. If the reader reflects only a little bit about my objective, I will consider my effort successful and be contented.

[There follows a five-page essay on conjugal love]

Box 6 My Opinion on Matters Related to *Stri-Dharma-Shikshak*[12]

—Rajbahadur

Śrīmatī Shail Kumari Devi beware.

The article that Śrīmatī Shail Kumari Devi has written about the paper *Stri-Dharma-Shikshak* in *Stri Darpan*'s past issue of 1 October 1917, has astonished and saddened me.

It is not my objective to write a defence of the paper *Stri-Dharma-Shikshak*. However, I also do not consider it appropriate that a paper may be destroyed in such a way. This is not appropriate for fine people and I do not wish to suggest that there are no faults in *Stri-Dharma-Shikshak*. It is also not my intention to offend Śrīmatī Shairl [sic] Kumari Devi, but her thoughts cannot be left uncommented upon. She has completely misinterpreted the poem written by Śrīmatī Govindi Devi from Moradabad. Truth is that this poem (parts of which are reprinted in *Stri Darpan*) is extremely well written. I am sorry to say that my sister was taken by rage and has defamed the editor of *Stri-Dharma-Shikshak*, as well as the esteemed author of the poem. I wonder what the reasons are?

[There follows a two-page interpretation of three stanzas of the poem]

Essays, Speeches, and Advice texts

Three- to six-page essays on topics that can be subsumed under the umbrella of the woman question as well as virtue and morality were in vogue in all women's periodicals. Often, they appeared under such headings as *strījagat* (woman's world), *strīsudhār* (woman's reforms), *strīśikṣā* (woman's education), *samājik samācār* (news pertaining to society), or simply *akhyāyikā* (report). They demonstrate that even in the period marked by nationalist discourse, articles on unresolved matters of social reform were a major thrust of women's periodicals. Women writers did not agree with supposed nationalist 'resolutions' of women's issues that, as Chatterjee (1989) describes them, relegated women's issues to an inner 'depoliticized' domain of sovereignty. To them each such issue was pressing and had to be discussed in public.[13]

Essays on virtue and morality were geared towards the improvement of character and conduct. They bear similarities to British Victorian behavioural texts while also drawing upon popular Sanskrit texts such as the *Hitopadesha* and the *Panchatantra*. The contributions generally condemned vice and singled out moral and virtuous behaviour. While stories and poems also highlighted virtues (see Box 21 'Grandmother's Stories: The Selling of a Virtue', pp. 302–5), moral essays focused primarily on one particular virtue, such as honesty, intelligence, contentment, and love. The texts were not solely geared towards women per se, even though virtuous behaviour such as being respectful, modest, humble, and polite was often described in specific gendered contexts. Friendship and companionship was held in high regard and women were encouraged to establish such relationships between women and with their husbands. This required that they be honest, intelligent, and capable of giving advice. Not only were women asked to be chaste and loyal towards their husbands (Box 7 'Chastity and Loyalty, the Prime Dharma of Women', pp. 255–7); men also had responsibilities towards women (Box 8 'A Husband's Duty Towards his Wife', pp. 257–61). Most of the virtues linked education and women's happiness. Wealth was defined as being blessed with education, wisdom, satisfaction, and gratitude, and not in material terms. The dangers of excess jewellery and indulging in foreign products was frequently highlighted. Several of the essays described the consequences of greed, jealousy, anger, bad habits, and laziness for a woman and her family. Women were also urged to be brave and courageous and to speak out against injustice. Other contributions in the periodical, most prominently fiction and advice literature, took the message of moral and virtue further by illustrating what it could mean for women to be virtuous (see Box 22 'Patni-vrata—Loyalty and Chastity Towards the Wife', pp. 306–10).

As the educational background of the contributors was diverse, the essays also differed in style and content. Some highlighted that they had been specifically written for publication in a women's periodical (Box 9 'Women and the Service of Literature', pp. 261–4). Readers also contributed essays and launched new debates or participated in raging ones (Box 10 'The Atrocities of Men over Women' pp. 264–6). Furthermore, essays could be part of an exchange between writers and readers, such as the one on women's responsibility for food preparation (Box 11 'Why Women Should Prepare the Food with their Own Hands', pp. 267–9).

Box 7 Chastity and Loyalty, the Prime Dharma of Women[14]

—Ambikaprasad Shukla[+]

Generally, women are primarily devoted to all worldly customs—dharma, karma, and *vrata* [ritual fasting]. But according to the principles of the *shastric* texts and the sayings of sages and wise men, there is no dharma for a woman other than her husband, because the word *pati* [husband] in itself means nurturer, progenitor, and destiny. It is written in the *shastra* that a woman's god is none other than her husband. Brahma, Vishnu, and Mahesh, all dwell within the husband's body. Worship of the gods, fasting, charity, austerity, reciting passages from religious scriptures, bathing, pilgrimages, hospitality towards guests, and initiation into all the rituals and other grand virtues are considered the sixteenth part of *patiseva.* There is no better dharma than thriving on patiseva. The happiness of a woman who is not dear to her husband is of no use. Eating, drinking, sleeping, and other pleasures, in short, life itself becomes useless for a woman. A woman who does not love her husband is born into the world without a purpose. If amongst all her loved ones she does not most love her husband, then even her love for her mother, father, son, relatives, wealth, youthfulness, etc., is useless and in vain. The consorts of the gods sit on their vehicles and sing of the virtues of India's faithful wives. They happily distribute their blessings to increase the fortune of faithful wives and condemn and curse those who do not love their husbands. Be it the father, son, brother or any other relative, nobody should be dearer to a wife than her husband. A virtuous task turns into its opposite, that is, a vice if a woman performs it without receiving the order to do so from her husband. A woman who neglects to serve her husband in order to perform service or a fast in honour of the gods, only diminishes the life-force of her husband, because he is her mainstay. A woman does not even need to bathe;* the braid of a woman whose husband is alive is like the confluence of the three rivers Ganges, Yamuna, and Saraswati. Therefore, a woman can simply bathe in the waters of love for the husband. It is appropriate that a woman offer her body, mind, and wealth only to her husband. God in his grace decreed that a husband embodies god and that a woman who is faithful and devoted embodies Lakshmi. Regardless of the enmity towards a man, a woman without a husband is not useful

(Contd)

for any virtuous thing. Ill-tempered, unfortunate, evil, inert, diseased, or poor, whatever the characteristics of a husband may be, the wife must respect and serve him. She must serve him continuously and with a clear conscience. A devoted and faithful wife is sad when her husband is sad and she is happy when her husband is happy. When the husband is not at home she is weakened by his absence and suffers the anguish of separation. She falls asleep only after her husband, eats after he has, and wakes before him. She is silent when he is, she sits with her husband only when he tells her to and gets up once he has done so. When her husband asks something she speaks with the uttermost courtesy. She looks at none else than her husband. From the deepest part of her heart she loves her husband and always follows his supreme order. She takes care of her husband, worries about him, and does everything to please him.

She does not go out to attend musical or dance performances, or other respectable events without him and does not even desire to do so. Whatever she may be doing—bathing, eating, applying make-up, doing her hair, etc.—she will always focus her attention onto the husband. When she performs her offerings to the gods, her feelings are meant only for her husband. Her eyes, ears, hands and feet, and all other parts of her body are put to use only for him. She always looks in the direction of the husband's face and only feels happiness upon the sight of the husband's face. A chaste, faithful and loyal woman, she is devoted to her husband for her steps purify the earth and both families.

[There follow verses in Braj Bhāṣā from Tulsidas' *Ramcharitmanas*]

If women want to obtain happiness they also need to pay attention to the following:

(i) It is appropriate for women that they *immediately* do what their husband tells them to do. They should abandon whatever important thing they might be doing at that time, and immediately begin doing what their husband tells them to do. They should continue doing it until their husband tells them otherwise. If the work that the husband has ordered to do is not that pressing, he will himself say that it is fine to first complete what the woman was doing and to do the other thing afterwards.

(ii) If the husband is upset for some reason and speaks harsh words or abuses her in anger, it is appropriate for the woman to be upset about this and to condemn it, but she should not show her anger or fear in front of the husband. Rather, in that moment she should fill her heart with happiness and tolerate him and when she notices

(Contd)

that her husband is calming down and he appears happy again, she may say the proper and improper thoughts that she has to say in a humble and polite voice. Doing so, will make the husband himself feel ashamed about any lapses that may have happened in his state of anger and ignorance and he will always remember the effect of your sweet voice.

(iii) This topic has been printed in a previous issue of *Grihalakshmi* and I direct the readers' attention to it once again. It is appropriate for women that they never do anything that is against the orders of the husband. This goes to the extent that she should not obey her mother, father, and relatives such as younger and older brothers-in-law if their orders are contrary to those of the husband.

[The following remark at the end of the page is hardly legible and had to partly be pieced together.]

⁺ I am not worthy of imparting anybody with wisdom through my article, because many of my mothers and sisters are themselves educated. But along with the above points, it has to be stressed that whatever needs to be done cannot be completed by simply reading about it. One cannot benefit simply by reading about something. It is as if somebody who is ill seeks remedies in a compendium. Without preparing these remedies, he will never find relief. Reading in order to seek advice is definitely required, but one must also act upon it or else no benefit can be obtained.

* The readers should not conclude that women do not ever need to bathe. The author's intention is to stress that worship of a husband is even more important than another essential task, such as bathing.

Box 8 A Husband's Duty towards his Wife[15]

—Vidyarthi Banvarilal Gupta

Nowadays it appears that people are astir and that in most papers and periodicals articles are being published about the need for women to be faithful and devoted, about their responsibilities towards their husbands, their dharma, their quotidian lives and their conduct with their husbands. With regret I must say that I have not seen a paper or periodical published on the responsibilities of husbands towards their wives. Whilst an article entitled 'men's treatment of women' was published in *Grihalakshmi* (Āṣāṛh 1971) by a gentleman named 'Gupta', the article was not satisfying because, apart from one perspective, there was no other

(Contd)

advice for men to understand and learn about their dharma. Reflecting on this, I decided to write this article. It is my hope that gentlemen readers will be able to get some instruction from it and make my efforts fruitful.

A woman is the Lakshmi of the home. Without her, a home is a wild place. She is the better half of a husband. Thus the husband must always treat her best. A home in which women are sorrowful will soon break into pieces. Property and wealth will soon be destroyed and the benediction (*kalyan*) ruined. The only foundation of a man's entire happiness is a woman. This is why a husband should always keep his wife, who cares for his wealth, happiness, lineage, and benediction, content by giving her food, ornaments, and clothes. The primary duties of a husband are to respect her in all possible ways, to protect her, to love her, to desire the best for her, to trust her, and much more. Even if she makes a mistake, he should never show disrespect or contempt. He should not consider her a slave, but rather the mistress of the home, a Lakshmi and a companion in crossing the ocean of the world. The primary dharma of a husband is to entrust his wife with tasks appropriate for her female energy (*śakti*) and not with tasks that require a lot of physical strength. In the same manner that a husband makes an effort to adorn his body and keep it contented, he should do the same for his wife, considering her to be his other half. For a man there is no greater friend than his wife, no other shelter than that provided by her, and no support in the world for religious fastidiousness like a woman. When the husband faces obstacles in the world, he may not recognize this, but the woman's qualities of patience, intelligence, courage, etc., that are hidden inside her manifest themselves and show her master the path of duty by granting him patience and courage. Such a virtuous and pleasurable better half, who shares her husband's happiness and grief, should therefore be kept happy. This is the prime dharma of a husband. Many ignorant men walk an untruthful path and give their wives cause for concern. By reflecting on the sins of such men, the chastity and virtuousness of women never decreases, but such sinful husbands will lose their wives due to their bad conduct and they will face much sorrow. The shastras say, 'where women are revered the gods dwell' [originally in Sanskrit].

This means that the gods enter the houses of women who are respected. However, where the floor of a house is soaked from the tears of a woman, all deeds remain unsuccessful. Only the radiant face of a woman can truly remove blindness from a home. Keeping such faces content and cheerful is the duty of all noble men, according to the scriptures. A man should truly

(Contd)

love his dutiful wife. She alone should mean the world to him. Regardless of whether she may be one-eyed, deaf, crippled, or ugly to look at, once the vow of marriage has been taken in front of Agnidev [the god of fire] and the priest, he should consider it his primary dharma to nourish her until the end of her life. For his entire life, a learned and noble man should never forget his matrimonial vow or even break it by desiring a woman other than his faithful wife. Just as a woman should be concerned only with her husband with regards to looks, virtue and comportment, the man should also be concerned only with his wife. Just as the shastras teach women about *pativrat-dharma*, they also instruct a man in being committed to *ek-patnivrat-dharma* [devotion and faithfulness to one wife only]. Just as women are instructed and urged to always walk with their husbands, husbands are also told to walk with their wives. A man who disregards this dharma and gives his wife needless sorrow will not be successful. Maharshi Markandeva says that Maharaj Vipashvita abandoned his wife for no reason, with the consequence that he had to endure the unbearable agony of hell.

A husband should always read his wife instructive stories when he has the time. He should arrange for her education, attempt to heed to what she has to say when it is appropriate, and he should love his offspring.

It has never served anybody when a man and woman quarrel. Woman is the essence and light of the world and the light disappears from the home when it is blown out. When wealth is destroyed only sorrow remains. Where quarrel persists, the gods leave and demons take their place. There is a saying that once a frightful demon named Vaksha asked the father of the world, Brahmaji, for a place to live. He asked, 'Where should I live?' Brahmaji said in response that he should live forever where there is quarrel between husband and wife. On the other hand, a woman who is nurtured and cherished takes on the form of a Lakshmi of the home, meaning that the wealth and good fortune of a family increases. On this topic, Maharshi Vyas has said, a nurtured and cherished housewife turns into the Lakshmi of the home [in Sanskrit]. Punishing her turns her into an enraged woman.

Whenever a lawfully married wife (*dharm-patnī*) has made a mistake, a husband should consider her to be a delicate woman and he should be the one to forgive her. He should instruct her on how to avoid the mistakes in future. What can be achieved with love can never be completed in fear. An English poet says—'Better to love by love than fear' [in English]. [The following two paragraphs are hardly legible]. This

(Contd)

means that love (*prīti*) emerging from love grows and not love emerging from fear.

This is why as far as is possible, love, instead of fear, should be considered of greatest merit, because the happiness that ensues from love is indescribable. Accordingly, a wise man should truly love the mistress of his house and thus fulfil the obligations of his dharma as a husband. Dear readers! Please remember that once a king was separated from his beloved Madalasa. In his grief, he began to search for her in different countries, religious sites, rivers, and mountains, always crying out 'Dear Madalasa, Madalasa! Dear Madalasa, Madalasa!!' He renounced food and drink and lived as a *yogi*. His parents presented him thousands of women, as virtuous as Madalasa, and asked if he would marry one of them, but he did not accept any of them. Only when, after encountering countless misfortunes, he finally found Madalasa, did he let go of his pledge as a yogi and started to eat and drink. Friends! Is it not your duty, according to the scriptures, to follow exactly your dharma as a husband and to meet your responsibilities and to always be faithful to your only wife, just as the aforementioned king? To cherish monogamy (*ek-patnī-vrat*) earns a man reputation and advancement, and will reform the world to come. This is why men need to always remember the vow given at the time of marriage, and cherish the bonds of true love to their devoted wives. They should never do anything that would be unjust to their wives. There is a saying that the master who respects his wife will always be held in high esteem and that is the way for him to experience complete happiness.

[...]

To keep one's wife uncivilized (*jaṅglī*) in this world or to molest her will render the entire family and country uncivilized and subjugated. Consider France, Germany, England, and other countries: men there cherish their dharma as husbands, and thus these countries are clearly at the pinnacle of progress. A wise person said that he is a beast who tells his wife that he brought her to serve him; and he is a true husband who includes his wife in his happiness and sorrow. That husband is a god who tells his mistress that he married her out of selfless love and in order to make her happy. Therefore a husband who holds to the highest standard should demonstrate selfless love towards his faithful wife, keep her content, consider her a blessing for his own family, and protect her purity.

Making a wife grieve destroys the peace of the home and sows the seed that will land the sons of the world's Lakshmis in hell, closing all the doors of men's progress, and also destroying the peace and prosperity of

(Contd)

the family. As food remains tasteless without salt, the world is devoid of flavour without women. The world can attain complete happiness only through its women. This is why an intelligent man should foster a trustful relationship with his faithful wife and keep her happy on all counts. For a man, this is the highest duty, and only if he completely cherishes his vow of monogamy and fulfils his duty, will the ancient beneficent state be re-established.

Gentlemen! If you ignore this article's shortcomings and take at least some instruction from it, I will consider my effort successful and I will promptly write another article for you. I now bid you goodbye.

Box 9 Women and the Service of Literature[16]

—Pandit Satyabhakt

The service of literature is one of the best and most meritorious tasks of humankind. Social work, teaching, moral-religious education, and the promotion of equity and moral conduct are considered a personal adornment. Those involved in these above-named activities are often described as charitable and noble, and are respected and venerated by the people at large; the same holds true for those involved in the service of literature. The service of literature benefits humankind immensely. Through literature, people enhance their knowledge and intellect, and their hearts become filled with joy. This is why a servant of literature is highly respected in the world. He holds an important and revered position. People consider him to be a national leader. One's character is also enhanced through the service of literature. Thus, man considers it very important to pursue and support such projects, and creates the best books and treatises possible for the benefit of the country as well as for his personal happiness.

Today, it is mostly men who undertake the service of literature: they compose various kinds of books and essays, edit periodicals and papers, and organize associations and societies to discuss literature. Only recently have women begun to participate in such activities, but now, they are also taking part in this virtuous task and their involvement is increasing steadily.

However, there is much disagreement amongst the public with regard to women serving literature. There is naturally no complaint from those who

(Contd)

believe in equality amongst women and men; they are delighted when they see women employing their right to participate in their literary pursuits. Amongst those who disagree, there are some who do not generally involve themselves in these debates. But there also exist a number of people who consider it extremely inappropriate for women to engage in the service of literature. In their opinion, women's education is entirely improper and harmful, and literature should be off-limits for them. According to these people, a woman should find satisfaction only in her household chores. They consider female participation in the male arena of literature and intellectual activities to be unequivocally improper and harmful.

But if we take a closer look at the opinions of such people, we will realize that these are the result of narrow-mindedness. Without knowledge, there would be no true humanity, nor accurate reflection upon religion and irreligion, nor upon the progress of the present world and the world thereafter. This is why the main reason for rendering service to literature is to obtain knowledge. This is an equal responsibility of both women and men. Certainly, the education for women and men differs, but it is nevertheless appropriate for Aryan women to engage in literary pursuits. What harm, after all, can occur through literature? What would be injurious about women creating literature? One should rather consider it a blessing for the language and literature of a country.

There is one more thing I wish to say: for women to be educated as servants to literature is not unprecedented. Women enjoyed this right in ancient times. To deny this right would insult those highly educated women and capable *devi*s who have always lived in India and other countries and who have already benefited the world through the creation of brilliant and sophisticated books. We have had Maitreyi, Gargi, Lilavati, Mandanmishra's wife and many other highly educated women rendering service to literature. It would be beyond this short essay to provide detailed accounts of these women, but in medieval times, too, there were learned women like Mirabai, Rani Bamkavati, Bibi Ratnakumari, Rani Pratapkumari, Chatrakumar Bai, and others, who very skilfully dipped into the ocean of Hindi poetry. Thus, to question the fact that women have served literature is unjustified and untruthful.

In this regard, the examples of England, America, and other European countries are remarkable. There, women do not lag behind men in the literary arena. They have composed many important works and are continuing to do so. The beauty and literary standard of their writing can only be found in the works of a few men. There exist thousands of

(Contd)

masterpieces written by women. Which learned mind is not forced to acknowledge the brilliance of Stowe's *Uncle Tom's Cabin*? The impact of this work was that it contributed to the abolition of slavery in America. Thousands of Negroes were freed from the claws of terrible slaveholders and they obtained independence. Even today, we find writers like Marie Corelli and Annie Besant, whose talents are exceptional.

Like Europe and America, Asia too, has its share of women writers. Since ancient times, Japanese women have served literature and are continuing to do so. Even China does not lack women writers, nor do Muslim countries such as Iran. Many women of these countries study and serve literature, and thus benefit their countries.

Women's education on moral-religious matters has long been common in India, but gradually this custom has declined. It is for this reason that we now lack educated women. But contemporary India can no longer remain unaffected by the rapid winds of change. For the past fifty to one hundred years women have begun to receive more modern education. Even though this education is still imperfect and can cause much harm, it is extremely necessary for this country and society to research it further. Furthermore, there is no doubt that this new education has produced many learned women. Women have contributed significantly to literature given their limited capabilities. As far as I know, the number of educated women is the highest in Bengal and, accordingly, in no other province of India do we find such capable women writers.

An investigation of the contemporary literature in all the provinces of India reveals that women are in one capacity or another part of the production of literature in Bengali, Marathi, Gujarati, and in the languages of other provinces. In the motherland of the national language Hindi, the United Provinces, Rajputana, and Madhya Pradesh, women lag the furthest behind in literary production. Perhaps there does exist excellent and meritorious works of Hindi literature by women we are not aware of. In our United Provinces, Rajputana, and other provinces, there is an enormous lack of education, especially of the higher education of Aryan women. In addition, the custom of purdah remains very common. Therefore, one hardly even hears the name of a female writer. The few Hindi books like *Kusum-Saṅgrah*, *Vaijñānik Kheti*, *Rājyog*, *Bhaktiyog* are all written by Bengali women. Is this not a shame? Even the women who give speeches and write essays at our literary assemblies are generally Bengali, Marathi, or Gujarati. As a matter of fact, this Province will never be praiseworthy or worth mentioning if the women of the United Provinces

(Contd)

pay no attention towards the sacred task of serving literature. The women of the Hindi-speaking provinces should engage in literary pursuits and promote the Hindi language. Hopefully, this province will then no longer lag behind and, like other provinces, will produce capable female writers who render service to their mother tongue. This will be of advantage to the common people.

Box 10 The Atrocities of Men over Women[17]

—A Reader

Mothers and sisters of the country! I submit this article as my humble attempt to serve you. If my contribution can be of any use to you, I will consider my efforts successful. Arya women! It is time to awaken from our extreme ignorance. Look at our present state. Dear sisters! Who are we and what state have we reached? Look, there were devis and durgas amongst us, some of whom are being worshipped as goddesses today. In comparison, women are now considered by many to be impure. It is sad that we have still not caste off such ignorance. Dear sisters! The atrocities that many men inflict upon women can no longer be kept hidden. Such men are responsible for our state. When sons are born to them, they prompt great celebrations. Their fathers not only celebrate, but also spend hundreds of rupees. It is sad but true: when we are born, they say a pebble or a stone is born and they find excuses to conceal their disappointment about our birth. Alas! Are we of no use that there is so much lament? They are not even ashamed about their disappointment. If we daughters did not exist, there would be no women and without women, there would be no sons. Every man desires in his heart that he may only have sons and never daughters. Just imagine the state of our country if the righteous god made this wish come true. Everywhere, only men would be seen. How could the cycle of Creation be maintained? Without us, the lives of these great men would be miserable. Luckily, the omniscient god is more intelligent than these 'great' men. Men have fallen prey to many vices and commit many terrible wrongs. The downfall of states and empires often happens through the misconduct of men. Can it be said of a woman that she destroyed a state through a game of dice or through adultery? We may eat dried up leftovers, but we will always feed the men well. For twenty-four hours a day we serve and attend to them. Would a paid servant ever tolerate all

(Contd)

that we put up with for the well-being of men? For us, our husbands are to be venerated forever. At all times, we give up our existence for the sake of theirs. Yet, men treat us badly in spite of our self-sacrifice. But god is just. This is why the lives of men have also become trouble-stricken. Someone has rightly said:

'Do not trouble the weak, whose curses are so powerful
The breath of this dead body can turn everything into ashes.'

This is something to think about: some reflection tells us that we were also born as a part of Brahma. Dear sisters! Before god, a son and a daughter are of equal worth. It is man who is responsible for our present condition. Men hold their own gatherings and give speeches. It is a matter of regret that when all the great men return home, they think that women are fools and cowards. If you tell them a ghost is around, they are frightened to death. Eminent men have written hundreds of great works, books and articles that argue against those who are hostile to the female community, but it is a matter of regret that the assemblies consider our community low-born and view women as fools and cowards. A daughter is not *born* as a fool or a coward. Thinking this is foolish, because if a daughter were educated in the same way as a son, she would probably not be foolish and a coward. All this is the result of ignorance. They give the sons the required education that turns them into religious, devout, and righteous *brahmacharis* [students]. They send them to religious and modern schools and make them complete their BA, doctorate, or law degrees. What else can there be written? Wherever one casts the eye, one sees BA or MA graduates, yet, it is a matter of regret that for us illiterates, those black letters are unobtainable. Nowadays we find some ostentatious supporters of women's education. I call them ostentatious because they do not have the courage to impart comprehensive education. They teach a couple of books and then withdraw; this way, they impart incomplete education and cast a slur on to the concept of education. They say, 'Is it not that in spite of your education you are ignorant.' Many say, 'Your community was obedient when women were not educated.' Had they received the exact same comprehensive education as our sons, would our condition still be the same? If yes, then the fault would certainly lie upon us. I am of the opinion that the condition would never be the same because knowledge always brings about respect, whereas ignorance is similar to the condition of an animal. Dear sisters! Nowadays, men walk around as noble souls, but inside, they are like whirlwinds.

(Contd)

Many men say that shudras and uncivilized people, drums, animals and women deserve to be beaten. Do you see how they consider women inferior even to shudras? This is the condition of our brothers, who do not grant us knowledge and on top of that accuse us of stupidity. It needs to be carefully assessed who carries more guilt. If anyone suggested sending a daughter to a religious or modern school, these brothers would first of all say that they are unable to spend that much money. Furthermore, they will say that a woman will be corrupted when she leaves the home. They don't even consider that their [male] community could be at fault. Why would a woman be corrupted in public if a man is not? Please tell me where the guilt lies. Dear brothers! If you want your community to progress, then please educate women. I request you not to display sorrow upon the birth of a daughter, but to happily raise and educate her. You will do much good. You say that the women of ancient times, such as Sita, Savitri, Anusuya, Damayanti, Gargi, Sulabha, Taramati, and so forth no longer exist. Alas! What a pity. Were they not educated? Were they uneducated the way women are today? Did they live in seclusion? Did anyone listen to them? Were they told from men that speaking out aloud was shameless? And if she walked by in front of someone else, what trouble would it cause! They will find all sorts of faults and reproach her for walking by such and such man, they will ask her whether she does not feel the slightest shame for walking in front of him while he was sitting there, and they will say that the women's community is shameless for not knowing when to walk by someone and when not.

Alas! Is it our duty to stay inside? Just think about your reaction if someone told you to sit inside the house for only one day: you would not be ready to do so. We women have agreed to stay at home instead of you men. This does not mean that we are not allowed to speak and walk around. Alas! This is the veil that you have imposed upon women. To control the senses, to maintain a modest gaze, to not show anger, to stay happy, to serve everyone duly and to speak softly is true modesty, but you judge the status of your home based on the length of the veil and based on whether we appear and speak in front of others. Alas! What a pity that this is called shame or honour. You give others advice, but you yourself stick to such customs. Someone has rightly said that in advising others, men are experts, but there are only few who also live according to their own advice. Dear mothers and sisters of the country! There is no need for me to say any more. The intelligent will understand what I wished to say.

Box 11 Why Women Should Prepare the Food with their Own Hands[18]

—Satyavati Devi

In the July issue of *Darpan*, I read an article by Śrīmatī Kamla Kumari Ji ('Why Women Should Prepare Food with their Own Hands') and the September issue of *Darpan* carried an article on the same topic by Śrīmatī Bishanpati Musharam. I would also like to share my opinion on the subject. I agree with Śrīmatī Kamla Kumari Ji and Śrīmatī Bishnupati Ji and thank both sisters very much that, in this modern world, they have directed their attention to the ancient custom of cooking, which today a large number of women and men often consider to be a worthless task. People often do not see that women are respected as *grihalakshmi*s precisely because they fulfil household duties par excellence. It is the primary duty of a woman to skilfully organize the household. Amongst all their household chores, the most important one is the preparation and organization of food, because it is the body that must confront all worldly challenges. To keep the body healthy and strong by virtue of the best and purest food is therefore absolutely necessary.

The intelligentsia is of the opinion that earning money is as difficult as spending it in a way that keeps the pot boiling. But our female readers can see how nonsensical it is to be indifferent towards cooking high quality and tasty food, considering that half of the money that our fathers, brothers, husbands, and sons earn is spent on it.

It is widely understood that a family will quickly lose all wealth and fall into suffering if the income is not spent carefully. This is why it is important that all our sisters cast off laziness and learn the art of cooking and food preparation according to custom, quality, season, and taste. A number of expenditures are being made necessary by the changing times, and it is impossible to compensate for their expense without women taking on the task of cooking themselves. If women agree that this important occupation is their responsibility, they can save four annas per rupee from the expenditure required for this task.

Śrīmatī Kamla Kumari writes that in joint families, women should cook only for their own sons and husband. I believe that family unity and mutual love can never be maintained in this way. Virtuous women should organize the household together, since there will probably be several women in a joint family. With the exception of sick, old, and pregnant women, as well as women who have recently given birth, all the other women should

(Contd)

be dedicated to household and kitchen chores. In doing so, they will avoid even a spark of jealousy or hostility from each other.

Dear sisters! Together, the women of a joint family can manage the various tasks of the household. If there is a highly respected, elderly mother or mother-in-law, work can be distributed according to her orders and the other women can complete it quickly and with greater simplicity.

Śrīmatī Bishanpati Ji writes that much pure food can be readily obtained from a certain group amongst the Mishra community, but I believe that a housewife should take care of her own house. Before cooking, she should check that all kitchen utensils are completely clean and make sure that the pulses, rice, vegetables, and other ingredients are washed properly. If a housewife takes this responsibility, all should be fine.

[...]

All wives should be the true ladies of their houses, regardless of whether their husbands are wealthy or poor. It is important that every mistress has a good attitude towards the family. In my opinion, there are now many ways to protect affluent people from the heat [of the oven] or other inconveniences, thanks to appliances and equipment that prevents fire and smoke. The kitchens of the wealthy are equipped with skylights and large windows so that smoke cannot accumulate. Also, if these families so choose, they can spend more money on an English stove, which works easily with only a few coals and a small flame that does not give off much fume. It is not difficult to quickly prepare all kinds of tasty meals on it. Furthermore, it is unlikely that a Mishra woman or man would pay much attention to the health of the family members and to the taste of the food the way a wife would. In addition, it is difficult to keep track of the expenditures when dependent on the work of a Mishra.

It is true that in many wealthy families it is customary that women prepare the food only for the family, whilst Mishras cook for the employees. There is no discernible harm done if servants are employed for cleaning the kitchen and doing the dishes, dusting, separating the husk from the grain, grinding and threshing it. But the lady of the house should certainly keep an eye on them, else their work can cause more harm than good.

Dear sisters! It is clear to me that the day turns dull and joyless when one does not work and sits idly instead. The body turns lazy and weak, and illness often follows. The mind turns dull. Therefore, all our sisters should keep in mind that nothing is better for women than preparing food with their own hands. Through this, their own bodies, as well as those of their

(Contd)

family members, will remain healthy and sturdy. Expenditures will be curtailed and the food will be tasty. It is my hope that all our sisters will gladly welcome this noble and sacred task.

Speeches

Speeches in reprints were so common in women's periodicals that they allow for a separate categorization as sub-genre, though it also needs to be noted that they were often summarized in the periodicals' editorials and accompanied by commentary. The speeches stemmed for the most part from meetings of women's and girl's associations in the Allahabad vicinity (Box 12 'How Long will the Women's Community be Content to Serve as Shoes?', pp. 269–74). Speeches held at literary gatherings such as the Hindī Sāhitya Sammelan and on national platforms or even 'abroad' (such as the speeches of Rameshwari Nehru in Burma) reached an audience that had mostly not attended such events in person. In the course of the 1920s, speeches not only held by women on woman-related topics found entry into the periodicals, political speeches by national leaders were also often reprinted. Regardless of their venue, there were also speeches that sought to set normative standards for women (Box 13 'The Model Girl', pp. 274–7).

The speeches in women's periodicals were marked by the frontal address of their audiences. They made frequent use of rhetorical questions, exclamations, and interjections. This is not to say that other subgenres in the periodical did not attempt to connect with their readers—the majority of contributions in women's periodicals, including advice texts and fiction, were dialogic and interactive in nature.

Box 12 How Long will the Women's Community be Content to Serve as Shoes?*[19]

—Hukma Devi

Dear sisters and revered mothers! India's old civilization is not hidden from anybody. Simple men and women watch the Ramlila and Krishnalila performances and revere their heroes simply after hearing about them

(Contd)

from others. This holy land has had women such as the faithful Sita, the well-educated Sumitra, and the devout Kaushalya. But the contemporary condition is grievous. In contemporary times, the women's community is in a miserable plight, the main reason for which is ignorance, which keeps women trapped. Apart from eating and clothing herself, she does not know anything. She has completely forgotten her duties and never reflects about her inferior position. Seeing this condition, duteous men have openly begun to tyrannize women, snatching all the rights of women and considering them equivalent to shoes for their feet. It is a principle of the world that a community, country, or society floating in the stream of ignorance easily becomes subjected to others imposing their will on them and trampling upon them. Men in this instance have just such an opportunity. This is the reason why today even animals are treated better than women are. When a parrot escapes a cage or when a cow or ox or aviculture dies, there is grief. Major and sincere grief!! The unfortunate women's community has fallen even lower than the animals. When a wife falls ill, the husband says 'Let her die and the botheration will cease and I will remarry. The money that would be wasted on remedies can be spent on bringing a new wife into the house and replenishing delight.' This is his only thought and he worries about finding a girl in order to not spend any time as a widower. In this way, the husband has already pronounced the ill woman dead.

This is the place to reflect on what Maharaj Manu has to say on the topic of women. 'The gods dwell at a place where women are respected and honoured; everything becomes fruitless where women are not respected.' Our great authorities, seers and wise men, consider man and woman one body with one half of it being woman and the other man; this is why woman is called the other half of man. Without a woman in proximity a man cannot perform ritual sacrifice in the authority of the *agnihotra* [priest] because he is not complete. The sisters who read the Ramayana will know that Ram, in order to perform the horse sacrifice, needed Sita whom he had initially abandoned. Why, then, should women be content with a rank equivalent to shoes for the feet? We must keep in mind that when a *jāti* [here: women's community] has lost its independence and is content upon seeing another *jāti* inflicting atrocities upon the *jāti* without any protest, and when the *jāti* has no interest in obtaining rights and does not show any effort to obtain the rank of goddesses, the entire *jāti* is powerless and ignorant and is cutting off its own feet and is the cause of its own destruction. Imagine a man who has always lived on top of a mountain.

(Contd)

If he were thrown into a salty lake, what would happen to him? This is exactly what is happening to the women's community. This is why they have to try to get out of the pond of ignorance. If a person falls into a deep well, people try to pull him out with ropes. But it needs to be remembered that as long as the person who has fallen into the well does not want to be rescued, those who wish to help will not succeed. Correspondingly, if the women's community does not on its own attempt to be taken out of the well of ignorance, if women do not clap their hands and feet for rescue from the atrocities imposed upon them by men, no success can be obtained. It will remain difficult for the women's community to progress.

Dear sisters and mothers! In our times, the women have forgotten about their duties and rights. They have become so accustomed to tolerating the atrocities inflicted upon them by men that they are holding the knife to their own necks. These are the daughters whom you have taken so much trouble to raise, whom you consider dearer than your own life. You see their lives destroyed in one instant before you can even sigh. All your love is in vain. You stay quietly seated upon seeing a young, chaste, and literate girl, pure like the waters of the Ganges, being bestowed into a dishonourable marriage to a seventy-year-old widower who has already offspring. You don't even reflect about right and wrong. It is possible that up to this day you have never considered such thoughts.

[The following paragraph is barely legible and therefore remains untranslated. It discusses mismatched marriage of young girls to widowers of advanced age.]

Let me give an example. The wives of men who married a second time may be forgiven. I don't feel hatred against those who remarry. I just think that in future this wrong should be stopped. A wealthy man was committed to turn the foal of a mare stout and robust. He had a beautiful cart made for him, studded with jewels. A second horse of age, old and weak, was tied to the cart. This is the place to reflect whether this old horse will thrive next to the young one and whether he will be able to complete the journey. Does this cart have equilibrium in front of any spectator? Can his master be called wise? Just as this cart without equilibrium, so are marriages with a severe age-gap. A man married for a second time to a young girl cannot obtain peace in his life. Sisters! There is no doubt that the best match for a young horse is another young horse. Everything has a pair in this world, but it needs to be remembered that only comparable things can form a pair. Today, the atrocity in guise of disharmonious marriages has rapidly

(Contd)

spread in India. No house is spared from one wife dying and a second coming in and when the second dies a third one stands ready. Proceeding in this manner people get older and reach up to seven marriages. And the especially 'fortunate' marry, even with the wife and offspring present. A discussion about who pays for this injustice is at stake. Is this not the predicament of the women's community? But the condition of the women's community may be described with an image of thieves who have burgled a house and removed all the wealth and goods. In the end, they even take off the clothes of the inhabitants, but the inhabitants' eyes are just not opening. Every day our delicate and fragile daughters are struck by this calamity, which is crushing their tender hearts. But the women's community is not paying attention to this.

Dear mothers! Awaken from your sleep. Enough years have passed in vain. Respect, dignity, and dharma have all been plundered. This is not the time to sleep. The world is changing. Everywhere, the signs of awakening are visible. In all provinces, communities are emerging to fight for their rights. This is the reason for Europe's major battles. Have you not heard that even in our backward India waves of *svarajya* [self-rule] are spreading? So why are only you content with being equivalent to the shoes of the feet? You need to get ready to stand up and to try to stop your community from being crushed underfoot. Ask any intelligent young girl and see whether she wants to marry a doter or not. I have asked many girls and the response was that they preferred to stay unmarried than to enter into such a marriage. Are they then not forced into this wrong? All sisters in whose laps girls are playing should vow that from now on they will not bestow their dear girls into the hands of an old man or widower. Such a vow will open the eyes of men and they will cease crushing women under the soles of their shoes and instead respect them as their better halves.

Dear sisters and revered mothers! This thought has been in my mind for a long time, but I considered it particularly appropriate to voice it today, on this happy occasion, because on this occasion, many of our sisters, old and young, are present. My advice is not just for *Arya* sisters. I think that regardless of whatever faith a woman belongs to and whatever community she may be from, it is appropriate for her to think about this. The women of Dehradun town especially have to pay attention to this question because men here lead in this matrimonial atrocity in comparison with other towns. The custom of marriage of old men, married men, fathers and grandfathers', as well as widowers is very common. This is why

(Contd)

poor and innocent girls have to suffer these atrocities every day. When one looks around there will be no unfortunate man who has not tied the crown [worn by a bridegroom at marriage] around his head two, three, four or five times, mounted on a horse with beautiful garlands hanging around him and with the sound of drums around him. In addition, there is also no dearth of brothers who have up to two or three wives. But what grief! Grief!! It is appalling that the women of Dehradun are unable to recognize this injustice and instead accept it—completely oblivious. If a large number [of people] accepts an atrocity on a regular basis then this atrocity increases day by day. This is why it is important that all women of Dehradun jointly reflect on this issue, and invest the effort to think about a way this injustice may be removed. Sisters! At the time when this thought first occurred to me, I was alone; but now it has reached your ears from my heart. It is my hope that you will give it a place in your heart and that you will not forget it. Even if I have not been able to state my intention clearly, I am hopeful that you will have understood its true meaning by virtue of your intelligence and wisdom. Whenever any sister takes this topic to other sisters and explains it adequately, I will be delighted and thank her deep from my heart. This is all I had to say. Now I ask my capable sisters to forgive any improper words that I might have uttered today. I will always be thankful for any suggestions and advice that you might have for me on this matter.

Note: I am publishing my humble thoughts in *Grihalakshmi* so that they may reach the ears of the sisters of the country and attract their attention. My insignificant opinion is that a Kanyā Hitkāriṇī Sabhā [Society for the Welfare of Girls], should be established through which disharmonious marriage may be stopped. This society should not be sectarian or communal, and it should be the duty of the members to stop such unjust marriages and to spread this idea in all the towns. I have previously written an article in *Stri Darpan*'s August first-issue with the same intention. I received letters from some sisters who agreed with me and some also expressed the thought that this society should be established in Prayag [Allahabad] and then branch out to other towns. This is why I also request the learned devis of Prayag to think about this and to write articles about this topic for different periodicals published in Prayag, thus attracting attention of the country's sisters to this topic. This work cannot be completed by a single person. But if many sisters come together and stand up, there is hope that this society can be established successfully. It would also be wonderful if

(Contd)

the sisters who are travelling the country and delivering speeches paid attention to this. For further correspondence my address is given below.

'Shanti Bhavan'
Dehradun

* I delivered this speech at the fifth anniversary of the Women's Society (*Stri Samaj*) in Dehradun on 9 November 1917.

Box 13 The Model Girl[20]

—Śrīmatī Kailash Rani Vatal*

Kumaris! Future mothers! Leaders of the nation! The life and death of *Bhāratvarṣ* is in your hands, as are the reins of the nation. The first generations of women stepped into life in a state of illiteracy and ignorance. Inspired by the women of other countries, they reformed themselves bit by bit, for better or for worse. But you are the next generation and your virtue impacts the esteem and grace of this community. It is therefore my wish that this generation emerges prepared and enlightened. With body, mind, and wealth, we must aspire towards obtaining the absolute best for our offspring. Even though we are at the far end of victory, you know that our esteem depends on you and it is your duty to correct our mistakes. May your community be full of strength and knowledge to quench the thirst of afflicted *Bhārat*. You should be prepared to lead the country forward and remove the blemishes of this holy land which has long been disgraced. May these lifeless institutions regain strength by virtue of the courage, enthusiasm, and efficiency of your community and flourish again. You are the ones who will rescue *Bhārat* and therefore you are of greatest importance. Like the *gaū mātā* [sacred cow] you will be the one to feed the children of *Bhārat* with *amṛt* [holy nectar] and your bull calves will be of use on the fields like the bull calves of the *gaū mātā*. The bull calves of the gaū mātā will fill the stomachs of *Bhārat*. They will make your Bhārat prosperous and grand. In the past, many bull calves were good-for-nothing due to the nescience and ignorance of their mothers, but the good-for-nothings of your generation will be seen as a disgrace. You will have to be at your best and at your most generous and magnificent, lest there be even more harm done to the women's community and the older generation, grandmothers and *daīs*, will turn even paler. Become a model—you are worthy to be called such. Only a model girl can become a

(Contd)

model woman. Under the guise of the daughter you have come to redeem the parents; all countries and scriptures have felicitated you and for those who insult you the door to hell is open. You are born to gratify your mother, father, country, and lineage. The country in particular is investing a lot of hope in you, focusing on *Bhārat* and awaiting your arrival since a very long time. It is already very late. *Bhārat* cannot be consoled by only a handful of unselfish daughters—there are so many other daughters whose dissatisfaction increases day by day. The country requires that all ascend on to the same path so that they all set an example. From there, the path is clear for you. In our times there were many bushes and shrubs, which did not allow us to progress, but it is a matter of great fortune that the obstacles are no longer there for you. Every day, capable people speak out for you. The society is giving you a lot of independence. Many will still obstruct your progress, but the number is decreasing. The big leaders are smoothening out the path for you. In all four cardinal directions, the reservoirs of knowledge, benevolence, love and service towards the country, and self sacrifice are filled; you need to immerse yourself in them, drink their waters, and then re-emerge. Taste *amṛt jal*, accept your new destiny, and let go of laziness and idleness. Thrive in every possible way and be on the lookout for every virtue. Show the light to the women and sisters who have lost their path in the dark night. Human beings at large should benefit from your unequalled devotion—stand up on the path of duty and lift up all the fallen sisters, because to create a new civilization, new ingredients and new materials need to be put together, which you alone cannot accomplish without the support of others. Solve your monstrous problems together, care about your neighbours, disentangle each others' problems—this will be your highest dharma. In short, everybody will have to properly look after all the change occurring in the human beings' civilization in entire *Bhārat*. Then you will find out that you have set out on the path of guidance and duty. The only thing remaining is to walk on it.

Goddesses! There are high expectations towards you and in order to accomplish them a lot of sacrifice is necessary. First of all, it is your duty that along with obtaining knowledge you prepare your body, mind, and wealth just as much as your parents will allow you to. Just by climbing the ladder to knowledge you can obtain exemplary status and become a role model. Your knowledge should be modern, meaning that it should not blindly follow in somebody else's footsteps and repeat what is read out; a complete education needs to be such that you can complete the work

(Contd)

of your country in the way it is appropriate for your country and in the way it is reflective of your community (*jātīyatā*). Never wear the 'jewels' of such knowledge that will make you and your community lose face. Shallow attitude lasts just for a few days, but true community spirit is forever. For the Indian girl to protect her community, religious education is very important. Reciting the religious scriptures will develop the mind and spirit, through which your conduct will be based on a solid and secure foundation. Only through cultivating dharma can duty be attended to and attending to one's duty is not only extremely necessary for the country, but also for the *maikā* [parent's home] and *sasurāl* [in-laws' home].

You know of the horrors of the Hindu household, which has encountered much critique. A patient and calm girl can massacre such invasions [sic]. In such times of sorrow and pain, many girls also commit suicide, but for those who are aware of the religious principles, this torture is insignificant. Through her conduct—through the power of her compassion, happiness, sweet speech, selflessness, cleverness, and empathy—she is able to win over the hearts of the members of the household; and even while doing household chores she doesn't turn her face away from the matters concerning the country.

Second, it is also necessary for you to foster benevolence, charity, love, hospitability towards guests, and show devotion to the country. A woman without these virtues is not complete. For the model girl these virtues are as important as the air we breathe. Selfless love, love towards brothers and sisters, sensible spending, and not wasting money on foreign clothes is the responsibility of an intelligent daughter. If a girl has demonstrated such conduct from the beginning and cherished such tasks she will face no worry. But it will be difficult to care for a poor husband and what charity and care for the family can she attend to in such a state? The arrival of a guest will be as if torrential waters rained upon a leaky hut. How can one be even superficially hospitable when one suffers the pangs of hunger? As against this, a woman who lives a simple and unpretentious life and whose needs are fulfilled with very little money, lives happily, and by virtue of her charity, engages in the service of the country.

Third, I want to return to love and service of the country and lay some more emphasis on this point. Girls! You need to be prepared to suffer for the sake of the country. The state of the country is not hidden from you: learn from this how much self sacrifice is required from your side. The time has come for you to consider your country equivalent to a large sasurāl. Consider its members as your family and the entire Hindu race

(Contd)

as your lineage. Consider the leaders as your model. Put on the clothes of true civilization and join your brothers and fathers in the work force. There is much work for you; in fact, there is double the work than there is for men. They only have one task, you have two. Why two? One is the house, the other the country. The same work that you accomplish at home needs to be done for the country. *Bhārat*'s tasks are manifold. Many sons and daughters are needed for it. A community of model girls will accomplish these tasks and redeem *Bhārat*.

* *Śrīmatīji* delivered this speech at the second anniversary of the Kumārī Sabhā on 5 August.

Advice Texts

Advice literature on cookery, hygiene and health, childcare, responsibilities towards the family, and the prudent financial management of household affairs constituted a further subject of women's periodicals. How detailed this section was, depended on the character of the periodical. Central to advice texts was that women were held accountable for running a household, raising children, and keeping a family together. Furthermore, women's responsibility for the domestic sphere was validated by her intelligence and education. The advice genre was the most prescriptive and authoritative of all texts found in women's periodicals. It had the least fluid boundaries when compared to the other sub-genres of the periodical. This made it relatively difficult to spread controversial messages for the modern woman in the traditional form of the genre. Roy (1995: 95) has aptly described prescriptive literature as 'reflecting the anxieties of a period of change where gender roles far from being settled, manifested domains of contest and struggle'. Gupta (2001: 23) also points to 'a sense of disquiet and increased patriarchal insecurities' emerging from publications on domesticity. After all, pamphlets and manuals on domesticity were the most circulating literature for middle-class women and girls. When they appeared in women's periodicals, however, their 'closed' character acquired a new and more open form by virtue of being published in the women's periodical where they stood next to other contributions (see also Chapter Four).

The texts selected as demonstration give advice on how to prepare a healthy sweet dish (Box 14 'Tasty Food—Laḍḍūs Made with Gram-Flour', p. 278), hygiene and health (Box 15 'Management of the Home', p. 279), as well as the responsibilities of women towards the family (Box 16 'The Impact of Women', pp. 279–81).

Box 14 Tasty Food—*Laḍḍūs* Made with Gram-Flour[21]

Laḍḍūs made with gram-flour are commonly prepared, but this style of preparation with *mung* bean gram-flour can be given to children without concern.

Required ingredients: ½ *ser* of clean and good quality ground *mung* beans, ¼ clean semolina that has been checked for insects or worms, which like to dwell there; one full or half *pāv*[22] of clarified butter and as much sugar; four big cardamom seedpods; some raisins; almonds; and pistachios.

Preparation: Clean the frying pan properly and preheat it before melting the clarified butter in it. Once the clarified butter is heated, mix the ground mung beans and the semolina and add the mixture to the frying pan. With a clean iron scraper stir the mixture to prevent it from burning. It will remain dry at first and then it will roast. Don't overheat. Reduce the heat once fragrance emerges and continue stirring. When the clarified butter begins to separate consider the mixture about to be ready, but not roasting sufficiently will impact the taste and reduce the storage life to only a few days. Take the pan off the heat and continue to stir, then pound the cardamom, wash the raisins and add them. Soak the almonds in hot water, then peel and cut them and add them along with the cut pistachios. Gradually sweeten and continue to stir. Then press the mixture with the hands.

Once everything is solid, test the sweetness and then form small *laḍḍū*-balls with the hands.

Because of the semolina, the *laḍḍūs* are tasty and not unhealthy. When the clarified butter separates and the mixture turns soft, one may regard it as an indication that the gram-flour is roasted. Be cautious that the mixture does not catch fire or turn black.

Their storage life is fifteen to twenty days.

Box 15 Management of the Home[23]

[...]

2. Saline rinse

Doctor Shaman recommends rinsing the sinus with a saline solution. He claims that all lung and sinus-related diseases can be prevented and treated acutely when a person has fallen sick. Along with that, drinking a teacup of water with the amount of salt that fits on to a one-paisā coin calms down the bile and gall. These two methods have proven effective in keeping the lungs and mind clear and in preventing fevers. Salt also cleans the blood. The eminent doctor holds that if all doctors prescribed this treatment, cholera and influenza would never spread.

Box 16 The Impact of Women[24]

—Anadidhan Bandyopadhyay

It is well known how great an impact a mother has on her child. But fewer people know of the impact of marriage on a couple. All over the world, women raise and educate children from a very early age on. The capacity of a mother to educate young boys cannot be equalled by a father. This is why the English (from whom we still have a lot to learn) employ female teachers in schools for the education of children.

Reading the biography of world renowned writer Sir Walter Scott, one discovers that during his childhood, his maternal grandmother used to tell him stories that later inspired him to write novels. Had she not told these stories, Scott might not be renowned today.

A similar case is the life of the country's famous historian Lord Macaulay. When he began to write articles at the age of thirteen, his perceptive mother recognized that her son would one day be celebrated in the world. She protected him from vanity and false pride, and encouraged him to aspire to flawless writing. Her advice made it possible for her son to achieve success during her lifetime.

I am of the opinion that if asked about the source of their success, all great people would certainly answer 'mother'. Furthermore, I suggest that a woman also influences her husband.

The relationship of husband and wife begins with marriage, and since love is a central component of a marriage, some attention should be paid

(Contd)

to it at this point. Even though love is not embodied in a specific practice, it is important to devote time to particular rituals in order to develop the right attitude and to distinguish true and false love, in order to ultimately live a contented life. Love should not be considered, as it often is, a foolish and selfish feeling. In its sacred, elevated, and pure state, love is bereft of self-interest, and acquaints you with religious virtue. It is first a spark kindling in a corner of the heart and then, slowly, it turns into a blaze in the lives of women and men. Anyone who does not attribute this meaning to love harbours false love. An English poet has said that generally 'all virtuous people were true lovers'.

This is absolutely true. Look at Bharatendu Babu Harishchandra, for example. How did he write his plays? How could the translation of *Vidyasāgar* turn out so excellent and how could Chandravali in 'Puneet' be filled with so much love?[25] The answer is love. On the path of love one arrives at a place where eternal happiness and reciprocal empathy are the only emotions. Babu Harishchandra was not the only follower of love; all poets, seers, and good writers were. The biography of Goswami Tulsidasji recalls his love for his wife. One night he felt the urge to be next to his wife. What should happen next! Love compelled him to go straight to the house of the in-laws that very night. You met many obstacles on the way, but what could make you tolerate them other than love? Seeing him in this state, his wife managed to calm him down through her capable influence (*strī prabhāv*). This was an excellent opportunity to do so. It is not necessary to repeat what she actually said or to detail how she actually calmed him down. Suffice it to say that had his learned and intelligent wife not given him advice, there would be no epic works like the Ramayana in Hindi today.

In many homes marriages are mismatched and the house then becomes akin to a battlefield. A solution should be devised to keep such quarrels out of the house. Patience is a virtuous remedy. Whether peace is established or the quarrelling and sorrow persist, all depends on the wife. If she wants to, she can reform her husband, and indeed she even has the power to spoil, corrupt, and ruin him. This is why women need to watch their every step in the domestic sphere. It is advisable and proper that a woman keep her husband out of worldly quarrels. By all the means at her command, she should never incur debt. She should make the home a place for refuge and protection. This does not simply mean overseeing things related to the house, raising the children and cleaning; it also includes caring for her own body. That is, a woman must also keep in mind her looks and what

(Contd)

she wears so that she may keep her husband content. One must always remember the impact that a woman can have on her husband.

Most of us agree that in this world there is an abundance of sorrow and the good fortune of happiness is rare. It is the dharma of a woman to keep the home organized and tranquil for her master. If he cannot rest at home, the home is of no avail to him. He is required to work hard outside and thus desires peace at home. Our women should pay special attention to this, because mostly, when men come home exhausted after a difficult workday, they must deal with quarrelling rather than being greeted by the comfort of a fan and instead of enjoying sherbet they are forced to listen to grievances.

This essay has been written exclusively for women, but it is necessary to discuss a few more topics to which men can also relate. The women of our country have no rights in their lives. Men make the laws, and therefore law-makers also need to be addressed in a few words.

My first request is directed at the father, that he may arrange a proper education for his daughter. The second request is directed at the brothers that they may impart knowledge to their sisters and thus also become virtuous. The third request is directed at the husband that he learns to respect his virtuous wife. As long as these three [types of] men don't awaken, it will be difficult to reform the condition of the women of our country.

There are many fools that don't realize how they hurt their Lakshmis with a few loveless and harsh words. It is absolutely necessary to avoid aversion and ignorance. A wise man once said that when I see a man of irascible temper, I pity his wife and when I see a happy person I am delighted by his happiness, as well as that of his wife and his relatives.

It is the hope that the men of irascible temper will change their temperament upon reading this article and that their wives will use their good influence to reform them.

(Auto)biographical Accounts, Fiction, and Poetry

(Auto)biographical accounts (*jīvanī, caritramālā*) of Indian and European female as well as male celebrities from the present and past (including social reformers, politicians, and women pioneers in politics) were another common feature of women's periodicals. The accounts were commonly accompanied by portraits and photographs. Besides the conventional biographical accounts (such as Box 17 'Kumari Mrinalini Chattopadhyay', pp. 282–3) that were often reprinted from mainstream Hindi periodicals, women's periodicals encouraged women (and girls) to submit stories from their lives or the lives of relatives and neighbours. Das (1991: 268) mentions the autobiographies of 'ordinary' women such as Rassundari Devi (in Bengali), a courtesan (in Urdu), and women activists such as Ramabai Saraswati (in English and Marathi), which began appearing in the late nineteenth century, indicating that some of the first autobiographies of the time were actually written by women (such as Box 18 'A Chapter of My Life', pp. 283–93). The periodical thus not only offered accounts of exceptional people to the readers, but asked the readers to also contribute in spreading information about women and girls who had acquired fame and recognition in their ordinary lives (Box 19 'A Thief in the House—A True Story', pp. 293–4).

Box 17 Kumari Mrinalini Chattopadhyay[26]

—Krishna Kumari

Kumari Mrinalini's father was well known. His name was Śrīyut Aghornath Chattopadhyay. Mrinalini Devi's older sister is Sarojini Naidu. Śrīmatī Sarojini is known all over India today. She is very competent on the political scene and doing better work than some male leaders. Kumari Mrinalini is an equally competent sister. Mrinalini was first educated by her father. He taught her mathematics, chemistry, and sciences, and she learned Urdu, English, French, and other languages.

In 1908, Mrinalini published two small books for the convenience of students at the ISC [Indian School Certificate]. With these books students receive a comprehensive introduction to chemistry and sciences. In 1911, Mrinalini travelled to England with a stipend from the Mahila Samiti in Calcutta. She wanted to excel in the field of learning. After passing the *training* in England, she prepared for the Tripos Exams in psychology and politics at Cambridge University, which she passed with honours. In England, Mrinalini wrote a small book. In it, her inclination towards anarchism became apparent, which upset the government of India. It thus became impossible for her to teach at a government educational institution or at one that received government funds.

Upon her return from England, Mrinalini went to Madras. There she did some very good work with Annie Besant and the venerable Subrahmanya

(Contd)

Aiyyar. For the last two years she has been successfully editing the beautiful tri-monthly paper, *Śāmā-Ā*. She is also contributing to the association that was established for the support of coolies and labourers. As learned and powerful pioneering women of our country, these two sisters are truly the epitome of glory.

Box 18 A Chapter of My Life[27]

—Charushila Devi (Translator Girijakumar Ghosh);
Translated from the Bengali for *Stri Darpan*

Often, the life story (*jīvan-caritra*) of a famous person is written after his death. Nobody has ever written a biography of an illiterate Bengali woman such as me, and nobody ever will. Knowing this very well, I have sat down to write my own biography (*jīvanī*). I also know that my sisters will turn up their noses and knit their brows on reading my strange laughable life-story. It might even be that they would want to spit fire into my mouth. In spite of such possible reactions, there is a good reason for writing my life-story: If there is a dear girl from a rich family, such as I was, or one with less understanding, she may benefit from reading my story. My unfortunate history is being written for this purpose.

My father was a well-known barrister. He was immensely wealthy. He had countless servants, carriages, horses, and motorcars; clothes and ornaments; there was comfort and opulence; enjoyment and merriment, we did not lack anything at our place. I have five brothers and I am the only daughter. This is why there was no shortage of love and affection for me. Servants, peons, doorkeepers—all of them obeyed my orders. My father was of the new type—a *fashionable* man. His ways and lifestyle were all adapted to the new *fashion*. This is why people made fun of him behind his back. But father did not bother about it at all. There is a famous saying that behind his back even the king's mother is called a witch, but it doesn't do her any harm. This is also how my father followed the wise saying that 'If a low-caste person is bitter and loud, a wise man ignores him with a smile on his face.' The fear of sharp tongues did not make him change his ways.

Growing up, we learned to imitate our father and he was glad about this. Who could have told upon seeing us that we were from a Bengali Hindu family background? Upon seeing our clothes and attire or hearing us speak, people would say 'children of the Sahib' and make fun of us. We

(*Contd*)

did not care. We went wherever we pleased—father did not forbid us to do so. In the mornings the servant placed tea, biscuits, cake, etc. on the side-table; we all paid our respects and greeted father according to the custom and I sat on the *piano* and played songs for father. At ten o'clock, I wore my outdoor shoes, tied up a loose braid and stepped into the '*bus*'-carriage and left to study at Bethune College. We also had a teacher who taught us brothers and sisters twice a day at home and an English woman taught me to sing. In the late afternoon, we put on our festive clothing and sat in a decorated *motor* car to go for a stroll with our father in Eden Gardens, Zoological Gardens, and the gardens of the Fort. Every Sunday evening, father's friends were invited to dinner at our place and there was music and dance. I had completely adopted English customs and manners. Our father hated the worship of gods and gurus, Bengali customs and rites, and even the Bengali language. My lifestyle and attitude was deeply influenced by my father. He even gave us English names.

But mother was against all this. She was devoted to the gods and goddesses. Whenever a new food or drink came into the house, she would not let us eat it before sending a piece of it to the shrine. Every morning at dawn she sat in the carriage to go to the Ganges for her bath. On the third floor, next to the stairs, a little store room was allotted to her for her prayers. Mother never let us sneak into this storeroom. Once I secretly snuck into it and got a glimpse of everything inside it. In the middle of the storeroom there were many pictures and statues of the Hindu gods and goddesses. In a niche, a big brass pot held water from the Ganges, and a second niche was reserved for sandalwood, stone slabs, and incense. In one corner there were a light of brass in a lamp-stand also made of brass, a box of matchsticks, a seat made of blankets, a vessel for offering water, a utensil for sipping water, a conch-shell, an alligator, and a few brass utensils. There were some Bengali books on a small *shelf.* I identified them as the Gita, the Bhagavata [Purana], the Ramayana, the Mahabharata, the Vishnu Purana, and more of such singular productions with titles that were unknown to me. I did not know anything about the contents of those books. Father often said, 'Does a man ever read a Bengali book?' In my mind the thought had also taken root that whatever was written in Bengali books was all rubbish, indecent, and sinful. When I was very small I had read a couple of books with my mother. After that all my ties to the Bengali language were broken. I was a student in the higher classes of Bethune College and was full of self-pride. Alright—Where was I? Right—In mother's devotional storeroom. There were statues of stone and

(Contd)

toys placed on a throne. It was said that these were all mother's personal gods (*ṭhākur*).

Mother lit the incense daily and made her offerings to all the deities with flowers and sandalwood. When she came out of the devotional storeroom after worship, wearing her yellow silken sari, marked with vermillion, and sandalwood, and her freshly-washed hair still spread [over her shoulders], she appeared as a goddess herself. But in my unfortunate state I was not capable of appreciating the sweetness of her purity. When father saw her appear thus, he used to burst out laughing. Like him, we also made fun of our mother, rolling around in laughter. Mother would get annoyed and disappear from our sight.

Mother was not fond of engaging in much conversation. Seeing her in this austere state we were intimidated; when we turned away from father and looked at mother, none of us ever had the courage to say anything. Just as father had English names for each of us, mother had named us after the gods and goddesses. The name she gave me was Lakshmi. But the name Lakshmi was to me bitter as poison. We also had a menial servant working in our house whose name was Lakshmi. I was not a servant! I was not a slave! My brothers made me mad when they shouted out this name. I was by no means ready to accept the name Lakshmi. After all, I was my Daddy's 'Bella'! I kept taking the vow that I would not respond when mother called me by the name 'Lakshmi'. But when mother, in her firm and austere, but also peaceful and soft voice called out 'Lakshmi', I found myself unable to ignore her.

Father's *library* was filled with stacks of English *novels*. As I grew older, I began to read more and more novels. I did not miss out on a single novel whether it was of literary value or not. I did not care for the household; life to me meant to eat, drink, stroll around, sing, play an instrument, write, and read *novels*. Reading *novels* day and night made me live in a dream world. Father, too, sometimes could not put a book down. Of all the English books I read, Shakespeare's 'Othello' was the best. Othello's love story, became a part of my physical and mental state. I kept thinking what if I were Desdemona. I was obsessed. My heart stirred when I thought of becoming Desdemona. But where was my Othello? Thanks to father I was completely independent and free; I wandered unhampered in different market places; but never spotted anybody who could be like Othello. I became depressed thinking of Othello. I could no longer concentrate on the books I was supposed to be reading, which is why I did not pass my exams with distinction. I yearned desperately for Othello. Where

(Contd)

was Othello? Othello? Would I not find Othello in this lifetime? Then all this independence would be to no effect. My education would also be meaningless. Even reading novels would bring me nothing. No, my entire life would be in vain. Where is my dark Moor, my well-built, strong hero? Othello! The entire Bengali community did not know anything about the meaning of heroism. Under British rule people lived without apprehension. There was not even a vestige of war and fighting. True, the evil war led by the German Reich left Europe a smouldering battlefield. Bengalis had also participated in this war, but there also they quietly gave up. Could none of these people be my Othello? It seemed that my life would be spent in vain.

In this state, I caught sight one day of the school's new coachman, Karim Baksh. I saw him when I was mounting the carriage after school had ended: only this Karim had the qualities of my Othello! Muscular, young, tall, dark, with an impressive turban tied around his head, wearing Indian shoes, a girdle tied around his waist, the reins of the horse in both his hands, what more could one wish for? Yes, what a powerful image! This is my Othello! Who knows whether my Othello had ever been to war or not? There was no opportunity to converse with him. How could I find out whether he had been to war or not? When the Bengalis started going to war it would not have been impossible for this Othello to join them. I let my thoughts roam—now that I had found Othello I would have to see what would happen next. I changed my school clothes, lay down on the sofa, and started thinking. I felt like writing a poem for Othello, but I had never written a poem. English or Bengali, it didn't matter as I didn't know how to write either type of poem. What was I to do? After thinking for a long time I decided to write a poem in Bengali. I immediately pulled a chair to the table, brought ink and a pen, and sat down to write the poem about my Othello alias Karim Baksh. I could find neither rhyme nor metre. Nor did I want to. After all, Shakespeare did not compose in a set rhyme scheme. So, what harm would it do if my poem did not rhyme either? Despite all my ambitions, the poem would not find an end. My younger brother who was eleven years old came to me and asked: 'Sister, to whom are you writing a letter?' Then he saw the poem and asked: 'Who is Othello Karim, sister? Whom are you addressing as my dearest?'

In the adjoining room mother was doing her hair. It is possible that she overheard our conversation. She slowly approached me and said: 'Let me see what type of letter this is.' Her earnest tone struck my ears like lightening. I could not respond. Maybe my body was trembling at the

(Contd)

time, my hands and feet were numb. Mother instantly picked up the sheet from the table and read it. She did not say anything. She left the room with the same earnestness and with the sheet in her hand. I was so ashamed I wanted to die. Fie! What had I done? I was not sure what mother thought about it. Who knows whether father would also see the sheet. What would he do? What had I done? I felt a lot of anger towards my younger brother. It was his fault. Had he not read the sheet out aloud, nobody would have ever found out.

I do not know what exactly mother told father, but he took me out of school. I thought paying attention to my lessons for a while would rid me of some of my shame, but this was not the case. Father also no longer asked me out for a stroll. For several days he was not seen much in the house. Perhaps he was occupied with some particular work. When he came home, he consulted oddly with mother and then left. Mother constantly kept an eye on me. My younger brother was also with me all day. I was held captive.

After that event, news broke one day that I was to be married! Upon hearing this, I was enraged. My body caught fire. I had had no clue, had not heard and seen any signs, and then, all of a sudden, marriage! How unjust this was. Under what compulsion was this happening! If that was what Daddy intended, why did he give me English education? All my education worthless! Destiny would now not allow me to become Desdemona. The bud of love was plucked before it could bloom! I wept with anger and sorrow. But nobody paid attention to my sobs. Nobody came to wipe my tears. In the end, I had to dry them myself.

One night, for good or ill, I was married in pomp and splendour. Like a common Bengali girl I was decorated with clothes and jewellery, veiled, and left behind with my husband in the house of the in-laws. Fie! What hatred this had turned into! Alas, what ending my novel-like-life had taken? Inside, I was burning with rage. My mother-in-law introduced me to the customs of the family. I was in the midst of crowds of women. Almost all of them lifted my veil to look at my face and to put money, gold coins or some jewellery in my hands. My heart was filled with anger. Was I a spectacle, or a toy?

When I realized that there was no way out, I decided to erase my longing for Othello for the sake of my husband. I had yet to see the face of my husband. At the time of *shubhdṛṣṭī** I had kept my eyes closed in contempt. I was performing the rite of the 'bed of flowers' when I first saw my husband. But, my god! Where was my Othello? There was a world of

(Contd)

difference between the two. There was absolutely no resemblance between my husband's and Othello's stature. My husband was thin and fair. His two eyes stretched up to his ears, his nose was upright, the hair on his head oily and silky, a big smile on his face; other than tenderness I did not detect any traces of bravery. He put much effort into conversing with me, but somehow I could not say a single word. I turned my back upon him, hid my face, and stayed on the bed. Several more days passed in exactly that way. After that I returned home to my parents' place. But I could not stay for long. After two months my mother-in-law sent a letter asking me to bid farewell to them. According to her, I was a big girl, not a child, and it was appropriate to live with my in-laws. My parents agreed. What was I to do? I had to go to the house of my in-laws. I had no right to object to anything. What destiny!

My father-in-law had been a landholder and was well-known in twenty-four villages of the district. After his death, my husband was in charge of the entire wealth. Being in charge of such a big landed estate at such a young age had not made him change in any way. It was as if his higher education and his abundant wealth had adorned him even more with the virtue of modesty. The household of my mother-in-law was a devotional Hindu household. There was an image of Radhagovind, the house deity since generations. There was also a Radhagovind temple and a guest house [for devotees]. Every day, the poor and grief-stricken filled their stomach with *prasād* [blessed food], that was distributed after it had been offered to the *ṭhākurjī* [master] as food. Whosoever wanted could receive prasād. To serve the ṭhākur, three or four Brahmin priests were employed. Just like my mother, my mother-in-law also bathed every morning at dawn. But there was no Ganges here, which is why she had to bathe in the waters of the river that flowed close to the village. It also took her about two to three hours to complete the worship. After that she was busy with household chores. There was no shortage of servants in the house, but nevertheless, my mother-in-law barely had any free time. I wondered about the purpose of all her arduous work. After worship, she put together the ingredients for light refreshment, and distributed it amongst all. Then she went to the kitchen and oversaw things there. There was no dearth of work for her even there. Taking out things from the storage or arranging for things to be taken out, preparing *pān*,[28] checking what had been consumed by whom and what was still left, distributing milk and sweets amongst everybody after breakfast, distributing pān—these were all her responsibilities. Even when the servants were eating she was present and oversaw them all.

(Contd)

After everybody had eaten, she would sit down somewhere and have food herself. In the afternoon she would rest for a little while and then resume her work.

Our household was small: there were only my mother-in-law and my husband. I was the third member to arrive. I had one sister-in-law who sometimes visited for a few days with her children. But the big house was always filled with kith and kin. My mother-in-law never got angry at anybody. She was always affectionate and respectful towards everybody. I never lent her a hand in any of her work. I never had social contact with people. I did not even speak to anybody. I took my imaginary life into my bedroom and let it burn in loneliness. I was an educated lady from Calcutta. The quietude of the village and its villagers, the shade of the cool groves of the village goddess, the dark green fields, none of this or anything else meant anything to me. True, I lived here, but my heart had stayed behind in father's *library*.

Once, as my sister-in-law was about to return to her in-laws' house, she took both my hands and said humbly, 'Leave your sorrow behind and cheer up. Sister, show some affection towards Devendra. He did not want to marry. We kept pushing him and forced him into marriage. If you continue to be the way you are, you will break his heart. You have been married to a husband whom others would usually only be granted after a lot of penance. Look, sister, don't lose him by being disrespectful.' My husband was a devotee of Sri Ramakrishnaji Paramahamsa. Sometimes he took a vow of service and took off to many places to help the poor and sick. He also donated huge sums in support of the *Ramakrishna Mission*. For this reason, his dear friends often worried that he might one day leave his home and put on the clothes of a Hindu *sanyasi*. Then my sister-in-law said, 'Sister, please look after mother. You are her very dear daughter-in-law. After the death of five of her sons, Devendra is the only one left. You are the only bride in this house. If you don't care about her, who else will? On *ekādaśī*[29] she fasts without even drinking water. Don't let her work that hard on such days. Take half of the workload from her.' When my sister-in-law still lived here, she used to share the chores with her mother. But after listening to what she had to say, my body was aflame. I was the daughter of a *barrister* in Calcutta. Had I been born to care for and serve uncouth and uncivilized ghosts (*bhūt*)? In their household, the mother-in-law was the head of the house and my arrival was only recent, right? And what could I do for my husband? His food, rest, and relaxation was taken care of by my mother-in-law, and he also always followed his mother like

(Contd)

a little child. Whatever he needed, his mother would immediately bring. What was I to contribute? It is unnecessary to say that I did not say a word in response to my sister-in-law. She went on chattering, unrestrained, and I kept standing there and listening quietly.

I have said before that I never joined in the household work. Every day after the bath, I sat in my room like a lifeless puppet all day except when it was time for the meals. From my room's window one could see the compound of our ṭhākur. In the big courtyard of the compound, orphans, guests, the blind, the crippled, and others gathered for prasād. I stood at the window to see the spectacle of the coming and going of numerous people. I was not showing devotion towards the ṭhākur; I was just passing my time. How was I living my life born as a woman and devoid of love, spirit, and purpose? Inside my heart, I constantly felt the burning pain of an awful restlessness. My imaginary life lived on without a heroine! Neither had I found Othello, nor were Romeo or Hamlet the writ of my forsaken destiny. Nobody had ever died for me, nor had anybody ever returned my feelings, nor even had anybody ever expressed contempt. Alas, my love had neither been reciprocated nor had it been rejected. In the manner of an uneducated Bengali woman, the conch shell had sounded, a lot of tumult made, and I had been married off! My birth as a woman was in vain! This realization filled my eyes with tears.

One day before dawn, I was standing close to the window, worrying about something when I suddenly turned around and saw my husband standing there. I turned my face away. He took my hands and placed a Bengali book in them. He said, 'Don't spend day and night like this, alone, quietly and filling your heart with sorrow. Take a book and read a little bit. It will cheer you up.' He left. Seeing that Bengali book I was full of disdain and threw it against the cabinet. Father used to say, 'The Ramayana and Mahabharata are full of useless and indecent matters. How can a person in his right mind read such a book?' I also believed in this, which is why I had no idea what was inside the Ramayana.

After a few days, my husband asked, 'Did you read the book? When you are done I will bring another one.' I did not respond. I had not even touched the book. It was still lying where I had thrown it down. But time seemed to crawl and the days seemed even longer when sitting around idle. One day, I took the Ramayana my husband had given me and started to read it. It was not that bad. I read all of it. What did I see? The renouncement of all comfort and luxury, a journey into the forest with the husband; unprecedented self-abandonment to carry the debt of the

(Contd)

husband; suffering thousands of difficulties in the house of the Brahmin and spending the time as a servant. Alas, how beautiful! What selfless love towards the husband! And then, the daughter of Janak, Sita! The constant seduction from the king of demons; endless sorrows in the Ashoka Tree forest (*aśokvan*)[30] caused by the maidservants; at the end abandoned by her husband without even being at fault, and yet, sincere affection for him, extraordinary veneration and endless love! She is the celestial Mandakini; the confluence of Ganges and Yamuna. What an astonishing story this was! I had read so many English *novels*, but never gotten the flavour of such selfless love. Why did Daddy condemn Bengali books? My husband is intelligent. This is why he is planting the right seeds on the designated land by giving me the books. I finished reading the book and returned it to my husband. Next, I received the Mahabharata. Needless to say that I got a sense of the importance of reading Bengali books. I also read the Mahabharata in only a few days. In the Mahabharata, I saw Damayanti, worry, Savitri, disappearances, and so many other things! Unequalled devotion towards the husband, astonishing affection for the brother, reverence for elder people and gurus, devotion for the gods and the twice-born! The Mahabharata is a sparkling jewel of the Hindu dharma! I was reborn.

I read about Bengali literature, history, and many other topics. Gradually, a veil fell over my imaginary life and I stepped into a new kingdom. Thinking about my conduct I began cursing myself a hundred times. Was I not the daughter of a country in which women happily burned their bodies to ashes on the funeral pyre of their husbands in order to please others? There are those who take a vow of poverty out of their own free will to serve others and who don't even debate the pros and cons; and was I born to this country to turn into a good for nothing? Even as the daughter of a king, Savitri did not neglect to serve her father-in-law, mother-in-law, and master out of her own free will, even when living in the forest and being in poverty; and through my lethargy I was destroying such great female power (*nārīśakti*)? Shame on me! A well-educated daughter of a king who was used to a diversity of pleasurable activities was capable of change, spontaneously, and I, born into an ordinary household was unable to do so? Conceited about my education, I was unable to fit in? Damn my education!

From that day on, I engaged in household activities. Seeing me suddenly turn into a true 'Lakshmi', all the women of the house laughed a little, but I did not care. I woke up very early and took a bath. Then I

(Contd)

gathered the ingredients for my mother-in-law's worship. Seeing this, my mother-in-law was delighted. She said, 'Daughter, this is the work of a Lakshmi of the house. The household is all yours. How will it run if you don't consider it your own?' From that day on I began to take part in all my mother-in-law's chores. While he was eating, my husband took note that I was busy doing my mother-in-law's work. Needless to say, he was delighted. I guessed it by looking at his eyes. After food, when he went for repose and when I placed the box of pān into his hands, he took a betel leaf in his mouth and said laughing, 'Hmm, today's pān is exceptionally tasty. Who has prepared it? Have you?'

I performed my chores at the regular times and during repose I spent my time reading Bengali books. My husband was delighted upon seeing my perseverance in reading books. He brought new books daily. Reading about the virtuous conduct of Arya men and women, the unprecedented greatness of Hinduism (*Hindutva*) started developing in my heart. I understood that I was also a Hindu woman. I realized that my birth and my life were not in vain, but that I also had a responsibility. And I also understood that education had to adjust to the changes taking place in the country. We are Hindu women, we are the community of mothers, we are born to fill the lives of all with endless love and nectar. People call us *Grihalakshmi*, Lakshmi of the home. It is our prime responsibility to live up to this name and to fill our homes with happiness and peace. Just reading English *novels* is not the end to our education. Instead of Shakespeare and Milton, Kashidas, and Krittavas, or for the Hindi readers, Tulsidas, should be used for our education. The fog had lifted from my eyes.

Self-remorse, secret repentance. From the pain of this strong whip my heart was crushed day and night. When I now think about the state of ignorance and the lack of understanding in my unfortunate story and when I try to understand my actions, my heart fills with terrible pain. For my prior sins, the image of the hell as described in the Ramayana and other works kept appearing before me day and night. Did I not know how to seek penance for my sins? Narayana! Which door to hell had you kept open for me? I resolved that I would admit all my wrongdoings in front of my husband and thus lighten the weight of my sin. One day after dawn my husband was lying down and reading a monthly journal. When I entered he said, 'Look at this, Lakshmi, this time your article has also been published. The editor has lauded your article'.

I had written an article about the responsibilities of a Hindu wife and sent it to a monthly. My husband was reading it very carefully. Upon

(Contd)

hearing my husband, I felt as if a nail punctured my heart. I myself was blind and had set out to teach others? What audacity! I whispered, 'You deserve this acclaim'.

My husband lifted his gaze from the journal and looked at me. He said, 'How is that, your majesty?' I said, 'I am not worthy of being called a Hindu woman. I knew nothing about the do's and don'ts nor about the responsibilities, rules, and things forbidden for a Hindu woman; whatever I learned, I owe it to you. I am an insect in hell. You are the god in heaven. You took pity on me and showed me the right path.'

As he had done before, my husband laughed a little and said, 'What is the matter? Say it. It seems you also learned how to *lecture*. Let me hear how you became unworthy of being a Hindu woman. To me it seems you are the model Hindu woman. Mother praises you to no end in front of everybody.'

I could no longer hold back and broke out in tears. I thought that I was in no way worthy of his pure love. I held his feet tightly and said, 'No, no, I am really not worthy of being called a Hindu woman. I am a sinner. I am not even worthy of being yours. If you hear my story you will repent you ever touched me.' Having said this, I told my husband the unvarnished truth of my former life. He did not hold the story against me. He was not the slightest bit angry. With his naturally sweet laughter, he hummed into the room and pulled me in his direction. 'Oh, you are the daughter of a Hindu home, the woman of a dignified Hindu family, in your body flows Hindu blood, in your breath and in each of your bones and veins, Hindu dharma is deeply rooted. You show such strength in venerating me.' I felt at peace. Thus, this chapter of my life came to an end.

* A Bengali rite during the *kanyadān* [literally, the giving away of the daughter] at which the bride and groom may look each other in the eyes.

Box 19 A Thief in the House—A True Story[31]

—Anadidhan Bandhyopadhyay

Tarachand lives at Kabir Chaura. Kabir Chaura is the name of a ward in Kashi. Tarachand is a telegraph employee. He has to work at the station at night from 10 p.m. to 3 a.m.

Tarachand's wife's name is Jyanvati. She is very smart, educated and intelligent, which is why her mother named her Jyanvati, the knowledgeable

(Contd)

one. Jyanvati is never scared or in distress; she always thinks of ways to solve a problem. And usually, she finds an answer to the problem at hand.

Jyanvati's in-laws were becoming slowly acquainted with her virtue. Through her good conduct, she kept her mother-in-law and her husband content. Jyanvati took good care of her mother-in-law and never let her do any work.

Seeing how her home was neat and well-managed, all the women of the ward followed Jyanvati's example and tried to keep their homes neat and tidy. But there was one incident for which Jyanvati's name resounded throughout the entire city of Benares:

One day, after dinner at around nine or ten o'clock, Jyanvati and her mother-in-law were sitting in the house and preparing *pān*. Tarachand had left for work. After a while, Jyanvati noticed a man hiding behind the bed. She did not tremble from fear, but continued to converse and joke around with her mother-in-law.

Jyanvati thought that if she told her old mother-in-law what she had just discovered, the old woman would scream out of fear and the thief would be alerted. It would be unpredictable how he would react. With this in mind she thought of another plan and continued to talk to her mother-in-law. 'Mother, once a thief broke into our place, but our father caught him and screamed out "a thief, a thief".' Jyanvati put extra emphasis on the word 'thief' and shouted it out aloud. Her mother-in-law did not know a thief was hiding in the house and laughed at her daughter-in-law's shouting. Jyanvati also laughed.

The thief who was listening from his hiding place thought of it all as a story.

But after a little while five men entered the house and inquired about the whereabouts of the thief. 'Where is the thief'?

The mother-in-law was about to say that there was no one of the kind and that the daughter-in-law was just telling a story. But Jyanvati pointed in the direction of the thief. The men then caught and interrogated him.

It is said that when asked by the collector sahib who had caught him, the thief responded, 'God'!

Sisters, you should always be fearless like Jyanvati and act thoughtfully. Had Jyanvati screamed out of fear at seeing the thief it would not have been surprising if the thief had killed the mother-in-law and wife or escaped. The mind cannot function in fear; this is why you should always remain fearless.

Fiction

Fictional literature such as short stories and novels—new genres in Hindi literature—or simply stories (*kathā*) and fictional dialogues narrated over a few pages were abundant in women's periodicals. The short story genre developed out of these different types of narratives (Das 1991: 302) that were also present in women's periodicals. Moreover, there were stories, tales, fables, character sketches, and anecdotes narrated by readers themselves. Like in literary periodicals such as *Saraswati*, realism dominated the fictional writing in women's periodicals, but it also needs to be noted, as Trivedi (2003: 1001) has for longer fictional narratives, that 'there are perhaps half a dozen different prose narratives in Hindi, all of which approximate in some but not all respects to the generic expectations of a western novel'. In women's periodicals, too, we find headings for prose narratives such as *upanyās* (the Hindi term for novel) and *nāval* (the English term in transliteration), as well as *kathā* (story, tale, legend) and *purāṇa* (referring to Sanskrit legend and mythology), amongst others. The texts themselves intersect in tone and style with moral essays and advice texts (Box 20 'The Model Friend', pp. 296–302). Writers selected from a pool of prose genres depending on their own familiarity with a genre and the purpose they had in mind.

All longer contributions were serialized. The themes featured were diverse and linked to other topics of the periodical. Some contributions concluded with a moral lesson. Not always did virtue triumph; we encounter as many tragic stories of murder, suicide, and social injustice. The range of contributors (female and male, students, writers from the world of Hindi letters, and lay-writers) accounts for the diversity of literary styles and topics in the fiction section.

The following four examples on marriage and loyalty, virtue, and patriotism by better- and less-known writers are each enjoyable to read, but also clear on the message they impart. 'The Model Friend' (Box 20) conveys that a young woman can change the fate of her girlfriend against the wishes of the latter's greedy father and brother. 'Grandmother's Stories: The Selling of a Good Deed' (Box 21, pp. 302–5) is about a poor Brahmin couple that is rewarded for the kindness and the honesty displayed by the husband in front of the king. 'Patni-vrata—Loyalty and Chastity Towards the Wife' (Box 22, pp. 306–10) is a story in which a husband shows exemplary devotion towards his wife, and 'Swadeshi Sari'

(Box 23, pp. 310–2), a serialized story, is set in the form of a dialogue between a rather unkind husband and his outspoken wife. This last story falls in between the grid of an advice text, moral essay, and fiction.

Box 20 The Model Friend[32]

—Gulabdevi Chaturvedi

1

It is evening. The Sun god is moving west. Exhausted from the day, the farmers are returning home along with their ploughs and oxen. Today the sun had been burning. Now, the poor birds that had fallen silent all day are happily springing from tree to tree and twittering joyful songs. At the same time, in the attic of Babu Shyamkishor's house, we can see a beautiful young girl in distress, moving in a room. The door to the room is open. The beauty's eyes are filled with tears. She keeps looking towards the door as if she were expecting someone. One hour has passed, but still no one has come. Suddenly, filled with fear, the girl lets out a piercing shriek. In fear, she screams, 'Why did I have to end up like this? Father! What have I done wrong that today you don't show compassion for your only daughter and that you care for no one's humility? Friend! At this time you also have left me behind, grief-stricken and motherless. In this world, I consider only you my companion in good and bad times. Alas! What wrong have I done to you that you have abandoned me? I have become an orphan without a mother. Is this why you have abandoned me?' Saying this, the beauty fainted and fell onto a bed. Not even five *seconds* had passed that a girl of sixteen years of age came running towards the beauty and said, 'Sister, don't be scared. As long as I live, I will not allow you to suffer.'

2

Babu Shyamkishor is one of the wealthy and respected residents of Ramgarh. He is currently around sixty years of age. He has married twice. The first wife passed away, leaving one son behind. The second wife bore a girl. Some years passed and his second wife passed away leaving behind the eighteen-year-old stepson and a beautiful daughter aged 14. Since childhood the son had been impudent. He had associated with bad company and ruined his life. As Kamla's sixteenth birthday approached, Shyamkishor's 'worthy' son Mahesh came to his father and said, 'Father! Kamla has reached a marriageable age, how can you be so careless? Your daughter is no longer an innocent girl!'

(Contd)

Shyamkishor: Mahesh! I do understand that the girl has reached a marriageable age. I will send the *nāī* [barber] to arrange for a suitable boy.

Mahesh: What is the need of sending a nāī or anyone else? I have already been on the lookout for a boy.

Shyam: Tell me, who is the noble boy that you have found?

Mahesh: It is Rupkishorji's worthy son Babu Yugalkishor.

Shyam: Of what age is he? And what is his current occupation?

Mahesh: He is nigh on forty, but he is very handsome; his father has left so much wealth behind, that they will live their entire lives in happiness. And it is particularly gratifying that he has a ten-year-old daughter and a five-year-old son from his first wife. Our Kamla will immediately obtain the rights of a mother. What do think?

Shyam: Son, I like the boy. I remember that I have met him before. He is attractive. But he has inherent vices; he loves alcohol and he passes his time gambling. But, I mustn't worry about that. Our Kamla will herself set this right. The house seems to be suitable. With god's grace, there will be no shortage of money.

Mahesh: So, should I apprise Yugalkishor of the matter?

Shyam: What is the hurry! We will send a letter in due time. Let's first also ask Kamla.

Mahesh: (frowning) Then we might lose the boy. What is the need of asking Kamla? It's not that we are sending her off to a lower-caste family.

Shyam: Alright, let it be. Inform him that your father would like to bestow his daughter to him in marriage.

Upon hearing his father's order, Mahesh left the house and cheerfully set out in the direction of Yugalkishor's house. The marriage proposal was approved.

From the above two matters the readers will have learned quite a lot about Yugalkishor's life. At this place it should also be mentioned that one day Kamla had suddenly caught Yugalkishor's eyes. Since then he had been enthralled by her. He had lured Mahesh into a trap with money and was in happy anticipation of obtaining Kamla so easily.

3

As Kamla's friend Sheila heard the news that the virtuous maiden girl would be bestowed in marriage to a wealthy gambler, she was furious. She was overcome with sorrow at the thought of Kamla facing such hardship.

(Contd)

She pledged to herself that she would save Kamla from this atrocity even if she herself would carry harm from this act.

The next day, Sheila finished her work, sat in a vehicle and rushed to Kamla's house to clear the air about Yugalkishor for Kamla's father. First, that he was doomed to death, that he had married three times and that his three wives had died of sorrow; second, that he was of bad character and that he also had two children. It is true that he was rich, but a little thought would make it apparent that wealth does not stay long with a gambler. Considering all expenses, even Kuber's treasure troves would dry out. Consider placing your daughter into the hands of a worthy young man. You won't have to search very far. It would be best to marry your daughter to the worthy Kamalnayan Babu, son of the local Dayanidhi. He recently returned from Lucknow with a medical degree. He is twenty-five-year old.

Even after hearing all that Sheila had to say, the old Shyamkishor did not understand anything. He was irritated and asked, 'What right do you have to interfere in our business?'

Sheila conceded defeat and told Kamla all that had been said. Kamla was at a loss and sat there quietly. Finally, she could feel herself sink into the ocean of sorrow and she nervously clung to Sheila. She wept and said, 'Sister, only you can release me from this sorrow or else I will commit suicide'.

Sheila consoled her and said, 'It's alright, don't cry. Listen to what I have to say.' She dried Kamla's tears with the end of her sari and said, 'Do you know Kamalnayan?'

Kamla: (hesitating) Yes, I do. The eldest son of Dayanidhi.

Sheila: Will you marry him?

Kamla: Sister, why are you poking fun at me? I am not worthy of him.

Sheila: Listen to this! Oh, how could you not be worthy? One day, while talking, Kamalnayan said in passing that he had never seen an intelligent and beautiful girl as Kamla. He said she appeared to be a Lakshmi.

Kamla lowered her big eyes in bashfulness. In the ocean of her heart, waves undreamed of undulated. She was staring at the floor. Sheila interrupted her thoughts and said, 'Sister, I have come to understand that you want to have only him as your husband. But confirm this verbally at least once.'

Kamla: Do you think I won't tell you what I feel? I accept all that you say, but father and brother have arranged my marriage. What will you be able to do about that?

(Contd)

Sheila: (laughing) I am pleased that you have given this worthy boy a place in your heart. He is worthy of you. Now, don't be scared. I am ready to give my life for your well-being. I shall leave. We will meet soon.

Kamla: (stopping her) Sister, listen! You are saying that there are only four to five days left until the wedding. What will you be able to do in these few days?

Sheila: The marriage will be called off. If it is god's wish, it will all work out and I will release you of this atrocity.

Sheila then returned to her own house. The feelings aroused in our Kamla's heart slowly settled.

Sheila, who had just taken leave from Kamla, went to Dayanidhi's house and told Kamalnayan the entire story. 'It is in your hands to save Kamla's life. If you don't protect her she will commit suicide.' Kamalnayan is a very intelligent and wise individual. He is not yet married. His father had passed away recently and left him behind with the burden of his old mother and a few female relatives on his shoulders. He was troubled by all that Sheila had told him. 'If I don't rescue Kamla, she will certainly commit suicide and misery will spread amongst all of us.' He considered it of utmost importance to help Kamla and said to Sheila, 'Sheila! Your role will be very important in this matter. What do you have to say?'

Sheila said, 'As for me, I am ready to give my life for Kamla.'

'Alright, I will write a letter today. Please deliver it to Kamla's father.' Kamalnayan wrote a letter and put it in Sheila's hands, 'Be careful! And don't let anybody find out about this pact. There are four days left till the wedding. I will take Yugalkishor to Prayag. You inform Kamla that I will not have her be strangled by this demon.'

Sheila had Kamalnayan's letter delivered to Shyamkishor. In the meantime, Kamalnayan went to Yugalkishor's house and exclaimed, 'Brother! A serious lawsuit has been brought up against you. If you don't come to Prayag immediately, you will be sent to prison.' Upon hearing this news Yugalkishor thought about the message and decided to leave for Prayag the following morning. He took five to ten bottles of alcohol along with him and informed Shyamkishor by a letter that he was leaving for Prayag.

4

Today, there are only two days left till the wedding, but Sheila has not heard back from Kamla and Kamalnayan has also not returned from Prayag. Why has Sheila not come? This very question tears Kamla's heart

(Contd)

apart with each passing moment. Kamla is overcome with sorrow. In the meanwhile, Sheila receives a letter in the post, which reads, 'Dear friend, do not worry. I will be meeting you this evening. Then, I will update you on everything.'

The readers will surely have understood for whom Kamla is waiting. We have already narrated that Kamla had fainted on the bed because of her worries. At that time, Sheila had come and said, 'My sister, don't be too scared. As long as I live, I will not allow that any atrocity shall happen to you.'

As Kamla regained consciousness, she was embracing Sheila and weeping on her shoulder. In a sweet voice, Sheila said, 'Sister, don't worry. Yugalkishor has gone to Prayag for some important business. Kamalnayan has joined him. They might arrive here by tomorrow night.'

Kamla: I don't understand what this is all about. Why did Yugalkishor go to Prayag and along with him this ... (she could not speak any further).

Sheila: Matters will be resolved slowly.

Kamla: What about the possibility of delaying the wedding? The auspicious time has been set for day after tomorrow. The preparations have begun.

Sheila: The wedding has been cancelled because Yugalkishor will not be able to return in time.

Kamla: (irritated) Sister! What you say makes no sense. Say it clearly.

Sheila: Well, now I see that you have become furious! Listen, Yugalkishor is involved in a lawsuit because he broke a wedding arrangement with a *kulin* Brahmin wife. He will not be able to arrive in time for the wedding. A short while thereafter, Kamalnayan will come for the wedding.

Kamla: Does father know about all this?

Sheila: Yes, why wouldn't he? Do you not want to marry? Kamla, have you forgotten all you said? Are you worried?

While they were speaking Shyamkishor entered the room. He was exasperated upon seeing Sheila seated next to Kamla. He furiously hissed at Sheila, 'You wicked person! You have concocted this plan. You have incited Kamla. Wicked! Get out of my house. (Looking in Kamla's direction) I am also finished with you.'

At first Sheila trembled upon witnessing Shyamkishor's rage. But then, courageously, she said, 'Babuji! As for me, I will leave. But what wrong has Kamla done that you want to kick her out?'

(Contd)

Shyamkishor: Listen to this girl! You have ruined Kamla's life. And you ask what her fault is.

Kamla: Babuji! I beg you, don't be angry. I will certainly follow your orders. But don't offend Sheila. She has not committed any fault.

Shyamkishor: I always knew that Sheila would ruin you. Sheila, I am finished with you. Get out of here and don't ever show your face again.

Sheila could no longer endure Shyamkishor's sharp words and she stood up. On her way out she said to Shyamkishor in a loud voice, 'Babuji! You are wrong to accuse Kamla and me. You will regret this.' Sheila left.

The readers may very well imagine the state Kamla was left in at that point.

5

Some months have passed since Sheila was accused, but nothing happened with regard to Kamla's wedding. Day and night, Kamla suffered from having been separated from her friend. She became weaker every day. But Sheila stayed quietly at home.

One day a letter arrived in the mail. Sheila rejoiced. She wrote to Kamla without any hesitation informing her of the following: 'Yugalkishor had been charged for breach of promise to a *kulin* woman. Kamalnayan will return tomorrow and this full moon will for sure mark your rite of passage into marriage.'

Kamla was moved to tears. Sheila had also sent the letter she had received to Kamla's father. The servant who had delivered the letter said upon his return, 'Respected Sheila! Shyamkishorji is on the way to you, in person!' Sheila began to tremble. But she tried to keep calm and said to the servant, 'Ask him to come upstairs.' Shyamkishor came upstairs and saw Sheila in her frightened state. He said, 'My dear daughter. Whatever I have said to you, I ask you to forgive me. Sheila! I will always be indebted to you. Daughter, I have done you injustice. I was unable to see your virtues. Will you forgive me for this glaring mistake of mine?'

Sheila's eyes filled with tears. She said, 'Babuji! You are not at fault. I have always respected you as a revered father. Don't feel disheartened. I had to carry out my duty. Now, please announce the preparations for Kamla's wedding.'

Shyamkishor said, 'Sheila! Please go to Kamla. She will be very worried otherwise.'

Could Sheila object to this gesture? She went to the house of her friend and embraced her.

(Contd)

6

There is no need to continue with this account. Due to Sheila's commitment Kamla was saved from a serious atrocity and was married with great pomp and grandeur to the worthy, educated, and wise groom Kamalnayan.

Dear sisters! How sacred, how high, how important is the bond of friendship. You may yourself judge this from your heart. Do you also know what it means to share the pain and happiness of a friend? Do you also consider it appropriate to help friends who are hit by injustice? It is my hope that you will keep in mind Sheila's conduct and that you will always maintain pure, truthful and loving relationships with your friends. If you ever see a friend of yours getting married to a dishonourable man, you should try to save her to the best of your abilities and not turn away. Our country is being destroyed by inappropriate marriages. Our sisters are being trampled over by the atrocity of inappropriate marriage. It is your *dharma* to prevent this atrocity to the best of your ability.

BOX 21 Grandmother's Stories: The Selling of a Good Deed[33]

—Champalal Jauhari (reprint from *Sudhakar*)

In a village there lived a Brahmin and his wife. They were very poor. Even though they begged, door to door, all day long, it was always very difficult for them to collect enough food for a single meal. As such, they faced many days of hardship. One day, the Brahmini said to her husband, 'Maharaj! How long will we have to put up with our hardship? We have suffered all our lives. Now, we have grown old and we have yet to experience happiness, even in our dreams. Will we not obtain even the slightest happiness in this life?' The Brahmini wept and wept. Seeing the dolour of his wife, the Brahmin tried to appease her and said, 'Devi, I try my best to obtain more alms every day. Sometimes, I even visit several villages to beg for alms, but I remain unsuccessful. We have to accept whatever is written in our fate. What else can we do? Can you think of a solution? If you have a suggestion about how we can obtain happiness, I would certainly follow it.' The Brahmin woman responded: 'Maharaj! I have heard that Seth Dharmapal of Vaikunthpur is buying good deeds. If you could go there and sell a couple of your good deeds then we might be able to obtain some wealth. The Seth gives those who sell a virtue whatever they ask for. It is my hope that this way we can obtain happiness.' The

(Contd)

Brahmin responded: 'Devi! We hardly have food; how could we possess good deeds? If we have not done any good deeds, what should we sell? Cheating is not appropriate.' Hearing the Brahmin's words of despair, the Brahmini said, 'Maharaj! Why are you so desperate? If you have not, in reality, done good deeds, there must be some good deeds deep within you. Selling those deeds will provide us with sufficient wealth. You should definitely go to Vaikunthpur. Let us hope that you do not return empty handed.'

Because his wife was so insistent, the Brahmin decided to go to Vaikunthpur. The Brahmini asked for some flour from houses in the neighbourhood and prepared *roṭīs* [unleavened bread]. Along with some chutney and pickles, she gave the packet to the Brahmin and said: 'If you feel hungry on your way, eat these roṭīs.' Then, he bid farewell.

The respected Brahmin took the roṭīs and set off on the path to Vaikunthpur. He arrived there in the evening. He thought it would not be appropriate to approach the Seth at this hour. So he decided to rest in an ashram outside the town and meet the Seth the next morning. As he was fully exhausted from his trip, he immediately fell asleep. The next morning, he completed his daily cleansing rituals. He did not know how long it would take to return from the Seth's place, so he decided to take his meal before leaving. Moreover, he had slept on an empty stomach the night before and felt hungry. He unwrapped his food and sat down to eat. He was about to take a piece of his roṭī, as a bitch delivered a litter of puppies outside the hostel. It is the nature of dogs and cats that after delivery they immediately eat one of their puppies or kittens out of hunger. The bitch, too, had snatched one of her puppies to eat it. Seeing this, the revered Brahmin was deeply moved. He quickly threw a piece of his roṭī in front of the bitch. As the bitch saw the roṭī, it cast aside the puppy and ate the roṭī instead. But it remained unsatisfied with one roṭī and so the revered Brahmin gave it a second one. Continuing this way, he fed his entire food to the bitch. He himself drank some water and stood up. After saving the lives of several puppies, he set off to meet the Seth.

Upon arrival at the Seth's place, the revered Brahmin said, 'Sethji! We have heard that you buy good deeds. I am a very poor Brahmin. I have come to sell one of my good deeds to relieve myself from poverty. Would you be so kind and let me know of the good deed in which you are interested?'

The Seth responded to the words of the Brahmin, 'Maharaj! For a certain reason I am unable to buy a good deed from you today. Please

(Contd)

come tomorrow. I will then buy a couple of good deeds from you and take heed of your wish.' The poor Brahmin lost hope and left. He begged for alms in the town to fill his stomach.

Readers! Let the poor Brahmin find nourishment. As long as he concerns himself with finding food, let us introduce you to Seth Dharmapal. The Sethji is bestowed with offspring and wealth. Through the grace of god, he does not lack anything in life. He has four well-educated sons and daughters-in-law. His youngest daughter-in-law is extraordinarily virtuous and smart. She is renowned in the entire Province for her devotion to her husband. Her devotion has even made her all knowing. Whatever she says about the past, present, or future, turns out to be true. The Sethji embarks on every task, however big or small it may be, only after consulting his youngest daughter-in-law. Even today, he has to consult her with regard to the good deeds offered to him by the Brahmin. He told the Brahmin to come the next day, so that he could talk to her and then buy the good deed she suggested. Consequently, on that very day in the evening, after having taken his meal, the Sethji asked his youngest daughter-in-law, 'Dear daughter-in-law! Today, a revered Brahmin came to sell one of the good deeds that he collected in the course of his life. Which good deed should I buy?'

The daughter-in-law thought for a while and responded, 'Respected father, tell the revered Brahmin that you will buy off the good deed that he performed yesterday. In exchange, he shall have as much wealth as he wishes.' With this advice in mind, the Sethji went off to sleep.

The next morning, after completion of his purification rituals, the Sethji went to his shop. At that time, the revered Brahmin, who had overcome his anxieties, also arrived. Seeing the revered Brahmin arrive, the Sethji said, 'Maharaj! I would like to buy the good deed that you performed yesterday. In exchange, you can have any amount of riches from my treasury that you are able to carry in your hands.'

Hearing the words of the Sethji, the revered Brahmin was in total dismay. He thought, 'The Sethji is making fun of me. I did not do any good deed yesterday, how could I lie and make a pact with sin? Perhaps the Sethji does not even want to buy a good deed, which is why he imposed this condition.' With these thoughts in mind, he said, 'Sethji! Yesterday, I did not do any good deed. There is nothing I could sell.'

The Sethji replied: 'Maharaj! I do not wish to buy any other deed except the one from yesterday. If you have something to give then give the good deed from yesterday.'

(Contd)

The Brahmin did not respond. He got up and left. He believed that the Sethji did not want to buy a good deed and that the condition had been set up under false pretext. Desperate, the Brahmin decided to return home to his village. On the way, he saw an amla tree. The tree was full of ripe amlas and the revered Brahmin decided to pick some amlas in order to earn some pennies from selling them. This would suffice for one meal. He climbed up the tree and picked the amlas, which he kept in a cloth bundle. Then he returned home. At home, he put them in the storage room. At that time, the Brahmini was not at home. She had gone to visit someone in the neighbourhood. The revered Brahmin thought 'I went to sell good deeds, but was unable to succeed. What will I tell my wife?' He was deeply ashamed and went on the roof-deck for a rest.

After a while, the Brahmini returned home. As she opened the storage, her eyes became dazzled from the splendour she saw! She was not seeing the amlas, but a heap of pearls, so she assumed that her revered husband had sold all his good deeds and had not even kept a single one. She felt ashamed and covered her face. However, she thought, he must be hungry. She set out to buy ingredients to prepare some food.

She took one of the pearls, sold it, and bought the ingredients. Then she prepared the food and went on the roof-deck to tell the revered Brahmin that the food was ready. The Brahmin had closed the door and was sleeping. The Brahmini said from outside, 'Maharaj! Why are you ashamed? I know that you sold all your good deeds. It might have been better if you had kept at least one good deed for yourself. But what has happened is irreversible. There is no point in repenting now. Come downstairs! You must be hungry. Food is ready. Wash yourself and have your meal.'

The words of the Brahmini did not make any sense to the revered Brahmin. He wondered why she was talking of having sold all of his good deeds whilst he had not sold even a single one. 'Let me find out what she is talking about. Right now I do not understand anything.' The revered Brahmin descended from the roof-deck and saw the pearls. He was startled. He told the Brahmini his entire story and concluded with the words that the Seth had not bought a single good deed. 'So what is this all about', he asked. The Brahmini responded, 'Maharaj, this is the reward for the lives that you saved at the ashram.' The saying of the Mahatmas that the root of all virtue lies in the nethermost world carries much truth. This is why, dear readers, you should be concerned about the well-being of others, whenever it is possible for you. This is the highest of all virtues.

Box 22 Patni-vrata—Loyalty and Chastity Towards the Wife[34]

—Pandit Ishwari Prasad Sharmma

For the past few days, Bhuvanmohan's wife Kishori has been ill. In the last four days she has been unable to eat even a morsel of food. No one could understand how her health could have deteriorated so rapidly. Kishori is very dear to her parents-in-law. Bhuvanmohan loves and respects her more than anyone else. It seems Kishori is about to die and all the members of the family have gathered. Their faces appear sad. Bhuvan cannot find peace during the day and is unable to sleep at night. He does not leave the bedside of his beloved wife. He takes care of her. Whenever the need arises, he consults the doctor and he cares for Kishori according to the doctor's advice.

Bhuvan is about twenty years old. He studies at the Prayag Muir Central College. The moment his exams were over, he was informed about the bad condition of his wife. Bhuvan became restless when he got the news. His big, lotus-like eyes filled with tears. He quickly packed his things and departed. His house is two to three hours away from Prayag, so he arrived at dusk. Upon arrival he saw that his life's companion, his friend in times of sorrow and in times of happiness, his dear beloved wife, was lying on her deathbed. When he saw the condition of this distressed woman his heart was shattered. All his happiness and joy vanished.

But men should not lose hope in times of crisis. Bhuvan realized that it would not be wise to be scared at this stage. 'It is my uppermost duty to take care of Kishori's suffering.' Relinquishing his worries and doubts, he supervised the medical treatment of his wife in a sensible and compassionate way. He thought: 'I see the distress that has befallen my beloved. She would sacrifice her own life for my happiness. I cannot sit here passively. I will take care of her now, the way she has taken care of me. Should it not be a husband's duty to keep the wife happy, just as it is her duty to make her husband happy? Why should it not be that way?! I am of the opinion that men who treat their wives like low-caste slaves have bad character. They are selfish and obstinate. Just as the happiness of her husband has been the prime goal of my wife, my prime goal should be the happiness of my wife.'

With these thoughts in mind, Bhuvan took care of the patient himself, despite the assistance of all the servants and his parents. People may call him a worshipper of *Strī-Devtā*, the wife-goddess, but Bhuvan feels satisfied that he has fulfilled his duty. People devoted to their duty do not concern themselves with the gossip or praise of other people.

(Contd)

2

The course of time does not take personal plight into consideration. Whatever happens, the course of time cannot be halted. The wheel of time will continue to turn. This is how fifteen days passed without anyone noticing it. Kishori's state had not improved. None of the medicines had shown any effect. The illness worsened every day.

Bhuvanmohan is sitting alone in his study. His head is bowed, his hands are on his cheeks, and he is engulfed in deep worry. The reader should not be surprised by this. The ill health of his beloved wife is the cause of all his worries. At this time, his eyes don't seem to have eyelids; his gaze is fixed in the direction of mother earth. He does not understand how a good-hearted, pure and simple woman like Kishori could fall into such life-threatening danger! Was she paying off bad deeds? Who knows?

Bhuvan is still sitting. All of a sudden, the door to his study opens and a twelve-year-old girl enters with a cry of distress. It is Indumati, Bhuvan's only sister. Seeing Indumati weep without restraint, Bhuvan sinks in despair. For a while they have lost their voices and remain silent. As Bhuvan begins speaking, he asks slowly, 'What has happened? Sister! What has happened? Indu!! Why are you crying in distress?'

But Indu can only respond 'Brother! Brother!!' Nothing else escapes her lips. Seeing her, Bhuvan's eyes also fill with tears. He is completely worn down. Hearing his mother weep along with the lamentation of the other women, Bhuvan understands that there is no more hope. He runs inside the house. A number of women have surrounded Kishori's bed. They are beating their heads with their palms and lamenting. Doctor Raghunath is standing next to them trying to calm them down, but without success. Bhuvan approaches and asks the doctor: 'Raghunath Babu! Is there any hope left?'

Doctor: 'Bhuvan Babu! Very little hope remains, but "as long there is breath, she is alive". She is not yet dead.'

All of a sudden, Kishori opens her clear, tender, and deer-like eyes, from which an extraordinary flame emerges. But these eyes stir up fear rather than joy. Those dear and joyful eyes that once evoked the holy confluence of faith, devotion and love, now cause a tremble to the heart!!! Oh blessed time! You are full of extraordinary powers!!

As Kishori opens her eyes, Bhuvan approaches her and drowned in tears, he speaks: 'My dear! Are you forever leaving me behind with my love and letting me float alone in the ocean of the world? Kishori, tell me what wrong have I done to you?'

(Contd)

Before a flame extinguishes, it suddenly flares up. Similarly, Kishori's flame of life that was preparing for salvation suddenly blazed. Upon hearing Bhuvan's loving and grief-stricken words, Kishori, even on the verge of death, smiled. At that moment, her lifeless body gained new strength. She took a breath and said: 'It scares me even more to see this crowd. Please stop the hustle and bustle so that I can say something.'

Everyone acceded Kishori's last request. Only wife and husband remained in the room. Kishori's cold limbs gathered unforeseen new strength and, after all the people had left, she sat down in the bed in which she had been lying. In a soft voice, she said, 'My dear! I am leaving, there is no hope that I can be saved. I can clearly see the messenger of the god of death standing in front of me. But my dear! Will you show sympathy and accept the last wish of this dying person?'

Bhuvan replied: 'My beloved! What are you asking for? Have I not always agreed to your words? You could ask me to ignite myself on a pyre, and I would not try to escape.'

Kishori could no longer sit, so she lay down again. She stayed quiet for a long time because speaking required much effort. She closed her eyes again. Bhuvan observed the scene without moving. Then, Kishori gathered new strength and said: 'My beloved! I have one request. You have had sympathy for me and fulfilled all my longings and desires. It is my wish that you now show as much sympathy and fulfil the request of your dying *dāsī*.'

Bhuvan interrupted the flow of her words and said: 'I will certainly agree to whatever you have to say.'

Kishori respectfully took his tender palm in her hand and said: 'My god! This is our destiny. Today, we are bidding farewell. I do not know when I will be able to once again press my heart on your venerable feet, but if the Vedas, Puranas, and *shastras* are to be believed, then I can say with certainty that I will be the dāsī of your feet even in my next birth. Be it so, in this life, god has not bestowed upon me the joy of offspring and I could not give you the happiness of a child. This is why I want to make sure that after I pass away, someone will be there to take care of you. It might be difficult for you to deal with the sorrow. There should be no hardship in your life. This is why I ask you to remarry. Whichever world I live in, I will remain concerned about your happiness. If you are happy, then my soul—wherever it may be—will obtain peace. Otherwise, it will be distressed.'

Hearing this, the grace around Bhuvan's face disappeared. Darkness spread in his eyes. In a choked voice he said, 'My beloved! I have told

(Contd)

you countless times that I am not that sort of a man to whom a woman is merely an object of sexual pleasure and who treats a god-given woman as an unpaid servant. I think that god has created man and woman as equals. Both should enjoy the same rights and responsibilities in society. This is why I think that the remarriage of a woman whose husband has died is as wrong, immoral, and improper as the remarriage of a man whose wife has died.'

Kishori was quiet. With her eyes half opened and half closed, she looked at Bhuvan's appearance as Bhuvanmohan and listened to him. Bhuvan said: 'My dear! There is only one heart. It cannot be given away twice. You fill my heart! How could I ever remove you, whose heavenly statue is presiding deep in my heart, in favour of someone else? Is your Bhuvan that vile?'

Kishori remained quiet. In a wave of emotion Bhuvan continued, 'Oh giver of life! If destiny has decided that I shall live in separation from you, then no one has the power to oppose this. But my love! You can be certain that I will always preserve you in the dearest of memories. Nothing can remove this memory from the tender heart of a person like me. Only those with a demonic nature can do so.'

Now Kishori began to speak: 'My dear! This is a day of joy for us. You have floated in the river of heavenly joy. At this moment, death appears to me to be worth more than a hundred thousand pleasures. But, oh god of the unfortunate, until I take my last sigh, I will keep asking you to marry and enter into family life so that you produce offspring, which is necessary to fulfil your debt to the forefathers.'

Bhuvan said, 'Oh my idol of love! Do not inflict injustice on me. If you truly care for my happiness, do not speak such cruel words.'

At that moment, Bhuvan's mother entered the room. From the agitation, Kishori lost her consciousness. After a short while, her condition worsened and she began breathing heavily. Doctor Raghunath Babu was called, but as he arrived Kishori's body turned cold, her pulse weakened, and her soul departed from her physical body. Bhuvan was still holding the goddess of his heart in his lap at that time.

3

After Kishori's death, all happiness in Bhuvan's life vanished forever. He never forgot the conversation at the time of his wife's death and how she had taken her last agonising breath in his lap. He always lived in loving memory of his wife. Whenever he remembered his wife, for whom he had

(Contd)

felt more love than for his own life, his eyes filled with tears and he wept. Bhuvan was completely devoted to his wife. He remained steadfast in his vow and stayed a widower throughout his life.

The women of India have since time immemorial been renowned for their devotion towards their husbands. This virtue has given them an elevated position amongst women of the entire world. But in these unfortunate times, this dharma is declining and with it widow remarriage is being advocated. A major reason for this is that men are to an increasing extent forgetting what it means to be devoted to their wives. But even in these bad times, there are examples of men like Bhuvan, who are devoted to their wives. It will be a day of utmost happiness when men who are devoted to their wives and women who are devoted to their husbands inhabit every house in India.

Box 23 Swadeshi Sari[35]

—'A well-wisher of the country'

Kishorchandra said to his wife Kamla: 'Listen, is this fine? Look at it properly. Do you like this sari or not?I don't have the time to keep running to the market nowadays. If you complain later, it will be no use.'

Kamla: 'You are really nagging. If I don't like it you *will* have to go. (She looks at the fabric). Alas, after asking you for so many days you have managed to buy a sari, but one that I don't like. Neither is the cloth fine nor does it look good. If I wear such a coarse cloth and mingle with people, what will they say?'

Kishor: 'So, this fondness for foreign clothes will not let go of you. I have explained to you so often that *swadeshi* clothes are of better quality than foreign ones. But you don't seem to understand. When finally something sank in your mind, your sister-in-law, her highness, honoured us and since then the stench of foreignness fills your mind.'

Kamla: 'Oh my lord! Purify my mind by uttering "swadeshi, swadeshi". I will go on asking you for whatever I like.'

Kishor: 'So, I can already imagine that after a while you won't want to live in Hindustan.'

Kamla: 'Why don't you listen? All I am saying is that you brought a piece of cloth because you thought it was nice, but I happen to not like it. The country it was made in does not make a difference.'

(Contd)

Kishor: 'I am sorry you have met her highness. Whenever a thing is not labelled "Made in Germany", "Made in France", you don't like it.'

Kamla: 'You are worrying for no reason.'

Kishor: 'Listen, I am not fond of making fun for no reason. I get angry when you irritate me at the wrong time.'

Kamla: 'Then please take your anger and put it permanently away.'

Kishor: 'You do not want to understand.'

Kamla: 'The thing is that wearing a fine and glittering sari makes me look better.'

Kishor: 'To me, you look very good when wearing a swadeshi, hence pure, sari. You are so beautiful. I don't have any desire for you to become more beautiful. Enhance your inner beauty. You will not receive as much respect from civilized society by increasing your outer beauty.'

Kamla: 'And you, who is covered from top to bottom with *European dress*.'

Kishor: 'But my clothes are swadeshi clothes. They are not labelled "Made in Germany" or "Made in France".'

Kamla: 'Alright, my sister-in-law likes such clothes. Brother has explained things to her very often, but she does not agree.'

Kishor: 'Alright. I will explain it to her.'

At that moment there was the sound of laughter. Turning back, Kamla saw her sister-in-law Śrīmatī Sushila Devi standing at the door, hidden and smiling. Kamla ran towards her and stood behind her. Kishorchandra said to Sushila: 'You are the wife of a barrister, aren't you? But your mind is filled with foreignness and now you are also corrupting your innocent sister-in-law.'

Sushila: 'Oh, wait a minute. There are only a few more days left before you become a barrister and my sister-in-law the wife of a barrister.'

Kishor: 'That is right, but the honourable barrister should also have some influence upon you. It seems, though, that this is where you have learned to argue.'

Sushila: 'Listen, if you continue to rave at me, I will have a letter written to our principal to declare you *restricted*.'

Kishor: 'I see! You are even acquainted with our principal.'

Sushila: 'Why would I not be? After all, he is a distant relative of mine.'

Kishorchandra laughed: 'Let me stop laughing and you tell me whether the honourable barrister has stopped you from wearing swadeshi clothes,

(Contd)

or whether you don't please him without foreign clothes. Please tell the truth.'
Sushila: 'How would I know? Ask him and see. The fact is that I am used to wearing fine cloth. Coarse cloth does not fall properly.'

(To be continued)

Arguably a separate category, translation into Hindi from prominent English and Bengali works also featured in women's periodicals. Such translations had been popular from the time of the Fort William College in the early nineteenth century, effectively broadening the initial audiences of a literary work. Many women's periodicals, however, also deplored that translations and renderings from other works were often not marked as such but falsely promoted as original works. The editor of *Stri Darpan* addressed the issue of plagiarism as follows:

Love for the Hindi language has spread amongst our sisters; there is a lot of evidence of this. Our sisters have great hopes of publishing their writings in *Stri Darpan*. [...] But often, the same article written by the pen of more than one author reaches us. It seems that our sisters and girls do not understand the wrong involved in just copying an article and submitting it. Sometimes we receive an article from a book or from some paper and, not having been bestowed with the omniscience of god, we consider it an original work and print it. It should be remembered that even we can be held guilty of plagiarizing. We hope that in future our sisters will pay more attention to this matter and never again claim authorship for an article that has been published elsewhere by someone else.[36]

The lyrical section contained prayers, songs, poems, and rhymes, occasionally also nursery rhymes, in varying poetic metres and verse patterns, covering mostly topics of social reform and nationalism. Some poems were also inspired by English romantic poetry, Indian devotional and religious poems, as well as a few bhajans in Braj Bhāṣā. Erotic poetry is not found in the women's periodicals that I consulted. The poems fall into a time period that marked a shift in themes from romanticism to social criticism and patriotism as well as poetic language. This shift came with a shift in the language of Hindi poetry from Braj Bhāṣā to Khaṛī Bolī Hindi, a development of the Dwivedi period (1893–1918) (Schomer 1983: 1). The new poetry broke away from the Braj poetic tradition, without necessarily breaking entirely with one of the common themes of that tradition, namely religious devotion (Schomer 1983: 9). Characteristic, however, were the new themes inspired by socio-political movements of the time that also constituted the topics of Kharī Bolī Hindi poetry. While none of the canonical works of Kharī Bolī Hindi poetry were reprinted in women's periodicals, major poets of the period such as Harioudh, Shridhar Pathak, and Maithilisharan Gupta published their poems in women's periodicals.

Most of the poetry still followed the form and metres of medieval Hindi poetry, the *dohā* featuring as the most common verse form. The *dohā* was a self-contained rhyming couplet 'eminently suitable for concise statement, aphoristic comment, or succinct characterization' (Schomer 1983: 13). Such *dohā*s were also found as interspersions in prose narrative. Two other common verse forms were the *kavittā* and *savaiyā* that consisted of four-line rhymes. Occasionally, the poetry named the metre it was set in (*savaiyā, gīt, kāvya*), which included Persian poetic forms that were especially prevalent in Urdu poetry (*ğazal, qasīdā*). Hindi women's and girls' periodicals also carried poems that borrowed from folk poetry, for example the *lāvanī* and *birahā*. Schomer (1983: 17) has described the poetry that was promoted primarily in the literary periodical *Saraswati* as ideological, but not programmatic poetry. Ideological, because it reflected a cultural ideology of the times and was imbued with socio-political ideals and didactics. This observation also holds true for women's and girls' periodicals, in which poems for the newly emerging middle-class female reader were published. Free verse, a development of the 1920s, is not found in women's periodicals.

The following two examples call out to women and men respectively. First, women are urged to awaken from their sleep (Box 24 'A Plea to Women', pp. 313–14); then, men are critiqued for their hypocritical politics (Box 25 'You Want Home Rule?', pp. 314–15).

Box 24 A Plea to Women[37]

—Matadin Shukla

Wake up women, the morning has come
Awaken your senses
Look at the birds, they will teach you

(Contd)

Leave the ignorance caused by sleep behind and
Familiarize yourself with politics and dharma
Regard the condition of the fallen country as your domestic work

A man may be wise, yet he cannot achieve anything alone
He will always await your support
Just like the cart cannot move with one single wheel
One person alone cannot maintain the relation between society and the home

He keeps you illiterate but then calls you a fool
He himself is unjust and on the wrong path
He cuts the roots of the tree, which he expects to take care of him
This is how he falls into darkness and suffers

He considers you the scum of the earth and humiliates you
As if in this world you were living half of your life as an animal
Can the scum of this world ever give birth to precious sons?
Can they ever be wise, become queens, heroines or renounce the world?

Men are not without fault, however, you also need to participate
Born as a human being will you die due to the sins of others?
Are you ready to endure the troubles of the world for the sake of your motherland
Or will you live cooking, sleeping, in worldly enjoyments and in fear?

Box 25 You Want Home Rule?[38]

—Jyandevi

You are clapping and want Home Rule
You boast and want Home Rule
How many of you want Home Rule?
You do nothing but will readily accept Home Rule
You debate in assemblies as busybodies
But you cannot live in peace. Yet you want Home Rule
You will do no hard work and you fight with each other
In this state you want Home Rule?
You have split into Moderates and Extremists and you combat each other
And you want Home Rule?
You yourself have earned MA degrees and keep us as fools

(Contd)

To obtain independence you want Home Rule?
You marry early and leave behind many widows
Upon whom you do not show mercy, and you want Home Rule?
The poor Shudras are being trampled over
Treating them this way, you want Home Rule?

Advertisements and Book Reviews

A four- to five-page compendium on the back and front pages of a periodical was kept for advertisements and job opportunity listings. These advertisements indicate that a new market for consumer products for middle-class women ranging from books to cosmetics was on the rise. The advertisements undoubtedly vied for female readers' attention.[39] While periodicals were certainly not a commercial enterprise with the selling of goods as the primary focus, their advertisements were a regular feature. The income generated from advertisements, along with revenue from subscriptions and private donors, was important to cover the printing and distribution costs of periodicals. Some periodicals proudly announced that they were self-supporting. Others were supported through high number subscriptions, for example, from British colonial educational departments.[40] The rates for advertisements ranged between four to eleven rupees per page, depending on the placement and size of the advertisement. The advertisement itself provided information on the product and where to obtain it. The layout was simple and advertisements, sometimes, came with illustrations.

As Pugh (1992: 209) has argued, the advertisement sections in British periodicals relied on a surplus of income amongst subscribers that could be spent to improve the quality of living. Particularly common in women's periodicals were products for women's health, beauty, and education. Perfumes, ayurvedic (hair) oils (Box 26 'Fragrant Pushpavilas Hair Oil', p. 316), oriental soaps, herbal and western toothpastes as well as books (Box 27 'Complimentary Gifts on the Occasion of the New Year', pp. 316–17) were promoted, at times at discounted rates or in special gift-wraps. British-Indian companies offered remedies to cure anaemia, hysteria, and weakness, as well as western manufactured pills for all-round health, dysentery, and pain. There were no advertisements for aphrodisiacs, which were common in newspapers and magazines of the early twentieth century (Gupta 2001: 72).[41]

The Hindi women's periodicals did not explicitly appeal to women's roles as decision-makers when it came to buying products for the household to the extent that Sarkar (2001: 262) has pointed out for Bengali advertisements addressing women. But products available in gift-wraps suggest that these products could be gifts for others. Regardless of who ultimately sanctioned the purchase of a product, advertisements ranging from women's body-care products to books indicate that it also required a woman's initiative and request, before an item was bought.

The majority of products were manufactured in the major cities of the British Indian Provinces by local producers in the United Provinces, as well as suppliers in Bombay, Calcutta, and Madras. Very rarely, products could also be ordered from North America. Besides health products, periodicals occasionally listed job postings looking for women teachers (Box 28 'Seeking', p. 317) or mill workers (Box 29 'Lucrative Employment at Cawnpore Woollen Mills Co. Ltd.', p. 318). Though the latter employment would not have been for the typical middle-class reader, it was important for her to have this information to pass it on to women who might be in economic need.

Box 26 Fragrant Pushpavilas Hair Oil[42]

This oil has wondrous effects: it replaces lost hair, it stimulates hair growth, and makes black curly hair soft and shiny. It keeps the brain cool and refreshed. Its fragrance beats every perfume. One bottle costs ten annas plus postage. Free shipping with purchase of three bottles. A Varma clock with purchase of six. A wrist watch with purchase of twelve.

Box 27 Complimentary Gifts on the Occasion of the New Year[43]

For customers of *Kanya Manoranjan* books worth one and a half rupees for only twelve annas! How precious books are! These books should be kept in every home. Books are very useful. They make women and girls modest, righteous, sweet-spoken, truthful, polite, humble, healthy, cheerful, morally aware, proficient in stitching, needle work, household work, and hygienic ways of living. It is advisable for all parents that they

(Contd)

order these books along with *Kanya Manoranjan* so that their daughters may attain the above-mentioned virtues.

1. A glimpse of the family
In this book Krishna Devi creates such an ideal family by virtue of her wonderful qualities that simply by reading the account, girls and women become acquainted with a new ideal life. A book of 200 pages for only twelve annas.

2. A beautiful *kumari*
This book is an unusual one in its own way. In it a beautiful kumari has to go through several hardships, but never turns away from dharma. This book is also very beneficial for women. Its price only five annas.

3. The moral conduct of girls
In it good advice is given to girls on topics such as the worship of gods and reverence of gurus, obedience towards the parents, modesty and politeness, goodness of character, sweet speech, the value of time, and health. This book is very suitable for girls and women. It will be of great help to girls who seek advice on how to deliver speeches and write essays. The price is only four annas.

4. Amusing stories
Children and adults who buy this book cannot let go of it. Many stories make the readers burst out in laughter while reading. Others require reflection and thought. The stories stand out because the moral of every story is thoroughly developed. Certainly order this book for your children's and your own mind's pleasure. The price is worth the sacrifice—it is only four annas.

—Manager, *Kanya Manoranjan*

Box 28 Seeking[45]

A capable and educated woman for the position of *Lady Superintendent* at King Edward Hindu Girl's School, and teachers with a degree from a Hindi Middle or Normal examination board, as well as a woman skilled in sewing work, are being sought. Salary depends on the applicant's qualifications. An application should be sent to the address given below.

—Śrīyut Ambaprasad Ji Mantri,
King Edward Hindu Girl's School
Saharanpur

FIGURE 29 Advertisement: Puspabilash [Pushpavilas] hair oil, Jaswant Brothers, Mathura (*Grihalakshmi*, December/January 1913/1914 [Pauṣ 1970])

Box 29 Lucrative Employment at Cawnpore Woollen Mills Co. Ltd.[46]

Lucrative employment for 3,000 Indians at Cawnpore Woollen Mills Co. Ltd., to produce Lalimli All Wool wear—the materials that are made in India by Indian labour under healthful, hygienic conditions, and which are a tribute to the land which produces them.

It was common to promote other publications that circulated in the Hindi public sphere: *Kanya Manoranjan* (November 1914) promoted the special national issue (*rāṣṭriya aṅk*) of *Pratap* and a special issue of *Jayaji Pratap*. It also promoted other Hindi weekly papers such as *Vijay* (edited by Harishchandra Vedalankar in Delhi) and *Rajbhakt* (edited from Benares by Birendrabahadur, BA, LLB). These advertisements were different from the ones found in children's periodicals in that young readers, and presumably adult members of the family, were envisioned here as the readers of Hindi mainstream literature.[44]

The advertisement section also laid emphasis on the promotion of periodicals and books. *Stri Darpan* (March 1914, October 1914, January 1917, November 1918) promoted a diversity of periodicals such as *Strishiksha*, a monthly periodical first edited in October 1914 from Kanpur by Mrs Nanhibhai (*Stri Darpan*, March 1914); *Chand*, a monthly from Lahore; *Shishu*, a forthcoming children's periodical; *Priyambada*, a monthly; *Chitramaya Jagat*, a weekly periodical first edited in 1910; *Bal Sakha*, an illustrated-monthly children's periodical edited first in 1917 by Babu Badrinath Bhatt, BA, from the Indian Press in Allahabad; the monthly *Lalita*, edited by Manglik and Karunik in Meerut; *Kayasthmahilahitaishi*, a monthly edited by the wives of two advocates; and *Mahila Sarvasva*, a monthly edited by Pandit Devdatt from Aligarh. The last two periodicals, though, were not recommended because they apparently fell short in journalistic qualities and language (*Stri Darpan*, 1919 [January]: 56). *Stri Darpan,* occasionally also promoted geography textbooks in English.

Book advertisements ranged from 'suitable literature' (*upayogī sāhitya*) and enjoyable books (*haṅsīdillagī kī kitābeṅ*) to biographies, advice manuals, and pamphlets. Children's literature, too, was regularly promoted as enjoyable and instructive for children and their mothers.

Periodicals frequently created self-publicity (see opening quotes of the *Stri Darpan* and *Arya Mahila* case studies in Chapter Two, pp. 38, 66), and promoted new publications from the same publishing house. They placed emphasis on the quality of content, paper, and print, and commented on their size, cost, and number of illustrations. Quotes from the Hindi literati were listed to validate the advertised literature. An increasing number of periodicals also fuelled the competition for subscribers. But Hindi publishers and publicists understood their profession more as a mission than as a financially profitable venture and most editors and publishers in northern India even fell into debt.[47] Orsini (2002: 60) notes that the 'first professional class of salaried intellectuals in Hindi' emerged in the form of editors, writers, managers, literary advisors, and other employees in the early twentieth century. This observation might also hold true for some of the editorial staff of women's periodicals, less so, however, for the occasional contributors.[48] Central to *sahitya sevā*, the service of literature, to which the Hindi literati was jointly committed, was writing in the service of the community, including the women's community. Moreover, women's periodicals were regarded as part of the nation-building process.

Reviews of books and periodicals were mostly written by editors and regular contributors. They were a welcome opportunity to promote a range of publications of the publishing house with which the periodical was affiliated, as well as to inform readers about what was considered to be *suitable* literature for women.[49] Mahavir Prasad Dwivedi (1995: 119) distinguished critical book reviews (that were central to his literary periodical *Saraswati*) from book advertisements meant for sales promotion: 'In contemporary Hindi literature, there is no scarcity of book reviews. There is no newspaper or periodical that does not publish book reviews. But it is wrong to call them book reviews. They are just advertisements'.[50] Women's periodicals carried both types of reviews: extensive assessments of books and periodicals (Box 30 'Review of *Arya Mahila*', pp. 320–1), as well as short summaries that were more like advertisements and informed readers about new publications (Box 31 'Review of *Children's Lullabies*', p. 321). Further examples of promotions are in the advertisement section (Box 27 'Complimentary Gifts on the Occasion of the New Year', pp. 316–17).

Box 30 Review of *Arya Mahila*[51]

Arya Mahila is a tri-monthly periodical for women readers, which will soon become a monthly periodical. It is published by Śrī Mahāmaṇḍal Bhavan, Jagatganj in Benares. Its annual price is six rupees. It is the mouthpiece of the Śrī Āryamahilā Hitkāriṇī Mahāpariṣad and is published by educated women and female proponents of the eternal dharma (*sanātan dharma*). It is free for members of the society. From its outer form it appears that the periodical will soon occupy a place in the high ranks of literature. Apart

(Contd)

from the print and detail as well as the beautiful images, the articles are earnest and of high quality. The editor is the much lauded and honourable Maharani Śrīmatī Surath Kumari Devi. From the name it would appear that you are a Lakshmi from Bengal. It seems likely, therefore, that *Arya Mahila* will never be faced with failure due to the absence of a Lakshmi. Heretofore, no monthly periodical has provided education in pure eternal dharma as literature for women. *Arya Mahila* will no doubt be able to fill this gap. In its objectives, it states that 'if somebody asked us about our primary goal we would at once respond that it is important to impart the highest principles as proclaimed in the Ramayana, the Mahabharata and the Puranas'. The opinions of Indian women seeking the progress of the women's community will thus be different from those of European women. From its title, *Arya Mahila* is often assumed to be a periodical of the Arya Samaj. But this is not the case. As is apparent from its cover showing Durga carrying a trident and seated on a lion, the periodical is modelled after Uma, who is delicate but also as capable as the powerful Durga of attaining great power to split the heart of the enemy when required to do so. The goal of this periodical will be to make women virtuous like the presiding Mahadevi, powerful and delicate. The hope is that women supporters of the eternal dharma will thus benefit from this periodical.

In our opinion, the language of this periodical is far too sophisticated. If the language were more straightforward, even ordinary women could benefit from it. If not even a large number of men in this country can understand the language of *Arya Mahila*, ordinary women are bound to lag even further behind. We welcome this periodical.

Box 31 Review of *Children's Lullabies*[52]

Children's Lullabies is a forty-page booklet. It contains songs for the instruction of children, which when sung will make children 'righteous, resolute, heroic, brave, courageous, dutiful, virtuous, and intelligent'. The aims are laudable and the lullabies are of good intent. It is the hope that mothers order a copy of the booklet and make the best use of it. But it is our opinion that the booklet would have been better if the language had been simpler and more colloquial so that children would be able to understand it without help. In some places, the words are too difficult. It would be better not to have words such as *puṇḍarīk*, *urag*, and *khagpati*. Mail order to Banarasilal Gupta, Gupta Nāgarī Bhavan, No. 3, Kasganj. The price is two annas and three paise.

Conclusion

In mainstream literary discourses at the turn of the century, the Hindi literati were critical of the new publicity available for literature such as women's periodicals. A frequent critique was levelled precisely at the openness of periodical literature that allowed the representation of a variety of opinions and literary tastes (Orsini 1999a: 410). All of a sudden, 'anyone' could create literature and bypass literary conventions regarding language, style, genre, and content. The conservatism of the Hindi literati regarding the 'purity' of the Hindi language and literature was seldom adhered to in women's literature (see Chapter Five). Communication on a diversity of topics stood at the centre of women's periodicals and it was acknowledged even by the most influential literary critics such as Mahavir Prasad Dwivedi that different speech genres were needed to address women readers.

The female editor distinguished herself from the male editor-critics of literary periodicals. Sales and market interests notwithstanding, women's periodicals fall in between the grid of literary periodicals and popular literature, the latter of which, as Orsini (2002: 162) reminds us, was discredited by the literati even though it dominated the publication market. The contributors to women's periodicals created a new, critical literary field different to the one envisioned by the leading figures of the Hindi public sphere whose 'normative reformism' (Ibid.: 12) was directed at the standardization of Khaṛī Bolī Hindi.

Notes

1. The correlation between the affordability of periodicals and the rise of readership and the woman's press is not to be underestimated. For the British case, White (1970), Braithwaite (1995), and Shevelow (1989) point to the publishing venture of Samuel Beeton targeting women from the newly emerging middle classes as a new market. Beeton's monthly periodical *English Woman's Domestic Magazine* (first published 1852) was sold at the comparatively low cost of two pence. Two years after the first issue was published, the periodical counted as many as 25,000 sales, and after another two years the number rose to 37,000 (White 1970: 44) reaching a record high of 50,000 sales in 1860 (Braithwaite 1995: 12).

2. Amartya Sen (2005: 322) has argued that supposed Hindu calendars were also secular calendrical systems 'devised and used—for all purposes including, *inter alia*, religious ones—by people who happened to be Hindus'.

3. The question of classifying literature according to genres was also a concern of publishers. Stark has pointed out that in the nineteenth century, the catalogues of the Newal Kishore Press in Lucknow classified Hindi publications according to Sanskrit literary genres. Once new literary genres emerged in Hindi literature, these categories were expanded, 'grouping together willy-nilly all genres that no longer fitted the Sanskrit paradigm' (Stark 2004: 271).

4. Gopaldevi, 1913, '*Sampādakīya*' [Editorial], *Grihalakshmi* (April/May [*Vaiśākh* 1970]): 107–12.

5. A sweet made of curd and cheese and generally garnished with almonds, saffron, and cardamom.

6. A ser weighs a little over 2 lbs.

7. Rameshwari Nehru and Roop Kumari Vancu, 1922, '*Sampādakīya: Laṛkiyoṅ se bātcit*' [Editorial: Conversation with girls], *Kumari Darpan* (May): 39–40.

8. R. Nehru, 1917, '*Sampādakīya: Avaśyak sūcnā*' [Editorial: Important information], *Stri Darpan* (September): 113–15.

9. To Bakhtin, primary speech genres constitute most of everyday talk and secondary (complex) speech genres are primarily written, artistic, and scientific forms of communication. Bakhtin (1986: 65) writes that '[s]peech genres are the drive belts from the history of society to the history of language' which makes it a crucial point that speech genres in general—and not just literary genres—are responsive to historical developments. More than that, they act as dynamic forces rather than as stable regulative and prescriptive norms. Further, he says that '[d]uring the process of their formation ... [secondary speech genres] absorb and digest various primary (simple) genres that have taken form in unmediated speech communion' (Ibid.: 62).

10. It seems that the esteemed author suggests that English education has led to Shyama's downfall, but this is not correct. To be righteous and to be spoilt is a question of man's and woman's nature. There is no such education that teaches to disobey the parents. There are also Hindu girls who disobey orders without having received English education. One cannot blame their education or religion.

> Lekhak mahāśay kā vicār yah mālūm hotā hai ki aṅgrezī bhāṣā ke paṛhne se śyāmā kī yah durdaśā huī parantu yah ṭhīk nahīṅ hai. Strī yā puruṣ kā sambhalnā, bigaṛnā us ke svabhāv kī bāt hotī hai koī śikṣā aisī nahīṅ jo mātā pitā kī ājñāpālan karnā na sikhātī ho. Dekhā gayā hai ki hindū laṛkiyāṅ bhī aisī nikal jātī haiṅ jo binā aṅgrezī paṛhe baṛoṅ kī ājñā kā ullaṅghan kartī hoṅ kintu yah un ke dharm yā śikṣā kā doṣ nahīṅ hotā. (R. Nehru, 1917, *Stri Darpan* [August]: 101)

11. Anon., 1917, '*Dāmpatya prem*' [Conjugal Love], *Stri Darpan* (August): 104.

12. Rajbahadur, 1917, '*Stri-Dharma-Shikshak sambandhī kuch bātoṅ par merā vicār*' [My opinion on matters related to *Strī-Dharma-Śikṣak*], *Stri Darpan* (November): 230–2.

13. While the Maharashtrian case displays the dissolution of public/private distinctions by women holding religious ceremonies in public (Anagol 2005: 6), in the case of North India, where women's physical emergence in public was yet awaited, this dissolution can certainly be witnessed in the pages of the Hindi women's periodical.

14. A. Shukla, 1913, '*Striyoṅ kā mukhya dharmma [sic]—pātivrat*' [Chastity and loyalty—the prime dharma of women], *Grihalakshmi* (September/October [Āśvin 1970]): 361–5.

15. V.B. Gupta, 1917, '*Pati kā patnī ke prati kartavya*' [A husband's duty towards his wife], *Grihalakshmi* (August/September [Bhādrapad 1974]): 212–7.

16. Pandit Satyabhakt, 1918, '*Striyāṅ aur sāhitya sevā*', *Arya Mahila* (April/May/June/July [Vaiśākh/Jyeṣṭ/Āṣāṛh 1975]): 374–7.

17. Anon. [A reader], 1917, '*Puruṣoṅ ke striyoṅ par atyācār*' [The atrocities of men over women], *Grihalakshmi* (June/July [Āṣāṛh 1974]): 166–9.

18. Satyavati (Devi), 1917, '*Striyoṅ apne hāth se bhojan kyoṅ banāveṅ*' [Why women should prepare the food with their own hands], *Stri Darpan* (April): 221–4.

19. Hukma (Devi), 1917, '*Strī-jāti kab tak jūtī ban kar santuṣṭ rahegī?*' [How long will the women's community be content to serve as shoes], *Grihalakshmi* (October/November [Kārtik 1974]): 323–8. Hukma Devi, the author of this article, was principal of the Girls' School in Dehradun. Hukma Devi also published a similar article titled '*Ardhāṅginī yā pāoṅ kī jūtī?*' [Partner or foot's shoe] in *Stri Darpan* (April 1918).

20. K.R. Vatal, 1917, '*Ādarś kanyā*' [The model girl], *Stri Darpan* (September): 121–5.

21. Anon., 1921, '*Svādiṣṭ bhojan—besan ke laḍḍū*' [Tasty food—*Laḍḍūs* made with gram-flour], *Vanita Vinod* (November/December [Mārgśīrṣ 1978]): 441.

22. A pāv equals ¼ of a ser.

23. Anon., 1921, '*Gṛh prabandh*' [Management of the home], *Vanita Vinod* (November/December [Mārgśīrṣ 1978]): 442.

24. A. Bandyopadhyay, 1913, '*Strī prabhāv*' [The impact of women], *Grihalakshmi* (September/October [Āśvin 1970]): 383–6.

25. The author seems to be referring to the character Chandravali, a *gopī* madly in love with god Krishna, from the novel *Kulin kanyā athavā pūrṇaprakāś aur candraprabhā*, in most likelihood written by Mallika and published under Harishchandra's name (Dalmia 2004: 406).

26. Krishna Kumari, 1923, '*Kumārī Mṛṇālinī Chaṭṭopādhyāy*' [Kumari Mrinalini Chattopadhyay], *Madhuri* (January): 90.

27. Charushila (Devi) (trans. G. Ghosh), 1920, '*Mere jīvan kā ek adhyāy*' [A chapter in my life], *Stri Darpan* (June): 319–31.

28. Betel leaves filled with areca nut, flavours, spices, and mineral slaked lime.

29. The eleventh day of either fortnight of a lunar month.

30. The botanical name of the evergreen tree is Jonesia Asoka, also known as 'sorrowless tree'.

31. A. Bandyopadhyay, 1914, '*Ghar meṅ cor: Ek saccī kahānī*' [A thief in the house—a true story], *Kanya Manoranjan* (November): 34–5.

32. G. Chaturvedi, 1918, '*Ādarś sakhī*' [The model friend], *Stri Darpan* (July): 9–18.

33. C. Jauhari, 1914/1915, '*Puṇya-vikray*' [The selling of a good deed], *Grihalakshmi* (December/January [Pauṣ 1971]): 519–23.

34. I.P. Sharmma, 1911, '*Patnivratā*' [Patni-vrata—loyalty and chastity towards the wife], *Maryada* (April): 240–4. This is an early example of the way fiction processed and shaped texts on domesticity and virtuous behaviour, which is why I include it in this section though *Maryada* was not a women's periodical. The illustrated monthly was first edited 1910 by Purushottam Das Tandon (1882–1962). Tandon was also a regular contributor to women's periodicals and an advocate of Hindi. From 1911 to 1924, *Maryada* was edited by Krishnakanta Malaviya (1883–1941), a nephew of Madan Mohan Malaviya.

35. Anon. [A well wisher of the country], 1913, '*Svadeśī sāṛī*' [Swadeshi sari], *Grihalakshmi* (September/October [Āśvin 1970]): 387–9.

36. Hamārī bahinoṅ meṅ hindī bhāṣā kā prem bhī bahut phailne lagā hai, iske bhī pramāṇ hamko milne lage haiṅ. Hamārī bahineṅ strīdarpaṇ meṅ apne lekh chapvāne kī baṛī icchā rakhtī haiṅ. [...] Parantu bahudhā ek hī lekh ek se adhik lekhikā kī lekhaniyoṅ se nikle hue hamāre pās āye haiṅ. Is bāt se yahī jān paṛtā hai ki kahīṅ se koī lekh uṭhā kar bhej dene meṅ kyā doṣ hotā hai, hamārī bahineṅ yā kumāriyāṅ ise nahīṅ samajhtīṅ. Kabhī kisī pustak yā kisī dūsre patr meṅ chapā huā lekh hamāre pās ā gayā, aur sarvajñatā kā guṇ hamko bhagvān se na milne ke kāraṇ hamne usko nayā samajhkar chāp bhī diyā, to smaraṇ rakhnā cāhie ki ham bhī sādhāraṇ dṛṣṭi meṅ aparādhī ṭhaharāyī jā saktī haiṅ. Āśā hai ki hamārī bahineṅ is viṣay par āge viśeṣ dhyān deṅgī aur kisī dūsre ṭhaur par prakāśit yā kisī dūsre lekhak ke likhe hue lekhoṅ ko apnī sampatti kah kar kabhī hamāre pās na bhejeṅgī. (R. Nehru, 1917, '*Sampādakīya: lekhikāoṅ se prārthnā*' [Editorial: A request to the writers], *Stri Darpan* [December]: 286–7)

37. M. Shukla, 1917, '*Mahilāoṅ se nivedan*' [A plea to women], *Stri Darpan* (March): 132–3.

38. Jyandevi, 1918, '*Kyā homrūl loge?*' [You want home rule], *Stri Darpan* (December): 288.

39. Correspondingly, children's periodicals published advertisements with products particularly suited to children. *Bal Sakha* (first published 1917) contained advertisements for tonics for children (*bālāmṛt*) and special books (*bālopayogī pustakeṅ*) such as a children's Mahabharata, a children's Gita, and children's poems, songs, and grammars. Books were always promoted as

extremely precious and worth owning. Children's periodicals gave discounts on books to subscribers of their periodicals and to subscribers who attracted new readers.

40. This was the case with Harishchandra's women's periodical *Balabodhini* (Dalmia 2004: 407).

41. Certainly, such invigorating tonics catered to male consumers and not to the female readers, whose sexuality was rather contained than made public. In mainstream periodicals and newspapers of the times, however, the advertisements became a novel way to make information on sexuality available to men even though the Hindi literati campaigned for imposing a ban on the publications of such advertisements as well as on manuals on sexuality (Gupta 2001: 79).

42. Advertisement, 1913/1914, '*Sugandhit Puṣpāvilās*' [Fragrant Pushpavilas hair oil], *Grihalakshmi* (December/January [*Pauṣ* 1970]), back page. The title of the advertisement does not exactly correspond with the label, which is Puṣpavilās tel and in English, Puspabilash.

43. Advertisement, 1913, '*Naye varṣ kā uphār*' [Complimentary gifts on the occasion of the new year], *Kanya Manoranjan* (December): 33.

44. *Khilauna*, for example, carried many advertisements from the Indian Press that promoted textbooks (*skūlī pustakeṅ*) such as Hindi and Urdu primers, grammars, library books, books handed out as awards, and books that were especially useful (*atyupayogī*) for women (Advertisement, 1927, *Khilauna* [January], inner cover).

45. Advertisement, 1914, '*Zarūrat hai*' [Seeking], *Grihalakshmi* (April/May [Vaiśākh 1970]), back page.

46. Advertisement, 1914, 'Lucrative employment at Cawnpore Woollen Mills Co. Ltd.', *Stri Darpan* (March), back page. (This advertisement is originally published in English.)

47. Mahavir Prasad Dwivedi (1995: 122), in a speech at the Hindi Sāhitya Sammelan in 1911, addressed the hardships of professional writers and called for financial support of writers who had stepped into the national service of literature: 'In this wretched state of Hindi very few people have been able to make a living from their service to literature. This is why there is much need to support them financially'. [Hindī kī vartamān hīnavasthā meṅ bahut kam log sāhitya-sevā kā vyavsāy karke sukh se jīvikānirvāh kar sakte haiṅ. Ataeva sāhitya-sevakoṅ ke lie utsāh-dān kī baṛī āvaśyaktā hai.] Ramrakh Singh Sahgal, editor of *Chand*, still echoed such a call in the 1920s (Schomer 1983: 184).

48. Even though Mahadevi Varma as editor of *Chand* received no remuneration (Schomer 1983: 225).

49. Orsini points to a symbiosis of ephemeral periodicals and supposedly longer-lasting 'stable' (*sthāyī*) literature when stating that 'books enhanced and

confirmed the success of poems, short stories, or novels already familiar to the public through periodicals. They also multiplied the profit, since the same material could be used twice—and with no additional cost when the editor-publisher bought the rights of the work' (2002: 59–60).

50. 'Vartamān hindī-sāhitya meṅ samālocanāoṅ kī kamī nahīṅ. Koī samācārpatr, koī sāmayik, aisī nahīṅ jismeṅ samālocanāyeṅ na nikaltī hoṅ. Parantu unko samālocanā kahnā bhūl hai. Ve vijñāpan mātr haiṅ' (Dwivedi 1995: 119).

51. Anon., 1918, '*Samālocanā—Ārya Mahīlā*' [Review of Arya Mahila], *Stri Darpan* (October): 223–4.

52. Anon., 1918, '*Samālocanā—Śiśulorī*' [Review of Children's Lullabies], *Stri Darpan* (September): 168.

Bibliography

Primary Sources

Periodicals

Āryā Mahilā (Arya Mahila). Selected issues, 1918–23. Surath Kumari Devi (ed.). Benares: Śrī Mahāmaṇḍal Bhavan.

Cānd (Chand). Selected issues, 1922–27. Ramrakh Singh Sahgal (ed.). Allahabad: Chand Kāryālay.

Gṛhalakṣmī (Grihalakshmi). Selected issues, 1913–17. Sudarshan Acharya and Gopaldevi (eds). Allahabad: Sudarshan Press.

Jyoti. Selected issues, 1921–22. Vidyavati Seth (ed.). Lahore: Unknown Publisher.

Kanyā Manorañjan (Kanya Manoranjan). Selected issues, 1913–17. Omkarnath Vajpeyi (ed.). Allahabad: Omkar Press.

Khilaunā (Toy). Selected issues, January–August 1927. Ramji Lal Sharmma (ed.). Allahabad: Hindi Press.

Kumārī Darpaṇ (Kumari Darpan). Selected issues, 1916–22. Rameshwari Nehru and Roop Kumari Nehru (eds). Allahabad: Law Periodical Press.

———. Selected issues, 1925. Sumati Devi and Phulkumari Mehrotra (eds). Kanpur: Coronation Press.

Mādhurī (Madhuri). Selected issues, 1923–25. Dularelal Bhargava and Rupnarayan Pandey (eds). Lucknow: Newal Kishor Press.

Maryādā (Maryada). Selected issues, 1911, 1915. Purushottam Das Tandon and Krishnakant Malaviya (eds). Allahabad: Abhyuday Press.

Strī Darpaṇ (Stri Darpan). Selected issues, 1911–23. Rameshwari Nehru (ed.). Allahabad: Law Periodical Press.

———. Selected issues, 1923–8. Sumati Devi and Phulkumari Mehrotra (eds). Kanpur: Coronation Press.

The Indian Ladies Magazine. Selected issues, 1901–2. Kamala Sattianadhan (ed.). Madras: Methodist Episcopal Press.

Individual Articles and Other Primary Sources

Abhichandra. 1927 '*Ham vīr haiṅ*'. *Khilauna* (September), p. 233.

Ahmed, N. 1903. *A Tale of Domestic Life in Delhi Forty Years Ago*. London: Henry Frowde.

Annual Reports on Indian Papers Published in the United Provinces during the Years 1911 and 1919. 2 Vols. Allahabad.

Anon. (A well-wisher of the country). 1913. '*Svadeśī sāṛī*' (Svadeshi sari). *Grihalakshmi* (September/October [Āśvin 1970]), pp. 387–9.

Anon. 1913. '*Gṛhasth śāsan*' (House rule). *Grihalakshmi* (October/November [Kārtik 1970]), pp. 427–30.

Anon. 1914. '*Patnī kā pati-prem*' (A wife's love towards her husband). *Grihalakshmi* (November/December [Mārgśīrṣ 1971]), p. 363.

Anon. (A reader). 1917. '*Suśīlā*' (Sushila). *Grihalakshmi* (May/June [Jyeṣṭ 1974]), pp. 119–27.

Anon. (A reader). 1917. '*Puruṣoṅ ke striyoṅ par atyācār*' (The atrocities of men over women). *Grihalakshmi* (June/July [Āṣāṛh 1974]), pp. 166–9.

Anon. 1917. '*Vah kahāṅ*' (Where is he?), *Kumari Darpan* (July), pp. 2–3.

Anon. (A reader). 1917. '*Dāmpatya Prem*' (Conjugal Love), *Stri Darpan* (August), p. 104.

Anon. 1917. '*Samālocanā*' (Review). *Grihalakshmi* (September/October [Āśvin 1974]), p. 290.

Anon. 1917. '*Nayī paheliyāṅ*' (New riddles). *Kumari Darpan* (October), p. 32.

Anon. 1918. '*Jaganmātā*' (Mother of the world). *Arya Mahila* (January/February/March/April [Māgh/Phālgun/Caitra 1975]), p. 215.

Anon. 1918. '*Samālocanā—Śiśulorī*' (Review of Childrens' Lullabies). *Stri Darpan* (September), p. 168.

Anon. 1918. '*Samālocanā*' (Review). *Stri Darpan* (October), pp. 223–4.

Anon. 1918. '*Samālocanā: Āryā Mahilā*' (Review: *Arya Mahila*). *Stri Darpan* (October), p. 224.

Anon. 1920. '*Puraskār lo*' (Receive a prize). *Kumari Darpan* (March), p. 21.

Anon. 1920. '*Nayī paheliyāṅ*' (New puzzles/riddles). *Kumari Darpan* (January), pp. 6–7.

Anon. 1920. '*Pustakālocanā*' (Book review). *Stri Darpan* (January), p. 51.

Anon. 1921. '*Svādiṣṭ bhojan—besan ke laḍḍū*' (Tasty food—*Laḍḍūs* made with gram-flour). *Vanita Vinod* (November/December [Mārgśīrṣ 1978]), p. 441.

Anon. 1921. '*Gṛh prabandh*' (Management of the home). *Vanita Vinod* (November/December [Mārgśīrṣ 1978]), p. 442.

Anon. 1923. (Self-advertisement). *Arya Mahila* (April/May/June/July [Vaiśākh/Jyeṣṭ/Āṣāṛh 1980]), p. 380.

Ara, V. 1913. '*Paropkār*' (Charity). *Grihalakshmi* (April/May [Vaiśākh 1970]), pp. 82–6.

______. 1913. '*Saccī mitratā*' (True friendship). *Grihalakshmi* (April/May [Vaiśākh 1970]), pp. 88–90.

Avasthi, R. 1920. '*Āgāmī "strī-śāsan" kī kalpanā*' (The lament of an approaching women's rule), *Stri Darpan* (January), pp. 1–4.

Balaji. 1918. '*Hindī meṅ striyoṅ ke yogya sāhitya*' (Suitable literature for women in Hindi). *Stri Darpan* (November), pp. 242–9.

Bandyopadhyay, A. 1913. '*Strī prabhāv*' (The impact of women). *Grihalakshmi* (September/October [Aśvin 1970]), pp. 383–6.

______. 1913. '*Ghar meṅ cor—Ek saccī kahānī*' (A thief in the house—a true story). *Kanya Manoranjan* (November), pp. 34–5.

Bhagvati (Devi). 1925. '*Vartamān paristhiti*' (Contemporary circumstances). *Madhuri* (September), pp. 394–5.

Bhatt, M. 1915. '*Pāk-vidyā*' (The art of cooking). *Kanya Manoranjan* (January), pp. 121–2.

Bihari, D. 1917. '*Inglenḍ kī bahū aur beṭiāṅ*' (England's wives and daughters). *Stri Darpan* (May), pp. 231–2.

Buddhimati (wife of Lala Vankelal). 1893–1895. *Nārīsudaśāpravartak* (The education and moral and physical training of women), 4 parts. Allahabad: Government Press.

Charushila (Devi) [trans. G. Ghosh]. 1920. '*Mere jīvan kā ek adhyāy*' (A chapter in my life). *Stri Darpan* (June), pp. 319–31.

Chaturvedi, G. 1918. '*Ādarś sakhī*' (The ideal friend). *Stri Darpan* (July), pp. 9–18.

Devi, P. 1917. '*Bhūgol kī kahānī*' (The story of geography). *Kumari Darpan* (February), pp. 9–13.

Devraj (Lala). 1899. *Patra Kaumudī* (A guide to letter writing). Lahore: Punjab Economical Press.

Devsakar, G. 1913. '*Iṅglenḍ kī striyāṅ*' (England's women). *Grihalakshmi* (September/October [Āśvin 1970]), pp. 365–7.

Divaniya, C. 1927. '*Suśīlā*' (Sushila). *Stri Darpan* (January), pp. 7–16.

Dwivedi, M. 1995 [1911]. *Mahāvīrprasād Dwivedī Racnāvalī* (Collected Works of Mahavir Prasad Dwivedi), Vol. 1. New Delhi: Kitab Ghar.

Dwivedi, P.N. 1914. '*Laṛkiyoṅ kā khel*' (Girls' games). *Kanya Manoranjan* (December), pp. 71–4.

Gajapuri, M.D. 1911. '*Hindī samāj meṅ striyāṅ*' (Women in the Hindi society). *Stri Darpan* (December), pp. 339–42.

Gandhi, M.K. 1965. *Our Language Problem*. Bombay: Bharatiya Vidya Bhavan.

Gangaram. 1914. '*Lālā aur chor*' (Lala and the thief). *Kanya Manoranjan* (November), pp. 44–7.

Garg, P. 1913. '*Kyā kyā sīkhnā cāhiye?*' (What all should be learned?). *Grihalakshmi* (May/June [Jyeṣṭ 1970]), pp. 145–51.

Ghosh, G.K. 1911. '*Puruṣ caritra*' (The character of men). *Stri Darpan* (December), pp. 363–4.

———. 1913. '*Bahādur laṛkī*' (The brave girl). *Kanya Manoranjan* (October), pp. 24–9.

Gopaldevi. 1913. '*Sampādakīya*' (Editorial). *Grihalakshmi* (April/May [Vaiśākh 1970]), pp. 107–12.

Grierson, G.A. (ed.). 1904. *Linguistic Survey of India. Indo–Aryan Family: Mediate Group, Specimens of the Eastern Hindi Language*, Vol. 6. Calcutta: Office of the Superintendent of Government Printing.

Gupta, V.B. 1917. '*Pati kā patnī ke prati kartavya*' (A husband's duty towards his wife). *Grihalakshmi* (August/September [Bhādrapad 1974]), pp. 212–17.

Harishchandra, B. 1893. *Hindī Bhāṣā* (The Hindi Language). Benares: Khadagvilas Press.

Hukma (Devi). 1917. '*Strī-jāti kab tak jūtī ban kar santuṣṭ rahegī?*' (How long will the women's community be content to serve as shoes?). *Grihalakshmi* (October/November [Kārtik 1974]), pp. 323–8.

———. 1918. '*Ardhāṅginī yā pāoṇ kī jūtī?*' (Partner or foot's shoe). *Stri Darpan* (April), pagination not available.

Jain, M. 1914/1915. '*Gahnā gale kī phāṅsī. Mātāoṅ kī mūrkhtā*' (Jewellery, death by hanging. The folly of mothers). *Grihalakshmi* (December/January [Pauṣ 1971]), pp. 512–14.

Jauhari, C. 1914/1915. '*Puṇya-vikray*' (The selling of a virtue). *Grihalakshmi* (December/January [Pauṣ 1971]), pp. 519–23.

Jaysaval, G. 1913. '*Parde kī cāl*' (The custom of veiling). *Grihalakshmi* (April/May [Vaiśākh 1970]), pp. 94–103.

Jhingaran, R.K. 1917. '*Ablā yā sablā*' (Weak or strong). *Stri Darpan* (March), pp. 133–6.

Jyandevi. 1918. '*Kyā homrūl loge*' (You want home rule). *Stri Darpan* (December), p. 288.

Kumari, K. 1923. '*Kumārī Mṛṇālinī Chaṭṭopādhyāy*' (Kumari Mrinalini Chattopadhyay). *Madhuri* (January), p. 94.

Kaul, S. 1920. '*Gahno se hānī*' (The harms of jewellery). *Stri Darpan* (May), pp. 268–73.

Manorama. 1914. '*Ek gharāū ghaṭnā*' (A domestic incident). *Grihalakshmi* (November/December [Mārgśīrṣ 1971]), pp. 466–70.

Mehrotra, G.P. 1917. '*Śyāmā*' (Shyama). *Stri Darpan* (August), pp. 86–101.

Mehrotra, P. 1925. '*Zevar kī cāh*' (The desire for jewellery). *Kumari Darpan* (July), pp. 50–1.

Mill, J. 1975 [1817]. *The History of British India*. Delhi: Associated Publishing House.

Mishra, J. 1920. '*Pañjāb prānt meṅ devanāgarī kī āvaśyaktā*' (The necessity of *Deva Nāgarī* in Punjab). *Stri Darpan* (April), pp. 197–8.

Mitra, B.K. 1917. '*Brahmāṇḍ aur saur jagat*' (The cosmos and the solar system). *Kumari Darpan* (January), pp. 1–7.

Mohandevi. 1913. '*Kām ke khel*' (Work games). *Kanya Manoranjan* (October), p. 13.

Mohini, H. 1917. '*Strī śikṣā par Akbar ke vicār*' (Akbar's thoughts on women's education). *Stri Darpan* (July), pp. 53–6.

Nagar, S. 1913. '*Bānūbāī kā sāhas*' (Banubai's courage). *Kanya Manoranjan* (November), pp. 56–7.

Nehru, J. 1960. *The Discovery of India*. London: Meridian Books Limited.

Nehru, R. 1917. '*Sampādakīya: Strī Darpaṇ*' (Editorial: *Stri Darpan*). *Stri Darpan* (February), pp. 57–60.

———. 1917. '*Sampādakīya: Śrīmatī Sarojinī Devī Naiḍū kā vyākhyān*' (Editorial: The speech of Mrs Sarojini Devi Naidu). *Stri Darpan* (February), pp. 60–3.

———. 1917. '*Strī kā kartavya*' (Women's duty). *Stri Darpan* (July), pp. 2–6.

———. 1917. '*Sampādakīya: Avaśyak sūcnā*' (Editorial: Important information). *Stri Darpan* (September), pp. 113–15.

———. 1917. '*Sampādakīya: Lekhikāoṅ se prārthnā*' (Editorial: A request to the writers). *Stri Darpan* (December), pp. 286–7.

———. 1918. '*Sampādakīya: Rāṣṭra-bhāṣā Hindī*' (Editorial: Hindi, the national language). *Stri Darpan* (July), p. 6.

———. 1918. '*Sampādakīya: Rāṣṭra-bhāṣā Hindī*' (Editorial: Hindi, the national language). *Stri Darpan* (October), pp. 169–71.

———. 1918. '*Sampādakīya: Striyāṅ aur voṭ*' (Editorial: Women and vote). *Stri Darpan* (November), pp. 225–30.

———. 1920. (Untitled editorial comment). *Stri Darpan* (January), p. 4.

———. 1920. (Untitled editorial comment). *Stri Darpan* (February), p. 113–14.

———. 1920. '*Ek sampādikā kā svapna*' (An editor's dream). *Stri Darpan* (May), pp. 277–83.

———. 1922. '*Sampādakīya*' (Editorial). *Stri Darpan* (February), p. 58.

Nehru, R. and R.K. Vancu. 1922. '*Laṛkiyoṅ se bātcit*' (Conversation with girls). *Kumari Darpan* (May), pp. 39–40.

Nehru, S.K. 1917. '*Deśbhakti*' (Patriotism). *Kumari Darpan* (October), p. 30.

Nehru, S.K. (ed.). c1938. *Our Cause. A Symposium by Indian Women*. Allahabad: Kitabistan.

Nehru, U. 1918. '*Hamāre samāj sudhārak*' (Our social reformers). *Stri Darpan* (March), pagination not available.

_____. 1918. '*Hamāre sāmājik sāñce*' (Our social organization). *Stri Darpan* (April), pagination not available.

_____. 1918. '*Hamāre hṛday*' (Our hearts). *Stri Darpan* (May), pagination not available.

_____. 1920. '*Hamāre zewar*' (Our jewellery), Part 1 of 2. *Stri Darpan* (January), pp. 5–11.

_____. 1920. '*Hamāre zewar*' (Our jewellery), Part 2 of 2. *Stri Darpan* (March), pp. 144–52.

Nehru-Hutheesing, K. (with A. Hatch). 1967. *We Nehrus*. New York: Holt, Rinehart and Winston.

N.N. 1913. '*Nārīcaryā*' (The conduct of women, Part I). *Grihalakshmi* (April/May [Vaiśākh 1970]), pp. 104–7.

_____. 1913. '*Nārīcaryā*' (The conduct of women, Part II), *Grihalakshmi* (May/June [Jyeṣṭ 1970]), pp. 159–62.

_____. 1913. '*Striyoṅ ko apne hāth se bhojan banānā cāhiye*' [Women should prepare food with their own hands], *Grihalakshmi* (September/October [Aśvin 1970], pp. 389–90.

_____. 1913. '*Sudhar aur phūhar*', *Kanya Manoranjan* (November), pp. 53–4.

_____. 1914. '*Ek patr*' (Letter). *Kanya Manoranjan* (December), pp. 92–3.

Pal, R.P. 1917. '*Striyoṅ ko hom rūl pahile dījiye*' (First give women 'home rule'). *Stri Darpan* (February), pp. 72–6.

Pandey, A.P. 1914. '*Ghar aur mātā*' (The home and the mother). *Stri Darpan* (October), pp. 242–6.

Pandey, Raj Bahadur. 1917. '*Striyāṅ aur deśbhakt*' (Women and patriotism), *Stri Darpan* (January), pp. 9–14.

Parvar, D. 1913. '*Rūpvati aur Guṇvati* (Rupvati and Gunavati). *Kanya Manoranjan* (October), pp. 2–4.

Purandas, V. 1914. '*Pativratā Māltī*' (Malti, the Pativrata). *Grihalakshmi* (June/July [Āṣāṛh 1971]), pp. 138–43.

Pushpavati. 1917. '*Nānī kī kahānī*' (Grandmother's stories). *Grihalakshmi* (May/June [Jyeṣṭh 1974]), pp. 103–8.

Rajbahadur. 1917. '*Strī-dharma-śikṣak sambandhī kuch bātoṅ par merā vicār*' (My opinion on matters related to Stri-Dharma-Shikshak). *Stri Darpan* (November), pp. 230–2.

Ram Lala (Munshi). 1872. *Putrīśikṣopakārīgranth* (A treatise on the education and social duties of women). Allahabad: Government Press.

Ramakrishna. 1871. *Strīśikṣā* (Women's education). Allahabad: Government Press.

Rameshprasad. 1920. '*Daśam Hindī sāhitya sammelan meṅ striyāṅ*' (Women at the tenth meeting of the Hindī Sāhitya Sammelan). *Stri Darpan* (May), pp. 283–5.

Richey, J.A. 1965 [1922]. *Selections from Educational Records, Part II. 1840–1859*. New Delhi: Government of India Press.

Risley, H. 1915. *The People of India*. Calcutta: Thacker, Spink and Co.

Sagar, D.V.D.D. 1917. '*Vīrāṅganā-Rūp Kumārī*' (Roop Kumari, the heroine). *Stri Darpan* (August), pp. 72–7.

Sahay, S. 1919/1920. '*Pati aur patnī kā paraspar sadbhāv*' (Mutual feelings between husband and wife). *Arya Mahila* (October/November/December/January [(Kārtik/Āgrahāyaṇ/Pauṣ 1976]), pp. 255–7.

Sahgal, R.S. 1923. '*Vidhvā-aṅk*' (Widows' issue). *Chand* (April).

______. 1925. '*Strī samāj aur sevā dharma*' (Women's society and seva dharma). *Chand* (April), pp. 5–8.

Saraswati, R. 1887. *The High-Caste Hindu Woman*. Philadelphia: The Jas. B. Rodgers Printing Co.

Satyabhakt (Pandit). 1918. '*Striyāṅ aur sāhitya sevā*' (Women and the service of literature). *Arya Mahila* (April/May/June/July [Vaiśākh/Jyeṣṭ/Āṣāṛh 1975]), pp. 374–7.

Satyavati (Devi). 1917. '*Striyoṅ apne hāth se bhojan kyoṅ banāveṅ*' (Why women should prepare the food with their own hands). *Stri Darpan* (April), pp. 221–4.

Secretary of State for India in Council (Publ.). 1908. *Imperial Gazetteer of India. United Provinces*, Vol. 1. Calcutta: Superintendent of Government Printing.

Selections from Indian-Owned Newspapers Published in the United Provinces, 1911, 1917, 1918.

Seth, J. 1920. '*Pardā*' (The veil). *Stri Darpan* (March), pp. 164–7.

Seth, Vidyavati. 1921. '*Vicār pravāh: Hindī Sāhitya Sammelan*'. *Jyoti* (November/December [Mārgśīrṣ 1978]), p. 431.

Shaksena, B. 1914. '*Pativrat dharma aur vartamān śikṣā kram*' (*Pativrat* dharma and the contemporary system of education). *Stri Darpan* (March), pp. 173–6.

Shaligram. 1913. '*Devi Suśīlā*' (Goddess Sushila). *Grihalakshmi* (September/October [Āśvin 1970]), pp. 343–52.

Sharma, Indumati. 1923. '*Strī kartavya*' (Women's duty). *Madhuri* (July), pp. 683–4.

Sharma, Pandit Thakur Prasad. 1914. '*Deśprem*' (Patriotism). *Kanya Manoranjan* (November), p. 39.

Sharmma, I.P. 1911. '*Patnivratā*' (*Patni-vrata*—loyalty and chastity towards the wife). *Maryada* (April), pp. 240–4.

Shiv. 1927. '*Deś kī bāt*' (Matters of the country). *Khilauna* (June), pp. 190–1.
Shrivastav, G.P. 1913/1914. '*Kālī mem*' (The black madam). *Grihalakshmi* (December/January [Pauṣ 1970]), pp. 515–19.
———. 1914. '*Manorañjan tum ham ko maṅgā do*' (Please order *Manoranjan* for us). *Kanya Manoranjan* (November), pp. 54–5.
Shrivastav, V.M. 1928. '*Sukhiyā kā vyāh*' (Sukhiya's marriage). *Stri Darpan* (June), pp. 819–24.
Shukla, A. 1913. '*Striyoṅ kā mukhya dharma—pātivrat*' (Chastity and loyalty—the prime dharma of women). *Grihalakshmi* (September/October [(Āśvin 1970]), pp. 361–5.
Shukla, M. 1917. '*Mahilāoṅ se nivedan*' (A plea to women). *Stri Darpan* (March), pp. 132–3.
Shukla, R. 1928. '*Sampādakīya*' (Editorial). *Stri Darpan* (June), pp. 871–3.
Singh, Upadhyaya 'Hariaudh'. 1919/1920. '*Hariaudh*', *Arya Mahila* (October/November/December/January [Kārtik/Āgrahāyan/Pauṣ 1976])
Steel, F.A. and G. Gardiner. 1909. *The Complete Indian Housekeeper and Cook*. London: William Heinemann.
Subhadradevi. 1928. '*Yorop kī striyāṅ*' (European women). *Stri Darpan* (June), pp. 848–57.
Surathkumari (Devi). 1923. '*Sampādakīya*' (Editorial). *Arya Mahila* (April/May/June/July [Vaiśākh/Jyeṣṭh/Āṣāḍh 1980]), pp. 382–4.
Vajpeyi, Omkarnath. 1913. (Editorial comment). *Kanya Manoranjan*, (September/October [Āśvin 1970]), p. 30.
Varma, S.C. 1917. '*Kiśorī*' (Kishori). *Grihalakshmi* (May/June [Jyeṣṭ 1974]), pp. 114–18.
Vasu, T. 1923. '*Strī kā sthān*' (The place of women). *Madhuri* (January), pp. 91–2.
Vatal, K.R. 1917. '*Ādarś kanyā*' (The model girl). *Stri Darpan* (September), pp. 121–5.
Vidyarthi, K. P. 1917. '*Bhūt nahīṅ billī—galp nahīṅ saccī ghaṭnā hai*' (Not a ghost, but a cat—not a story, but a true incident). *Stri Darpan* (March), pp. 147–51.
Vivekananda (Swami). 1918. '*Jīvan hiṇḍola*' (Life's swing). *Arya Mahila* (January/February/March/April [Māgh/Phālgun/Chaitra 1975]), pp. 297–301.

Secondary Sources

Agnew, V. 1979. *Elite Women in Indian Politics*. Delhi: Vikas Publishing House.
Anagol, P. 2005. *The Emergence of Feminism in India, 1850–1920*. Hampshire: Ashgate.

Anderson, B. 1983. *Imagined Communities. Reflections on the Origin and Spread of Nationalism*. London: Verso.

Andrews, R.H. 1967. *A Lamp for India: The Story of Madame Pandit*. London: Arthur Baker Ltd.

Armstrong, N. 1987. 'The Rise of the Domestic Woman.' In N. Armstrong and L. Tennenhouse (eds). *The Ideology of Conduct: Essays on Literature and the History of Sexuality*. New York: Methuen, pp. 96–141.

Armstrong, N. and L. Tennenhouse. 1987. 'The Literature of Conduct, the Conduct of Literature, and the Politics of Desire: An Introduction.' In N. Armstrong and L. Tennenhouse (eds). *The Ideology of Conduct. Essays on Literature and the History of Sexuality*. New York: Methuen, pp. 1–24.

Bailey, T.G. 1936. 'Does *Khaṛī Bolī* Mean Nothing More than Rustic Speech?' *Bulletin of the School of Oriental Studies*, Vol. 8, No. 2/3, pp. 363–71.

Bakhtin, M.M. 1986. 'The Problem of Speech Genres.' In C. Emerson and M. Holquist (eds). *Speech Genres and Other Late Essays*. Austin: University of Texas Press, pp. 60–102.

———. 1996 [1975]. *The Dialogic Imagination*. Austin: University of Texas Press.

Ballaster, R., M. Beetham, E. Frazer, and S. Hebron. 1991. *Women's Worlds: Ideology, Femininity and the Woman's Magazine*. London: MacMillan.

Bandyopadhyay, S. 1995. 'Caste, Widow-remarriage and the Reform of Popular Culture in Colonial Bengal.' In B. Ray (ed.). *From the Seams of History*. Delhi: Oxford University Press, pp. 8–36.

Banerjee, Sumanta. 1989. 'Marginalization of Women's Popular Culture in Nineteenth Century Bengal.' In K. Sangari and S. Vaid (eds). *Recasting Women: Essays in Colonial History*. New Delhi: Kali for Women, pp. 127–79.

Banerjee, Swapna. 1996. 'Exploring the World of Domestic Manuals: Bengali Middle-Class Women and Servants in Colonial Calcutta.' *SAGAR* 3.1.

———. 2004. *Men, Women, and Domestics: Articulating Middle-Class Identity in Colonial Bengal*. New Delhi: Oxford University Press.

Bannerji, H. 1991. 'Fashioning a Self: Educational Proposals for and by Women in Popular Magazines in Colonial Bengal.' *Economic and Political Weekly*, Vol. 26, WS 50–62.

———. 1992. 'Mothers and Teachers: Gender and Class in Educational Proposals for and by Women in Colonial Bengal.' *Journal of Historical Sociology*, Vol. 5, No. 1, pp. 1–30.

———. 1998. *The Mirror of Class: Essays on Bengali Theatre*. Calcutta: Papyrus.

Barannikov, A. 1936. 'Modern Literary Hindi.' *Bulletin of the School of Oriental Studies*, Vol. 8, No. 1/2, pp. 373–90.

Barthes, R. 1981. *Camera Lucida: Reflections on Photography*. New York: Hill and Wang.

Basu, A. 1974. *The Growth of Education and Political Development in India, 1898–1920*. New Delhi: Oxford University Press.

______. 1976. 'The Role of Women in the Indian Struggle for Freedom.' In B. R. Nanda (ed.). *Indian Women. From Purdah to Modernity*. New Delhi: Vikas Publishing House, pp. 16–40.

Bayly, C.A. 1975. *The Local Roots of Indian Politics: Allahabad, 1880–1920*. Oxford: Clarendon Press.

Beauvoir, S. de. 1970. *The Second Sex*. New York: Alfred A. Knopf.

Beetham, M. 1990. 'Towards a Theory of the Periodical as a Publishing Genre.' In L. Brake, A. Jones, and L. Madden (eds). *Investigating Victorian Journalism*. London: The Macmillan Press, pp. 19–32.

______. 1996. *A Magazine of Her Own? Domesticity and Desire in the Woman's Magazine, 1800–1914*. London: Routledge.

Beetham, M. and K. Boardman (eds). 2001. *Victorian Women's Magazines. An Anthology.* Manchester: Manchester University Press.

Bhatnagar, R.R. c1947. *The Rise and Growth of Hindi Journalism, 1826–1945*. Allahabad: Kitab Mahal.

Blackburn, S. 2004. 'The Burden of Authenticity: Printed Oral Tales in Tamil Literary History.' In S. Blackburn and V. Dalmia (eds). *India's Literary History*. New Delhi: Permanent Black, pp. 119–45.

Blackburn, S., and V. Dalmia (eds). 2004. *India's Literary History: Essays on the Nineteenth Century*. New Delhi: Permanent Black.

Borthwick, M. 1984. *The Changing Role of Women in Bengal, 1849–1905*. Princeton: Princeton University Press.

Braithwaite, B. 1995. *Women's Magazines: The First 300 Years*. London: Peter Owen Publishers.

Butler, J. 1990. *Gender Trouble: Feminism and the Subversion of Identity*. New York: Routledge.

Calhoun, C. (ed.). 1992. *Habermas and the Public Sphere*. Cambridge: MIT Press.

Carroll, L. 1989. 'Law, Custom and Statutory Social Reform: The Hindu Widows' Remarriage Act of 1856.' In J. Krishnamurty (ed.). *Women in Colonial India. Essays on Survival, Work and the State*. Delhi: Oxford University Press, pp. 1–26.

Chakrabarty, D. 1994. 'The Difference-Deferral of a Colonial Modernity: Public Debates on Domesticity in British India.' In D. Arnold and D. Hardiman (eds). *Subaltern Studies VIII: Essays in Honour of Ranajit Guha*. Delhi: Oxford University Press, pp. 50–88.

Chakrabarty, D. 2000. *Provincializing Europe: Postcolonial Thought and Historical Difference*. Princeton: Princeton University Press.

Chakravarti, U. 1989. 'Whatever Happened to the Vedic *Dasi*? Orientalism, Nationalism and a Script for the Past.' In K. Sangari and S. Vaid (eds). *Recasting Women*. Delhi: Kali for Women, pp. 27–87.

_____. 1998. *Rewriting History: The Life and Times of Pandita Ramabai*. New Delhi: Kali for Women.

Chandra, N. 2001. 'Siting Childhood: A Study of Children's Periodicals in Hindi, 1920–50.' Unpublished PhD Thesis, Jawaharlal Nehru University, New Delhi.

_____. 2007. 'Travel Writing as Nationalist Pedagogy in the Hindi Children's Periodicals (1920–1950).' *South Asia: Journal of South Asian Studies*, Vol. 30, No. 2, pp. 293–325.

Chandra, S. 1992. *The Oppressive Present: Literature and Social Consciousness in Colonial India*. New Delhi: Oxford University Press.

Chartier, R. 1992. 'Laborers and Voyagers: From the Text to the Reader.' *Diacritics*, Vol. 22, No. 2, pp. 49–61.

Chatterjee, P. 1986. *Nationalist Thought and the Colonial World: A Derivative Discourse?* London: Zed Books.

_____. 1989. 'The Nationalist Resolution of the Women's Question.' In K. Sangari and S. Vaid (eds). *Recasting Women*. Delhi: Kali for Women, pp. 233–53.

_____. 1993. *The Nation and Its Fragments: Colonial and Postcolonial Histories*. Princeton: Princeton University Press.

Chin, C.C. 2006. 'Translating the New Woman: Chinese Feminists View the West, 1905–15.' *Gender and History*, Vol. 18, No. 3, pp. 490–518.

Cohn, B.S. 1985. 'The Command of Language and the Language of Command.' In R. Guha (ed.). *Subaltern Studies IV*. Delhi: Oxford University Press, pp. 276–329.

Dalmia, V. 1997. *The Nationalization of Hindu Traditions: Bharatendu Harishchandra and Nineteenth-century Banaras*. Delhi: Oxford University Press.

_____. 1999. 'A Novel Moment in Hindi: *Parīkṣhā Guru*.' In V. Dalmia and T. Damsteegt (eds). *Narrative Strategies*. Delhi: Oxford University Press, pp. 169–84.

_____. 2003. 'The Locations of Hindi.' *Economic and Political Weekly*, Vol. 38, No. 14, pp. 1377–84.

_____. 2004. 'Generic Questions: Bharatendu Harishcandra and Women's Issues.' In S. Blackburn and V. Dalmia (eds). *India's Literary History: Essays on the Nineteenth Century*. New Delhi: Permanent Black, pp. 402–34.

Dalmia, V., and T. Damsteegt (eds). 1999 [1998]. *Narrative Strategies: Essays on South Asian Literature and Film*. Delhi: Oxford University Press.

Dalmia-Lüderitz, V. 1992. '"Sati" as a Religious Rite: Parliamentary Papers on Widow Immolation, 1821–30.' *Economic and Political Weekly*, Vol. 27, No. 4, pp. 58–64.

Das, S.K. 1991. *A History of Indian Literature, 1800–1910: Western Impact, Indian Response*. New Delhi: Sahitya Akademi.

———. 1995. *A History of Indian Literature, 1911–1956: Struggle for Freedom, Triumph and Tragedy*. New Delhi: Sahitya Akademi.

Deleuze, G., and F. Guattari. 1990. 'What is a Minor Literature?', In R. Ferguson, M. Gever, Trinh T. Minh-ha, and C. West (eds). *Out There: Marginalization and Contemporary Cultures*. New York: MIT Press, pp. 59–69.

Forbes, G. 1981. 'The Indian Women's Movement: A Struggle for Women's Rights or National Liberation.' In G. Minault (ed.). *The Extended Family: Women and Political Participation in India and Pakistan*. New Delhi: Chanakya Publications, pp. 49–81.

———. 1988. 'The Politics of Respectability: Indian Women and the Indian National Congress.' In D.A. Low (ed.). *The Indian National Congress*. Delhi: Oxford University Press, pp. 54–97.

———. 1998. *Women in Modern India*. Volume 4.2 of *The New Cambridge History of India*. Cambridge: Cambridge University Press.

Foucault, M. 1997. 'Self-Writing.' P. Rabinow (ed.). *Ethics: Subjectivity and Truth*, Vol. 1. New York: The New Press, pp. 207 -22.

Fraser, N. 1992. 'Rethinking the Public Sphere: A Contribution to the Critique of Actually Existing Democracy.' In C. Calhoun (ed.). *Habermas and the Public Sphere*. Cambridge: MIT Press, pp. 109–42.

Freitag, S.B. 1991. 'Introduction: Aspects of "the Public" in Colonial South Asia.' *South Asia*, Vol. 14, No. 1, pp. 1–14.

Ghosh, S. 1986. '"Birds in a Cage": Changes in Bengali Social Life as Recorded in Autobiographies by Women.' *Economic and Political Weekly*, Vol. 21, No. 43, WS 88–96.

Goswami, M. 2004. *Producing India: From Colonial Economy to National Space*. New Delhi: Permanent Black.

Guha, R. 1988. 'The Prose of Counter-Insurgency.' In R. Guha and G. Spivak (eds). *Selected Subaltern Studies*. Oxford: Oxford University Press, pp. 45–88.

Gupta, C. 2001. *Sexuality, Obscenity, Community: Women, Muslims, and the Hindu Public in Colonial India*. New Delhi: Permanent Black.

Habermas, J. 1962. *Strukturwandel der Öffentlichkeit. Untersuchungen zu einer Kategorie der bürgerlichen Gesellschaft*. Berlin: Luchterhand.

Harlow, B. 1987. *Resistance Literature*. New York: Methuen.

Heimsath, C. 1964. *Indian Nationalism and Hindu Social Reform*. Princeton: Princeton University Press.

Helsinger, E. 1991. 'Using and Abusing Fiction.' J. Chandler, A.I. Davidson, and H. Harootunian (eds). *Questions of Evidence: Proof, Practice, and Persuasion across the Disciplines*. Chicago: University of Chicago Press, pp. 352–7.

hooks, b. 1981. *Ain't I a Woman: Black Women and Feminism*. Boston: South End Press.

———. 1984. *Feminist Theory from the Margin to Center*. Boston: South End Press.

Jahan, R. (ed.). 1988. *Sultana's Dream. A Feminist Utopia and Selections from The Secluded Ones by Rokeya Sakhawat Hossain (with an Afterword by Hanna Papanek)*. New York: The Feminist Press.

Jayawardena, K. 1994 [1986]. *Feminism and Nationalism in the Third World*. London: Zed.

Johnson-Odim, C. 1991. 'Common Themes, Different Contexts: Third World Women and Feminism.' In C.T. Mohanty, A. Russo, and L. Torres (eds). *Third World Women and the Politics of Feminism*. Bloomington: Indiana University Press, pp. 314–27.

Kalsi, A.S. 1990. 'The Influence of Nazir Ahmad's Mirat al-'Arus (1869) on the Development of Hindi Fiction.' *Annual of Urdu Studies*, Vol. 7, pp. 31–44.

Karlekar, M. 1991. *Voices from Within: Early Personal Narratives of Bengali Women*. Delhi: Oxford University Press.

Kellogg, S.H. 1893 [1876]. *A Grammar of the Hindi Language in which are treated the Standard Hindi, Braj, and the Eastern Hindi of the Ramayan of Tulsidas, also the Colloquial Dialects of Marwar, Kumaon, Avadh, Baghelkhand Bojpur, etc.; with Copious Philological Notes*. Allahabad: Allahabad Mission Press.

Kerkhoff, K. 1995. *Save Ourselves and the Girls! Girlhood in Calcutta under the Raj*. Rotterdam: Extravert.

King, C. 1994. *One Language, Two Scripts: The Hindi Movement in Nineteenth Century North India*. Bombay: Oxford University Press.

Kishwar, M. 1985a. 'Gandhi on Women.' *Economic and Political Weekly*, Vol. 20, No. 40, pp. 1691–1702.

———. 1985b. 'Gandhi on Women.' *Economic and Political Weekly*, Vol. 20, No. 41, pp. 1753–8.

———. 1986. 'Arya Samaj and Women's Education: Kanya Mahavidyalaya, Jalandhar.' *Economic and Political Weekly*, Vol. 21, No. 17, pp. 9–24.

Kumar, A. 2000. 'Representing the Popular: Ugra's *Chand Hasinon Ke Khatoot* (Letters from Some Beautiful People).' *Hindi: Language, Discourse, Writing*, Vol. 1, No. 1, pp. 133–49.

Kumar, N. 1994. 'Oranges for the Girls, or, the Half-Known Story of the Education of Girls in Twentieth-Century Banaras.' In N. Kumar (ed.). *Women as Subjects: South Asian Histories*. Calcutta: Stree, pp. 211–32.

Kumar, R. 1993. *The History of Doing. An Illustrated Account of Movements for Women's Rights and Feminism in India, 1800–1900*. New Delhi: Kali for Women.

Lal, M. 2003. '"The Ignorance of Women is the House of Illness": Gender, Nationalism, and Health Reform in Colonial North India.' In B. Andrews and M.P. Sutphen (eds). *Medicine and Colonial Identity*. London: Routledge, pp. 14–40.

Lelyveld, D. 1993. 'The Fate of Hindustani: Colonial Knowledge and the Project of a National Language.' In Carol Breckenridge and Peter van der Veer (eds). *Orientalism and the Postcolonial Predicament*. Philadelphia: University of Pennsylvania Press, pp. 189–214.

MacKinnon, C.A. 1982. 'Feminism, Marxism, Method, and the State: An Agenda for Theory.' *Signs*, Vol. 7, No. 3: 515–44.

Major, A. 2008. 'The Burning of Sampati Kuer: Sati and the Politics of Imperialism, Nationalism and Revivalism in 1920s India.' *Gender and History*, Vol. 20, No. 2, pp. 228–47.

Majumdar, R. 2002. '"Self-Sacrifice" versus "Self-Interest": A Non-Historicist Reading of the History of Women's Rights in India.' *Comparative Studies of South Asia, Africa and the Middle-East*, Vol. 22, No. 1/2, pp. 20–35.

_____. 2003. 'Marriage, Modernity and Sources of the Self. Bengali Women, c. 1870–1956.' Unpublished PhD Thesis. University of Chicago.

Mani, L. 1989. 'Contentious Traditions: The Debate on Sati in Colonial India.' In K. Sangari and S. Vaid (eds). *Recasting Women: Essays in Colonial History*. New Delhi: Kali for Women, pp. 88–126.

Mazumdar, V. 1976. 'The Social Reform Movement in India—From Ranade to Nehru.' In B.R. Nanda (ed.). *Indian Women: From Purdah to Modernity*. New Delhi: Vikas, pp. 41–66.

McGregor, R.S. 2004 [1993]. *Oxford Hindi–English Dictionary*. Oxford: Oxford University Press.

McLane, J.R. 1988. 'The Early Congress, Hindu Populism, and the Wider Society.' In R. Sisson and S. Wolpert (eds). *Congress and Indian Nationalism: The Pre-Independence Phase*. Berkeley: University of California Press, pp. 47–61.

Metcalf, B.D. 1990. *Perfecting Women: Maulana Ashraf Ali Thanawi's Bihishti Zewar (A Partial Translation with Commentary)*. Berkeley: University of California Press.

Metcalf, B.D. 1994. 'Reading and Writing About Muslim Women in British India.' In Z. Hasan (ed.). *Forging Identities: Gender, Communities and the State*. New Delhi: Kali for Women, pp. 1–21.

Minault, G. 1998. *Secluded Scholars: Women's Education and Muslim Social Reform in Colonial India*. Delhi: Oxford University Press.

Misra, B.B. 1961. *The Indian Middle Classes: Their Growth in Modern Times*. London: Oxford University Press.

Mohan, K. 2002. 'Fashioning Minds and Images: A Case Study of *Stree Darpan* (1909–1928).' In Aparna Basu and Anup Taneja (eds). *Breaking Out of Invisibility: Women in Indian History*. New Delhi: Council of Historical Research, pp. 232–71.

_____. 2005. 'A Juster India for Women: The Thought and Work of Pandita Ramabai and Rameshwari Nehru.' In Irfan Habib (ed.). *India: Studies in the History of an Idea*. New Delhi: Munshiram Manoharlal, pp. 204–31.

Mohanty, C.T. 1991a. 'Introduction. Cartographies of Struggle: Third World Women and the Politics of Feminism.' In C.T. Mohanty, A. Russo, and L. Torres (eds). *Third World Women and the Politics of Feminism*. Bloomington: Indiana University Press, pp. 1–47.

_____. 1991b. 'Under Western Eyes: Feminist Scholarship and Colonial Discourses.' In C.T. Mohanty, A. Russo, and L. Torres (eds). *Third Women and the Politics of Feminism*. Bloomington: Indiana University Press, pp. 51–80.

Mohanty, C.T., and A. Russo, and L. Torres (eds). 1991. *Third World Women and the Politics of Feminism*. Bloomington: Indiana University Press.

Moi, T. 1985. *Sexual/Textual Politics: Feminist Literary Theory*. London: Routledge.

_____. 1989. 'Feminist, Female, Feminine.' In C. Belsey and J. Moore (eds). *The Feminist Reader: Essays in Gender and the Politics of Literary Criticism*. London: Macmillan Education, pp. 104–16.

Moraga, C., and G. Anzaldua. 1981. *This Bridge Called My Back: Writings by Radical Women of Color*. Watertown: Persephone Press.

Mukherjee, M. 1988. 'The Unperceived Self: A Study of Nineteenth Century Biographies.' In K. Chanana (ed.). *Socialisation, Education, and Women: Explorations in Gender Identity*. Delhi: Orient Longman, pp. 247–72.

_____. 1994 [1985]. *Realism and Reality: The Novel and Society in India*. New Delhi: Oxford University Press.

Murshid, G. 1983. *Reluctant Debutante: Response of Bengali Women to Modernization, 1849–1905*. Rajshahi: Sahitya Samsad.

Nagendra. 1998 [1973]. *Hindī Sāhitya kā Itihās*. Delhi: National Publishing House.

Naim, C.M. 1984. 'Prize-Winning *Adab*: A Study of Five Urdu Books Written in Response to the Allahabad Government Gazette Notification.' In B.D. Metcalf (ed.). *Moral Conduct and Authority: The Place of Adab in South Asian Islam*. Berkeley: University of California Press, pp. 290–314.

Naregal, V. 2002. *Language Politics, Elites, and the Public Sphere: Western India under Colonialism*. London: Anthem Press.

Nijhawan, S. 2004. 'Hindi Children's Journals and Nationalist Discourse (1910–1930).' *Economic and Political Weekly*, Vol. 39, No. 33, pp. 3723–9.

______. 2008. '"The touchstone of a nation's greatness is the status of its women": Responses to colonial discourses on Indian womanhood.' *South Asia Research*, Vol. 28, No. 1, pp. 73–88.

______. 2009. 'Global (?), Modern and Colonized: Indian Women Writers' and Activists' Networking in the Early Twentieth Century.' *The Global Modern: Transnationalism and the Media in Asia Symposium*, York University, Toronto, Canada. Unpublished paper.

______. 2012. 'At the Margins of Empire: Feminist Configurations of Burmese Society in the Hindi Public, 1917–1920.' *Journal of Asian Studies* (Forthcoming).

______ (ed.). 2010. *Nationalism in the Vernacular: Hindi, Urdu and the Literature of Indian Freedom*. New Delhi: Permanent Black.

O'Hanlon, R. 1991. 'Issues of Widowhood: Gender and Resistance in Colonial Western India.' In D. Haynes and G. Prakash (eds). *Contesting Power: Resistance and Everyday Social Relations in South Asia*. Berkeley: University of California Press, pp. 62–108.

______. 1994. *A Comparison between Women and Men: Tarabai Shinde and the critique of gender relations in colonial India*. Madras: Oxford University Press.

Offredi, M. 1992. 'The Search for National Identity as Reflected in the Hindi Press.' In M. Offredi (ed.). *Literature, Language and the Media in India*. Delhi: Oxford University Press, pp. 221–67.

Ong, W. 1982. *Orality and Literacy. The Technologizing of the World*. London: Routledge.

Orsini, F. 1999a. 'What did they mean by "Public"? Language, literature and the politics of nationalism.' *Economic and Political Weekly*, Vol. 34, No. 7, pp. 409–16.

______. 1999b. 'Domesticity and Beyond: Hindi Women's Journals in the Early Twentieth Century.' *South Asia Research*, Vol. 19, No. 2, pp. 137–60.

______. 2002. *The Hindi Public Sphere, 1920–1940: Language and Literature in the Age of Nationalism*. Delhi: Oxford University Press.

______. 2004. 'Detective Novels: A Commercial Genre in Nineteenth-century North India.' In S. Blackburn and V. Dalmia (eds). *India's Literary*

History: Essays on the Nineteenth Century. New Delhi: Permanent Black, pp. 435–82.

Paliwal, O.P. 1986. *Rameshwari Nehru: Patriot and Internationalist.* New Delhi: National Book Trust.

Pandey, G. 1988. 'Congress and the Nation, 1917–1947.' In R. Sisson and S. Wolpert (eds). *Congress and Indian Nationalism. The Pre-Independence Phase.* Berkeley: University of California Press, pp. 121–33.

Pandit, V.L. 1981 [1979]. *The Scope of Happiness: A Personal Memoir.* Delhi: Orient Paperbacks.

Pateman, C. 1988. *The Sexual Contract.* Cambridge: Polity Press.

Pollard, C.L. 1997. 'Nurturing the Nation: The Family Politics of the 1919 Egyptian Revolution.' Unpublished PhD Thesis. University of California, Berkeley.

——.1999. *Another Reason: Science and the Imagination of Modern India.* Princeton: Princeton University Press.

Prakash, G. 1996. 'Science Between the Lines.' In S. Amin and D. Chakrabarty (eds). *Subaltern Studies No. 9: Writing on South Asian History and Society.* New Delhi: Oxford University Press.

Pugh, M. 1992. *Women and the Women's Movement in Britain, 1914–1959.* New York: Paragon House.

Rai, Alok. 2001. *Hindi Nationalism.* New Delhi: Orient Longman.

Rai, Amrit. 1984. *A House Divided: The Origin and Development of Hindi/Hindavi.* Delhi: Oxford University Press.

Ramanujan, A.K. 1992. 'Wo Spiegel Fenster sind: Versuch einer Anthologie der Reflexionen.' In S.N. Eisenstadt (ed.). *Kulturen der Achsenzeit II. Ihre institutionelle Dynamik. Teil 2. Indien.* Frankfurt: Suhrkamp, pp. 158–88.

Ray, B. 1994. 'Collaboration and Protest: Women in the Nineteenth and Early Twentieth Centuries in Colonial Bengal.' In L. Kasturi and V. Mazumdar (eds). *Women and Indian Nationalism.* Delhi: Vikas Publishing House, pp. 75–93.

——. 1995. 'The Freedom Movement and Feminist Consciousness in Bengal, 1905–1929.' In B. Ray (ed.). *From the Seams of History: Essays on Indian Women.* Delhi: Oxford University Press, pp. 174–217.

Ray, R. 1995. 'Conformity and Rebellion: Girls' Schools in Calcutta.' In B. Ray (ed.). *From the Seams of History: Essays on Indian Women.* Delhi: Oxford University Press, pp. 149–73.

Robinson, F. 1993. 'Technology and Religious Change: Islam and the Impact of Print.' *Modern Asian Studies,* Vol. 27, No. 1, pp. 229–51.

Roy, A. 1995. *Gendered Citizenship: Historical and Conceptual Explorations.* New Delhi: Orient Longman.

Sahgal, M.Z. (ed. by G. Forbes). 1994. *An Indian Freedom Fighter Recalls Her Life*. London: M.E. Sharpe.

Sangari, K. 1999. *Politics of the Possible: Essays on Gender, History, Narratives, Colonial English*. Delhi: Tulika.

Sangari, K., and S. Vaid (eds). 1989. *Recasting Women: Essays in Colonial History*. Delhi: Kali for Women.

Sarkar, T. 1989. 'Politics and Women in Bengal—The Conditions and Meaning of Participation.' In J. Krishnamurty (ed.). *Women in Colonial India: Essays on Survival, Work and the State*. New Delhi: Oxford University Press, pp. 231–41.

_____. 1992. 'The Hindu Wife and the Hindu Nation: Domesticity and Nationalism in Nineteenth Century Bengal.' *Studies in History*, Vol. 8, No. 2, pp. 215–35.

_____. 1996. 'Educating the Children of the Hindu Rashtra: Notes on RSS Schools.' In P. Bidwai, H. Mukhia, and A. Vanaik (eds). *Religion, Religiosity and Communalism*. New Delhi: Manohar, pp. 237–47.

_____. 1999. *Words to Win: The Making of Amar Jiban, A Modern Autobiography*. New Delhi: Kali for Women.

_____. 2001. *Hindu Wife, Hindu Nation: Community, Religion, and Cultural Nationalism*. New Delhi: Permanent Black.

Schomer, K. 1982. 'Where Have all the Radhas Gone? New Images of Women in Modern Hindi Poetry.' In J.S. Hawley and D.M. Wuff (eds). *The Divine Consort: Radha and the Goddesses of India*. Berkeley: University of California Press, pp. 89–116.

_____. 1983. *Mahadevi Varma and the Chhayavad Age of Modern Hindi Poetry*. Berkeley: University of California Press.

Scott, J.W. 1988. *Gender and the Politics of History*. New York.

_____. 1992. 'Experience.' In J. Butler and J.W. Scott (eds). *Feminists Theorize the Political*. New York: Routledge, pp. 22–40.

_____. 1996. *Only Paradoxes to Offer: French Feminists and the Rights of Man*. Cambridge: Harvard University Press.

Sen, Amartya. 2005. *The Argumentative Indian: Writings on Indian History, Culture and Identity*. New York: Picador.

Sen, Samita. 1993. 'Motherhood and Mothercraft: Gender and Nationalism in Bengal.' *Gender and History*, Vol. 5, No. 2, pp. 231–43.

Shackle, C., and R. Snell. 1990. *Hindi and Urdu Since 1800: A Common Reader*. London: School of African and Oriental Studies.

Shaw, G. and M. Lloyd (eds). 1985. *Publications Proscribed by the Government of India: A Catalogue of the Collections in the India Office Library and Records and the Department of Oriental Manuscripts and Printed Books, British Library Reference Division*. London: British Library.

Shevelow, K. 1989. *Women and Print Culture: The construction of femininity in the early periodical*. London: Routledge.

Showalter, E. 1999 [1977]. *A Literature of Their Own: British Women Novelists from Bronte to Lessing (Expanded Edition)*. Princeton: Princeton University Press.

Shukla, S. 1991. 'Cultivating Minds: 19th Century Gujarati Women's Journals.' *Economic and Political Weekly*, Vol. 26, No. 43, pp. 63–6.

Sinha, M. 1994. 'Reading *Mother India*: Empire, Nation, and the Female Voice.' *Journal of Women's History*, Vol. 6, No. 2, pp. 6–44.

———. 1995. *Colonial Masculinity. The 'Manly Englishman' and the 'Effeminate Bengali' in the Late Nineteenth Century*. Manchester: Manchester University Press.

———. 1997. 'Agency and Accommodation: Contradictions in Words and Actions of Three South Asian Women.' *American Historical Association Conference*, New York City, 2–5 January. Unpublished Paper.

———. 1999. 'Suffragism and Internationalism: The Enfranchisement of British and Indian Women under an Imperial State.' *The Indian Economic and Social History Review*, Vol. 36, No. 4, pp. 461–84.

———. 2000. 'Refashioning Mother India: Feminism and Nationalism in Late-Colonial India.' *Feminist Studies*, Vol. 26, No. 3, pp. 623–44.

———. 2006. *Specters of Mother India: The Global Restructuring of an Empire*. Durham: Duke University Press.

Smith-Rosenberg, C. 1986. 'Writing History: Language, Class, and Gender.' In T. de Lauretis (ed.). *Feminist Studies/Critical Studies*. Bloomington: Indiana University Press, pp. 31–54.

Spivak, G.C. 1985a. 'The Rani of Sirmur: An Essay in Reading the Archives.' *History and Theory: Studies in the Philosophy of History*, Vol. 24, No. 3, pp. 247–72.

———. 1985b. 'Can the Subaltern Speak?' In P. Williams and L. Chrisman (eds). *Colonial Discourse and Postcolonial Theory: A Reader*. New York: Columbia University Press, pp. 66–111.

———. 1993. 'The Interview with Ellen Rooney.' *Outside in the Teaching Machine*. New York: Routledge.

Sreenivas, M. 2003. 'Emotion, Identity, and the Female Subject: Tamil Women's Magazines in Colonial India, 1890–1940.' *Journal of Women's History*, Vol. 14, No. 4, pp. 59–82.

Stark, U. 1995. *Tage der Unzufriedenheit. Identitaet und Gesellschaftsbild in den Romanen muslimischer Hindischriftsteller (1965–1990)*: *Beitraege zur Suedasienforschung*. Stuttgart: Franz Steiner Verlag.

———. 2000. 'Educating Women, Educating a Daughter: Babu Navincandra Rai, *Lakshmi–Sarasvati Samvad* (1869), and Hemantkumari Chaudhurani.'

In A. Copley (ed.). *Gurus and their Followers: New Religious Reform Movements in Colonial India*. Delhi: Oxford University Press, pp. 33–56.

Stark, U. 2004. 'Hindi Publishing at the Heart of an Indo–Persian Cultural Metropolis.' In S. Blackburn and V. Dalmia (eds). *India's Literary History*. New Delhi: Permanent Black, pp. 251–79.

———. 2007. *An Empire of Books: The Naval Kishore Press and the Diffusion of the Printed Word in Colonial India*. New Delhi: Permanent Black.

Tagore, R. [trans. S. Tagore]. 2005 [1916]. *The Home and the World*. New York: Penguin.

Talwar, V.B. 1989. 'Feminist Consciousness in Women's Journals in Hindi, 1910–1920.' In K. Sangari and S. Vaid (eds). *Recasting Women*. New Delhi: Kali for Women, pp. 204–32.

———. 1993. *Rāṣṭrīya Navjāgaraṇ aur Sāhitya: Kuch Prasaṅg, Kuch Pravṛittiyāṅ*. Delhi: Himācal Pustak Bhaṇḍār.

Thapar-Björkert, S. 2006. *Women in the Indian National Movement: Unseen Faces and Unheard Voices, 1930–1942*. New Delhi: Sage Publications.

Tharu, S., and K. Lalita (eds). 1991. *Women Writing in India: 600 BC to the Present*. Delhi: Oxford University Press.

Trinh, M.T. 1989. *Woman, Native, Other: Writing Postcoloniality and Feminism*. Bloomington: Indiana University Press.

Trivedi, H. 2003. 'The Progress of Hindi, Part 2.' In Sheldon Pollock (ed.). *Literary Cultures in History: Reconstructions from South Asia*. Berkeley: University of California Press, pp. 958–1022.

Turner, R.L. 1966. *A Comparative Dictionary of the Indo–Aryan Languages*. London: Oxford University Press.

Varma, M. 2000 [1969]. *Mahādevī Sāhitya Sāmagra*, Vol. 3. New Delhi: Vani Prakashan.

Vedalankar, S. 1969. *The Development of Hindi Prose Literature in the Early Nineteenth Century (1800–1856)*. Allahabad: Lok Bharati Publications.

Visweswaran, K. 1996. 'Small Speeches, Subaltern Gender: Nationalist Ideology and its Historiography.' In Shahid Amin and Dipesh Chakrabarty (eds). *Subaltern Studies IX: Writings on South Asian History and Society*. New Delhi: Oxford University Press, pp. 83–125.

Walker, A. 1983. *In Search of Our Mother's Gardens: Womanist Prose*. San Diego: Harcourt Brone Jovanevich.

Walsh, J.E. 1997. 'What Women Learned When Men Gave Them Advice: Rewriting Patriarchy in Late-nineteenth-century Bengal.' *Journal of Asian Studies*, Vol. 56, No. 3, pp. 641–77.

———. 2004. *Domesticity in Colonial India: What Women Learned When Men Gave Them Advice*. Lanham: Rowman and Littlefield.

Wellek, R., and A. Warren. 1956. *Theory of Literature*. New York: Harcourt, Brace and World.

White, C. 1970. *Women's Magazines 1693–1968*. London: Michael Joseph.

Winship, J. 1996. 'Women's Magazines: Times of War and Management of the Self in *Woman's Own*.' In C. Gledhill and G. Swanson (eds). *Nationalising Femininity: Culture, Sexuality, and British Cinema in the Second World War*. Manchester: Manchester University Press, pp. 127–39.

Wolpert, S. 1988. 'The Indian National Congress in Nationalist Perspective.' In R. Sisson and S. Wolpert (eds). *Congress and Indian Nationalism: The Pre-Independence Phase*. Berkeley: University of California Press, pp. 21–46.

Index